WORLD TRADE ORGANIZATION

Dispute Settlement Reports

2002
Volume V

Pages 1819-2070

CAMBRIDGE
UNIVERSITY PRESS

University Printing House, Cambridge CB2 8BS, United Kingdom

One Liberty Plaza, 20th Floor, New York, NY 10006, USA

477 Williamstown Road, Port Melbourne, VIC 3207, Australia

314-321, 3rd Floor, Plot 3, Splendor Forum, Jasola District Centre, New Delhi - 110025, India

103 Penang Road, #05-06/07, Visioncrest Commercial, Singapore 238467

Cambridge University Press is part of the University of Cambridge.

It furthers the University's mission by disseminating knowledge in the pursuit of education, learning and research at the highest international levels of excellence.

www.cambridge.org
Information on this title: www.cambridge.org/9780521854641

© World Trade Organization 2002, 2005

This publication is in copyright. Subject to statutory exception and to the provisions of relevant collective licensing agreements, no reproduction of any part may take place without the written permission of Cambridge University Press.

First published 2005

A catalogue record for this publication is available from the British Library

ISBN 987-0-521-85464-1 Hardback

Cambridge University Press has no responsibility for the persistence or accuracy of URLs for external or third-party internet websites referred to in this publication, and does not guarantee that any content on such websites is, or will remain, accurate or appropriate.

THE WTO DISPUTE SETTLEMENT REPORTS

The *Dispute Settlement Reports* of the World Trade Organization (the "WTO") include panel and Appellate Body reports, as well as arbitration awards, in disputes concerning the rights and obligations of WTO Members under the provisions of the *Marrakesh Agreement Establishing the World Trade Organization*. The *Dispute Settlement Reports* are available in English, French and Spanish. Starting with 2002, each volume contains a cumulative index of published disputes.

This volume may be cited as DSR 2002:V

TABLE OF CONTENTS

Page

India – Measures Affecting the Automotive Sector (WT/DS146, WT/DS175)

Report of the Appellate Body 1821

Report of the Panel 1827

United States – Definitive Safeguard Measures on Imports of Circular Welded Carbon Quality Line Pipe from Korea (WT/DS202)

Award of the Arbitrator under Article 21.3(c) of the DSU 2061

Cumulative Index of Published Disputes 2063

INDIA – MEASURES AFFECTING THE AUTOMOTIVE SECTOR

Report of the Appellate Body
WT/DS146/AB/R, WT/DS175/AB/R

*Adopted by the Dispute Settlement Body
on 5 April 2002*

India – *Appellant*	Present:
European Communities – *Appellee*	Ganesan, Presiding Member
United States – *Appellee*	Sacerdoti, Member
Korea – *Third Participant*	Taniguchi, Member

1.   This appeal concerns the Panel Report, *India – Measures Affecting the Automotive Sector* (the "Panel Report").[1] The Panel was established to consider complaints by the United States and the European Communities relating to certain aspects of India's automotive components licensing policy as set forth in India's Public Notice No. 60[2] and the Memoranda of Understanding signed pursuant thereto. Public Notice No. 60 required each passenger car manufacturer in India to sign a Memorandum of Understanding ("MOU") with the Director General of Foreign Trade, and specified a number of conditions to be included in such MOUs.[3]

2.   This dispute concerns two of the conditions stipulated by Public Notice No. 60 and included in each MOU, namely: (i) an "indigenization" requirement, whereby each car manufacturer was obliged to achieve indigenization, or local content, of a minimum level of 50 percent by the third year from the date of its first import of cars in the form of completely and semi-knocked down kits ("CKD/SKD kits"), or certain automobile components, and 70 percent by the fifth year from that date; and (ii) a "trade balancing requirement", whereby each car manufacturer was obliged to balance, over the period of the MOU, the value of its imports of CKD/SKD kits and components with the value of its exports of cars and components.[4] At the time Public Notice No. 60 was issued, India maintained import restrictions and a discretionary import licensing scheme for, *inter alia*, automobile CKD/SKD kits and components. A manufacturer that failed to comply with the conditions set forth in Public Notice No. 60 and the MOUs could be denied a licence to import CKD/SKD kits and components. India abolished its import restrictions and related discretionary import licensing scheme,

---

[1]   WT/DS146/R, WT/DS175/R, 21 December 2001.

[2]   Public Notice No. 60 was issued on 12 December 1997 by the Government of India's Ministry of Commerce, acting pursuant to the Foreign Trade (Development and Regulation) Act of 1992. (Panel Report, para. 2.4)

[3]   Panel Report, paras. 2.4 and 2.5 and Annex Tables 1 and 2.

[4]   *Ibid.*

Report of the Appellate Body

including the restrictions and licensing requirements applicable to CKD/SKD kits and components, on 1 April 2001. This occurred during the course of the Panel proceedings. The relevant factual aspects of this dispute are set out in greater detail in paragraphs 2.1 through 2.5 of the Panel Report.

3.   On 15 May 2000, the United States requested the establishment of a panel to examine the consistency of the measures at issue with Articles III:4 and XI:1 of the *General Agreement on Tariffs and Trade 1994* (the "GATT 1994"), and Articles 2.1 and 2.2 of the *Agreement on Trade-Related Investment Measures* (the "*TRIMS Agreement*").[5] On 12 October 2000, the European Communities requested the establishment of a panel to examine the consistency of the measures at issue with Articles III:4 and XI:1 of the GATT 1994, and Article 2.1 of the *TRIMS Agreement*.[6] The European Communities also specifically requested the Panel to find that the measures at issue were inconsistent with these provisions of the covered agreements as of the date of establishment of the Panel, and that they had remained so after 1 April 2001.[7] Pursuant to Article 10.2 of the *Understanding on Rules and Procedures Governing the Settlement of Disputes* (the "DSU"), Korea and Japan reserved their third party rights in the dispute.[8]

4.   In its Report, circulated on 21 December 2001, the Panel found that:

(a)   India acted inconsistently with its obligations under Article III:4 of the GATT 1994 by imposing on automotive manufacturers, under the terms of Public Notice No. 60 and the MOUs signed thereunder, an obligation to use a certain proportion of local parts and components in the manufacture of cars and automotive vehicles ("indigenization" condition);

(b)   India acted inconsistently with its obligations under Article XI of the GATT 1994 by imposing on automotive manufacturers, under the terms of Public Notice No. 60 and the MOUs signed thereunder, an obligation to balance any importation of certain kits and components with exports of equivalent value ("trade balancing" condition); [and]

(c)   India acted inconsistently with its obligations under Article III:4 of the GATT 1994 by imposing, in the context of the trade balancing condition under the terms of Public Notice No. 60 and the MOUs signed thereunder, an obligation to offset the amount of any purchases of previously im-

---

[5]   WT/DS175/4.

[6]   WT/DS146/4. At its meeting on 17 November 2000, the Dispute Settlement Body agreed, in accordance with Article 9.1 of the *Understanding on Rules and Procedures Governing the Settlement of Disputes*, that the Panel established on 27 July 2000 to examine the complaint by the United States should also examine the complaint by the European Communities. (Panel Report, para. 1.4; WT/DSB/M/92)

[7]   Panel Report, para. 3.5.

[8]   *Ibid.*, para. 1.6.

1822   DSR 2002:V

ported restricted kits and components on the Indian market, by exports of equivalent value.[9]

5. In the light of its findings that the measures at issue were inconsistent with Articles III:4 and XI:1 of the GATT 1994, the Panel was of the view that it was not necessary to address the claims made by the European Communities and the United States under the *TRIMS Agreement.*[10]

6. The Panel then went on to give "separate consideration" to:

> ... whether the events which took place subsequently, including on or after 1 April 2001, might have affected the existence of any violations identified and ... whether those events affect the nature or range of any recommendations [the Panel] may make to the DSB in accordance with Article 19.1 of the DSU.[11]

7. More specifically, the Panel:

> ... felt that it would not be making an "objective assessment of the matter before it", or assisting the DSB in discharging its responsibilities under the DSU in accordance with Article 11 of the DSU, had it chosen not to address the impact of events having taken place in the course of the proceedings, in assessing the appropriateness of making a recommendation under Article 19.1 of the DSU.[12]

8. Having considered the events that took place during the Panel proceedings, the Panel found that:

> ... the indigenization conditions contained in Public Notice No. 60 and in the MOUs, as they have continued to exist and apply after 1 April 2001, have remained in violation of the relevant GATT provisions.[13]

> ...

> ... the trade balancing conditions contained in Public Notice No. 60 and in the MOUs, as they have continued to exist and apply after 1 April 2001, have remained in violation of the relevant GATT provisions.[14]

9. The Panel consequently recommended that the Dispute Settlement Body (the "DSB") request India to bring its measures into conformity with its obligations under the *Marrakesh Agreement Establishing the World Trade Organization* (the "*WTO Agreement*").[15]

---

[9] Panel Report, para. 8.1.
[10] *Ibid.*, para. 7.324.
[11] *Ibid.*, para. 8.3.
[12] *Ibid.*, para. 8.28.
[13] *Ibid.*, para. 8.47.
[14] Panel Report, para. 8.61.
[15] *Ibid.*, para. 8.65.

Report of the Appellate Body

10.   On 31 January 2002, India notified the DSB of its decision to appeal certain issues of law covered in the Panel Report and certain legal interpretations developed by the Panel, pursuant to paragraph 4 of Article 16 of the DSU, and filed a Notice of Appeal with the Appellate Body pursuant to Rule 20 of the *Working Procedures for Appellate Review* (the *"Working Procedures"*). In this Notice of Appeal, India stated that:

> India seeks review by the Appellate Body of the Panel's conclusion that Articles 11 and 19.1 of the DSU required it to address the question of whether the measures found [to] be inconsistent with Articles III:4 and XI:1 of the General Agreement on Tariffs and Trade 1994 ("GATT") had been brought into conformity with the GATT as a result of measures taken by India during the course of the proceedings.
>
> India further seeks review by the Appellate Body of the Panel's conclusion that the enforcement of the export obligations that automobile manufacturers incurred until 1 April 2001 under India's former import licensing scheme is inconsistent with Articles III:4 and XI:1 of the GATT.
>
> India considers these conclusions of the Panel to be in error and based upon erroneous findings on issues of law and related legal interpretations. [16]

11.   On 11 February 2002, India filed an appellant's submission. [17] The European Communities and the United States each filed an appellee's submission on 25 February 2002. [18] On the same day, Korea filed a third participant's submission. [19]

12.   On 25 February 2002, the Appellate Body received a letter from Japan indicating that Japan would not be filing a written submission in this appeal, but that Japan wished to attend the oral hearing. [20] By letter dated 27 February 2002, the Appellate Body Secretariat informed Japan, the participants and the third participant that the Division hearing this appeal was "inclined to allow Japan to attend the oral hearing as a passive observer, if none of the participants or third participants object." On 1 March 2002 and 4 March 2002, respectively, the Appellate Body received written responses from the European Communities and the United States.

13.   Taking account of the views expressed by the European Communities and the United States, the Division on 5 March 2002 informed Japan, the participants, and the third participant, that although Japan had not filed a written submission as a third participant, Japan would be allowed to attend the oral hearing

---

[16]   WT/DS146/8, WT/DS175/8, 31 January 2002.
[17]   Pursuant to Rule 21(1) of the *Working Procedures*.
[18]   Pursuant to Rule 22(1) of the *Working Procedures*.
[19]   Pursuant to Rule 24 of the *Working Procedures*.
[20]   Japan had reserved its rights to participate as a third party in the proceedings before the Panel; Panel Report, para. 1.6.

1824   DSR 2002:V

as a passive observer, that is, to attend the oral hearing and hear the oral statements and responses to questioning by the participants and the third participant in this appeal.

14.   In accordance with the Working Schedule for Appeal communicated to the parties and the third parties on 1 February 2002, the oral hearing in the appeal was scheduled to be held on 15 March 2002.[21]

15.   On 14 March 2002, the Appellate Body received a letter from India, in which India stated that:

> Pursuant to Rule 30(1) of the *Working Procedures for Appellate Review*, this is to inform the Appellate Body that India is withdrawing the above-mentioned appeal; oral hearing on this is scheduled for 15 March 2002. Inconvenience caused to the Appellate Body, Secretariat, the other parties and the third participants is deeply regretted.

16.   Rule 30(1) of the *Working Procedures* provides that:

> At any time during an appeal, the appellant may withdraw its appeal by notifying the Appellate Body, which shall forthwith notify the DSB.

17.   Upon receipt of India's letter of 14 March 2002, the Appellate Body on the same day notified the DSB, pursuant to Rule 30(1) of the *Working Procedures*, that India "has notified the Appellate Body that India is withdrawing its appeal" in this dispute[22], and simultaneously informed India, the European Communities, the United States, Korea and Japan that the oral hearing in this appeal was cancelled.

18.   In view of India's withdrawal of the appeal by its letter of 14 March 2002, the Appellate Body hereby completes its work in this appeal.

---

[21]   Pursuant to Rule 27 of the *Working Procedures*.
[22]   WT/DS146/9, WT/DS175/9, 14 March 2002.

INDIA – MEASURES AFFECTING THE AUTOMOTIVE SECTOR

Report of the Panel
WT/DS146/R, WT/DS175/R

*Adopted by the Dispute Settlement Body
on 5 April 2002*

TABLE OF CONTENTS

			Page
I.	INTRODUCTION		1832
II.	FACTUAL ASPECTS		1834
	A.	The Licensing Regime	1834
	B.	Public Notice No. 60 and the MOUs	1835
III.	PARTIES' REQUESTS FOR FINDINGS AND RECOMMENDATIONS		1836
	A.	US Claims and Requests for Findings	1836
	B.	EC Claims and Requests for Findings	1836
	C.	India's Requests for Findings	1837
IV.	ARGUMENTS OF THE PARTIES		1839
	A.	Factual Arguments	1839
		1. The Licensing Regime	1839
		2. Public Notice No. 60 and the MOUs	1841
		(a) The "indigenization" Requirement (paragraph 3 (iii) of Public Notice No. 60) and paragraph III(IV) of the MOU)	1842
		(b) The "trade balancing" Requirement (paragraph 3 (iv) of Public Notice No. 60 and paragraph III (vi) of the MOU)	1844
	B.	Has The Matter Been Settled and Adjudicated?	1849
		1. Has the Matter Been Settled?	1852
		2. Has the Matter Already Been Adjudicated?	1860
		(a) India – Quantitative Restrictions	1860
		(i) The Notion of Res Judicata	1866
		(b) The Provisions Are an Inherent Part of the Licensing Scheme that Must be Eliminated	1868
		(i) The Notion of Abusive Splitting	1872

DSR 2002:V

Report of the Panel

				Page
C.	Are the Measures within the Terms of Reference of the Panel?			1877
	1.	Do the Measures Applied After 1 April 2001 Fall Outside the Terms of Reference?		1877
		(a)	The Method of Enforcement before and after 1 April 2001	1880
D.	Claims under GATT 1994 and TRIMs			1898
	1.	Article III:4		1898
		(a)	The Indigenization Requirement	1900
		(b)	The Trade Balancing Requirement	1905
	2.	Article XI:1		1908
		(i)	The Indigenization Requirement	1908
		(ii)	The Trade Balancing Requirement	1908
		(a)	Are the Measures Justified by Article XVIII:B of the GATT and Articles 3 and 4 of the TRIMs Agreement?	1920
		(i)	Procedural Requirements of the Balance of Payments Provisions	1924
		(ii)	Substantive Requirements of the Balance of Payments Provisions	1925
		(iii)	The Burden of Proof	1929
		(iv)	Relevance of the India – Quantitative Restrictions Case	1934
	3.	TRIMs Agreement		1936
V.	ARGUMENTS OF THE THIRD PARTIES			1943
	1.	The Agreements Regarding the Indian Measures Must be Respected and Enforced		1943
	2.	The Measures that India May Take by 1 April 2001 are not, and as a Matter of Logic Cannot be, Properly before the Panel.		1944
	3.	Prospective Measures		1945
VI.	INTERIM REVIEW			1946
A.	Comments on the Descriptive Part			1947
	1.	Comments by the United States		1947
	2.	Comments by India		1947
	3.	Comments by the European Communities		1948
B.	Comments on the Findings and Conclusions			1948
	1.	Comments by the United States		1948

India – Autos

				Page
	2.		Comments by the European Communities................	1949
	3.		Comments by India...	1950
		(a)	General Comment in Respect of India's Procedural Rights in the Proceedings	1951
		(b)	India's Argument that the Matters Addressed in the Recommendations Section Should be Left to a Compliance Panel........................	1953
		(c)	India's Argument that the Panel could not "properly" Conclude that the Violation is Still in Existence..	1955
		(d)	India's Argument that the Panel Inappropriately Prescribes a "retrospective" Remedy..	1957
VII.	FINDINGS			1958
A.	Clarification of the Claims in the Course of the Proceedings and Requests for Preliminary Rulings			1959
B.	Clarification of the Measures within the Terms of Reference of this Panel..			1962
	1.		Measures Identified in the Complainants' Requests for Establishment of a Panel	1963
	2.		Evolution of the Measures in the Course of the Proceedings...	1965
	3.		Measures not within our Terms of Reference	1967
C.	The Panel's Competence to Consider the Matter before it			1969
	1.		Are any of the United States' Claims Barred by the Principle of *res judicata*?...	1970
		(a)	Arguments of the Parties and Scope of India's Invocation of the Doctrine of *res judicata*	1970
		(b)	Role of India's Import Licensing System in the United States' Claims..............................	1971
		(c)	General Approach to the *res judicata* Arguments	1972
			(i) The Matter before this Panel	1977
			(ii) The Matter Ruled on by the India – Quantitative Restrictions Panel	1979
			(iii) Comparison between the Matter Ruled on by the India – QRs Panel and the Matter before this Panel	1981

DSR 2002:V

1829

Report of the Panel

			Page
		A Comparison of the Measures Expressly Considered	1982
		A Comparison of the Express Claims	1983
		Are the Matters the Same?	1984
		Conclusion	1987

1. Has Any Part of the Matter before this Panel Been Settled Through a Mutually Agreed Solution? 1988

    (a) The Mutually Agreed Solution in the *India – Quantitative Restrictions* Dispute with the EC 1988

    (b) Relevance of Mutually Agreed Solutions in Subsequent Proceedings 1989

    (c) The Scope of the Mutually Agreed Solution Between the European Communities and India 1990

    (d) Conclusion 1995

2. Measures to be Eliminated in the Course of Implementing the Results of the India ☐ Quantitative Restrictions Dispute and Abusive Splitting of a Dispute 1996

    (a) Abusive Splitting 1996

    (b) Unnecessary Litigation 1997

3. Conclusion 1999

D. Order of Examination of the Claims 1999

E. Consistency of the Indigenization Condition with the GATT 1994 2003

1. Claims under Article III:4 of GATT 1994 2004

    (a) Like Products 2005

    (b) "Laws, regulations or requirements" 2005

        (i) The Notion of "requirement" within the Meaning of Article III:4 2006

        (ii) The Indigenization Condition as a "requirement" 2008

    (c) ... Affecting the Internal Sale, Offering for Sale, Purchase (...) of the Products 2010

    (d) Whether Imported Products are Accorded Less Favourable Treatment 2010

    (e) Conclusion 2012

2. Claim under Article XI 2012

India – Autos

					Page
F.		GATT Claims Concerning the Trade Balancing Condition ..			2013
	1.	Factual Aspects of the Measure			2013
	2.	Order of Analysis of the Claims			2014
	3.	Relationship between Articles III and XI			2015
	4.	Claims under Article XI:1			2016
		(a)	Scope of the European Communities' Claim ..		2016
			(i)	The Scope of the Trade Balancing Obligation	2017
			(ii)	The Continued Enforceability of the MOUs after 1 April 2001	2019
		(b)	Arguments of the Parties		2020
		(c)	Scope of Article XI:1		2021
			(i)	The Notion of "measures" within the Meaning of Article XI:1	2021
			(ii)	"Restriction on importation" within the Meaning of Article XI:1 and "border measures"	2023
		(d)	The Trade Balancing Condition as a "restriction ... on importation"		2025
			(i)	The Notion of "restriction ... on importation"	2025
			(ii)	Analysis of the Trade Balancing Condition	2029
	5.	Balance-of-Payments Defense			2030
	6.	Claims under Article III:4			2032
		(a)	Purchases of Restricted Imported Kits and Components on the Domestic Market		2033
			(i)	Like Products	2034
			(ii)	Laws, Regulations or Requirements	2034
			(iii)	Affecting Internal Sale, Use, ...	2034
			(iv)	Whether the Measure Affords Less Favourable Treatment to Imported Products	2036
	7.	Ruling on the Consistency of Public Notice No. 60 with the GATT 1994			2036
		(a)	Consistency of Public Notice No. 60 with Article III:4 of GATT 1994		2037

DSR 2002:V

Report of the Panel

			Page
(b)	Consistency of Public Notice No. 60 with Article XI:1 of the GATT 1994 in so far as it Contains the Trade Balancing Condition		2038

G. Claims under the TRIMs Agreement 2039

VIII. CONCLUSIONS AND RECOMMENDATIONS 2039

    A. Conclusions 2039

    B. Consequences of Events Having Taken Place in the Course of the Proceedings 2040

        1. Presentation of the Issue: Arguments of the Parties 2040

        2. Approach of the Panel 2043

        3. Analysis 2046

            (a) Indigenization Provisions 2047

                (i) The Cessation of the Application of Public Notice No. 60 and the MOUs as Private Contracts 2048

                (ii) Achievement of the Required Levels of Indigenization by MOU Signatories 2050

            (b) Trade Balancing Provisions 2051

                (i) Accrued Obligations as Independent from Imports 2051

                (ii) Cessation of the Application of Public Notice No. 60 and the MOUs as Private Contracts 2052

    C. Recommendations 2053

TABLE 1 2054

TABLE 2 2057

I. INTRODUCTION

1.1 In a communication dated 12 October 1998 (WT/DS146/1), the European Communities requested consultations with India pursuant to Article 4 of the Understanding on Rules and Procedures Governing the Settlement of Disputes (DSU), Article XXII:1 of the General Agreement on Tariffs and Trade 1994 (GATT 1994) and Article 8 of the Agreement on Trade-Related Investment Measures (TRIMs Agreement), concerning certain measures affecting the automotive sector. On 21 and 22 October 1998, Japan and the United States, respec-

1832

DSR 2002:V

tively, lodged requests to join in the consultations.[1] The European Communities and India held consultations in Geneva on 2 December 1998. The United States and Japan participated in the consultations under DSU Article 4:11.

1.2   In a communication dated 2 June 1999 (WT/DS175/1), the United States requested consultations with India pursuant to Articles 1 and 4 of the Understanding on Rules and Procedures Governing the Settlement of Disputes (DSU), Article XXII:1 of the General Agreement on Tariffs and Trade 1994 (GATT 1994) and Article 8 of the Agreement on Trade-Related Investment Measures (to the extent it incorporates by reference Article XXII of the GATT 1994) regarding certain measures affecting trade and investment in the motor vehicle sector. The United States and India held such consultations, in which Japan and the European Communities joined, on 20 July 1999. The consultations provided some helpful clarifications but failed to settle the dispute.

1.3   On 15 May 2000, the United States (WT/DS175/4) requested the Dispute Settlement Body to establish a panel with standard terms of reference as set out in Article 7.1 of the DSU. The Panel was established on 27 July 2000. On 12 October 2000, the European Communities (WT/DS146/4) also requested the DSB to establish a panel pursuant to Article 4.7 and 6 of the DSU.

1.4   At its meeting of 17 November 2000, the DSB agreed that, in accordance with Article 9.1 of the DSU, the Panel established on 27 July 2000 to examine the complaint by the United States should also examine the complaint by the European Communities contained in WT/DS146/4 and agreed that the Panel should have standard terms of reference. The terms of reference of the Panel were therefore as follows:

> "To examine, in the light of the relevant provisions of the covered agreements cited by the United States in WT/DSB/175/4 and by the European Communities in WT/DS146/4, the matters referred to the DSB by the United States and the European Communities in those documents and to make such findings as will assist the DSB in making the recommendations or in giving the rulings provided for in those agreements."

1.5   On 24 November, in accordance with Article 8.7 of the DSU, the Director-General composed the Panel as follows:

Chairman: Mr. John Weekes

Members: Ms. Gloria Peña

Mr. Jeffrey Waincymer

1.6   Japan and Korea reserved their third party rights in the dispute.

1.7   The Panel met with the Parties on 21 and 22 March 2001 and 17 and 18 May 2001. The Panel held a third-party session on 22 March. Korea presented its submission. Japan did not make a submission.

---

[1]   WT/DS146/2 and WT/DS146/3.

Report of the Panel

II.   FACTUAL ASPECTS

A.   The Licensing Regime

2.1   For many years, India applied import restrictions for balance of payment reasons. On 24 July 1997 the European Communities requested consultations with respect to all the import restrictions maintained by India on balance-of-payment grounds, including those on passenger cars, and chassis and bodies therefore.[2] As a result of those consultations, the European Communities and India reached a mutually agreed solution on 25 November 1997 (the "1997 Agreement").[3] The 1997 Agreement stipulated that the import restrictions on passenger cars, and on chassis and bodies therefor, were to be eliminated no later than 31 March 2003. The 1997 Agreement, nevertheless, had to a large extent been superseded by the agreement concluded between India and the United States on 24 December 1999[4] referred to below.

2.2   On 22 July 1997 the United States requested consultations under the DSU with respect to quantitative restrictions maintained by India for balance-of-payments reasons on 2,714 agricultural and industrial product tariff lines.[5] A panel was established on 18 November 1997.[6] The panel concluded that the restrictions applied by India, violated GATT Article XI:1 of GATT and were not justified by GATT Article XVIII:B.[7] The Appellate Body upheld those findings.[8]

2.3   On 24 December 1999 India and the United States agreed, pursuant to Article 21.3(b) of the DSU, that the reasonable period of time for complying with the recommendations and rulings of the DSB would expire on 1 April 2001.[9] Accordingly, India was required to eliminate the current system of non-automatic licenses for imports of passenger cars, and chassis and bodies therefor, no later than 1 April 2001. At the time when the United States (15 May 2000) and the European Communities (12 October 200) submitted their requests for the

---

[2]   WT/DS96/1. The United States (WT/DS90/1), Australia (WT/DS91/1), Canada (WT/DS92/1), New Zealand (WT/DS93/1) and Switzerland (WT/DS94/1) also requested consultations with respect to the same measures.

[3]   The Agreement was notified under Article 3.6 DSU (WT/DS96/8). India reached similar Agreements with Australia, Canada, New Zealand, Switzerland and Japan, but not with the United States.

[4]   Paragraph 3 of the 1997 Agreement provides that:
"India shall grant to the EC treatment no less favourable than that granted by India to any other country with respect to the elimination or modification of import restrictions on the products in the Annex and those in Annex II of document WT/BOP/N/24, under any form, either autonomously or pursuant to agreement or understanding with that country, including pursuant to the settlement of any outstanding dispute under the WTO Understanding on Rules and Procedures Governing the Settlement of Disputes".

[5]   WT/DS90/1.

[6]   WT/DS90/8 and WT/DS90/9.

[7]   Panel Report on *India – Quantitative Restrictions on Imports of Agricultural, Textile and Industrial Products*, (hereinafter "*India – Quantitative Restrictions*"), WT/DS/90/R, adopted 22 September 1999, DSR 1999:V, 1799, at para. 6.1. The report addresses the compatibility with GATT Article XI:1 of the licenses required for the importation of "restricted" items at paras. 5.125 *et seq.*

[8]   Report of the Appellate Body in *India – Quantitative Restrictions,* WT/DS90/AB/R, adopted on 22 September 1999, DSR 1999:IV, 1763.

[9]   WT/DS90/15.

India – Autos

establishment of this panel, India applied discretionary import licensing to 715 tariff line items, including cars imported in the form of completely and semi-knocked down ("CKD/SKD") kits. The import licensing scheme for cars imported in the form of CKD/SKD kits was abolished on 1 April 2001 in accordance with the agreements reached with the European Communities and the United States under Articles 3.6 and 21.3(b) of the Dispute Settlement Understanding ("DSU").

B.   Public Notice No. 60 and the MOUs

2.4   On 12 December 1997, the Ministry of Commerce adopted Public Notice No. 60, the auto components licensing policy, issued under the Foreign Trade (Development and Regulation) Act of 1992 (the "FTDR Act").

2.5   The Notice, effective from the date of issue, requires any passenger car manufacturer wishing to import SKD/CKD kits to sign a Memorandum of Understanding (MOU) with the Director General of Foreign Trade ("DGFT") (see Annex Tables 1 and 2). A car manufacturer that does not sign an MOU or does not perform the obligations assumed under an MOU may therefore be denied a license for the importation of SKD/CKD kits. Subparagraphs 3(i) through (iv) of Public Notice No. 60 set out four requirements which an MOU must impose on the manufacturing company:

(i)   establishment of actual production facilities for manufacture of cars, and not for mere assembly.

(ii)   a minimum of foreign equity of US$50 million to be brought in by the foreign partner within the first three years of the start of operations, if the firm is a joint venture that involves majority foreign equity ownership.[10]

(iii)   indigenization (i.e. local content) of components up to a minimum level of 50% in the third year or earlier from the date of first import consignment of CKD/SKD kits/components, and 70% in the fifth year or earlier.

(iv)   broad trade balancing of foreign exchange over the entire period of the MOU, in terms of balancing between the actual CIF value of imports of CKD/SKD kits/components and the FOB value of exports of cars and auto components over that period. While a firm that signs an MOU has an export obligation equivalent to the total CIF value of the imports made by the firm over the period of the MOU, there is a two-year moratorium during which the firm does not need to fulfill that commitment. The period of export obligation therefore begins from the third year of commencement of pro-

---

[10]   Paragraph 3(ii) also provides that this condition applies to new joint venture companies only. In response to a question from Japan, India stated that "this condition has been imposed on new joint venture companies because the existing companies have already invested more than their minimum stipulation." *Replies by India to Questions Posed by Japan*, G/TRIMS/W/15, circulated 30 October 1998, response to Question 18.

DSR 2002:V

Report of the Panel

duction. However, imports made during the moratorium count towards the firm's total export obligation under the MOU.

III. PARTIES' REQUESTS FOR FINDINGS AND RECOMMENDATIONS

A. US Claims and Requests for Findings

3.1 The **United States** contended that the local content and trade balancing requirements in Public Notice No. 60 and the MOUs, together with the Indian domestic legislation under which they had come into force, were inconsistent with the obligations of India under the General Agreement on Tariffs and Trade 1994 ("GATT 1994") and the Agreement on Trade-Related Investment Measures ("TRIMs Agreement"). The United States requested the Panel to find that the measures at issue in this dispute, the indigenization and the trade balancing requirements, imposed by Public Notice No. 60 and the MOUs, were inconsistent with Article III:4 and XI:1 of GATT 1994 and Articles 2.1. and 2.2 of the TRIMs Agreement.[11] The United States requested this Panel to make findings to this effect, and to recommend that India bring all such measures into conformity with its obligations.

3.2 The United States considered it would be appropriate for the Panel to rule on Public Notice No. 60 given that the requirements were still in place through the MOUs. The United States said it was not requesting the Panel to make findings on Public Notice No. 60 that were separate from its findings on the MOUs executed thereunder. The United States was, however, requesting that the Panel's findings encompass both Public Notice No. 60 and the individual MOUs. A comprehensive ruling by the Panel would apply to both Public Notice No. 60 (the source of the WTO-inconsistent requirements) and the MOUs (by which individual companies were bound to those WTO-inconsistent requirements), especially since Public Notice No. 60 was, as all the parties to this dispute agreed, in force at the time this Panel was established. However, the Panel need not analyze Public Notice No. 60 separately from the MOUs in order to make its findings.[12]

B. EC Claims and Requests for Findings

3.3 The European Communities said that its complaint was directed primarily against the indigenization and balancing requirements contained in the MOUs concluded under Public Notice No. 60.[13]

---

[11] See also Questions 1 and 17 of the Panel.
[12] See also US response to Question 72 of the Panel.
[13] The EC's complaint did not extent to the MOUs "as a whole". More precisely, the European Communities did not challenge the other two requirements imposed by the MOUs (i.e. the minimum foreign equity requirement and the manufacturing requirement).

1836   DSR 2002:V

- The European Communities claimed that the indigenization requirement violated Article III:4. It had not claimed that this requirement violates also Article XI:1.

- The European Communities claimed that the balancing requirement was inconsistent with both Article XI:1 and Article III:4 because the signatories were required to balance the value of the automotive products which they import themselves, as well as the value of any imported automotive products which they purchase from vendors within India[14].

- To the extent that the balancing requirements required the signatories to balance the value of the imported products which they purchase within India they were inconsistent with Article III:4.

- To the extent that the balancing requirements required the signatories to balance the value of the automotive products which they imported themselves, they restricted the importation of such products, thereby violating Article XI:1.

3.4   It also requested the Panel to make an express factual finding regarding the product scope of the trade balancing requirement.

3.5   The European Communities reiterated its request to the Panel to find that the trade balancing and indigenization requirements contained in Public Notice No. 60 and in the MOUs concluded thereunder were inconsistent with Articles III:4 and XI:1 of the GATT and Article 2.1 of the TRIMs Agreement as of the date of establishment of this Panel and had remained so after 1 April 2001. Furthermore, the European Communities requested the Panel to find that, at the time when the Panel was established, Public Notice No. 60 was inconsistent with Article XI:1 and III:4 of GATT and Article 2.1 of the TRIMs Agreement. It clarified that the measures applied after 1 April 2001 continued to be inconsistent with the GATT and the TRIMs Agreement because they were the same as the measures applied before that date.[15]

C.   India's Requests for Findings

3.6   As to the claim that Public Notice No. 60 and the trade balancing provisions of the MOUs are inconsistent with Articles III and XI of the GATT, India requested the Panel to make the following findings and recommendations:

3.7   If the Panel were to conclude that the matter before it is the operation of Public Notice No. 60 and the trade balancing provisions of the MOUs under India's former licensing regime, it should reject the complaints as inadmissible because this matter had already been satisfactorily resolved and settled as a result of the previous invocations of the DSU by the complainants. Specifically, India requested the Panel to find that:

---

[14]   See EC First Submission, at paras. 32 and 74.
[15]   See Question 87 of the Panel.

Report of the Panel

- the matter raised by the European Communities had already been settled through a mutually agreed solution jointly notified by the European Communities and India to the DSB in accordance with Article 3.6 of the DSU,

- the matter raised by the United States had already been adjudicated by the DSB in the proceedings on *India - Quantitative Restrictions on Imports of Agricultural, Textile and Industrial Products* (hereinafter "*India – Quantitative Restrictions*") (WT/DS90), and

- the re-invocation of the DSU in respect of the matters raised by the European Communities and the United States was inadmissible.

3.8   If the Panel were to conclude that the matter before it was the operation of Public Notice No. 60 and the trade balancing provisions under India's former licensing regime and were to regard the complaints as admissible, it should examine India's invocation of Article XVIII:B of the GATT and, in accordance with the precedent set by the Panel in *India – Quantitative Restrictions*, consult with experts under Article 13 of the DSU, including the IMF.[16]

3.9   If the Panel were to conclude that the operation of Public Notice No. 60 and the trade balancing provisions under India's former licensing regime was inconsistent with the GATT, it should - following the practice of previous panels[17] - note that the licensing regime had been abolished on 1 April 2001, that the Public Notice and the trade balancing provisions no longer applied since 1 April 2001 and that it was therefore not necessary for the Panel to recommend to the DSB in accordance with Article 19:1 of the DSU that it request India to bring these measures into conformity with the GATT.

3.10   If the Panel were to conclude that the matter before it is the operation of Public Notice No. 60 and the trade balancing provisions of the MOUs outside India's former import licensing regime, the Panel should reject the complainants' claims as factually baseless. Specifically, it should find that, in the absence of an import licensing regime, Public Notice No. 60 is not operational because it merely states how the former restrictions were to be administered and the trade balancing provisions do not entail any export obligation and hence do not restrict imports or favour domestic over imported products because they do not apply to freely importable products.

3.11   *As to the claim that the indigenization provisions set out in the MOUs are inconsistent with Article III of the GATT,* India requested the Panel to find that the Government of India had, since the abolition of the import licensing regime the discretion whether or not to apply its contractual rights under the MOUs and that this raised new legal issues not covered by the Panel's terms-of-reference. If the Panel were to rule that the indigenization requirements in the MOUs are in-

---

[16]   See the Panel Report on *India – Quantitative Restrictions,* WT/DS90/R, DSR 1999:V, 1799, paras 5.11 through 5.13.
[17]   See the Panel Report on *Indonesia – Certain Measures Affecting the Automobile Industry,* (hereinafter "*Indonesia – Autos*"), WT/DS54/R, WT/DS55/R, WT/DS59/R, WT/DS64/R, adopted 23 July 1998, para. 14.9 and the reports cited therein (DSR 1998:VI, 2201).

1838   DSR 2002:V

consistent with Article III:4, it should find that, according to the evidence submitted by the parties, there remained as of May 2001 only one company that was still bound by the indigenization requirement with respect to one car model. India therefore requested the Panel to limit any recommendation under Article 19:1 of the DSU to the indigenization requirement that remains to be performed by that particular company with respect to that model.

3.12   *As to the claims related to the TRIMs Agreement*, India requested the Panel to find that the provisions on trade balancing and indigenization set out in Public Notice No. 60 and the MOUs are trade measures and not investment measures and therefore do not fall within the framework of the TRIMs Agreement.

IV.   ARGUMENTS OF THE PARTIES

A.   *Factual Arguments*

1.   *The Licensing Regime*

4.1   The **European Communities** noted that, at the time the Panel was established, India regulated the imports of goods by means of a Negative List contained in the Export-Import Policy (the "EXIM Policy)[18]. The Negative List[19] consisted of "prohibited"[20] items, "restricted" items and "canalized"[21] items. "Restricted" items were permitted to be imported only against a specific import license issued by the Director General of Foreign Trade in India's Ministry of Commerce ("DGFT"[22]). The granting of import licenses for "restricted" items was not automatic[23]. Licenses were granted on a discretionary basis or, in some cases, subject to the conditions set out in advance in a Public Notice.

4.2   Under the EXIM Policy 1997-2002, passenger cars (HS[24] 87.03), and chassis (HS 87.06) and bodies (HS 87.07) therefor, were classified as "restricted" items in the Negative List. In contrast, parts and accessories for passenger cars (including *inter alia* those falling within HS 87.08, 40.11, 40.12, 40.13, 70.07,

---

[18]   The EXIM Policy is formulated and announced from time to time by the Indian Government on the basis of the authority conferred by the Foreign Trade Development and Regulation Act, 1992 (hereinafter the "FTDR" Act) (cf. Section 5 of the FDTR). The policy currently in effect is the Export and Import Policy 1 April 1997 – 31 March 2002.

[19]   Chapter 16 of the EXIM Policy. The Negative List is further specified in the "ITC (HS) Classifications of Export and Import Items", published and notified by the DGFT (cf. Section 4.1 of the EXIM Policy).

[20]   Section 4.4 of the EXIM Policy ("Prohibited items in the Negative List of imports shall not be imported [...]").

[21]   Section 4.8 of the EXIM Policy ("Any goods, the import or export of which is canalized, may be imported by the canalizing agency specified in the Negative Lists [...]").

[22]   Section 4.5 of the EXIM Policy ("Any goods, the export or import of which is restricted through licensing, may be exported or imported only in accordance with a license issued in this behalf").

[23]   Section 4.7 of the EXIM Policy ("No person may claim a license as a right and the Director General of Foreign Trade or the licensing authority shall have the power to refuse to grant or renew a license in accordance with provisions of the Act and the Rules made thereunder").

[24]   The term "HS" refers to the Harmonized Commodity Description and Coding System evolved by the World Customs Organization.

DSR 2002:V

Report of the Panel

70.09, 90.29, and 94.01) were not included in the Negative List and could, therefore, be freely imported.

4.3   In accordance with Rule 2(a) of the General Rules for the Interpretation of the HS nomenclature[25], the Indian customs authorities classify within HS 87.03 complete passenger cars that are presented unassembled ("CKD" kits), as well as incomplete passenger cars, whether assembled or disassembled ("SKD" kits), provided that they have the "essential character" of a complete car[26]. According to the Indian Government, imports of parts and components were considered to have the "essential character" of a passenger car where, at least, all the following seven items were imported: engine, gear box, chassis, transmission assembly system, body/cab, suspension system and axles front and rear[27].

4.4   The **United States** stated that India applied licensing requirements both to finished vehicles as such and to SKD/CKD kits/components for such vehicles. Consequently, when Public Notice No. 60 was issued, no one was permitted to import finished motor vehicles, or kits and components in SKD/CKD form for such vehicles, into India without a license. At the time Public Notice No. 60 was issued, 90 tariff line items in Chapter 87 ("vehicles other than railway or tramway rolling-stock, and parts and accessories thereof") of India's tariff schedule were "restricted" and therefore subject to import licensing requirements.[28] At the time the panel was established, these import licensing requirements still applied to approximately 75 tariff line items in Chapter 87.

4.5   **India** clarified that some tariff lines covering cars in the form of CKD/SKD kits that were identified as restricted for "AUTO/BOP-XVIII-B" reasons in India's notification to the BOPs Committee (WT/BOP/N/24) required licenses under the MOUs. All tariff lines covering components for cars that were identified in the notification as restricted, including for "BOP-XVIII :B" reasons, also required licenses under the MOUs. Apart from CKD/SKD kits of cars, chassis with engines mounted for passenger motor cars and bodies (initial equipment and replacement parts) were also under Restricted Category requiring an import licence. As per Chapter 87, parts and accessories of motor vehicles like bumpers, safety seat belts, mounted brake linings, gear boxes, drive-axles, non driving axles, road wheels, suspension shock absorbers, radiators, silencers and exhaust

---

[25]   Rule 2(a) of the General Rules for the Interpretation of the HS reads as follows:
"Any reference in a heading to an article shall be taken to include a reference to that article incomplete or unfinished, provided that, as presented, the incomplete or unfinished article has the essential character of the complete or finished article. It shall also be taken to include a reference to that Article complete or finished (or falling to be classified as complete or finished by virtue of this rule), presented unassembled or disassembled"
[26]   India's responses to Questions by the EC (hereinafter "EC Questions"), dated 9 May 1999, Response to Question 1(a) .
[27]   See Public Notice No. 3/98 issued by the Delhi Customs House on 6 January 1998.
[28]   *E.g.,* tariff heading 870321.01 ("Other vehicles, with spark-ignition internal combustion reciprocating piston engine; Of a cylinder capacity not exceeding 1,000 cc; Motor car, new, assembled") is classified as "Restricted: Not permitted to be imported except against a licence or in accordance with a Public Notice issued in this behalf."

India – Autos

pipes, clutches, steering wheels, steering columns and steering boxes, etc. were under free category.[29]

2. Public Notice No. 60 and the MOUs

4.6 **India** explained that Public Notice No. 60 clarified policies first adopted in 1995. The revision of the MOU scheme in 1997 was designed to render the existing policies more uniform and transparent. The parameters applied in 1995 were individually negotiated with each car manufacturer wishing to import CKD/SKD kits. As from 1997, the parameters followed a common format; the product coverage was the same.[30] Public Notice No. 60 improved upon the 1995 MOUs by removing the discretionary element from licensing, by stipulating uniform commitments for all MOU signatories, and by making the granting of licenses "automatic" upon fulfilment of the conditions stipulated therein.[31]

4.7 India went on to explain that Public Notice No. 60 was adopted to ensure the uniform and transparent administration of these restrictions. It declared that only car manufacturers that had signed an MOU with provisions on foreign equity, assembly operations, indigenization and trade balancing would obtain a license and that a license could be denied if the MOU provisions were not observed.[32] India explained that only the car manufacturers that wished to import SKD/CKD kits were required to sign an MOU. This requirement did not apply to any manufacturer that did not wish to import such kits. By accepting the commitments set out in the MOUs, a car manufacturer obtained a significant economic advantage, namely the quota rents associated with the importation of SKD/CKD kits within the framework of India's restrictive licensing scheme. The quota rents enjoyed by the manufacturers, on the one hand, and the commitments to take actions to mitigate the adverse balance-of-payments impact of their imports, on the other hand, constituted a balanced whole.

4.8 The European Communities pointed out that Public Notice No. 60 had no termination date.[33] Nevertheless, according to the Indian Government, "once the quantitative restrictions which cover autos and auto parts in the phase out plan are removed, the Public Notice. 60 shall cease to operate".[34] By its own terms, Public Notice No. 60 applied only to joint ventures between Indian and foreign investors.[35] Nevertheless, the Indian Government had indicated that companies

---

[29] It should be noted that any part/component of a car e.g., gear box, radiator, silencer, etc. which were under free category could be imported without any licence as long as these were imported individually. However, in case, these parts/components formed a part of a CKD/SKD kit of a car itself was under restricted category and required a licence for its import into the country prior to 31.3.2001.

[30] Response to Question 43 of the Panel.

[31] Response to Question 45 of the Panel.

[32] In practice, the Director-General of Foreign Trade never denied a license to a signatory for failing to meet the indigenization or trade balancing requirements. (Panel Question 51).

[33] India's responses to Questions from the United States dated 10 May 1999 (hereinafter "US Questions"), response to Question 10.

[34] Ibid.

[35] Public Notice No. 60, at paras. 1 and 2.

DSR 2002:V

1841

Report of the Panel

wholly owned by Indians are subject to the same requirements.[36] Public Notice No. 60 applied to both "existing" (i.e. those established before 12 December 1997) and "new" joint ventures.[37]

4.9   The **United States** noted that Paragraph 4 of Public Notice No. 60 provided that the MOU scheme was to be enforced through the import licensing mechanism. Paragraph 5 provided for MOU signatories to submit annual reports and for Indian officials to conduct an annual review of signatories' progress towards meeting their MOU obligations. The United States noted that Paragraph 8 of Public Notice No. 60 required MOUs to be signed in a standard format, which was appended to the Notice.[38] The MOU was to be signed by the Government of India acting through the Director General of Foreign Trade and by the managing director of the manufacturing company on its behalf. Paragraph III of the standard MOU format reconfirmed each of the requirements of Public Notice No. 60. The requirement to establish actual manufacturing facilities, and not mere assembly facilities, appeared in MOU paragraph III, clause (iii); the US$50 million equity requirement appeared in MOU paragraph III, clause (ii); the indigenization obligation appeared in MOU paragraph III, clause (iv); and the trade balancing obligation appeared in MOU paragraph III, clause (vi). All or virtually all companies manufacturing automobiles in India had signed an MOU in accordance with the standard format, and it was easy to see why. Because companies were not granted an import license for CKD/SKD kits until an MOU was signed, India's policy effectively prohibited any company from importing CKD/SKD kits and components unless it abided by the terms and conditions of Public Notice No. 60 and the MOU.

(a)   The "indigenization" Requirement (paragraph 3 (iii) of Public Notice No. 60) and Paragraph III(IV) of the MOU)

4.10   The **European Communities** described its understanding of the "indigenization" requirement as follows: the MOU signatories must achieve a level of indigenization of 50% in the third year from the first import or earlier, and of 70% no later than the fifth year.[39] The Indian Government had confirmed that "indigenization" meant "local content"[40]. The European Communities understood that in practice the percentage of indigenization was computed in accordance with the following formula:

(CIF value of imported parts and materials assembled into the passenger car / ex works value of the passenger car) x 100

---

[36]   US Questions. In response to Question 3, India stated   that   "Indian companies importing CKD/SKD kits are also being subjected to the same requirements of indigenization as well as foreign exchange trade balancing". See also India's response to Question 16.
[37]   Public Notice No. 60, at para. 2.
[38]   See Table 2.
[39]   *Ibid.*, para (iii).
[40]   US Questions, response to Question 6.

1842   DSR 2002:V

India – Autos

4.11   The European Communities further understood that the numerator in-cluded not only the value of the parts and materials imported directly by the MOU signatory but also the value of any imported parts and materials purchased in India by the joint ventures from local vendors. Public Notice No. 60 did not prescribe whether the percentage of indigenization was to be measured on a model, category or manufacturer basis. It appeared that, in practice, the Indian authorities might allow the manufacturers to meet the requirement on any of those bases.[41]

4.12   The **United States** noted that once an MOU signing firm had reached an indigenization level of 70%, there would be no need for further import licenses. By implication, licenses would be withheld if the targets were not met. India had confirmed that the MOU limited the importation of SKD/CKD kits/components when a firm failed to meet the indigenization requirement. The standard MOU format also imposed other requirements on the manufacturing firm (e.g.,, it re-quired the firm to state its intended level of indigenization year by year). Signifi-cantly, the MOU also required that the firm "shall aggressively pursue and achieve as soon as possible the development of the local supply base and in-creased local content". This requirement highlighted the intentions that underlay the MOU scheme: to induce manufacturing firms to abandon imported goods and to favor domestic goods instead. With respect to automotive components, the Secretariat's report for the Indian Trade Policy Review noted that the value of their production rose from Rs33.6 million in 1990/91 to Rs67.5 billion by 1994/95 and Rs91 billion in 1995/96. Indian authorities estimated the level of indigenization in the automobile components sector at around 90%. This high level of indigenization was due in part to a number of previous requirements that companies investing in the automobile sector in India must agree to increase the level of indigenization in their units within a certain period of time. Public No-tice No. 60 and the MOUs continued in this tradition of nurturing the domestic auto parts and components industry. Indeed, that was the very reason that Indian officials gave for the adoption of Public Notice No. 60: "The objective of the new policy is to encourage local production of auto-components and thus, bring in modern technology and develop this key segment, explain ministry offi-cials"[42].

4.13   **India** pointed out that the signatories of the MOUs were required to reach a level of 70 per cent of indigenization. An MOU was effectively terminated on the date of the achievement of an indigenization level of 70 per cent, except for the export obligations that accrued before that date. In this regard, it was perti-nent to note that, according to the WTO Secretariat report prepared for the 1998 Trade Policy Review of India, the level of indigenization in the automobile com-ponents sector was estimated to be around 90 per cent.[43] Moreover, according to as yet unverified reports received from car manufacturers in the autumn of 2000,

---

[41]   *Ibid.*
[42]   "Car Makers Have to Sign New MOUs in Accordance with New Automobile Policy", *Business Standard*, December 11, 1997.
[43]   Trade Policy Review, India: Report by the Secretariat (WT/TPR/S/33), 5 March 1998, para. 109.

DSR 2002:V   1843

Report of the Panel

most of the signatories had almost reached the 70 per cent threshold. By 1 April 2001, there might consequently no longer be any signatory bound by an indigenization requirement. India was examining this situation. India was committed to resolving it in a manner that did not entail any inconsistencies with its WTO obligations. In late April and early May of 2001, officials of the Ministry of Commerce and Industry met with the most important car manufacturers from the EC, Japan and the United States to verify their performance under the MOU. Subsequent to these meetings, these signatories confirmed in writing that they had all achieved or exceeded the 70 per cent threshold. The only exception was General Motors India, which had achieved only a 60 per cent level of indigenization in respect of one of its car models. However, this company wrote in a letter dated 4 May 2001 to the Commerce Secretary:

> Localization for any player is imperative in order to be competitive in the market. Keeping this in mind, we have . . crossed 70% location in the case of Astra much before the target date as envisaged in the MOU. . .In the case of Corsa, although launched only about a year back, we had already localized 60.31 % and intend to cross 70 % localization during this fiscal year . . .

4.14   The results of the survey clearly confirmed that car manufacturers had had no difficulty meeting the 70 per cent threshold and that, except in respect of one recently launched car model, all surveyed manufacturers reached the threshold in the meantime. Indeed, the survey showed that indigenization was part of the manufacturers drive towards greater competitiveness.

(b)   The "trade balancing" Requirement (paragraph 3 (iv) of Public Notice No. 60 and Paragraph III (vi) of the MOU)

4.15   The **European Communities** understood that the requirement to achieve "broad trade balancing of foreign exchange" translated into the obligation to balance the CIF value of imports of "CKD/SKD kits/Components" and the FOB value of exports of "cars and auto components" over the entire period of duration of the MOU.[44] The MOU signatories were not required to start exporting until the third year from the commencement of production.[45] But the value of imports made during the first two years must be balanced in subsequent years.[46] Public Notice No. 60 further specified that from the fourth year onwards "the value of imports of CKD/SKD may be regulated with reference to the export obligation fulfilled in the previous years as per the MOU". The precise meaning of this provision, however, remained unclear.[47] The wording of Public Notice No. 60 suggested that the balancing obligation extended not only to imports of "CKD/SKD kits" but also to imports of "components". That interpretation had been corrobo-

---

[44]   Public Notice No. 60, para 3 (iv). See also Japan's Questions, response to Question 23.
[45]   *Ibid.*
[46]   *Ibid.*
[47]   See Japan's Questions, response to Question 24, and US Questions, response to Questions 7 and 8.

India – Autos

rated to the European Communities by some signatories of MOUs. During the consultations, however, India asserted that "the signatories have to neutralize only the value of imported CKD/SKD kits and not of those components which are freely imported".[48] It was also unclear whether the balancing requirement applied to imported kits and components purchased by the signatories within India, or only to those which they import themselves. Before the TRIMs Committee India explained that "[b]road trade balancing of foreign exchange ... includes the purchases in India of the imported components or CKD/SKD kits"[49]. Yet, during the consultations, India answered to a question from the United States that "the signatories of the MOU have to neutralize only the value of CKD/SKD imported by them ...."[50]

4.16 The **United States** added that Public Notice No. 60 also made clear that the trade balancing obligation remained in place independently of the indigenization obligation: "However, they [i.e. firms that have achieved 70% indigenization] will discharge the export obligation corresponding to the import made by them till that time." India had confirmed that a company's imports could be limited under this provision if it had not met its export obligations. India did not intend to terminate the requirements of Public Notice No. 60 or the MOUs on 1 April 2001. India had told the United States directly that the MOUs remained effective even after 1 April 2001. Moreover, Indian officials had told the press that automobile manufacturers who had entered into MOUs in the past would have to honour their commitments in terms of exports, localization level, and minimum capital invested in the venture. India's Director-General of Foreign Trade himself had confirmed India's intentions. According to published reports, in response to "domestic auto-ancillary units, who felt threatened by the removal of QRs [and] have appealed to the government to protect their interests", the Director-General had "hinted that manufacturers using a large percentage of local components are likely to benefit from several incentives to be announced as part of the new policy". He added that "under all circumstances, the auto industry will have to fulfill the outstanding export commitments even after quantitative restrictions are removed".[51]

4.17 **India** explained that imports of cars in the form of CKD/SKD kits and of components subject to import restrictions were taken into account for calculating the value of imports for trade balancing purposes.[52] This included purchases in India of imported components or CKD/SKD kits.[53] That is, if an MOU signatory purchased a component that was subject to import restrictions in India from ei-

---

[48] EC Questions, response to Question 8. See also US Questions, response to Questions 7 and 8.

[49] Japan's Questions, response to Question 23.

[50] US Questions, response to Questions 7 and 8.

[51] "India's New Automobiles Policy Will Protect Domestic Industry Using Tariffs, Officials Say," *BNA Daily Report for Executives*, 22 August 2000.

[52] The following tariff lines in Chapter 87 that were notified as restricted for AUTO/BOP reasons cover cars in the form of CKD/SKD kits: 870321.04; 870322.04; 870323.04; 870331.04; 870332.04; and 870333.03. The tariff lines covering components for cars that were identified as restricted for BOP-XVIII-B reasons such as 870600.01, 870600.09, 870710.01 and 870710.02 would also have been subject to MOU signatory license privileges.

[53] WT/G/TRIMS/W/15, p. 9, 30 October 1998.

DSR 2002:V

Report of the Panel

ther a trading company or another MOU signatory that had imported such a component on the basis of an import license, the value of such components would be taken into account for purposes of the trade balancing requirement. In every case, the license clearly specified that it was subject to the trade balancing requirement. Components that were not subject to import restrictions under the EXIM Policy 1997-2002 were not taken into account for purposes of the trade balancing requirement.

4.18   India considered that it should ensure that all car manufacturers that had accepted MOUs were treated equally. It was therefore not the intention of the Government of India to release the car manufacturers from the commitments they had assumed under the MOUs as a result of imports of SKD/CKD kits prior to 1 April 2001. India intended to require the signatories of the MOUs to continue to perform after 1 April 2001 those provisions of the MOUs that were consistent with India's WTO obligations. India was also of the view that to require the signatories of the MOUs to perform the obligations they had assumed as a result of imports of SKD/CKD kits *prior to 1 April 2001 wa*s perfectly consistent with India's obligations under WTO law. The trade balancing requirement did not remain in place after 1 April, 2001. As a result of the abolition of the import licensing regime, there remained only a WTO-consistent obligation to discharge export obligations that accrued as a result of imports prior to 1 April 2001. As from 1 April 2001, the signatories of the MOUs would continue to be required to discharge the export obligations corresponding to the imports made by them *before* that date. They would thus be required to discharge the export obligations they had already assumed *but would no longer incur any new export obligations as a result of the further importation of SKD/CKD kits*. From 1 April 2001, the right to import SKD/CKD kits would consequently no longer in any way depend on, or vary with, the level of exports achieved. For this reason, the export requirements would no longer create any incentive to purchase local products. Since 1 April 2001, the import restrictions for SKD/CKD kits and car components had been abolished and no licenses referring to the trade balancing requirement had been issued. The signatories of the MOUs had therefore no longer incurred any new export obligations as a result of the importation of SKD/CKD kits or components.

4.19   The **European Communities** noted that India had declared that, as from 1 April 2001,

> The signatories of the MOUs will be required to discharge the export obligations they have already assumed but will no longer incur any new export obligations as a result of the further importation of SKD/CKD kits. Since 1 April 2001, the right to import SKD/CKD kits will consequently no longer in any way depend on, or vary with, the level of exports achieved.[54]

4.20   The interpretation of the obligations imposed by the balancing requirements after 1 April 2001 made by India in the reply to Panel Question 33 could

---

[54]   India's response to Question 33.

1846   DSR 2002:V

not be reconciled with the wording of paragraph 3(iv) of Public Notice No. 60 and paragraph III(iv) of the MOUs. The European Communities's interpretation of those two provisions had been confirmed by India's answer to Question 50(c), when India explained that

> Under paragraph 3(iv) of Public Notice 60 and paragraph III (iv) of the MOUs, the MOU signatory goes "outside the ambit of the MOU" and will not require any import licenses once it achieves a 70% indigenization level. However t*he MOU signatory will be required to achieve trade balancing of the foreign exchange obligation incurred on imports made up to that date.*[55]

In the European Communities's view, the wording of the MOUs did not support the interpretation that the signatories were not required to balance the imports of CKD/SKD/components made after 1 April 2001. Even if it were correct that the parties agreed in the MOUs that imports of components not subject to licensing at that time would not be covered by the balancing requirements, it would not follow necessarily that the elimination of the import licensing as of 1 April 2001 entailed automatically the elimination of all the balancing requirements agreed in the MOUs. As regarded the different issue of whether imports of "CKD/SKD kits/components" made after 1 April 2001 had to be balanced, the European Communities had shown that the MOUs contained no provision stipulating that the balancing requirements would cease to apply in respect of any product which ceased to be subject to import licensing. The European Communities understood that in the MOUs the signatories assumed the commitment to export an amount equivalent to the value of imports estimated for the entire duration of the MOU. Those estimates included imports of "CKD/SKD kits/components" to be made after 1 April 2001, since at the time when the MOUs were concluded it was not anticipated that the import licensing would have to be eliminated as of that date.[56]

4.21   Paragraph III(vi) of the standard format for MOU attached to Public Notice No. 60 stipulated in relevant part that

> "... the party shall achieve broad trade balancing of foreign exchange *over the entire period* of the MOU in terms of balancing between the actual CIF value of imports of CKD/SKD Kits/components and the FOB value of export of cars and auto components over the said period."[57]

4.22   Thus, the signatories must neutralize all the imports made "over the entire period of the MOU", and not just those made before 1 April 2001. Paragraph 3(iii) of Public Notice No. 60 further provided that

> "... as and when the time firms achieve 70% indigenization, they would go outside the ambit of the MOU automatically. However,

---

[55]   India's response to Question 50 (c). [Underlining added].
[56]   EC's response to Questions 93 and 94 of the Panel.
[57]   Emphasis added.

DSR 2002:V

Report of the Panel

they will discharge the export obligation corresponding to the imports made by them till that time."

4.23   This indicated clearly that the signatories must balance all the imports made until they achieved an indigenization level of 70%. Thus, any signatory which, as of 1 April 2001, had not achieved that threshold would be required to balance imports made after that date. In other words, the signatories were required to balance all the imports made by them until they achieved a 70% indigenization level. Since some signatories had not achieved that level as of 1 April 2001 (and had not achieved it yet), the imports made by those signatories after 1 April 2001 must still be balanced with exports, contrary to India's contention. India recognized expressly that, after 1 April 2001, the signatories continued to be required to meet the same indigenization commitments.[58] Nevertheless, it argued once again that

> ... according to as yet unverified reports received from the car manufacturers in the autumn of last year, most of the signatories have almost reached the 70 per cent threshold. At present, there may consequently no longer be any signatory bound by the indigenization requirements.[59]

4.24   This was mere speculation, which could neither form the basis for an informed panel decision nor give satisfaction to the complainants. The European Communities encouraged India to verify, once and for all, the reports in question, instead of complaining about the supposed "inappropriateness"[60] of bringing this dispute. India had also stated that the balancing requirements applied not only with respect to imports of CKD/SKD kits but also of those "components" which were subject to discretionary import licensing until 1 April 2001.[61] The European Communities would note, nevertheless, that the relevant provisions of Public Notice No. 60 and of the MOUs referred to all "components", without any further qualification. Should the Panel accept India's explanations regarding the product scope of the balancing requirements, the European Communities would reiterate its request that the Panel make an express factual finding to that effect in its report.

4.25   The **United States** continued to see some difficulties with India's position. First, paragraph III, clause (vi) of the MOU required MOU signatories to balance their imports of SKD and CKD kits and components "over the entire period of the MOU". India had said that it did not apply a balancing obligation to kits and components importable without a license – but India did not address the phrase "over the entire period of the MOU", even when the Panel expressly asked it to do so.[62] India had yet to explain how this phrase functioned under its domestic law, and how India ensured that a car manufacturer whose MOU was still in force was not accruing further export obligations for current imports. Sec-

---

[58]   India's response to Question 33, at p. 3, para. 2.
[59]   India's response to Question 33, p. 4 *in fine* and p. 5, para. 1.
[60]   *Ibid.*, at p. 5, para. 2.
[61]   India's response to Questions 47-49.
[62]   India's response to Question 50(a) of the Panel.

1848

DSR 2002:V

ond, even if it were true that no new or additional export obligations were accruing after 1 April 2001, the United States disagreed with India's contention that the level of an MOU signatory's imports was not restricted by the level of its exports. It was still doubtful whether an MOU signatory was permitted to import CKD/SKD kits in excess of the signatory's *accrued but not yet discharged* export obligations.

4.26   **India** confirmed that, in respect of freely importable products, the MOU signatory did not assume any export obligations that might limit its right to import or create an incentive to purchase domestic components. The European Communities and the United States interpreted the trade balancing provisions in the MOUs differently. Their reading of the MOUs was that they entitled the Government of India to require the signatory to offset through exports the foreign exchange expenditures for all imports of CKD/SKD kits and components whether subject to licensing or not.[63] This was not, and had in practice never been, the interpretation of the Government of India. The Government of India had never requested any of the MOU signatories to apply the trade balancing requirement to freely importable car components and had ceased applying the requirement in respect of all imports of cars and car components after 1 April 2001. This practice confirmed that the trade balancing requirement in the MOUs had always been understood by the Government of India to apply only to imports subject to licensing. India could not be required to prove the negative. India could not, therefore, be asked to prove that it had *not* required trade balancing in respect of freely importable products. It was consequently for the complainants to demonstrate that the Government of India had requested MOU signatories to apply the trade balancing requirements in respect of freely importable products. The MOUs had now been in place since 1996 and car companies had during this period imported freely importable components. If the complainants were correct, they should be able to indicate at least one instance in which the Government of India had required trade balancing for freely importable components. So far, they had failed to do so and had therefore not met their burden of presenting a *prima facie* case of violation.[64]

B.   Has The Matter Been Settled and Adjudicated?

4.27   **India** considered that the matter that the complainants had presented to the Panel in their first submissions concerned the application of the discretionary licensing system which had already been the subject of complaints brought by each of the complainants under the DSU. Both complaints concerned the application of India's discretionary licensing system to automobiles imported in the form of semi-knocked down or completely knocked down components or kits (SKD/CKD kits). This licensing system had already been the subject of complaints brought by each of the complainants under the Dispute Settlement Under-

---

[63]   Responses to the Questions of the Panel to the European Communities after the First Meeting with the Parties, paras. 10-14. US response to Panel Questions, paras. 31-33.
[64]   India's response to Question 111 of the Panel.

Report of the Panel

standing (DSU). India noted that the European Communities[65] and the United States[66], together with other developed country Members,[67] brought complaints in July 1997 under the DSU against all of India's import restrictions notified under Article XVIII:B, including cars. Basing themselves on a determination by the International Monetary Fund that India's foreign exchange reserves were adequate, the European Communities and the United States claimed that India's import restrictions were no longer justified by Article XVIII:B.

4.28   According to Article 21.3(b) of the DSU, the recommendations and rulings of the DSB must be implemented within a reasonable period of time, the length of which may be determined by agreement between the parties to the dispute. India and the United States agreed that India would remove its restrictions in stages and that the reasonable period of time would expire on 1 April 2001.[68] India must therefore bring its import restrictions, including those applied to SKD/CKD kits, into conformity with its WTO obligations by that date. According to the mutually agreed solution with the European Communities, India must accord to the EC treatment no less favourable than that accorded to any other country in respect of the elimination of the restrictions.[69] As a consequence, the implementation period effectively ended on 1 April 2001, both under the solution agreed with the European Communities under Article 3.6 of the DSU and under the agreement reached with the United States pursuant to Article 21.3(b) of the DSU.

4.29   In the complaint brought by the European Communities, a mutually agreed solution was found which was notified to the Dispute Settlement Body (DSB). In the complaint brought by the United States, the DSB issued rulings on the basis of panel and Appellate Body findings. Under Articles 3.6 and 21.3(b) of the DSU, India agreed with both the European Communities and the United States to bring the licensing system into conformity with its WTO obligations as of 1 April 2001. This commitment covered also the application of India's discretionary licensing system to SKD/CKD kits. In India's view, the matter raised by the European Communities and the United States in the case before this Panel had therefore already been settled and adjudicated in accordance with the DSU.

4.30   India considered that the dispute with the European Communities had been settled through an exchange of letters notified to the DSB on 7 April 1998 as a mutually agreed solution under Article 3.6 of the DSU. The exchange of letters stipulated that the import restrictions applied to specified products would be phased out in stages by 31 March 2003. It further stipulated that, as long as

---

[65]   WT/DS96/1.

[66]   WT/DS90/1.

[67]   Australia (WT/DS91/1), Canada (WT/DS92/1), New Zealand (WT/DS93/1) and Switzerland (WT/DS94/1).

[68]   WT/DS90/15.

[69]   Paragraph 3 of the mutually agreed solution provides that: "India shall grant to the EC treatment no less favourable than that granted by India to any other country with respect to the elimination or modification of import restrictions on the products in the Annex and those in Annex II of document WT/BOP/N/24, under any form, either autonomously or pursuant to agreement or understanding with that country, including pursuant to the settlement of any outstanding dispute under the WTO Understanding on Rules and Procedures Governing the Settlement of Disputes".

1850   DSR 2002:V

India complied with its phase-out commitments, *"the European Communities will refrain from action under GATT Article XXII or Article XXIII" as regards the restrictions notified by India under Article XVIII:B.*[70] The joint notification of this settlement to the DSB also made clear that the European Communities and India had reached a mutually agreed solution with respect to the whole of the dispute on which the European Communities had requested consultations. India had fully complied with every aspect of the mutually agreed solution notified in accordance with Article 3.6 of the DSU. Notwithstanding the fact that India had fully complied with the notified solution, the European Communities had re-invoked the DSU with respect to the application of the discretionary licensing to one of the items notified under Article XVIII:B.

4.31   It was not clear from the submission what precisely *the scope of measure at issue* was. The complainants referred to the import licensing regime, Public Notice No. 60 and the MOUs. They acknowledged that the import licensing regime applied to CKD/SKD kits would not be applied after 1 April 2001. They also seemed to acknowledge that Public Notice No. 60, which implemented that licensing regime, would no longer be operational after that date. Their concern seemed to relate primarily to measures India might take after 1 April in respect of the MOUs *outside the framework of the import licensing regime and Public Notice No. 60.* India asked the Panel to request the complainants to clarify whether in their view the measure at issue in this proceeding was the enforcement of MOUs through the import licensing regime and Notice No. 60 or whether it was limited to the enforcement of MOUs outside the licensing regime and Notice No. 60. If the complainants were to respond that their complaints related to *the enforcement of MOUs through the import licensing regime and Public Notice No. 60*, India would ask the Panel to issue a preliminary ruling to the effect that both complaints were inadmissible because the DSU cannot be invoked in respect of the same matter twice. In this context, India requested the Panel to ask the complainants to clarify whether or not, in their view, India must cease the application of its import licensing regime to CKD/SKD kits after 1 April 2001 as a result of the agreements that India concluded with the complainants under Article 3.6 and 21:3(b) of the DSU. In particular, India asked the panel to request the United States to answer the following questions: Would the United States consider itself entitled to suspend concessions in accordance with Article 22 of the DSU if India were to maintain its licensing regime for CKD/SKD kits and Public Notice No. 60 after 1 April 2001 contrary to the findings of the panel on *India - Quantitative Restrictions.* If so, what additional rights did the United States expect to obtain from the present proceeding? If not, should India await the results of the present proceeding before acting on this matter?

---

[70]   WT/DS96/8, p. 2.

Report of the Panel

1. Has the Matter Been Settled?

4.32 From the start, the **European Communities** had made it clear that the measures in dispute were not allowed by the 1997 Agreement[71]: in the first place, the 1997 Agreement only allowed India to maintain restrictions on imports and not on the internal purchase or use of already imported products; second, the 1997 Agreement only authorized India to maintain restrictions with respect to passenger cars (including in CKD or SKD form), and chassis and bodies therefor, but not with respect to other "components" for passenger cars; and third, the 1997 Agreement, read in conjunction with the 1999 Agreement, required India to eliminate all the import restrictions on passenger cars, and chassis and bodies therefor, no later than 1 April 2001. Yet, according to India's own explanations, the MOUs would nevertheless remain valid and legally enforceable after that date.

4.33 **India** responded to the European Communities' arguments as follows: first, the European Communities argued that the mutually agreed solution "only allows India to maintain restrictions on imports and not on the internal purchase or use of already imported products". This argument could not be reconciled with the fact that the European Communities was asking the Panel to find that the measures at issue constituted import restrictions and that the alleged restrictions on the internal purchase and use of imported products were part and parcel of the import restrictions that India must in any case eliminate as a result of the mutually agreed solution. Second, the European Communities had argued that the mutually agreed solution "only authorizes India to maintain restrictions with respect to passenger cars (including in CKD or SKD form), and chassis and bodies therefor, but not with respect to other "components" for passenger cars". In fact India confined its import restrictions to CKD/SKD kits. Therefore, India was in full compliance with the mutually agreed solution. Moreover, as noted above, the joint notification made to the DSB confirmed that the mutually agreed solution resolved the whole of the dispute on which the European Communities had requested consultations. Third, the European Communities had argued that the mutually agreed solution "was not a 'covered agreement' within the meaning of Articles 1 and 2 of the DSU; therefore, India could not invoke that Agreement in order to justify the violation of its obligations under the GATT and the TRIMs

---

[71] The European Communities recalled that, in any event, the 1997 Agreement between the European Communities and India was not a "covered agreement" within the meaning of Articles 1 and 2 DSU Therefore, India could not invoke that Agreement in order to justify the violation of its obligations under the GATT and the TRIMs Agreement. See the Report of the Appellate Body on *European Communities – Measures Affecting the Importation of Certain Poultry Products*, WT/DS69/AB/R, adopted on 23 July 1998, paras. 79-80 (DSR 1998:V, 2031), where the Appellate Body concluded that a bilateral agreement concluded by Brazil and the European Communities under Article XXVIII of GATT was not a "covered agreement". See also the Panel Report on *Korea – Measures Affecting Imports of Fresh, Chilled and Frozen Beef*, (hereinafter "*Korea – Various Measures on Beef*"), WT/DS161/R, WT/DS169/R, para. 539 (DSR 2001:I, 59), where the Panel emphasized that it had examined the provisions of the "Records-of-Understanding" concluded by Korea with some other Members "not with a view to 'enforcing' the contents of these bilateral agreements, but strictly for the purposes of interpreting an ambiguous WTO provision, i.e. Note 6 to Korea's schedule".

Agreement. In India's view, it was however completely irrelevant that the mutually agreed solution was not a covered agreement within the meaning of Article 1 of the DSU and that it could therefore not provide an exemption from the obligations under the GATT and the TRIMs Agreement. The issue was whether the DSU could be invoked again in respect of a matter formally raised under the DSU and settled through a mutually agreed solution notified under the DSU. This issue was related to the European Communities's procedural rights under the DSU, not India's substantive obligations under a covered agreement.

4.34   India went on to say that, under the DSU, mutually agreed solutions were clearly a formally recognized procedure for reaching settlement. The following paragraphs of Article 3 of the DSU left no doubt in that respect:

> "3.   *The prompt settlement* of situations in which a Member considers that any benefits accruing to it directly or indirectly under the covered agreements are being impaired by measures taken by another Member *is essential to the effective functioning of the WTO* and the maintenance of a proper balance between the rights and obligations of Members.
>
> 6.   Mutually agreed solutions to matters formally raised under the consultation and dispute settlement provisions of the covered agreements shall be notified to the DSB and the relevant Councils and Committees, where any Member may raise any point relating thereto.
>
> 7.   .....The aim of the dispute settlement mechanism is to secure a positive solution to a dispute. A solution mutually acceptable to the parties to a dispute and consistent with the covered agreements is clearly to be preferred.
>
> 10.   .....if a dispute arises, all Members will engage in these procedures in good faith in an effort to resolve the dispute. . . "

The above provisions made clear that mutually agreed solutions notified under Article 3.6 of the DSU were a formal part of the dispute settlement process set out in the DSU. In fact, they declared them to be the *preferred* method of resolving disputes. These provisions must be given effect and their objectives must be realized. This meant *a mutually agreed solution to a matter formally raised under a covered agreement and jointly notified to the DSB as such by the disputant parties in accordance with Article 3.6 of the DSU must be regarded as a formal settlement of the dispute that made the re-submission of the same dispute inadmissible.*

4.35   India wondered if the European Communities took the view that it could bring its complaint *notwithstanding* the solution agreed with India under Article 3.6 of the DSU or whether that solution *did not cover the matter* raised before this Panel. If the European Communities agreed that a mutually agreed solution to a matter formally raised under a covered agreement and jointly notified to the DSB as such by the disputant parties in accordance with Article 3.6 of the DSU must be regarded as a formal settlement of the dispute that made the re-submission of the same dispute inadmissible then India wished to know from the

Report of the Panel

European Communities which measures taken by India were not covered by the mutually agreed solution. If the European Communities took the view that it had the right to re-invoke the DSU in respect of a matter even if it had formally agreed under Article 3.6 of the DSU not to do so, India wondered if the European Communities could explain why India, or any other Member of the WTO for that matter, would ever want to negotiate a mutually agreed solution with the European Communities again and how this approach could be reconciled with the objectives of the DSU.

4.36   In response, the **European Communities** argued that the 1997 Agreement did not preclude the European Communities from pursuing this dispute and India's defence was wrong already as a matter of fact. The 1997 Agreement dealt with different measures and different claims. At any rate, the European Communities considered that, even if the matter in dispute were the same, that would still not render the European Communities's complaint inadmissible. The 1997 Agreement settled a dispute concerning the system of discretionary import licenses applied by India with respect to a large number of products, including passenger cars, on alleged BOP grounds. In essence, the European Communities claimed that those measures were inconsistent with Article XI:1 of GATT and could not be justified under Article XVIII: B. Public Notice No. 60 and the MOUs were not the subject of that dispute and were not covered by the 1997 Agreement. Indeed, Public Notice No. 60 and the MOUs had not even been adopted by India when the 1997 Agreement was concluded. The "1997 Agreement" had authorized India to apply discretionary licensing with respect to imports of passenger cars until 1 April 2001; it did not authorize India to apply the balancing or indigenization requirements contained in the MOUs either before or after that date. Nevertheless, to the extent that the balancing requirement obligated the manufacturers to balance the value of the imports of passenger cars, its effects did not go beyond the potential restrictive effects on imports of passenger cars which could have resulted from the application of the discretionary licensing for those products permitted by the 1997 Agreement until 1 April 2001. For the above reason, the European Communities did not consider it necessary to challenge the application of the balancing requirement before 1 April 2001, in so far as imports of passenger cars were concerned. This was not because, as a matter of law, the 1997 Agreement allowed the application of that measure before 1 April 2001, but rather because the elimination of the balancing requirements in respect of import of passenger cars before 1 April 2001 would have provided no effective relief to the European Communities, since in any event India could have continued to restrict the importation of passenger cars through discretionary licensing.

4.37   The scope of the matter settled by the 1997 Agreement was defined in the request for consultations submitted by the European Communities on 18 July 1997[72] and in the 1997 Agreement itself. Neither of those documents referred to the balancing and indigenization requirements. Moreover, those requirements were never discussed during the consultations or during the negotiations leading

---

[72]   WT/DS96/1.

1854   DSR 2002:V

to the 1997 Agreement. According to the European Communities, there was, therefore, no basis for India's contention that the 1997 Agreement covered also those measures. The request for consultations of 18 July 1997 had made no reference to the balancing or the indigenization requirements. It described the measures in dispute as

> "[the] quantitative restrictions maintained by India on importation of a large number of agricultural, textile and industrial products. The restrictions include those notified to the WTO in document WTO/BOP/N/24 of 22 May 1997."

Document WTO/BOP/N/24 contained a notification made by India under paragraph 9 of the *Understanding on the Balance-of-Payments Provisions of the GATT 1994* (the Understanding). Annex I, Part B of document WTO/BOP/N/24 listed the import restrictions applied by India on BOP grounds as of the date of the notification. It described the import regime applicable to passenger cars falling within HS 8706[73] as "AUTO/BOP-XVIII:B", which means that

> "Imports of passenger cars and automotive vehicles are permitted without a license on fulfilment of conditions specified in a Public Notice issued in this behalf, and restrictions on import through NAL are otherwise maintained."[74]

As of 18 July 1997, when the European Communities made its request for consultations, no such Public Notice had been issued. Therefore, the conditions to be imposed by India were unknown to the European Communities. The import regime of chassis (HS 87.06) and bodies (HS 87.07) was described in document WTO/BOP/N/24 as "BOP-XVIII:B", which meant that imports were "regulated though NAL"[75] (i.e. through non-automatic licenses). There had been no mention in document WTO/BOP/N/24 that the importation of chassis or bodies was subject to balancing requirements or that their internal use or purchase was restricted through the application of indigenization or balancing requirements. Most parts and accessories for the assembly of passenger cars were not listed in Annex I, Part B[76]. There had been no indication in document WTO/BOP/N/24 that the importation of these products or their internal use or purchase was restricted for BOP reasons through the application of balancing or indigenization requirements or in any other manner. As regarded the claims submitted by the European Communities, the request for consultations mentioned the following provisions: Articles XI, XIII, XVII and XVIII of GATT 1994; Article 4.2 of the Agreement on Agriculture; Articles 1 and 3 of the Agreement on Import Licensing Procedures; and Articles 2, 3 and 5 of the Agreement on the Application of Sanitary and Phytosanitary measures.[77] Thus, the request for consultations had

---

[73] With the exception of ITC 870310.00 (snow and golf cars) and 870390.00 (a residual category covering "other passenger cars" not included in the preceding positions).

[74] See the Coding Diagram included at the end of document WTO/BOP/N/24.

[75] *Ibid.*

[76] See e.g., HS 87.08, 40.11, 40.12, 40.13, 70.07, 70.09, 90.29 and 94.01 in document WTO/BOP/N/24.

[77] The claims under the SPS Agreement reflect the fact that the request for consultations covered also the imports restrictions contained in Annex I, Part A of Document WTO/BOP/N/24, which were

Report of the Panel

not raised any claims under Article III:4 of GATT or under Article 2 of the TRIMs Agreement, contrary to what could have been expected if the request had been meant to cover also the balancing and indigenization requirements. Like the request for consultations, the 1997 Agreement made no reference to the balancing or to the indigenization requirements. The introductory paragraph of the 1997 Agreement specified that it was a settlement of

> "... the difference regarding the quantitative restrictions maintained by India on import of industrial, agricultural and textile products, as notified by India to the WTO by Annex I, Part B (Notification on Quantitative Restrictions Maintained on Imports Under the Export and Import Policy (as on 1 April 1997) of document WT/BOP/N/24."

As explained above, Annex I, Part B of document WT/BOP/N/24 had not mentioned anywhere the balancing or indigenization requirements. Although that document referred to the conditions specified in a Public Notice (not adopted when the 1997 Agreement was concluded), the European Communities could not be assumed to have settled in advance all possible claims with respect to whatever conditions India might see fit to include subsequently in that Public Notice. It would be unreasonable to interpret the 1997 Agreement as giving a blank check to India.

4.38   The 1997 Agreement had not settled the matter currently in dispute and, at any rate, was not a covered agreement enforceable by this Panel. Consequently, the 1997 Agreement did not preclude the European Communities from bringing this dispute. Even if the 1997 Agreement had settled the matter in dispute in the present case, that would still not preclude the European Communities from bringing this dispute. The 1997 Agreement was not a "covered agreement" in the sense of Article 1.1 of the DSU. Therefore, the rights and obligations of the parties under the 1997 Agreement were not enforceable under the DSU. The 1997 Agreement only allowed India to restrict the importation of passenger cars until 1 April 2001, in derogation of Article XI:1 of GATT. Public Notice No. 60 and the MOUs went beyond this in a number of respects:

- first, the indigenization requirements provided less favourable treatment to imported components and materials than to like domestic products with respect to their purchase and use for the assembly of passenger cars, contrary to Article III:4 of GATT and Article 2.1 of the TRIMs Agreement;

- second, the balancing requirements provided less favourable treatment to the internal use and purchase of imported CKD/SKD kits and components for the assembly of passenger cars, contrary to Article III:4 of GATT and Article 2.1 of the TRIMs Agreement; and

---

applied by India on alleged sanitary grounds. This part of the dispute is not covered by the 1997 Agreement.

1856

DSR 2002:V

- third, the MOUs had been concluded for a period of time that extended beyond 1 April 2001 (in principle, five years). As a result, the restrictions on imports of passenger cars imposed by the balancing and indigenization requirements would be maintained beyond that date in violation of Article XI:1 of GATT and Article 2.1 of the TRIMs Agreement.

4.39 The manufacturers acceded to sign the MOUs in order to obtain import licenses for passenger cars. But this did not mean that the MOUs were part of the licensing system temporarily authorized by the 1997 Agreement. The MOUs constituted separate measures and imposed additional trade restrictions that were not permitted by the 1997 Agreement. In addition, the balancing requirements appeared to require the manufacturers to balance not only the imports of passenger cars in CKD/SKD form but also of components, in violation of Article XI:1 and Article 2.1 of the TRIMs Agreement. The trade restrictive effects of the balancing and indigenization requirements went beyond those resulting from the application of the discretionary import licensing for passenger cars that India was authorized to maintain pursuant to the 1997 Agreement until 1 April 2001. In particular, India would have infringed the 1997 Agreement by continuing to apply the balancing and indigenization requirements beyond 1 April 2001. That violation would have arisen, and would have been open to challenge by the European Communities, from the moment that India concluded the MOUs, since the MOUs stipulated a period of duration for the balancing and indigenization requirements that went beyond 1 April 2001.[78]

4.40 In the 1997 Agreement, the European Communities had expressly reserved its right to resort to dispute settlement in the event that India did not comply with the terms of that agreement. Therefore, even if the matter in dispute in this case had been settled by the 1997 Agreement (*quod non*), the European Communities would not be precluded by the terms of the 1997 Agreement from pursuing the present dispute with respect to those aspects of Public Notice No. 60 and the MOUs which were incompatible with that agreement. Furthermore, the European Communities recalled that the 1997 Agreement was not a "covered agreement" in the sense of Article 1.1 of the DSU. India did not dispute this. Therefore, this Panel could not rule on whether the measures in dispute were consistent with the 1997 Agreement. By the same token, this Panel could not rule on India's defence that the EC's complaint was "inadmissible" because it was a violation of the EC's obligation under the 1997 Agreement not to take dispute settlement action against India. India's defence essentially amounted to saying that the obligations imposed by the 1997 Agreement upon the European Communities were enforceable under the DSU, but those imposed upon India were not. India could not have it both ways: either the 1997 Agreement was a "covered agreement" enforceable by this Panel, or it was not. As recalled by India, the DSU encouraged Members to seek mutually agreed solutions. Nevertheless, the DSU did not attach to such solutions the legal effects alleged by India. It was nowhere stipulated in the DSU that where Members had notified a mutually

---

[78] See EC's response to Question 18.

Report of the Panel

agreed solution they could no longer request a Panel with respect to the same matter. This was only logical, given that the DSU provided no mechanisms to enforce mutually agreed solutions. Thus, if a complaining Member considered that the other party had failed to comply with a mutually agreed solution it did not have the option of requesting a "compliance" Panel under Article 21.5 of the DSU. Nor could the complaining Member request the establishment of a new Panel under Article 6.1 of the DSU to rule that the other party had violated the mutually agreed solution. The only remedy available to the complaining Member was to resume the original dispute settlement proceedings at the point where they were left. If that course of action were also barred to the complaining Member, the defending Member would enjoy complete impunity to violate the mutually agreed solution. Without the assurance that they could revert to dispute settlement under the DSU in the event that the other party failed to comply with a mutually agreed solution, no complaining Member would ever agree to any such solution. Thus, it was India's interpretation, and not the European Communities', that would defeat the DSU's objective to encourage mutually agreed solutions.

4.41   **India** expressed surprise that it was the considered position of the European Communities and its Member States that a WTO Member could request the establishment of a panel on a matter on which it had reached a settlement notified under Article 3.6 of the DSU even if the respondent had faithfully implemented the settlement. The European Communities claimed that this followed from the fact that the DSU provided for no mechanism to enforce the agreed solution. Of course, it did. If the solution was not faithfully implemented, the complaining Member could re-invoke the DSU to claim its rights under the WTO provisions that were not implemented. It was therefore simply incorrect to claim that the "defending Member would enjoy complete impunity to violate the mutually agreed solution". India believed that the European Communities was presenting arguments in this proceeding that – if accepted – would frustrate the objectives of the DSU, which explicitly favoured settlement over adjudication. Endorsing the EC's approach would seriously curtail the policy options of the European Communities and the other WTO Members under the DSU. India invited the European Communities and its Member States to reconsider their position on this important point in the light of their broader interests.

4.42   The **European Communities** noted that India's position had evolved during the course of the proceedings. At first, India had seemed to argue that, where a matter had been settled, the original complaint could not be re-submitted under any circumstances. Subsequently, India contended that a complaint could be re-submitted, if the Member complained against had infringed the settlement. Thus, on India's interpretation, the European Communities would have to show in this case, first, that India had violated the settlement and, second, that India had violated the WTO Agreement. In the view of the European Communities, India's more recent position was more reasonable. But, like the previous one, it had no basis whatsoever in the DSU. Moreover, India's new position could not be reconciled with the principle that it had asserted earlier, whereby a matter which had been settled could not be re-litigated again. If this were correct, the only remedy available to the complaining Member in the event of violation of the settlement

1858   DSR 2002:V

would be to request a panel to find that violation, and not a violation of the WTO Agreement. As already explained by the European Communities, mutually agreed solutions were not "covered agreements" within the meaning of Article 1.1 of the DSU. Therefore, the rights arising from a mutually agreed solution could not be enforced through the DSU. That meant that a complaining Member could not ask the establishment of a panel to find that the other party had violated the mutually agreed solution. It meant also that the Member complained against could not invoke the existence of a mutually agreed solution as a defence before a panel established to find a violation of the WTO Agreement. India's interpretation would create an unacceptable imbalance between the two parties to a settlement. Whereas panels could not enforce the rights of the complaining Member under the settlement (which can go beyond its rights under the WTO Agreement), they would be required to enforce the rights of the Member complained against (i.e. the correlative obligation of the complaining Member not to re-invoke the DSU).

4.43   The European Communities noted that India had asked why a Member complained against would agree to a settlement, if the other party was not prevented from re-invoking the DSU. The European Communities could ask why a complaining Member would agree to a settlement given that its rights under the settlement, even on India's interpretation, were not enforceable under the DSU. The answer was the same in both cases: the parties to an agreement might consider that enforceability was not indispensable, where it was in both parties' interest to comply with the agreement. India made the error of assuming that a settlement did not confer to the complaining Member any advantages and, therefore, that the complaining Member paid no price for re-invoking the DSU. India made much of the fact that the mutually agreed solutions was notified to the WTO. That notification, however, was made only for transparency purposes and did not confer any legal effects to the settlement. The notification allowed other Members to verify that settlements were consistent with the WTO Agreement[79], and in particular that any concessions negotiated with the complaining Member falling within the scope of the different MFN obligations provided in the covered agreements were duly extended to all Members. The European Communities continued that the status of mutually agreed solutions under the DSU could be usefully contrasted with that of the arbitration awards issued under Article 25 of the DSU. Article 25.4 of the DSU provided that Articles 21 and 22 of the DSU should apply *mutatis mutandis* to arbitration awards. No similar provision was made with respect to mutually agreed solutions. This proved the drafters' intention to maintain a clear distinction between those solutions which involved the adjudication of the parties' right under the WTO Agreement (panel reports and arbitration awards) and those which did not involve such adjudication. *De lege ferenda*, a case could perhaps be made that mutually agreed solutions should be made enforceable under the DSU. Indeed, some Members had already made proposals to that effect. As the law stood, however, mutually agreed solutions were not enforceable under the DSU. The Panel should reject India's request to re-

---

[79]   Cf. Article 3.5 of the DSU.

Report of the Panel

write the DSU in order to make settlements partially enforceable (only the rights of the party complained against!) on the basis of vague and unsubstantiated legal principles. As recalled pertinently by the Panel in *India – Patent Protection*,

> "the Panel is required to base its findings on the language of the DSU. [It] simply cannot make a ruling *ex aequo et bono* to address a systemic concern divorced from explicit language of the DSU".[80]

4.44   In conclusion, the European Communities noted that India had taken the position that, in order to bring a dispute with respect to a matter settled by mutually agreed solution, the complaining Member must establish first that the other party had infringed that solution.[81] Should the Panel agree with that view, and should the Panel conclude further that the 1997 Agreement settled the matter in dispute in this case, the European Communities submitted that the measures at issue would be incompatible with the 1997 Agreement for the reasons stated above.

2.   Has the Matter Already Been Adjudicated?

(a)   India – Quantitative Restrictions

4.45   **India** also argued that the dispute with the United States had been resolved by rulings adopted by the DSB on 22 September 1999 on the basis of the findings set out in the reports of the Panel and the WTO Appellate Body in the proceedings *India - Quantitative Restrictions*. The Panel, endorsed by the Appellate Body, had recommended that the DSB request India to bring the measures at issue into conformity with its obligations under the WTO Agreement.[82] The Panel had specifically identified discretionary import licensing applied to all the products notified under Article XVIII:B, including SKD/CKD kits, as one of the measures at issue.[83] The dispute with the United States concerned *all* of the restrictions notified by India under Article XVIII:B, including those applied under the discretionary licensing scheme administered by the Ministry of Commerce. The panel declared this regime, to the extent that it was applied to the notified import restrictions, "a measure at issue" in the proceedings and found it to be inconsistent with Article XI:1 of the GATT.[84] The panel, endorsed by the Appellate Body, found that India no longer had any balance-of-payments justification for the "measures at issue" and that they were therefore not justified by Article XVIII:B of the GATT. Consequently, it recommended that the DSB request India to bring the measures at issue into conformity with its obligations under the WTO Agreement. The United States had thus obtained a ruling that the discretionary licensing scheme administered by the Ministry of Commerce was inconsistent with Article XI of the GATT. The United States was now requesting the present Panel to rule that also the application of this licensing scheme to imports

---

[80]   *India – Patents (EC)*, para. 7.23 (DSR 2998:VI, 2661).
[81]   See EC's response to Question 24 of the Panel.
[82]   *India – Quantitative Restrictions* (WT/DS90/R), para. 6.2 (DSR 1999:V, 1799).
[83]   *Ibid.*, WT/DS90/R, paras. 6.1 and 5.117.
[84]   *Ibid.*, WT/DS90/R, para. 6.1.

of CKD/SKD kits was inconsistent with Article XI. However, the DSB ruling covered the operation and application of the discretionary licensing system in respect of *all* products that were notified under Article XVIII:B, including the products of which CKD/SKD kits were composed. The United States was thus requesting the present Panel to rule on a matter that had already been adjudicated by the DSB. If the Panel found that the inconsistency of India's licensing scheme with Article XI:1 of the GATT was not a settled and adjudicated matter, then India's invocation of Article XVIII:B of the GATT could also not be considered to be a settled and adjudicated matter. *The Panel could not declare, with regard to the same matter, the complainant's claim of inconsistency to be a new issue and the respondent's defense to be settled and adjudicated.* The two sides of the issue would have to receive the same treatment. Consequently, if the Panel were to decide to examine the consistency of the licensing scheme for SKD/CKD kits with Article XI, it would also have to examine its justification under Article XVIII:B. Before the Panel on *India - Quantitative Restrictions*, India had argued, *inter alia*, that:

- panels must exercise judicial restraint when examining measures subject to the jurisdiction of the Committee on Balance-of-Payments Restrictions,

- panels could not transfer the determination of the adequacy of foreign exchange reserves to the International Monetary Fund, and

- the provisions of the DSU on the implementation of DSB recommendations could not replace the mechanism for the phase-out of balance-of-payments measures set out in paragraph 13 of the Understanding on the Balance-of-Payments Provisions of the GATT 1994.[85]

All of these matters would have to be re-examined by this Panel if the inconsistency of India's licensing scheme with Article XI:1 of the GATT were not found to be a settled and adjudicated matter. Depending on the Panel's rulings on these issues, India's external financial positions in May and October 2000 would have to be examined, possibly with the advice of the International Monetary Fund, because they would be different from the India' s external financial position in November 1997 which the earlier panel examined.[86] This panel correctly found that "the determination of whether balance-of-payments measures are justified is tied to a Member's reserve situation as of a certain date".[87]

4.46   The **United States** responded that India had completely misconstrued the nature of its complaint. The measures at issue were not India's import licensing system; instead, the measures challenged were the indigenization and trade balancing requirements of Public Notice No. 60 and the MOUs. India could not avoid the complaint by defending measures that were not the subject of the case. Contrary to India's assertion, the rulings in the *India – Quantitative Restrictions*

---

[85]   See Section III.D of the Panel Report on *India – Quantitative Restrictions* (WT/DS90/R) (DSR 1999:V, 1799).

[86]   WT/DS90/R, para. 5.156 (DSR 1999:V, 1799).

[87]   *Ibid.*, para. 5.162.

Report of the Panel

dispute did not adjudicate the matter that the United States had brought before this Panel. Second, India was inviting the Panel to analyze legal issues that were not presented by the facts of this case and therefore were not necessary to the resolution of this dispute; the Panel should decline that invitation. Third, because the measures and claims at issue in this dispute were different from those at issue in *India – Quantitative Restrictions*, this Panel's rulings would apply to discrimination and import restrictions that the *India – Quantitative Restrictions* panel could not and had not addressed. The United States argued that the *India – Quantitative Restrictions* dispute did not overlap this one; for that reason alone, the Panel should conclude that India's arguments lacked merit. India had argued that the measures at issue in this case had already been the subject of a ruling by the Dispute Settlement Body, and for that reason could not be examined by this Panel. The premise for this argument, of course, was that the measures at issue in this case were India's import licenses, and that premise was incorrect. It was also worth pointing out that the terms of reference of the *India – Quantitative Restrictions* Panel were established on 18 November 1997.[88] Public Notice No. 60, on the other hand, was issued on 12 December 1997. Therefore, even under India's logic, these measures could not have been a part of the *India – Quantitative Restrictions* dispute. In the United States' view, the *India – Quantitative Restrictions* panel did not examine the measures that had been referred to this panel; consequently, the DSB recommendations and rulings in that dispute would not have required India to bring these measures into compliance. The United States had asked India whether they shared this view, or whether, since these measures remained in force after the end of the reasonable period of time for compliance in that dispute, India believed instead that the United States was entitled to request authorization to suspend concessions in accordance with Article 22 of the DSU on the basis of the *India – Quantitative Restrictions* ruling.[89]

4.47   In response to the Panel's Question 5, the United States had detailed the differences between the *India – Quantitative Restrictions* dispute and this one. In sum: in *India – Quantitative Restrictions*, the United States challenged the existence of India's non-automatic import licensing system as such, and not the application of specific criteria for licensing the importation of specific tariff line items. For example, the United States had noted in that case that "all that the United States knew was that the Indian licensing authority generally refused to grant import licences for 'restricted' items when it was considered prejudicial to the state's interest to do so."[90] India had the same view of the case: "which implied that the scope of this proceeding did not include the administration of the import restrictions....India concluded that the United States invoked the dispute settlement procedures only with respect to the justification of the import restrictions and not in respect of matters arising from their application. India, therefore, reserved its position on the allegations of the United States with respect to the application of India's import restrictions, in terms of both their factual basis and

---

[88]   WT/DS90/R, para. 1.2 (DSR 1999:V, 1799).
[89]   See Questions 4 and 5 of the United States to India.
[90]   WT/DS90/R, *op.cit*, para. 3.20 (DSR 1999:V, 1799).

1862   DSR 2002:V

their legal implications."[91] Furthermore, the *India – Quantitative Restrictions* panel's findings confirmed that the panel too had that view: "we note that it is agreed that India's licensing system for goods in the Negative List of Imports is a discretionary import licensing system, in that licences are not granted in all cases, but rather on *unspecified* 'merits'. We noted also that India conceded *this measure* is an import restriction under Article XI:1."[92] By contrast, the dispute before this Panel did not concern India's non-automatic licensing regime. It concerned instead different measures (those specified in the U.S. panel request, particularly Public Notice No. 60 and the MOUs) and different requirements (the indigenization requirement and the trade balancing requirement) that India imposed on car manufacturers and on automotive parts and components. Furthermore, this dispute raised different legal issues: first, did those requirements as such (apart from import licensing) impose prohibitions or restrictions on imports in violation of GATT Article XI:1? In the United States' view, those requirements did impose such import restrictions, but the particular restrictions at issue here (limitations correlated to projected and achieved export values and to the degree of local content) were different from the very existence of non-automatic licensing that was at issue in the *India – Quantitative Restrictions* dispute. Second, did those requirements as such (apart from import licensing) impose discrimination against imported goods in violation of GATT Article III:4? The US view was that these requirements treated imported goods less favorably than like domestic goods - and that was a claim that even India realized was not and could not have been a part of the *India – Quantitative Restrictions* dispute. The United States added that those measures and requirements came into force after the import licensing regime was put in place, and, as India had acknowledged, would remain in force after the import licensing regime expired. Moreover, those requirements existed because car manufacturers had undertaken to comply with them in order to obtain relief from the measures at issue in the *India – Quantitative Restrictions* dispute, but that point only confirmed that the measures at issue here were different from the ones *India – Quantitative Restrictions* considered. Furthermore, India's argumentation mixed up two quite separate concepts. On the one hand, India's licensing regime acted as a total ban on imports. So-called "restricted" items ordinarily could not be imported at all. That was the basis of the United States' complaint in the *India – Quantitative Restrictions* dispute. The present dispute, on the other hand, did not contest that import ban; instead, this dispute challenged the conditions that India attached to goods imported despite the ban. Simply put, the *India – Quantitative Restrictions* dispute was about India's efforts to keep goods out of India. This dispute was about what India did when goods actually got in.

4.48   In the view of the United States, this dispute was a logical successor to the *India – Quantitative Restrictions* case. After finally achieving access for their products into India by peeling away the import ban that India had been applying through its licensing regime, WTO Members were naturally concerned about the

---

[91]   WT/DS90/R, *op.cit*, para. 3.41 (DSR 1999:V, 1799).
[92]   *Ibid.*, paras. 5.130 (footnotes omitted) (emphasis added).

Report of the Panel

treatment their products would receive after importation - hence their desire to ensure national treatment for those products. And, Members were concerned about the durability of that access. They therefore wanted to ensure that India did not impede that access through an entirely new layer of barriers - such as, in this case, the independent import restrictions and prohibitions contained in Public Notice No. 60 and the MOUs.

4.49   The measures in this dispute were different, and the legal claims in this dispute were different. Consequently, in the terminology of DSU Article 7.1, the "matters" in the two disputes were different,[93] and therefore this dispute was not even addressed, let alone "adjudicated" (to use India's terms), by that prior panel. Therefore, the Panel should decline to undertake to clarify a legal issue that was neither presented by the facts before it nor necessary to the resolution of this dispute. The United States noted that in its responses to the Panel's question 36, India seemed to have accepted the distinction between its import licensing regime and the requirements at issue in this case:

> The complainants thus appear to accept that a Member cannot resort to DSU twice with respect to the same matter but that their claims are different from that those that were the subject of the prior DSU proceedings. They asserted in particular that Public Notice No. 60 and the MOUs impose requirements and restrictions within the meaning of Articles III:4 and XI:1 of the GATT and the corresponding provisions of the TRIMs Agreement even in the absence of the discretionary licensing scheme that India was obliged to eliminate as a result of the prior proceedings. India therefore assumed that the issue before the Panel was no longer the scope of the principle of *res judicata* but rather the question of whether Public Notice No. 60 and the MOUs impose requirements and restrictions even in the absence of the licensing scheme for CKD/SKD kits.

According to the United States, the legal consequences of the rulings in the *India - Quantitative Restrictions* report entailed the elimination of the licensing requirements for a large number of goods, including SKD/CKD kits. The legal consequences of a ruling in favor of the United States in this dispute would entail the elimination of separate import restrictions imposed by Public Notice No. 60 and the MOUs. Without such a ruling in this dispute, those separate import restrictions would continue to apply to car manufacturers as long as the MOUs remained in place.

4.50   Of course, India's import licenses for SKD and CKD kits did play a role in this dispute. In the context of this case, those licenses were, first and foremost, an "advantage" given to MOU signatories, as that term was used in the *European Economic Community – Regulation on Imports of Parts and Components* (here-

---

[93]   "The '*matter* referred to the DSB', therefore, consists of two elements: the specific *measures* at issue and the *legal basis of the complaint* (or the *claims*)." Report of the Appellate Body in *Guatemala – Anti-Dumping Investigation Regarding Portland Cement from Mexico*, (hereinafter "*Guatemala – Cement I*"), WT/DS60/AB/R, adopted on 25 November 1998, para. 72 (DSR 1998:IX, 3767).

1864   DSR 2002:V

inafter "*EEC – Parts and Components*") report. Companies willing to sign an MOU obtained an advantage not given to others - namely, the right to import SKD and CKD kits despite their "restricted" status. However, just as in the *EEC – Parts and Components* dispute, and in the *Canada – FIRA* dispute before it, it was not the "advantage" that was the subject of the complaint, but rather the conditions attached to the "advantage". In *Canada – FIRA*, for example, the "advantage" was authorization to invest - which, as India pointed out, was at the time not a subject of GATT disciplines at all. But that advantage was conditioned on local purchase undertakings, which in turn were examined by the *Canada – FIRA* Panel and were found to be contrary to GATT's national treatment disciplines. This case was no different: it was not the "advantage" - the import licenses - that this panel needed to examine, but rather the conditions attached to those licenses. Those conditions included undertakings by MOU signatories to comply with indigenization and trade balancing requirements, and for the reasons already given, those conditions were inconsistent with India's WTO obligations. The **United States** considered that India's confusion about the role that import licenses played in this case should not deter the Panel from that conclusion. Elsewhere, the United States had discussed how the indigenization requirement damaged the competitive position of *all* automotive parts and components imported into India. That point alone should by itself put to rest India's assertion that this dispute concerned its import licenses. After all, India licensed the import of *kits*; the discrimination at issue in this dispute affected *all automotive parts and components*. Public Notice No. 60 and the MOUs were harming the export interests of all car part manufacturers around the world - not just the interests of manufacturers of the SKD and CKD kits to which India's import licensing regime applied.

4.51   The **European Communities** pointed out that although the balancing and indigenization requirements were applied in conjunction with the discretionary import licenses at issue in *India - Quantitative Restrictions* until 1 April 2001, they were legally distinct and separate measures, as evidenced by the following:

- Public Notice No. 60 had not been issued when the United States requested the establishment of the panel in India – QRs;

- nothing in the EXIM Policy or in document WTO/BOP/N/24 required India to apply the balancing and indigenization requirements;[94]

---

[94]   Cf. Report of the Appellate Body on *United States – Import Measures on Certain Products from the European Communities*, (hereinafter "*US – Certain EC Products*") WT/DS165/AB/R, para. 60 *et seq.* (DSR 2001:I, 373) Although this report concerns the different issue of whether a measure taken after the consultations was within panel's term of reference, it may offer guidance for the application of the *res judicata* principle in this case. The Appellate Body concluded that, although "related" to the 3 March Measure, the 19 April Measure was outside the terms of reference of the panel because it was a "separate and legally distinct measure". In reaching that conclusion, the Appellate Body considered as particularly significant that nothing in the 3 March Measure required the United States to take the 19 April Measure (*ibid.*, para. 76). Likewise, the import licenses challenged in *India – Quantitative Restrictions* did not require India to impose the balancing and indigenization requirements at issue in this dispute.

Report of the Panel

- contrary to India's assertions, the balancing and indigenization requirements were not an "inherent part" of the discretionary import licensing scheme. It was perfectly possible to operate a discretionary import licensing scheme without applying any of those requirements. Most products subject to discretionary import licensing under the EXIM Policy were not subject to balancing and indigenization requirements;

- by the same token, the balancing and indigenization requirements could be applied and enforced in the absence of discretionary import licensing; and

- the balancing and indigenization requirements contained in the MOUs had remained binding and enforceable after the elimination of the import licenses, even though no additional action to achieve that effect had been taken by the Indian authorities after 1 April 2001.

4.52   Moreover, as conceded by India, the legal basis for the United States complaint in this case was also different, to the extent that it included also claims under Articles III:4 of GATT and Article 2 of the TRIMs Agreement.

4.53   In the course of the panel proceedings, **India** conceded that its argument that no WTO Member might resort to the DSU on the same matter twice was no longer relevant because the European Communities and the United States had made it clear that their case did not rest on the application of the discretionary licensing system. India assumed that the Panel would examine the operation of PN 60 and the MOUs as such, that is independently of the discretionary licensing system Specifically, India assumed that the panel would examine whether the trade balancing and indigenization provisions set out in PN 60 and the MOUs would have been inconsistent with Article III:4 and XI:1 even if India had not applied import licensing restrictions for cars imported in the form of CKD/SKD kits and for car components at the time when the request for the establishment of the panel was submitted. [95] (See also III.C)

4.54   The **European Communities** countered that the method of enforcement of the MOUs was not a constituent element to the violations claimed by the European Communities. The balancing and indigenization requirements were as such inconsistent with the GATT and the TRIMs Agreement, regardless of the method used to enforce them. The European Communities saw no merit in the hypothetical and speculative analysis proposed by India.

(i)   The Notion of Res Judicata

4.55   **India** made reference to the principle of "*res judicata*", quoting:

Interest republicae ut sit finis litigium, is an old maxim deeply fixed in the law of fundamentals; that it concerns the state that there be an end to litigation. This maxim has wide application; it . .

---

[95]   See also India's response to Question 102 of the Panel.

1866   DSR 2002:V

.is obviously based on common sense and sound policy. For if matters which have been solemnly decided are drawn again to controversy; if facts, once solemnly affirmed, are to again denied whenever the affirmant sees his opportunity, there can never be an end to litigation and confusion.[96]

For these very basic and fundamental reasons, all legal systems had developed principles to ensure that matters, once settled, could not be litigated again. India submitted that there were no legal procedures, national or international, under which a complainant would be entitled to do what the European Communities was doing in the present case, namely litigate a matter after having formally consented to a settlement of the matter. The Appellate Body had frequently resolved interpretative issues under the DSU by reference to generally applied principles of law. Thus, it ruled on the distribution of the burden of proof between the parties to a DSU proceeding on the basis of "a generally-accepted canon of evidence in civil law, common law and, in fact most jurisdictions"[97] The Panel should do the same in the present case. According to Article 3.4 of the DSU, the ". . . rulings made by the DSB shall be aimed at achieving a satisfactory settlement of the matter", and, according to Article 3.7 of the DSU, "the aim of the dispute settlement mechanism is to secure a positive solution to a dispute". The generally applied principle of *res judicata* must therefore be considered to constitute an inherent part of the WTO dispute settlement process. To quote Henry M. Herman again:

> The slightest reflection will show that if some point were not established at which judicial proceedings must stop, no one could ever feel secure in the enjoyment of his life, liberty and property; while unjust, obstinate and quarrelsome persons, especially such as are possessed of wealth or power, would have society at their mercy, and soon convert it into one vast scene of litigation, disturbance and ill will.[98]

In fact, the principle of *res judicata* was firmly established in international law. In the case of the International Court of Justice (ICJ), the scope of this principle is defined in Articles 59 and 60 of its Statute. Article 59 provided as follows: "The decision of the Court has no binding force except between the parties and in respect of that particular case." Article 60 provided as follows: "The judgment is final and without appeal .." .The ICJ made clear that the principle of *res judicata* applied also outside the scope of Articles 59 and 60. Thus, in the advisory opinion of the ICJ on the *Effects of Awards of Compensation made by the United Nations Administrative Tribunal case,* the Court ruled that a judgment rendered by a judicial tribunal such as the Administrative Tribunal of the United Nations

---

[96] Henry M. Herman, *Commentaries on the Law of Estoppel and Res Judicata*, F.D. Linn & Company, Jersey City, N. J. (1886), Vol. I, page 8.
[97] *United States - Measures Affecting Imports of Woven Wool Shirts and Blouses from India*, (hereinafter "*US – Wool Shirts and Blouses*"), (WT/DS33/AB/R), para. 4.6 (DSR 1997:I, 323).
[98] Henry M. Herman, *Commentaries on the Law of Estoppel and Res Judicata,* F.D. Linn & Company, Jersey City, N.J. (1886), Vol. I, page 8.

Report of the Panel

would be *res judicata* between the parties based on general principles of law.[99] This appeared to be also the view of the Appellate Body. It noted in a discussion of the status of panel reports adopted by the CONTRACTING PARTIES to the GATT 1947 that "the generally-accepted view under GATT 1947 was that the conclusions and recommendations in an adopted panel report bound the parties to the dispute in that particular case.[100] The parties' and the Panel's efforts would lead to a ruling on a measure that would no longer exist when the Panel issued its report. The waste of resources that a failure to apply the *res judicata* principle would entail in the present case would therefore be enormous.

(b)   The Provisions Are an Inherent Part of the Licensing Scheme that Must be Eliminated

4.56   **India** presented the argument that the provisions on which the European Communities and the United States were basing their claims were an "inherent" part of the licensing scheme. India noted that the European Communities and the United States claimed that the granting of import licences subject to indigenization and trade balancing was not only inconsistent with Article XI of the GATT but also with Article III:4 of the GATT and Article 2 of the TRIMs Agreement. Claims related to these provisions were not specifically mentioned in the mutually agreed solution negotiated with the European Communities nor in the DSB rulings obtained by the United States. However, the alleged violations of Article III:4 of the GATT and Article 2 of the TRIMs Agreement were an inherent part of the licensing scheme that India was obliged to eliminate as a result of the ruling on Article XI. By eliminating the licensing scheme, India would necessarily also eliminate those aspects of that scheme that the European Communities and the United States considered to be inconsistent with those provisions. India considered that it *would be completely pointless to go through a whole new dispute settlement proceeding for the sole purpose of adding two further legal grounds why the scheme must be eliminated.* In India's view, if the issue of the consistency of India's licensing scheme under Article III:4 of the GATT and Article 2 of the TRIMs Agreement had been raised before the panel on *India – Quantitative Restrictions*, the panel would probably have exercised judicial economy and declared a ruling on that issue unnecessary to resolve the dispute. India noted that Article 3:10 of the DSU provided that "if a dispute arises, all Members will engage in these procedures in good faith in an effort to resolve the dispute" and suggested that the Panel ask the complainants how they reconciled their approach with the principle of good faith set out in Article 3:10 of the DSU.

4.57   In this connection it was important to keep in mind that Article III:4 of the GATT could be violated only through "laws, regulations and requirements", and Article 2 of the TRIMs Agreement only through "measures" adopted by a Member. The MOUs, as such, and the conduct of firms under those MOUs, by

---

[99]   ICJ Reports (1954).
[100]   *Japan – Taxes on Alcoholic Beverages*, (hereinafter "*Japan – Alcoholic Beverages II*"), (WT/DS8/R, WT/DS10/R, WT/DS11/R), adopted 1 November 1996, as modified by the Appellate Body Report, para. 5.3 (DSR 1996:I, 125).

1868   DSR 2002:V

India – Autos

itself, were therefore not covered by these provisions of the GATT and the TRIMs Agreement. The only "requirement" and "measure" that the Indian government {currently} imposed in respect of the MOUs were set out in paragraphs 2 and 4 of the Notice, which provided in relevant part:

> ... import of components for motor vehicle in ckd/skd form, which is restricted for import under the current Export-Import Policy, shall be allowed for importation against a license and such a license will be issued only to joint venture automobile manufacturing companies on the basis of an MOU to be signed by these companies ...

> The MOU Scheme would be enforced through the import licensing mechanism and MOU signing firms would be granted import licenses by DGFT based on above parameters.

4.58   The MOUs were thus at the time when the requests for the establishment of a panel were submitted enforced exclusively through the denial of import licenses for CKD/SKD kits. The application of discretionary import licensing for CKD/SKD kits was consequently the only governmental measure related to the MOUs that was {currently} in place.

4.59   It followed from the above that, once the discretionary licensing system for CKD/SKD kits was eliminated, the only governmental measure currently in place in respect of the MOUs would be eliminated, and as a result also the factual basis on which the EC's and the US's claims of violation of Article III:4 of the GATT and Article 2 of the TRIMs Agreement rested. A separate legal finding of inconsistency with Article III:4 of the GATT and Article 2 of the TRIMs Agreement was for these reasons completely unnecessary. The new and different measures that India might take in the future in respect of the MOUs, including their enforcement through the courts, were not before the Panel.

4.60   The **European Communities** responded that, although recognizing that Public Notice No. 60 and the MOUs were not even mentioned in the 1997 Agreement[101], India contended that they "were an inherent part of the licensing scheme that India was obliged to eliminate as a result of [the 1997 Agreement]"[102]. Until 1 April 2001 the balancing and indigenization requirements had been applied in *conjunction with* the licensing scheme for passenger cars, but this did not make them an *inherent part* of that scheme. The term "inherent" meant "existing in someone or something as a natural and inseparable quality, characteristic or right"[103]. The balancing and indigenization requirements (those at issue in this dispute and, more generally, all similar requirements) were clearly distinct and separable from and, therefore, not "inherent" in discretionary import licensing: it was perfectly possible to operate a discretionary import licensing scheme without applying any balancing or local content requirements in conjunction therewith. Most products subject to discretionary import licensing under the

---

[101]   India's response to Question 37 of the Panel.
[102]   *Ibid.*
[103]   Webster's New World Dictionary, Third College Edition.

DSR 2002:V

Report of the Panel

EXIM Policy before 1 April 2001 were not subject to balancing and indigenization requirements; likewise, balancing and local content requirements could be operated in the absence of discretionary import licensing. That the balancing and indigenization requirements were not an "inherent part" of the import licensing scheme was further confirmed by the fact that the MOUs had remained binding and enforceable after the elimination of that scheme, even though no additional measure to achieve that effect had been taken by the Indian authorities either before or after 1 April 2001. Furthermore, assuming that the balancing and indigenization requirements were in fact an "inherent part" of the licensing scheme, they should have been eliminated automatically as of 1 April 2001.

4.61   The **United States** noted that India, despite acknowledging that the scope of "*res judicata*" was not an issue in this dispute once the United States claims were properly understood, nevertheless insisted that Public Notice No. 60 and the MOUs were "an inherent part of the licensing scheme" that India had now eliminated.[104] India also maintained that it "fails to understand what interest protected by the DSU the European Communities and the United States are pursuing by requesting rulings on the specific conditions attached to the grant of licenses for SKD/CKD kits when they have already obtained an agreement and a DSB ruling according to which the whole licensing scheme for such kits must be eliminated on 1 April 2001 and the scheme was in fact eliminated on that date."[105] For the United States too, there was nothing "inherent" about the indigenization and trade balancing requirements. Import licensing of the kind that India had maintained until 1 April 2001, could have easily been administered without imposing export requirements or requiring discrimination in favor of domestic goods. India had given the Panel no reason to believe otherwise. In any case, India had effectively confirmed this point by saying that "it would in any case have been totally impracticable for India to notify these details [i.e. the details of the licensing regime India applied to each restriction notified under Article XVIII:B] for 2,700 items and for the Committee on Balance-of-Payments Restriction to examine them." The fact that those details varied by item made clear that no one set of administrative details was inherent in the restrictions themselves. Moreover, the indigenization and trade balancing requirements were continuing in force even though the import licensing regime had been eliminated, as India had acknowledged. This too demonstrated that they were independent of, and not inherent in, that licensing regime. The fact that those requirements were continuing also answered India's second point. What the United States sought was a ruling whose legal consequences would entail the elimination of separate import restrictions imposed by Public Notice No. 60 and the MOUs, as well as the elimination of the less favorable treatment that Public Notice No. 60 and the MOUs accorded to imported automotive parts and components than to like domestic parts and components. By contrast, the legal consequences of the rulings in the *India - Quantitative Restrictions* report entailed the elimination of the import licensing requirement for a large number of goods,

---

[104]   India's response to Question 37 of the Panel.
[105]   Response to Question 38.

1870   DSR 2002:V

including SKD/CKD kits, a different matter entirely. Eliminating the latter would not eliminate the former.

4.62 In reply to a Panel question, the United States added that it had not been able to envision any situation in which a panel could have settled an issue on which it did not expressly make findings. Under DSU Article 11, the function of a panel was to "make such other findings as will assist the DSB in making the recommendations or in giving the rulings provided for in the covered agreements." The DSU did not give any legal status to findings that a panel does *not* make. Furthermore, GATT and WTO dispute settlement panels were authorized to exercise judicial economy and not to make a finding on a particular legal issue if the finding was not necessary to enable the Dispute Settlement Body to make sufficiently precise recommendations and rulings to allow for prompt compliance in order to ensure the effective resolution of the dispute. It was difficult to see how a finding that a panel chose not to make for reasons of judicial economy could settle the issue that would have been the subject of the finding if the panel had made it. It was equally difficult to see how a finding that a panel did not make *without* citing judicial economy could settle the issue that would have been the subject of the finding if the panel had made it.

4.63 **India** pointed out that the Appellate Body had ruled on the question of judicial economy in *United States - Measure Affecting Imports of Woven Wool Shirts and Blouses from India* (hereinafter *"US – Wool Shirts and Blouses"*) as follows:[106]

> ... the basic aim of dispute settlement in the WTO is to settle disputes. This basic aim is affirmed elsewhere in the *DSU*. Article 3.4, for example, stipulates:
>
> > Recommendations or rulings made by the DSB shall be aimed at achieving a satisfactory settlement of the matter in accordance with the rights and obligations under this Understanding and under the covered agreements.
>
> ... Article 3.2 of the *DSU* states that the Members of the WTO "recognize" that the dispute settlement system "serves to preserve the rights and obligations of Members under the covered agreements, and *to clarify the existing provisions of those agreements* in accordance with customary rules of interpretation of public international law" (emphasis added). Given the explicit aim of dispute settlement that permeates the *DSU*, we do not consider that Article 3.2 of the *DSU* is meant to encourage either panels or the Appellate Body to "make law" by clarifying existing provisions of the *WTO Agreement* outside the context of resolving a particular dispute. A panel need only address those claims, which must be addressed in order to resolve the matter in issue in the dispute.[107]

---

[106] WT/DS33/AB/R, page 18 (DSR 1997:I, 323, at 339).

[107] The "matter in issue" is the "matter referred to the DSB" pursuant to Article 7 of the *DSU*.

Report of the Panel

4.64   The ruling of the Appellate Body referred to the range of claims an individual panel should address. However, there was no reason why the principle that "*a panel need only address those claims which must be addressed in order to resolve the matter in issue in the dispute*" should not also apply when a panel was requested to rule on a matter already resolved or settled as a result of a prior invocation of the DSU. In the view of India, the Appellate Body ruling made clear that the matters "resolved" by a panel report were not only the matters on which the panel specifically ruled upon. The whole notion of judicial economy rested on the idea that a ruling on one matter could resolve another matter on which no ruling was made. For instance, if a panel ruled that a Member must eliminate its import licensing scheme, it had at the same time resolved all issues related to the administration of that scheme even if had not made rulings on the administration of the scheme.[108]

(i)   The Notion of Abusive Splitting

4.65   **India** considered that there was no legal system in which a complainant was permitted to do what the European Communities and the United States were doing in the present case, namely, challenge without good cause one legal aspect of a situation in one proceeding and then another legal aspect of the same situation in a new proceeding. All legal systems imposed limits to such an abusive "splitting" of a subject matter into separate proceedings. Here again, India wished to invite the Panel to draw on generally applied principles of law and the objectives of the DSU. If an abusive splitting of legal challenges under the DSU were permitted, WTO Members would be deprived of their right to "a satisfactory settlement of the matter", to which they were entitled in accordance with Article 3.4 of the DSU. The principle of the prohibition of abusive splitting must therefore be considered to be an inherent part of the DSU procedures. India drew the Panel's attention to the importance that the Appellate Body had attached to the concept of good faith. In *United States – Tax Treatment for "Foreign Sales Corporations"* (hereinafter "*US – FSC*"), the Appellate Body described the concept of good faith as a "pervasive principle" of general international law that guides the way in which Members should interpret their rights and obligations.[109] In *United States – Import Prohibition of Certain Shrimp and Shrimp Products* (hereinafter "*US – Shrimp*"), the Appellate Body explained as follows the way in which good faith constrains WTO Members' exercise of their rights under WTO law:

> This principle [of good faith], at once a general principle of law and a general principle of international law, controls the exercise of rights by states. One application of this general principle, the application widely known as the doctrine of *abus de droit*, prohibits the abusive exercise of a state's rights and enjoins that whenever the assertion of a right "impinges on the field covered by [a] treaty

---

[108]   India's responses to Questions 104 (b) and 108 of the Panel.
[109]   *US – FSC*, WT/DS108/AB/R, adopted on 20 March 2000, as modified by the Appellate Body Report, para. 166 (DSR 2000:III, 1619).

1872   DSR 2002:V

obligation, it must be exercised bona fide, that is to say, reasonably." An abusive exercise by a Member of its own treaty right thus results in a breach of the treaty rights of the other Members and, as well, a violation of the treaty obligation of the Member so acting.[110]

4.66   The Appellate Body quoted an author who wrote:

A reasonable and bona fide exercise of a right in such a case is one which is appropriate and necessary for the purpose of the right (*i.e.* in furtherance of the interests which the right is intended to protect). It should at the same time be *fair and equitable as between the parties* and not one which is calculated to procure for one of them an unfair advantage in the light of the obligation assumed. A reasonable exercise of the right is regarded as compatible with the obligation. But the exercise of the right in such a manner as to prejudice the interests of the other contracting party arising out of the treaty is unreasonable and is considered as inconsistent with the bona fide execution of the treaty obligation, and a breach of the treaty.[111]

India submitted that the European Communities' and the United States' exercise of their procedural rights under the DSU in the present case was abusive and did not meet the standards set by the Appellate Body. India urged the Panel to make the rulings necessary to protect India in this case, and other Members in future cases, against the use of the DSU procedures for the purpose of coercing developing countries into making concessions in policy areas not covered by WTO law.

4.67   The **European Communities** noted that India had invoked the existence of principles in all legal systems whereby "matters, once settled, cannot be litigated again" , but had offered no evidence of the existence of such principles, except a quotation from a Henry M. Herman dated 1886 concerning the maxim "*Interest republicae ut sit finis litigium*". That maxim meant simply that "there must be an end to litigation" (a platitude with which anybody would agree) and did not address specifically the issue in dispute. The European Communities agreed that where a matter had already been adjudicated in a panel report adopted by the Dispute Settlement Body, the complaining Member was bound by that report and could not request the establishment of another panel with respect to the same matter.[112] Nevertheless, the European Communities believed that panels should apply the principle of *res judicata* with great circumspection, especially where the complainant had been successful in the first dispute, as in

---

[110]   *US – Shrimp*, WT/DS58/AB/R, adopted on 6 November 1998, para. 158 and fn. 156 (DSR 2001:XIII) (internal footnote revised).

[111]   This quote in the Appellate Body report as explained in fn. 156 of *US – Shrimp*, comes from B. Cheng, *General Principles of Law as applied by International Courts and Tribunals* (Stevens and Sons, Ltd., 1953), Chapter 4, p.125.

[112]   See the Report of the Appellate Body on *Japan –Alcoholic Beverages II*, WT/DS8/AB/R, WT/DS10/AB/R, WT/DS11/AB/R, adopted on 1 November 1996, p. 24 (DSR 1996:I, 97, at 116-117).

Report of the Panel

the instant case. In those circumstances, the risk of unnecessary re-litigation should be of less concern than that of incurring in a denial of justice by depriving a Member of its right to a panel under the DSU. The application of the *res judicata* principle was subject to strict requirements. There must be complete identity between the parties and between the "matters" in dispute. The identity of the "matter" required that both the measures in dispute and the claims submitted in connection with those measures be the same. It is not sufficient, therefore, that the matters be merely similar or related. In the present case, both the measures and the claims were different. Therefore, the conditions for considering that the matter in dispute was *res judicata* were clearly not met. As acknowledged by India[113], the Panel Report on *India – Quantitative Restrictions* was not binding upon the European Communities. Therefore, that report would not have the effect of *res judicata* vis-à-vis the European Communities even if this Panel were to conclude that the matter brought by the United States in these proceedings had already been adjudicated in that panel report. It was still unclear to the European Communities which were the "general principles of law" invoked by India. India had mentioned a "principle of the prohibition of abusive splitting". Later, India no longer referred to that principle, but instead to the "principle of good faith set out in Article 3:10 of the DSU". There was no reason why a complaining Member would ever wish to request a new panel with respect to a measure that had already been found to be inconsistent by another panel. Such situation might arise only as a result of an error on the part of the complaining Member regarding the scope of the earlier panel's findings, and not of bad faith. The United States would derive no advantage from "splitting" the dispute. Rather, the opposite was true. If India's view that the balancing and indigenization requirements were covered by the rulings of the panel on *India – QRs* were correct, the United States could have asked directly for a compliance panel under Article 21.5 of the DSU. That the United States had asked instead for the establishment of this panel evidence, if anything, the good faith of the United States. In contrast, India's decision to continue to apply the balancing and the indigenization requirements after 1 April 2001, notwithstanding its position that they were an inherent part of the measure that was found to be inconsistent with Article XI:1 of the GATT by the Panel on *India – Quantitative Restrictions*, was difficult to reconcile with the requirements of Article 3.10 of the DSU. (Not to speak of India's totally unsupported invocation of Article XVIII:B.)[114]

4.68   The **United States** hoped that India would clarify what it meant by its use of the term *res judicata,* because while India referred to this "principle", India nowhere defined it. It was therefore not entirely clear what India had in mind when it used the term. Generally speaking, however, a principle of *res judicata,* if applicable, would presumably relate to the effect of a previously adopted panel report on a subsequent dispute involving the same matter between the same parties. India sought to support its "principle of *res judicata*" by reference to a decision of the International Court of Justice (ICJ) and a statement of the Appellate

---

[113]   India's response to Question 42.
[114]   Question 21 of the Panel.

1874   DSR 2002:V

India – Autos

Body in the *Japan – Taxes on Alcoholic Beverages* (hereinafter "*Japan – Alcoholic Beverages II*") dispute. But neither of those cases provided any help for India's position. In *Japan – Taxes*, the Appellate Body *rejected* a claim that prior GATT panel decisions constituted binding precedent.[115] As for the ICJ's advisory opinion in *Effects of Awards of Compensation Made by the United Nations Administrative Tribunal*, while that opinion mentioned *res judicata* it did not define what it meant by that term. In any event, the question posed to the ICJ in that case was "Having regard to the Statute of the United Nations Administrative Tribunal and to any other relevant instruments and to the relevant records, has the General Assembly the right on any grounds to refuse to give effect to an award of compensation made by that Tribunal in favour of a staff member of the United Nations whose contract of service has been terminated without his assent?[116] (i.e. was the General Assembly required to pay the award rendered by the tribunal?) The decision therefore did not address the question whether a tribunal hearing a subsequent dispute was in any sense bound by a previous tribunal decision, and therefore it is inapposite to India's contentions here.

4.69   The United States noted that India, despite acknowledging that the scope of "*res judicata*" was not an issue in this dispute once the US claims were properly understood, nevertheless insisted that Public Notice No. 60 and the MOUs were "an inherent part of the licensing scheme" that India had now eliminated.[117] India also maintained that it "fails to understand what interest protected by the DSU the European Communities and the United States are pursuing by requesting rulings on the specific conditions attached to the grant of licenses for SKD/CKD kits when they have already obtained an agreement and a DSB ruling according to which the whole licensing scheme for such kits must be eliminated on 1 April 2001 and the scheme was in fact eliminated on that date."[118] Even if the Panel were inclined to pursue the legal issue that India had raised, it would have to conclude that India's analysis was without basis in the text of the WTO Agreement. India gave no citation at all for its so-called "principle of abusive splitting"; its one textual reference - namely, to the phrase "satisfactory settlement of the matter" in DSU Article 3.4 - did not support its position, for the straightforward reason that the "matter" at issue in this dispute was different from the "matter" at issue in the *India – Quantitative Restrictions* dispute. The measures were different; the claims were different. India's removal of the import licensing at issue in the earlier case would not end the discrimination against foreign goods or the additional import barriers that Public Notice No. 60 and the MOUs imposed. These separate violations were the ones that this Panel must address; the previous panel did not, and could not, address them.

4.70   India's "good faith" argument was equally unavailing. India referred to the provision in DSU Article 3.10 that "if a dispute arises, all Members will engage in these procedures in good faith in an effort to resolve the dispute." The Appel-

---

[115] Report of the Appellate Body in *Japan - Alcoholic Beverages II*, WT/DS8/AB/R, WT/DS10/AB/R, WT/DS11/AB/R, adopted on 1 November 1996, Part E (DSR 1996:I, 97).
[116] (1954) I.C.J. Rep. 50.
[117] India's response to Question 37 of the Panel.
[118] *Ibid.*, response to Question 38.

Report of the Panel

late Body's construction and application of that phrase, however, did not help India's position. In its report in the *FSC* dispute, the Appellate Body said:

> By good faith compliance, complaining Members accord to the responding Members the full measure of protection and opportunity to defend, contemplated by the letter and spirit of the procedural rules. The same principle of good faith requires that responding Members seasonably and promptly bring claimed procedural deficiencies to the attention of the complaining Member, and to the DSB or the Panel, so that corrections, if needed, can be made to resolve disputes. The procedural rules of WTO dispute settlement are designed to promote, not the development of litigation techniques, but simply the fair, prompt and effective resolution of trade disputes.[119]

The Appellate Body was considering purely a question of timing - whether or not an objection to a consultation request had been timely raised. In a subsequent case the Appellate Body considered the application of Article 3.10 to another question of timing - whether or not a Member had asked for clarification of a panel request in a timely manner.[120] Nothing about Article 3.10 or the Appellate Body's construction of that provision had anything to do with "res judicata", "splitting", or the binding nature in a subsequent dispute of a ruling in an earlier one.

4.71   In effect, India was inviting this Panel to embark on an examination of "principles" that were not anchored in the text of the DSU. Previous panels had rejected similar attempts by India to obtain procedural rulings that were not based on the language of the DSU; as the United States had pointed out in its answers to the Panel's questions, the *EC – Mailbox* Panel properly concluded that a panel proceeding was not the appropriate forum to address systemic issues. The Panel explained that it was required to base its findings on the language of the DSU and could not make a ruling *ex aequo et bono* divorced from explicit language in the DSU.[121] In this case, not only had India failed to ground its argumentation in the text of the WTO Agreement, it had also not made any effort to deal with other DSU provisions that lead to the opposite conclusion. For example, India's position was at odds with DSU Article 3.7, which the Appellate Body noted in the *Bananas* report "suggests ... that a Member is expected to be largely self-regulating in deciding whether any such action would be 'fruitful'.[122] For similar reasons, India's position was also at odds with DSU Articles 3.3 and 7.1:

---

[119] Report of the Appellate Body in *US – FSC*, WT/DS108/AB/R, adopted on 20 March 2000, para. 166 (DSR 2000:III, 1619).

[120] Report of the Appellate Body in *Thailand – Anti-Dumping Duties on Angles, Shapes and Sections of Iron or Non-Alloy Steel and H-Beams from Poland*, WT/DS122/AB/R, adopted on 5 April 2001, para. 97 (DSR 2001:VII).

[121] Panel Report on *India – Patents (EC)*, WT/DS79/R, adopted on 22 September 1998, paras. 7.22-7.23 (DSR 1998:VI, 2661).

[122] Report of the Appellate Body in *European Communities – Regime for the Importation, Sale and Distribution of Bananas*, (hereinafter "*EC – Bananas III*") WT/DS27/AB/R, adopted on 25 September 1997, para. 135 (DSR 1997:II, 591).

1876   DSR 2002:V

Much like Article 3.7, DSU Article 3.3 emphasized the importance of resolving the claims that a complaining Member "considers" to be impairing its benefits under the WTO Agreement,[123] and DSU Article 7.1 allowed the complaining Member to define the measures challenged and the legal claims advanced. Furthermore, India's position was at odds with DSU Article 3.2, which, if India is correct, would be ignored in this case because violations of Article XI:1 and III:4 would go unaddressed.[124] The same considerations apply here as applied in *EC – Mailbox*: the text of the DSU required the Panel to examine the matter that the United States had placed before it. Nothing in the language of the DSU supported the argument that India had made.

4.72   The United States noted that in its responses to the Panel's questions, India seemed to have accepted the distinction between its import licensing regime and the requirements at issue in this case. Moreover, as India noted, the issue before the Panel was not the scope of *res judicata* (or any of the other "principles" that India invoked in aid of its argument) –regardless of the precise meaning of India's "principles", this case did not involve the reprise of a dispute that had already been adjudicated, nor the "splitting" of a single matter in two. In light of this common ground on the issues before the Panel, the Panel should not tarry over India's assertions earlier in this dispute that its position was justified by a " principle of *res judicata*" or a "principle of abusive splitting"; or a principle of "good faith" There was no need for the Panel to consider whether such principles existed under the WTO Agreement, and if so what their scope might be - those were legal issues that were neither presented by the facts before the Panel nor necessary to the resolution of this dispute.

C.   Are the Measures within the Terms of Reference of the Panel?

1.   Do the Measures Applied After 1 April 2001 Fall Outside the Terms of Reference?

4.73   **India** said that it was not clear whether the measures on which the European Communities and the United States were requesting rulings were those that India was applying at the time when the requests for the establishment of a panel were submitted to the DSB or the measures that India might be applying as from 1 April 2001. It requested the Panel to request the complainants to clarify this issue. If the complainants were to respond that they considered India's future measures to be part of the present proceedings, India would request the Panel to issue a preliminary ruling to the effect that these measures fell outside of its mandate.

---

[123]   Article 3.3 provides that "the prompt settlement of situations *in which a Member considers* that any benefits accruing to it directly or indirectly under the covered agreements are being impaired by measures taken by another Member is essential to the effective functioning of the WTO and the maintenance of a proper balance between the rights and obligations of Members" (emphasis added).

[124]   DSU Article 3.2 provides that "recommendations and rulings of the DSB cannot add to or diminish the rights and obligations provided in the covered agreements."

DSR 2002:V

Report of the Panel

4.74   India argued that, under the DSU, Members may not bring complaints on proposed measures[125] nor may they request advisory rulings on potential future issues. This followed from Article 7.1 of the DSU, according to which the mandate of a panel was to examine "the matter" referred to the DSB in the document containing the request for establishment of the panel. According to Article 6.2 of the DSU, the panel request must identify (a) "the specific measures at issue" and (b) the "legal basis of the complaint". The Appellate Body clarified that the requirement to identify the legal basis of the complaint meant that the legal claims in respect of the measures identified must be specified in the request for the establishment of the panel.[126] The reference of the DSU to "the matter" in the document requesting the establishment of the panel thus consisted of (a) the specific measures identified as the "measures at issue" and (b) the legal claims made in respect of those measures. It logically followed from this that both the measures at issue before a panel and the legal issues to which they gave rise must have existed at the time of the request for the establishment of a panel.

4.75   The Panel on *India – Quantitative Restrictions* had noted that:

> ... practice, both prior to the WTO and since its entry into force, limits the claims which panels address to those raised in the request for establishment of the panel, which is typically the basis of the panel's terms of reference (as is the case here).[127] In our opinion, this has consequences for the determination of the facts that can be taken into account by the Panel, since the complainant obviously bases the claims contained in its request for establishment of the panel on a given set of facts existing when it presents its request to the DSB. . . . it would seem consistent with such a request and logical in the light of the constraints imposed by the Panel's terms of reference to limit our examination of the facts to those existing on the date the Panel was established.[128]

In India's view, it followed from the above that the mandate of the present Panel was to examine the measures that existed at the time the panel requests were submitted by the European Communities and the United States and the legal claims that could be made in respect of those measures at that time. The relevant date for the United States was 15 May 2000 and 12 October 2000 for the European Communities.[129] It was thus clear that *the measures which India would ap-*

---

[125]   This contrasts with the dispute settlement provisions of the North American Free Trade Agreement, which permit complaints on "any actual *or proposed* measure" (Article 2006:1).

[126]   See *India – Patent Protection for Pharmaceutical and Agricultural Chemical Products*, (hereinafter "*India – Patents (US)*") (WT/DS50/AB/R), adopted on 16 January 1998, para. 89 (DSR 1998:I, 9).

[127]   Appellate Body Report on *EC – Bananas III*, (WT/DS27/AB/R), adopted on 25 September 1997, para. 143 (DSR 1997:II, 591), and Appellate Body Report on *India – Patents (US)*, (WT/DS50/AB/R), adopted on 16 January 1998, paras. 87-89 (DSR 1998:I, 9).

[128]   See *India – Quantitative Restrictions*, (WT/DS90/R), paras. 5.160-5.161 (DSR 1999:V, 1799).

[129]   WT/DS146/4. In *US – Certain EC Products*, the Appellate Body found that a measure which did not exist at the time when the consultations required under Articles 4 and 6 of the DSU were held could not be deemed to be a measure falling within the panel's terms of reference (WT/DS165/AB/R,

ply as from 1 April 2001 to comply with the mutually agreed solution negotiated with the European Communities and the DSB ruling sought by the United States fell outside the Panel's terms of reference.

4.76   Although the European Communities and the United States alleged that India was currently violating its obligations under the GATT and the TRIMs Agreement, many of their arguments related to measures that India might take after 1 April 2001 and legal issues that *might* consequently arise at that time. It was unclear whether the legal arguments of the claimants related to the factual situation before or after the elimination of the discretionary licensing regime for SKD/CKD kits.

4.77   The European Communities claimed that the "trade balancing" requirements stipulated in the MOUs were inconsistent with GATT Article XI:1 in that they restricted imports of passenger cars, and of components therefor, by the signatories of the MOUs. The European Communities had recognized that the solution it reached with India under Article 3.6 of the DSU and the United States' agreement with India under Article 21.3 (b) of the DSU allowed India to maintain import restrictions on passenger cars until 1 April 2001. Therefore, the European Communities explained, it made its claim of violation of Article XI only in so far as: the MOUs require the "trade balancing" of imports of "components" other than chassis and bodies[130]; *and the MOUs will remain binding and enforceable after 1 April 2001*, both with respect to passenger cars and components therefor. In India's view, this made it clear that the EC's complaint was really directed against measures which India *might* take to enforce the MOUs, but that were not yet in place, and legal issues that had therefore not yet arisen.

4.78   The United States' argumentation was equally contradictory. Thus, the United States "applauds the efforts that India is undertaking" in eliminating the licensing restrictions. However, the United States expressed regret that this would not resolve the dispute because "India *intends* to maintain and continue enforcing the requirements of Public Notice No. 60 and the MOUs after its import licensing regime ends". The United States explained that the dispute concerned discriminatory, trade-restricting conditions that India exacted from investors in the motor vehicle manufacturing sector - and that it *intends to continue to exact.* Citing press reports of statements by Indian policy makers, the United States claimed that "*India does not intend to terminate the requirements*" of Public Notice No. 60 or the MOUs when it eliminates the balance-of-payments restrictions on imports of SKD/CKD kits and components on 1 April 2001.

4.79   The prospective nature of the United States' complaint had become particularly evident when it argued that India might deny import licenses under the general enforcement and confiscation provisions of the FTDR Act even after 1 April 2001. It claimed that:

---

para. 70 (DSR 2001:II, 413)). This ruling suggested that the measures at issue in a panel proceeding must have existed even at the time of consultations.

[130]   India wished to point out that the MOUs did not require the trade balancing of imports of components except when such imports were in the form of SKD/CKD kits.

Report of the Panel

> *These additional import-restricting provisions* will evidently not disappear when India eliminates its balance-of-payments licenses on 1 April 2001, but *will instead, apparently, become the instruments* through which India carries out the import restrictions in Public Notice No. 60 and the MOUs (and thus prevents SKD/CKD kits/components from being brought into India to compete with domestic parts and components).[131]

The United States thus recognized that India would eliminate the import restrictions at issue on 1 April 2001, but nevertheless argued that India would "apparently" re-introduce new restrictions under the general enforcement provisions of the FTDR Act. It was on the basis of this alleged possibility of a future measure covered by Article XI of the GATT that it was asking the Panel to rule that India was acting inconsistently with this provision.

4.80   The above made clear that both the European Communities and the United States were satisfied with the way in which India had so far implemented the mutually agreed solution and the DSB rulings. Their complaints related to measures that India *might* in their view adopt as from 1 April 2001 and legal issues that *might* arise in this connection. However, for the reasons explained above, these complaints – should events substantiate them – should appropriately be made in a dispute settlement proceeding initiated after 1 April 2001. India concluded that the European Communities and the United States had brought their complaints to the DSU before the end of the agreed implementation period, and thus prematurely, because they claimed to have reason to believe that India *might* not bring the application of its licensing system for automotive parts and components into conformity with its WTO obligations as from 1 April 2001. India would demonstrate that this concern was unjustified. In any event, according to established WTO jurisprudence the Panel's terms of reference did not extend to measures that had not yet been adopted and claims on legal issues that had not yet arisen. For these reasons, India would request the Panel to reject both complaints as inadmissible.

> (a)   The Method of Enforcement before and after 1 April 2001

4.81   **India** stated that both Public Notice No. 60 and the MOUs themselves clearly and explicitly stipulated that the MOUs were to be enforced through the import licensing mechanism. They both contained the following clause:

> The MOU Scheme would be enforced through the import licensing mechanism and MOU signing firms would be granted import licenses by DGFT based on above parameters.[132]

4.82   As long as India maintained its import licensing regime for SKD/CKD kits, the only possible legal consequence of the non-observation of the terms of a

---

[131]   Underlining added.

[132]   See para. 4 of Public Notice No. 50 and para. V of the standard format for MOUs annexed to the Notice.

1880   DSR 2002:V

MOU was therefore the denial of an import license for such kits. An enforcement of the MOUs by other means would at that time have been contrary to the policy set out in Public Notice No. 60. Moreover, even if the Government of India had decided to enforce the MOUs through the courts, the automobile manufacturer concerned could have invoked the clause in the MOU according to which the licensing mechanism would be the exclusive mechanism of enforcement. If the European Communities and the United States were to state that their complaints related to the *enforcement of the MOUs outside the licensing regime and Notice No. 60*, India requested the Panel to ask them to clarify which enforcement measure India had taken outside the licensing regime and Notice No. 60 at the time when the panel requests were submitted was at issue in this proceeding. Specifically, the complainants should be asked to clarify what measure that India took outside the framework of the licensing regime and Notice No. 60 at that time constituted a "requirement" and "restriction" within the meaning of Articles III and XI of the GATT and the corresponding provisions of the TRIMs Agreement. In this context, India wished to emphasize that the MOUs were, prior to 1 April 2001, enforced exclusively through the denial of import licenses for CKD/SKD kits. *The application of discretionary import licensing for CKD/SKD kits was consequently the only governmental measure related to the MOUs that was in place at that time.* India was particularly interested in learning from the complainants how, in the absence of any import licensing regime for CKD/SKD kits, the MOUs could entail any restriction on the importation of such kits within the meaning of Article XI of the GATT. India continued by pointing out that compliance with the commitments made by car manufacturers under the MOUs was, under the regime applied by India prior to 1 April 2001, secured exclusively through the denial of import licenses for SKD/CKD kits. This method of securing compliance could of course no longer be applied when the restrictive licensing for such imports was abolished as from 1 April 2001. From then on, the MOUs would, if necessary, be enforced through the courts since they were binding contracts under Indian civil law. This method of enforcement would not entail any denial of import licenses. The MOUs potentially might now be enforced under the provisions of the Foreign Trade (Development and Regulation) Act, 1992 (the "FTDR Act") and the Foreign Trade (Regulation) Rules, 1993. However, none of the potential methods of enforcement would entail any import restrictions.

4.83   It followed from the above that the enforcement of the MOUs as contracts outside the import licensing scheme for SKD/CKD kits could not have arisen at the time when the European Communities submitted its request for the establishment of the Panel. The Panel would therefore be ruling on a prospective matter – that is, a legal situation which did not exist at the time of its establishment – if it were to examine the legal effects of MOUs after the abolition of the licensing regime. This prospective matter was outside its terms of reference. A panel may not rule: if the respondent were to do this or were to do that, then it would be acting inconsistently with this or that provision. Or: because the respondent has done this or that during the course of the proceedings, the respondent acted inconsistently with this or that provision. It must base its ruling on inconsisten-

Report of the Panel

cies that had already occurred at the time of the request for its establishment. After 1 April 2001, any measures that India might take to secure compliance with remaining obligations under the MOUs would no longer entail any limitation of the right of the signatories to import SKD/CKD kits. The enforcement of the MOUs after the abolition of the import licensing system would therefore be fully consistent with India's WTO obligations.

4.84   The Panel needed to take into account that the issue was the applicability of provisions of contracts to which the Government of India was a party. The Government of India had repeatedly stated, that the trade balancing provisions in Public Notice No. 60 and in the MOUs did not apply to freely importable products. This was, of course, also the position of the Government of India as the holder of contractual rights under the MOUs. The Panel should for this reason accept the position of the Government of India on the applicability of the MOUs.[133] India wished to stress that the measures outlined above were those actively being considered at the present time, but that no final decision on this matter had as yet been taken. None of the measures to secure compliance with remaining obligations under the MOUs described above had thus far been adopted and none of the legal issues discussed above has therefore arisen as yet. Moreover, as far as the indigenization requirement under the MOUs was concerned, it was presently not clear whether there was any need to take any action at all.

4.85   The **United States** responded that India's argument that the United States was challenging measures that India would take in the future was based on flawed premises. First, the United States was actually challenging measures that India had already taken – namely, the imposition of local content and trade balancing obligations on MOU signatories. And, while India said that import licensing would end on 1 April India had acknowledged that nothing about the MOUs would change after that date: they remained "binding" and "will, if necessary, be enforced". These measures were no different from the binding and enforceable purchase undertakings that the *Canada – FIRA* Panel found inconsistent with the GATT.

4.86   The distinction that India tried to draw between the situation before 1 April 2001, and the situation after 1 April 2001, was contradicted by India's acknowledgement that the MOUs would remain in force even after 1 April 2001, and by India's further acknowledgement that the trade balancing and indigenization requirements in the MOUs remained binding and enforceable after that

---

[133]   India would like to note in this connection that the Panel on *United States – Sections 301-310 of the Trade Act of 1974* (hereinafter "*US – Section 301 Trade Act*") based its interpretation of some of the most controversial provisions of United States trade law, *inter alia*, " on representations and statements by the representatives of the United States . . . solemnly made, in a deliberative manner, for the record, repeated in writing and confirmed in the Panel's second hearing." (WT/DS152/R, para. 7.122, adopted on 27 January 2000 (DSR 2000:II, 815)) Since the assurances given by United States regarding the content of its domestic law were accepted as decisive by a WTO panel, the United States should accept by the same token the position stated by the Government of India on the applicability of the MOUs.

1882

DSR 2002:V

date.[134] In fact, in addition to reconfirming that these requirements remained enforceable in Indian courts, India's answers to the Panel's questions also confirmed that they were enforceable through monetary penalties levied under Section 11 of the FT(DR) Act.[135]

4.87   Those acknowledgements necessarily meant that the trade balancing and indigenization requirements were legally independent of the licensing requirements that India previously imposed on imports of SKD/CKD kits and components. As the United States had made clear, it was not the licensing requirements but the indigenization and trade balancing requirements that were the subject of the US complaint in this dispute. Because the indigenization and trade balancing requirements did not change on 1 April 2001 (or on any other date), and because those requirements were independent of India's now-eliminated licensing regime, India's elimination of import licensing was not relevant to – and certainly did not resolve – this dispute. In its answers to the Panel's questions, India appeared to have finally recognized this point. India said, "there are requirements set out in the MOUs that apply also in the absence of any import restriction on SKD/CKD kits."[136]   The United States agreed: and it was those MOU requirements – and their inconsistencies with India's WTO obligations – that were the subject of this dispute. However, India regrettably persisted in arguing that the situation after 1 April 2001 (i.e. after elimination of the import licensing regime) was somehow different from the situation before that date. According to India, enforcement of the MOUs "could not have arisen at the time when the European Communities [or, presumably, the United States] submitted its request for the establishment of the Panel. The Panel would therefore be ruling on a prospective matter – that is, a legal situation which did not exist at the time of its establishment – if it were to examine the legal effects of MOUs after the abolition of the licensing regime. This prospective matter was outside its terms of reference."[137]

4.88   India's argument relied on several misunderstandings. First, the US complaint was not directed at any particular method or means of enforcing the MOUs and Public Notice No. 60. The US complaint was instead directed to the indigenization and trade balancing requirements as such, and these requirements had not changed. These requirements had imposed the same obligations on car manufacturers since the date that the MOUs were signed, and it was the US position that those obligations were themselves inconsistent with India's WTO commitments. What mattered was that those obligations were binding and enforceable; what means India chose or would choose to enforce them was simply not rele-

---

[134]   The position was less clear with respect to Public Notice No. 60; as far as the United States could tell, this notice had not been rescinded and thus remained in force. India had said only that "Public Notice No. 60 is no longer operational because the licensing scheme it was to administer no longer exists." India's response to Question 33 of the Panel.

[135]   "As pointed out above, after the abolition of import licensing for CKD/SKD kits on 1 April 2001, MOUs potentially can be enforced as contracts through the domestic courts. The companies may also be liable to monetary penalties under Section 11 of the FTDR Act." India's response to Question 52(d) of the Panel.

[136]   India's response to Question 33 of the Panel.

[137]   *Ibid.*

DSR 2002:V

Report of the Panel

vant to the US legal claims in this dispute.[138] The text of the GATT 1994 made this point clear. Article III:4 of the GATT 1994 was addressed to "... laws, regulations and requirements ... ." The indigenization and trade balancing requirements were indisputably "requirements"; and they remained "requirements" regardless of what methods India used to enforce them.[139] India's position – that the Panel should focus not on the requirements that the measures imposed but should look instead at changes in the means of enforcement – was simply not consistent with the GATT text. The situation was no different for Article XI:1: the scope of that article had always been interpreted to be broad, and it used the term " measures," the meaning of which was at least as broad as the term "requirement".[140]

4.89   India's position was also inconsistent with the conclusions reached by the *Canada – FIRA* Panel. That panel had found as follows:

> The Panel further noted that written purchase undertakings – leaving aside the manner in which they may have been arrived at (voluntary submission, encouragement, negotiation, etc.) – once they were accepted, became part of the conditions under which the investment proposals were approved, in which case compliance could be legally enforced. The Panel therefore found that the word "requirements" as used in Article III:4 could be considered a proper description of existing undertakings.[141]

It was the enforceability of the undertakings – not the specific means of enforcement – that led the *Canada – FIRA* panel to conclude that the undertakings were "requirements" within the meaning of GATT Article III:4. Notably, none of the undertakings examined in the *Canada – FIRA* dispute had ever actually been enforced by the Canadian Government; performance of unfulfilled undertakings had always been either postponed or waived, or the undertakings had been replaced by revised undertakings.[142] This fact did not change the Panel's legal conclusion that the undertakings imposed "requirements" that were inconsistent with the GATT.

---

[138]   Thus, even if it were true that before 1 April 2001, "as long as India maintained its import licensing regime for SKD/CKD kits, the only possible legal consequence of the non-observation of the terms of a MOU was therefore the denial of an import license for such kits" and that a manufacturer could have resisted court enforcement of the MOUs on that basis (Indian Panel Answers, response to question 33), the fact remained that the enforceability as such of the requirements in the MOUs had not changed.

[139]   Furthermore, Public Notice No. 60 was certainly also a "regulation".

[140]   *Cf. also* Panel Report on *Japan – Measures Affecting Consumer Photographic Film and Paper*, (hereinafter "*Japan – Film*") WT/DS44/R, adopted on 29 April 1998, para. 10.51 (DSR 1998:IV, 1179): "Given that the scope of the term *requirement* would seem to be narrower than that of *measure*, the broad reading given to the word *requirement* by the *Canada - Administration of the Foreign Investment Review Act* (hereinafter "*Canada – FIRA*") and *European Economic Community – Regulation on Imports of Parts and Components* (hereinafter "*EEC – Parts and Components*") panels supports an even broader reading of the word *measure* in Article XXIII:1(b)."

[141]   Panel Report on *Canada - FIRA*, adopted on 7 February 1984, BISD 30S/140, para. 5.4.

[142]   *Ibid.*, para. 2.11.

India – Autos

4.90   India was also wrong to say that the situation after 1 April 2001, was outside the Panel's terms of reference. This Panel's terms of reference were:

> To examine, in the light of the relevant provisions of the covered agreements cited by the United States in WT/DS/175/4 and by the European Communities in WT/DS146/4, the matters referred to the DSB by the United States and the European Communities in those documents and to make such findings as will assist the DSB in making the recommendations or in giving the rulings provided for in those agreements.[143]

The "matters referred to the DSB by the United States" in document WT/DS175/4 included "Public Notice No. 60 ((PN)/97-02) of the Indian Ministry of Commerce, published in the Gazette of India Extraordinary, effective 12 December 1997; ... memoranda of understanding signed by the Government of India with manufacturing firms in the motor vehicle sector pursuant to Public Notice No. 60 ... ." India's admission that "there are requirements set out in the MOUs that apply also in the absence of any import restriction on SKD/CKD kits " made clear that those requirements fell within the terms of reference of this panel. Furthermore, India's focus on the elimination of import licensing misapprehended the limited relevance of import licensing to this dispute. India used those licenses to induce car manufacturers in India to accept the indigenization and trade balancing requirements. Car manufacturers had to sign an MOU in order to receive those licenses and to import CKD/SKD kits. As a matter of factual background, therefore, it was relevant that import licensing existed in 1997 and 1998, when the MOUs were signed. With respect to the legal claims of the United States, the import licenses constituted an "advantage" that MOU signatories received in exchange for binding themselves to the indigenization and trade balancing requirements.[144] The *Canada – FIRA* panel considered an analogous situation: permission to establish an investment in Canada was conditioned on compliance after investment with various GATT-inconsistent undertakings. In this dispute, access to the import licenses played the same role as the permission to invest played in that one: as the one-time "advantage" provided by the government to induce companies to accept on-going WTO-inconsistent requirements.

4.91   In a related point, India also asserted that Public Notice No. 60 was no longer "operational"[145] As a matter of fact, the status of Public Notice No. 60 was not at all clear. To the best of the United States' knowledge, Public Notice

---

[143] *India – Measures Affecting the Automotive Sector*: Constitution of the Panel Established at the Requests of the United States and the European Communities: Note by the Secretariat, WT/DS146/5, WT/DS175/5, 30 November 2000, para. 2. These are standard terms of reference drawn up in accordance with DSU Article 7.1.

[144] *See, e.g.,* the Panel Report on *EEC - Parts and Components*, adopted on 16 May 1990, BISD 37S/132, para. 5.21 (those requirements "which an enterprise voluntarily accepts in order to obtain an advantage from the government constitute 'requirements' within the meaning of" GATT Article III:4). And, in the terms of the chapeaux to paragraphs 1 and 2 of the TRIMs Agreement Illustrative List, undertaking to comply with those two requirements was "necessary to obtain an advantage" – namely, the right to receive import licenses.

[145] India's response to Question 33 of the Panel.

DSR 2002:V

Report of the Panel

No. 60 had not been rescinded. India had not explained what it meant for an Indian regulation not to be rescinded and yet not be "operational". In any event, even if Public Notice No. 60 were no longer in force, it remained in force for several months after the establishment of this Panel (27 July 2000, for the US complaint) and the fixing of the Panel's terms of reference on that date; the Panel could and should make findings concerning it. As the United States explained in answering the Panel's question 7, past GATT and WTO panels had ruled on measures that were discontinued during the panel's examination.[146] It would be particularly appropriate for the Panel to rule on Public Notice No. 60 in this case, given that the requirements of Public Notice No. 60 were still in place through the MOUs, which all parties agreed remained in effect, binding and enforceable. The Panel would thus achieve no economy by omitting Public Notice No. 60 from its findings; to the contrary, as long as there was uncertainty over the status of Public Notice No. 60, such a ruling could help ensure clear implementation of the DSB's rulings and recommendations.[147] The United States added that the MOUs were directly binding on individual signatories because, according to India, they were contracts enforceable under Indian domestic law. However, the indigenization and trade balancing requirements had originally been established by Public Notice No. 60. In fact, the terms of the MOUs were mandated by Public Notice No. 60, paragraph 8 of which provides that "a standard format for MOU is enclosed as appendix to this Public Notice and *MOU is required to be signed as per this format*." Consequently, a comprehensive ruling by the Panel would apply to both Public Notice No. 60 (the source of the WTO-inconsistent requirements) and the MOUs (by which individual companies were bound to those WTO-inconsistent requirements), especially since Public Notice No. 60 was, as all the parties this dispute agreed, in force at the time this Panel was established.

4.92 In summary: as long as the MOUs remained in force, the WTO-inconsistent indigenization and trade balancing requirements remained in force. Second, as India had confirmed, the MOUs, and therefore also those two requirements, were binding and enforceable independently of the import licensing requirements, and would remain so even after the import licensing requirements were removed. Therefore, the date of 1 April 2001, had no relevance to the legal issues before this Panel and provided India no defense to the US claims.

---

[146] Such cases include: the Panel Report on *Argentina - Measures Affecting Imports of Footwear, Textiles, Apparel and Other Items*, (hereinafter "*Argentina – Textiles and Apparel*") WT/DS56/R, adopted as modified by the Appellate Body on other issues on 22 April 1998, para. 6.12 (DSR 1998:III, 1033); the Report of the Appellate Body in *US – Wool Shirts and Blouses*, WT/DS33/AB/R, adopted on 23 May 1997, page 1 (DSR 1997:I, 323); and the Panel Report on *Indonesia – Autos*, WT/DS54/R, WT/DS55/R, WT/DS59/R, WT/DS64/R, adopted on 25 September 1997, para. 14.9 (DSR 1998:VI, 2201).

[147] As the Appellate Body has explained, "A panel has to address those claims on which a finding is necessary in order to enable the DSB to make sufficiently precise recommendations and rulings so as to allow for prompt compliance by a Member with those recommendations and rulings 'in order to ensure effective resolution of disputes to the benefit of all Members.'" Report of the Appellate Body in *Australia – Measures Affecting Importation of Salmon*, (hereinafter "*Australia – Salmon*"), WT/DS18/AB/R, adopted on 6 November 1998, para. 223 (DSR 1998:VIII, 3327) (quoting DSU Article 21.1).

India – Autos

For the United States, what was relevant to the present dispute was that, both before and after 1 April 2001, those car manufacturers who signed MOUs before 1 April had been and would continue to be subject to the indigenization and trade balancing requirements. Both after and before 1 April 2001, compliance with these requirements had been necessary in order to comply with Indian law. Because those requirements were legally binding on MOU signatories and enforceable against them, they were measures that this Panel must rule upon.[148]

4.93   The **European Communities** noted that India contended that the EC's complaint did not relate to measures that were in place when the panel request was submitted, but rather to the measures which India might take to enforce the MOUs as from 1 April 2001. Therefore, according to India, the measures in dispute would fall outside the terms of reference of this Panel. The European Communities contended that any measures taken after 1 April 2001 would be outside the terms of reference of this Panel to the extent that they changed the essence of the measures in dispute.[149] It was common ground that the MOUs signed before the date of establishment of this Panel had remained in place after 1 April 2001 and continued to be binding upon the signatories. The only change was that the balancing and indigenization requirements had ceased to be enforceable though the denial of licenses. Nevertheless, those requirements had remained enforceable though other means. India's answers to the Panel's questions confirmed that:

- the MOUs had not been eliminated as of 1 April 2001, despite India's claims that they were an "inherent part" of the import licensing scheme for passenger cars eliminated on that date;

- after 1 April 2001, the signatories continued to be required to meet the commitments imposed by the MOUs[150];

- after 1 April 2001, the MOUs were enforceable as contracts through the domestic courts[151];

- in addition, the MOUs were also enforceable under the FD(TR) Act[152], in particular through the imposition of monetary penalties[153];

- India had taken no action in order to achieve the effect that the MOUs remained legally binding and enforceable after 1 April 2001[154], either before or after that date.

4.94   The method of enforcement of the MOUs was not a constituent element of the violations claimed by the European Communities. The European Communities did not claim that the balancing and indigenization requirements were in-

---

[148]   Question 12 of the Panel.
[149]   Cf. the Report of the Appellate Body on *Brazil – Export Financing Programme for Aircraft,* (hereinafter "*Brazil – Aircraft*"), WT/DS46/AB/R, adopted on 20 August 1999, at paras. 130 *et seq.* (DSR 1999:III, 1161).
[150]   India's response to Question 33, para. 5.
[151]   India's response to Question 52 (d).
[152]   India's response to Question 52 (a).
[153]   *Ibid.*
[154]   India's response to Question 56.

DSR 2002:V

Report of the Panel

consistent with the GATT and the TRIMs Agreement because they were enforced through the denial of licenses. Those requirements were always inconsistent with the GATT and the TRIMs Agreement, irrespective of the precise method used to enforce them. Therefore, the change which occurred as of 1 April 2001 did not give rise to a new "legal situation"[155]. It did not transform the MOUs into different measures and it did not bring them outside the scope of the terms of reference of the Panel, contrary to India's contentions. Any genuinely new measures taken by India after 10 October 2000 would be outside the terms of reference of this Panel. For the reasons explained elsewhere, a mere change of the method of enforcement of the balancing and indigenization requirements after that date would not transform those requirements into new measures beyond the terms of reference of this Panel.[156] The EC's claims were addressed against the balancing and indigenization requirements as such, and not against the method used by India in order to enforce those requirements. Even if it were true that, as India argued now, before 1 April 2001 the MOUs could be enforced exclusively through the denial of import licenses, the use of a different means of enforcement as from 1 April 2001 would not change the obligations imposed by the balancing and indigenization requirements and would not transform them into different measures falling outside the terms of reference of this Panel.[157] The measures applied by India after 1 April 2001 were the same as those that were the subject of the panel request submitted by the European Communities on 12 October 2000. The balancing and indigenization requirements continued to impose the same obligations upon the signatories of the MOUs. The only change occurring on 1 April 2001 concerned the method of enforcement of those obligations. That change, however, was without relevance for this dispute. The EC's complaint was not directed against any of the specific methods available to the Indian authorities in order to enforce the balancing and indigenization requirements, but against the requirements themselves.

4.95   The European Communities agreed with India that the DSU did not allow a Member to launch a dispute settlement proceeding on "the-WTO consistency of implementation measures before those implementation measures are taken"[158]. But that situation was not present here. The European Communities was quite simply not challenging any "implementation measures". As explained [repeatedly], the EC's complaint was not directed against the specific enforcement actions which India might be required to take in order to enforce the MOUs. In other words, the European Communities did not challenge the imposition of fines pursuant to the FT(DR) Act or the bringing of actions before the civil courts for breach of contract. Instead, the EC's complaint was addressed against the MOUs as such, regardless of the method used to enforce them. Contrary to India's assertion[159], the EC's complaint was not addressed against the enforce-

---

[155]   India's response to Question 33, at p. 4, para. 4.
[156]   EC's response to Question 18 of the Panel.
[157]   Cf. the Report of the Appellate Body on *Brazil – Aircraft*, WT/DS46/AB/R, adopted on 20 August 1999, paras. 130 *et seq.* (DSR 1999:III, 1161).
[158]   India's response to Question 37 of the Panel.
[159]   *Ibid.*

1888   DSR 2002:V

ment measures which India might take after 1 April 2001. [The panel request and the EC's First Submission to the Panel made it perfectly clear that] the EC's complaint was directed against Public Notice No. 60 and the MOUs *as such.* Public Notice No. 60 and the MOUs were adopted by India well before the European Communities submitted its panel request and were unquestionably within the terms of reference of this Panel. The European Communities did not contest that Public Notice No. 60 ceased to be effective as of 1 April 2001. Yet, by now it was a well established practice that Panels should rule on all the measures within their terms of reference, even if they were discontinued during the proceedings.[160] The European Communities saw no reason why this Panel should depart from that practice. The European Communities, therefore, reiterated its request to the Panel to find that, at the time when this Panel was established, Public Notice No. 60 was inconsistent with Articles XI:1 and III:4 of the GATT and Article 2.1 of the TRIMs Agreement. India's defence was premised on the mistaken assumption that the MOUs were not " measures", and that only the specific actions that India might take in order to enforce them could be subject to dispute settlement. That assumption was manifestly wrong, and so was India's defence. The MOUs were acts of the Indian Government. Moreover, they were binding upon the signatories and legally enforceable. In the light of well established case law, that was more than sufficient to conclude that they were, *as such*, "measures" in the sense of GATT Article XI:1 as well as "requirements" in the sense of GATT Article III:4. Since the MOUs were "measures" and " requirements" on their own, they could be the subject of dispute settlement from the moment of their conclusion and for as long as they remained enforceable, regardless of whether the Indian authorities needed to take any specific actions to enforce them. Indeed, it was very likely that, after 1 April 2001, India would not have to take any enforcement actions at all, because, just as they had done until now, the signatories would comply with the terms of the MOUs in order to avoid the imposition by the Indian authorities of the penalties provided for in the FDTR or to be sued by the Indian Government before a civil court.

4.96   The European Communities argued that until 1 April 2001, the Indian authorities had had the possibility to enforce the MOUs by denying import licenses for passenger cars in SKD/CKD form to the signatories who failed to comply with the indigenization and balancing requirements set out in their MOUs. But this was just one of the various enforcement mechanisms available to the Indian authorities. The European Communities noted that the Indian Government had indicated that "the obligation under the MOUs already entered shall continue to be valid even after the termination of Public Notice as they shall continue to be enforceable under the FT (DR) Act[161]. The enforcement mechanisms provided for in the FDTR Act included the cancellation or suspension of the Importer-Exporter Code Number[162] and of the import or export licenses[163], the im-

---

[160]   See e.g., the Panel Report on *Indonesia – Autos*, WT/DS54/R, WT/DS55/R, WT/DS64/R, adopted on 23 July 1998, para. 14.9 and the reports cited therein (DSR 1998:VI, 2201).
[161]   US Questions, TRIMs Committee, Response to Question 10.
[162]   Section 8 of the FTDR Act. Section 7 of the FTDR Act stipulates that "No person shall make any import or export except under an Importer-Exporter Code Number ....".

Report of the Panel

position of fines[164] and the confiscation of the imported or exported goods[165]. The terms of the MOU can be enforced in Indian courts as it is a legal contract between the Government of India and the joint venture car manufacturer.[166] During the consultations, India had said that the MOUs were enforceable under the Foreign Trade (Development and Regulation) Act of 1992 (the "FTDR Act"), and would remain so after 1 April 2001. Thus, according to India,

> "... the obligation under the MOUs already entered shall continue to be valid even after the termination of Public Notice No. 60 as they shall continue to be enforceable under the FT(DR) Act."[167]

> and

> "The conditions mentioned on the MOUs signed by different joint venture automobile companies are enforceable as per the provisions of the Foreign Trade (Development & Regulation) Act, 1992."[168]

Yet, at the first meeting with the Panel, India seemed to take the position that the MOUs were not, and indeed would have never been, enforceable under the FT(DR) Act. (India explained away the above statements as being made by technicians without legal expertise!). The European Communities noted that the Panel has asked several questions to India in order to clarify this issue.[169] During the consultations, India had also confirmed that the MOUs were binding contracts under India's civil law which could be enforced through the courts:

> "The terms of the MOU already entered into can be enforced even after 2001 in the Indian courts as it is a legal contract between the Government of India and the joint venture car manufacturer."[170]

It must be emphasized that, even on India's interpretation, the enforceability of the MOUs as contracts after 1 April 2001 was not the result of any action taken by the Indian Government after the establishment of this Panel. India appeared to admit that the MOUs had been binding contracts from the moment of their signature.[171] Nevertheless, it argued that before 1 April 2001 they could not be enforced through the courts, because of the clause contained in paragraph V of the standard format for MOUs. Following the elimination of the discretionary import licensing on 1 April 2001, the inhibitory effect of that clause would have ceased and the MOUs would have become enforceable through the courts automatically.

---

[163] Section 9 of the FTDR Act.

[164] Section 11 of the FTDR Act.

[165] *Ibid.*

[166] India's responses to Questions by the United States, 13 July 2000, responses to Supplemental Question 4.

[167] India's responses to Questions by the United States, 20 May 1999, response to Question 10.

[168] India's responses to Supplemental Questions by the United States, 30 July 1999, response to Question 3.

[169] Cf. Questions 52 (a) and (b) of the Panel.

[170] India's responses to Supplemental Questions by the United States, 30 July 1999, response to Question 4 .

[171] See India's responses to Supplemental Questions by the United States, 30 July 1999, response to Question 4.

In spite of the above, India now contended that, before 1 April 2001, the MOUs could be enforced exclusively through the denial of import licenses for CKD/SKD kit. According to India, this would result from paragraph V of the standard format for MOU, which provided that:

> The MOU scheme would be enforced through the import licensing mechanism and MOU signing firms would be granted import licenses based on the progress made in respect of the parameter mentioned at para. III above.

The European Communities considered that the wording of the above clause did not exclude the possibility for the Indian authorities to enforce the MOUs through other methods generally available under Indian law. Indeed, if the interpretation of paragraph V now made by India were correct, it would mean that, as from 1 April 2001, the MOUs would have become unenforceable, since any attempt by the Indian authorities to enforce them as contracts through the courts would amount to a breach of paragraph V. The European Communities doubted that it was in the interest of India to maintain that interpretation. At any rate, whether or not the MOUs were enforceable exclusively through the denial of import licenses prior to 1 April 2001 was ultimately irrelevant. As explained, a mere change in the method used to enforce the balancing and indigenization requirements was without consequences for the legal characterization of those requirements and did not transform them into new measures falling outside the terms of reference of this Panel.

4.97   The European Communities agreed with India that the Panel "must base its ruling on inconsistencies that had already occurred at the time of the request for [the establishment of the Panel]". However, the continued existence and enforceability of the MOUs after 1 April 2001 did not result from any additional measure taken by the Indian Government after that request, but exclusively from the terms of the MOUs concluded by the Indian Government before that date. Thus, the inconsistencies claimed by the European Communities existed from the moment of the conclusion of the MOUs. For the same reason, India's argument that the European Communities was requesting the Panel to rule on a "prospective matter" was also without merit. The European Communities was not asking the Panel to rule that India would infringe the GATT and the TRIMs Agreement if "India were to do this or were to do that" in order to enforce the MOUs. The European Communities claimed that already the existence of binding and enforceable MOUs was as such inconsistent with the GATT and the TRIMs Agreement, regardless of whether any specific enforcement action needed to be taken. It was well established in GATT/WTO law that mandatory measures could be challenged without having to wait until they were actually enforced.[172] Indeed, to hold the opposite, as India appeared to be suggesting,

---

[172]   See e.g., the Panel Report on *United States – Taxes on Petroleum and Certain Imported Substances*, adopted on 17 June 1987, BISD 34S/136, 160, para. 5.2.2 (the objective of Article XI:1 "could not be attained if contracting parties could not challenge existing legislation mandating actions at variance with the General Agreement until the administrative acts implementing it had actually been applied to their trade.").

Report of the Panel

would mean that the MOUs could only be challenged in the WTO if and when the signatories failed to observe their terms.

4.98   The **United States** recalled that India had advised it as early as May of 1999 – some twelve months before it requested this Panel, and almost two years before India abolished import licensing for SKD and CKD kits – that the requirements of the MOUs could be enforced through the provisions of the FT(DR) Act and through Indian civil courts. India reconfirmed the point in July 2000. As the United States mentioned at the outset it was led to pursue this complaint precisely because India had told it about these additional means of enforcement, and because the trade balancing and indigenization requirements in the MOUs would not come to an end at the same time as the import licensing regime. Despite all of India's discussion of 1 April 2001, nothing of substance had actually changed with the MOUs: The requirements were still in place; they were still binding and enforceable; companies faced the prospects of an action against them in court, or enforcement under the FT(DR) Act, if they did not comply; and India – though it said it could waive compliance with the requirements if it so chose – had in fact not yet chosen to do so.

4.99   **India** disagreed with the assertions by the European Communities and the United States that the precise nature of the method used to enforce the balancing and the indigenization requirements was without relevance for the legal characterization of those requirements. At issue was not merely a change in the method of enforcement of the MOUs. There was a substantial difference between a requirement that had to be fulfilled to obtain an import license under the Indian trade laws and a requirement that must be met under a private law contract with the Government of India. The Government of India was bound by its trade law. Once the restrictions on imports of cars had been imposed under the EXIM policy and conditions for the grant of import licenses were set out in Public Notice No. 60, the Government had no option but to act in accordance with that policy and that Notice. However, under the law of contract in India, it was always open to the Government of India, like any other party to a contract, to determine whether it would enforce or waive its rights under the MOUs.[173] With the removal of the restrictions on imports of cars in the form of SKD/CKD kits, the Government of India therefore acquired discretion with respect to the application of the indigenization requirements that it did not previously have.[174] This created a new legal situation which did not exist when the requests for the establishment of a panel were submitted and could therefore not be examined by the panel. India was entitled to the presumption that it would exercise its discretion under the MOUs in a WTO-consistent manner. If the European Communities and the United States were to consider any future action in respect of the contractual indigenization requirements to be WTO-inconsistent, they had the right to invoke the DSU in respect of that matter. However, they could not ask this Panel to rule

---

[173]   The only limitation on actions by the Government of India in the realm of contract was the right to equality contained in Article 14 of the Constitution of India, which would require the Government to follow a uniform policy with respect to all contracts that fall in the same class or category.

[174]   See also India's response to Question 127 of the Panel.

on that possible future action. India wished to recall in this context that, under the consistent jurisprudence of GATT and WTO panels, discretionary legislation as such could not be challenged, only the application of such legislation in a specific case. The practice of GATT panels was summed up in the report of the panel on *United States - Measures Affecting the Importation, Internal Sale and Use of Tobacco* as follows:

> ... panels had consistently ruled that legislation which mandated action inconsistent with the General Agreement could be challenged as such, whereas legislation which merely gave the discretion to the executive authority of a contracting party to act inconsistently with the General Agreement could not be challenged as such; only the actual application of such legislation inconsistent with the General Agreement could be subject to challenge.[175]

If WTO Members must be presumed to apply their discretionary legislation WTO-consistently, they must also be presumed to exercise their discretion in exercising their private contractual rights WTO-consistently. Subsidiarily, India pointed out that there was no reason why the discretion that the executive branch of a WTO Member had under its trade law and the discretion it had under its civil law should be treated differently. In both instances, it was only fair if other Members were required to await the application of the domestic law before resorting to the WTO dispute settlement procedures. India noted that the United States had vigorously defended this principle when its domestic law was challenged by other WTO Members - most recently in the WTO proceedings on Sections 301-310[176] of the Trade Act of 1974 and on the Anti-dumping Act of 1916.[177] The United States had in particular rejected the idea that the WTO obligations in respect of domestic discretionary law should be "interpreted by reference to a new-found obligation to avoid uncertainty and to ensure 'security and predictability'."[178] India was entitled to the presumption that it would exercise its discretion under the MOUs in a WTO-consistent manner just as the United States was deemed entitled to the presumption that it would apply its trade laws WTO-consistently. However, these were matters that this Panel need not resolve because they arose only after the requests for the establishment of a panel had been submitted.

4.100 India said that the MOUs were merely "private contractual arrangements" between the Indian Government and car manufacturers, and that because of the elimination of import licensing, India now had discretion to waive its rights to

---

[175] BISD 41S/131, para. 118. See also the jurisprudence cited in this report and the Report of the Appellate Body in *United States – Anti–Dumping Act of 1916,* (hereinafter "*US – 1916 Act*"), (WT/DS136/AB/R, WT/DS162/AB/R), adopted on 26 September 2000, paras. 84-102 (DSR 2000:X, 4793).

[176] Panel Report on *US – Section 301 Trade Act,* (WT/DS152/R), adopted on 27 January 2000, paras. 4.301-4.317 (DSR 2000:II, 815).

[177] Report of the Appellate Body in *US – 1916 Act,* (WT/DS136/AB/R, WT/DS162/AB/R), adopted on 26 September 2000, para. 13 (DSR 2000:X, 4793).

[178] Panel Report on *US – Section 301 Trade Act* (WT/DS152/R), adopted on 27 January 2000, para. 4.301 (DSR 2000:II, 815).

Report of the Panel

enforce the indigenization requirement. As a consequence, India argued the requirement was a "discretionary" measure that could not be challenged. In the view of the **United States**, India's argument was mistaken, however, for the fundamental reason that at no time had the indigenization and trade balancing requirements ceased to be binding and enforceable on MOU signatories. The fact that India's enforcement options might have changed did not mean the requirements themselves had changed. Moreover, the fact that India had the option of revoking these requirements did not change their mandatory nature. The situation here was no different than that of *any* WTO-inconsistent measure: a WTO Member generally had the power to withdraw such a measure, but that did not render the measure discretionary. For example, mandatory legislation could typically be repealed; but that fact did not mean that legislation was inherently discretionary. To support its argument, India invoked the "consistent jurisprudence of GATT and WTO panels" that "discretionary legislation as such cannot be challenged". India misconstrued that jurisprudence, however. For example, India cited the Appellate Body report in the *US – 1916 Act* dispute, but that report did not support India's position. In that case, the Appellate Body drew particular attention to the reasoning in one paragraph of the GATT 1947 *United States – Measures Affecting Alcoholic and Malt Beverages* Panel Report (hereinafter "*US – Malt Beverages*").[179] In that paragraph, the *US - Malt Beverages* Panel reasoned as follows:

> In respect of the United States contention that the Massachusetts measure was not being enforced and that the Rhode Island measure was only nominally enforced, the Panel recalled its discussion of mandatory versus discretionary laws in the previous section. The Panel noted that the price affirmation measures in both Massachusetts and Rhode Island are mandatory legislation. Even if Massachusetts may not currently be using its police powers to enforce this mandatory legislation, the measure continues to be mandatory legislation which may influence the decisions of economic operators. Hence, a non-enforcement of a mandatory law in respect of imported products does not ensure that imported beer and wine are not treated less favourably than like domestic products to which the law does not apply. Similarly, the contention that Rhode Island only "nominally" enforces its mandatory legislation *a fortiori* does not immunize this measure from Article III:4. The mandatory laws in these two states by their terms treat imported beer and wine less favourably than the like domestic products. Accordingly, the Panel found that the mandatory price affirmation laws in Massachusetts and Rhode Island are inconsistent with Ar-

---

[179] Report of the Appellate Body in *US –1916 Act*, WT/DS136/AB/R, WT/DS162/AB/R, adopted on 26 September 2000, para. 91, fn. 50 (DSR 2000:X, 4793).

ticle III:4, irrespective of the extent to which they are being enforced.[180]

Thus, even if India were actually not enforcing these requirements, the situation in this dispute would be the same as in *US - Malt Beverages*. As India had said, a car manufacturer that signed an MOU was legally obligated, under the contract law of India, to achieve 70% local content and to discharge its export obligations. The manufacturer could not do otherwise without breaching those contractual obligations; those obligations were mandatory. And, as in the *US - Malt Beverages* dispute, the fact that India might eventually decide not to enforce those obligations did not make them any less mandatory. This panel, like the *US - Malt Beverages* panel before it, should conclude that these requirements were inconsistent with India's WTO obligations. As a practical matter, if the Panel accepted India's argument, India's measures could never be examined unless manufacturers were willing to violate their contracts and expose themselves to the risk of enforcement by the Indian authorities – hardly a satisfactory outcome for them or for those WTO Members whose trade interests were undermined by these requirements.

4.101 A similar issue had also arisen in *Canada – FIRA*. That panel considered but rejected an argument that contractual undertakings like the MOUs in this case should be considered as private contractual obligations of particular foreign investors vis-à-vis the government. In particular, that panel concluded that such contractual obligations should not adversely affect the rights which GATT contracting parties possess under Article III:4.[181] In fact, many of the undertakings had actually been waived by the Government[182] but that did not change the Panel's legal conclusion that the undertakings were inconsistent with the GATT. The United States did not doubt that India could revoke the MOU requirements if it wished to do so. Of course, it had in fact *not* done so. Regrettably, India had reiterated that MOU signatories were still "bound" by those obligations. India's insistence on that point showed how far from "discretionary" the requirements of the MOUs really were and underscored the contradictory nature of India's arguments. If India actually took the welcome step of permanently rescinding the MOU requirements, it would indeed be changing the MOU signatories' mandatory obligations. But the fact that India could in principle take that step did not change the legal analysis: the requirements themselves were binding and enforceable, and thus they were not discretionary. And, India's refusal actually to take this step – as opposed to stating that it had the power to do so – reinforced the need for Panel findings that would confirm India's obligation to do so.

4.102 The **European Communities** said that Panels were not bound by a Member's interpretation of its domestic law.[183] Rather, Panels must treat the domestic law of a Member as a fact, the establishment of which was subject to the ordi-

---

[180] Panel Report on *United States – Measures Affecting Alcoholic and Malt Beverages*, (hereinafter "*US – Malt Beverages*") adopted on 19 June 1992, BISD 39S/206, para. 5.60.

[181] Panel Report on *Canada – FIRA*, adopted on 7 February 1984, BISD 30S/140, para. 5.6.

[182] *Ibid.*, para. 2.11.

[183] Panel Report on *US – Section 301 Trade Act*, WT/DS152/R, adopted on 27 January 2000, para. 7.19 (DSR 2000:II, 815).

Report of the Panel

nary rules on the burden of proof.[184] India could not ask this Panel to accept its interpretation of the MOUs simply because India was a party to the MOUs. Rather, India must prove that the MOUs actually said what India pretended now that they said. India made a similar argument in *India – Patents (US)*. The Appellate Body rejected it in categorical terms. According to the Appellate Body, India's position amounted

> "... to say that only India can asses whether Indian law is consistent with India's obligations under the WTO Agreement. This clearly cannot be so."[185]

India's reliance on *US – Section 301 Trade Act*[186] was inapposite. That case did not stand for the proposition that Panels were bound to accept whatever views were expressed by a Member with respect to the interpretation of its domestic legislation. In *US – Section 301 Trade Act*, the Panel found that the relevant statutory language (as interpreted by the Panel, and not by the United States) left a margin of discretion to the US Government. The Panel then relied upon the Statement of Administrative Action made to the US Congress at the time of the approval of the results of the Uruguay Round, and upon the statements made by the United States to the Panel to the effect that it would exercise that margin of discretion consistently with its WTO obligations in order to conclude that the measures in dispute were not inconsistent with the WTO Agreement.[187]

4.103 This case concerned an entirely different situation. The MOUs left no margin of discretion to the Indian Government for making the interpretation which it had presented to the Panel. The MOUs required to balance all the imports made by the signatories until they achieved a 70% indigenization level. This left no scope for India's interpretation. The Panel could not accept an interpretation which was at odds with the plain meaning of the MOUs simply because it had been put forward by India.

4.104 India argued that, since 1 April 2001, the indigenization requirements had become "discretionary legislation" not subject to dispute settlement because, from that date, the MOUs were enforceable only as contracts and, under Indian contract law, the Indian Government was free to decide whether or not to enforce them. This argument reflected an erroneous understanding of the notion of "discretionary legislation", was refuted by well established precedent and, moreover, would lead to a manifestly absurd and unacceptable result. In WTO law the term "discretionary legislation" was used to designate legislation which allowed, but did not mandate, the executive branch of the Government to take measures that were inconsistent with the WTO Agreement. In the present case, the European Communities did not claim that the MOUs were inconsistent with the GATT because they «allow» the Indian Government to take other, GATT inconsistent

---

[184] *Ibid.*, para. 7.18.
[185] Report of the Appellate Body in *India – Patents (US)*, WT/DS50/AB/R, adopted on 16 January 1998, at para. 66 (DSR 1998:I, 9).
[186] Panel Report on *US – Section 301 Trade Act*, WT/DS152/R, adopted on 27 January 2000 (DSR 2000:II, 815).
[187] *Ibid.*, para. 7.117.

1896   DSR 2002:V

measures. Rather, the European Communities claimed that the MOUs *as such* were GATT inconsistent, regardless of the measures that might be taken subsequently by the Indian Government in order to enforce them. There was a fundamental difference between the «discretionary legislation» considered in previous cases and the MOUs. "Discretionary legislation" did not, as such, impose any legal obligations upon the economic operators. The obligations for the operators arose exclusively from the measures taken subsequently by the executive branch on the basis of the authority granted by the "discretionary legislation". In contrast, the MOUs imposed binding obligations upon the signatories, which they must fulfil in order to avoid the risk of sanctions. The measures which the Indian Government might take pursuant to the MOUs would not create any new legal obligations for the operators, but served merely to enforce those obligations already imposed by the MOUs. Previous cases confirmed that the discretion to enforce or not to enforce a measure did not transform such measure into "discretionary legislation" immune to dispute settlement action. In *US – 1916 Act* the Appellate Body ruled that the discretion enjoyed by the US Department of Justice in order to initiate or not to initiate criminal proceedings was not

> discretion of such nature or of such breadth as to transform the 1916 Act into discretionary legislation, as this term has been understood for purposes of distinguishing between mandatory and discretionary legislation[188].

By the same token, the discretion enjoyed by India's Government to bring or not an action before a civil court in order to enforce the MOUs did not transform the MOUs into discretionary legislation.

4.105 Further confirmation was provided by *US – Malt Beverages*.[189] In that case the Panel found that the measures at issue were inconsistent with Article III:4, even though they were not being enforced in practice. The Panel reasoned that although the responsible authorities

> may not be currently using its police powers ... the measures continue to be mandatory legislation which may influence the decisions of economic operators.[190]

Furthermore, by now it was well established that a measure might be inconsistent with Article III:4 even if it was not legally enforceable. Thus, for example, in *Canada – Autos*, the Panel held that certain value added requirements contained in the "Letters of Undertaking" submitted to the Canadian Government by some car manufacturers were inconsistent with Article III:4, even though the Letters were not enforceable through sanctions in the case of non-compliance[191]. If non-enforceable local content requirements were inconsistent with Article III:4, then

---

[188] Report of the Appellate Body in *US – 1916 Act*, WT/DS136/AB/R, WT/DS162/AB/R, adopted on 26 September 2000, at para. 91 (DSR 2000:X, 4793).
[189] Panel Report on *US – Malt Beverages*, BISD 39S/206.
[190] *Ibid.*, para 5.60.
[191] Panel Report on *Canada – Certain Measures Affecting the Automotive Industry*, (hereinafter "*Canada – Autos*"), WT/DS139/R, WT/DS142/R, adopted on 19 June 2000, as modified by the Appellate Body Report, para. 10.120 *et seq.* (DSR 2000:VI, 2985)

Report of the Panel

enforceable ones must be *a fortiori* inconsistent with that provision, even if the authorities had discretion not to enforce them. Moreover, India's interpretation would lead to an absurd result. On India's interpretation, the European Communities could not challenge the MOUs unless and until India brought an action against a signatory before an Indian civil court for breach of contract. Yet the Indian authorities would not have to take any such action unless the signatories failed to comply with the MOUs. Thus, India's interpretation would have the paradoxical result that the MOUs could be subject to WTO dispute settlement if they were not complied with (i.e. if they are ineffective), but not if they are complied with by the signatories (i.e. if they were effective in discriminating against imported products). Ultimately, India's interpretation would lead Members to encourage their economic operators to disobey the domestic laws of other Members which they considered to be WTO inconsistent, as a pre-requisite for being able to challenge those laws in the WTO. The European Communities was convinced that no Member, including India, could regard this as a desirable development of WTO law.

D.   Claims under GATT 1994 and TRIMs

1.   Article III:4

4.106 The **United States** claimed that the indigenization and trade balancing obligations were "regulations" or "requirements" that "affect" the sale, use or purchase of automobile parts and components but that accord "less favourable treatment" to foreign products than to "like" domestic products.

- *"Regulations" or "requirements"*: First, the ordinary meaning of "regulation" included its use as a generic term for governmental measures that implement statutes and other domestic legal provisions. Public Notice No. 60 was such a measure. Second, Public Notice No. 60 fell within the ordinary meaning of the term "regulation" because it regulated the conduct of manufacturing firms (they must meet local content and trade balancing targets) and the conduct of the Indian import licensing authorities (they may issue licenses for CKD/SKD components and kits if those targets are met). Third, Public Notice No. 60 and the MOUs both imposed "requirements" on firms manufacturing cars in India. A firm that signed an MOU was required to achieve 50% local content during the first three years of the MOU, and 70% before the end of the fifth year. That firm was also required to export cars and auto components with an FOB value at least equal to the CIF value of their importations of CKD/SKD kits and components. Previous panels had considered similar situations. The *Canada – FIRA* panel[192] recognized that the term "requirements" properly described legally enforceable undertakings given to the Government of Canada by individual companies. In this case, as in *Canada –*

---

[192] Panel Report on *Canada –FIRA*, adopted on 7 February 1984, BISD 30S/140.

1898   DSR 2002:V

FIRA, the local content and trade balancing commitments in the MOUs were part of the conditions under which signatories can receive import licenses. India had confirmed that those conditions were meant to be enforced. The analysis was not affected by the fact that firms could in theory choose not to sign an MOU. Any firm that did so would forfeit the right to import CKD/SKD components and kits. Accepting and complying with the terms of an MOU were requirements that a firm must fulfill to take advantage of the opportunity to import SKD/CKD kits and components. The term "requirement" encompassed such preconditions to obtaining an advantage from the government. Previous panels addressing this issue had reached the same conclusion. For instance, the *EEC - Parts and Components* Panel recognized that requirements that an enterprise voluntarily accepts to gain government-provided advantages are nonetheless "requirements".

- *"Affecting"*: Ever since the *Italian Discrimination Against Imported Agricultural Machinery* report (hereinafter "*Italy – Agricultural Machinery*"), panels had recognized that the term "affecting" in Article III:4 had a broad meaning, which extended not only to laws and regulations which directly govern the conditions of sale or purchase but also to any laws or regulations which might adversely modify the conditions of competition between the domestic and imported products on the internal market. The measures at issue here "affect" the sale, etc., of domestic and imported goods, because they required manufacturers in India to increase their purchases and use of Indian-made automotive parts and components at the expense of like foreign parts and components. A company manufacturing cars in India could not import SKD/CKD kits and components unless it used a decreasing percentage of imported goods in its production – no more than 50% in the first three years, no more than 30% by the fifth year. Moreover, the more a car manufacturer bought or used imported kits and components, the more it had an obligation to allocate a portion of its output to export, regardless of its business preferences. Both of these requirements made it less attractive for a manufacturer to purchase or use imported parts and components.

- *"Like"*: Imported automotive parts and components were "like" automotive parts and components made in India. Domestic and imported components to be used in manufacturing a particular car share the same physical characteristics and commercial uses. Thus, while a clutch and a shock absorber differed from each other, a domestic clutch and an imported clutch to be incorporated in a particular car were "like" each other, just as a domestic shock absorber and an imported shock absorber to be incorporated into a particular car were "like" each other.

Report of the Panel

- *"Less Favourable Treatment"*: The indigenization obligation and the trade balancing obligation accorded a competitive advantage to Indian goods and thus accord "less favorable treatment" to imported automotive components and kits as described in paras 4.107 and 4.110 and 4.111."

(a)　The Indigenization Requirement

4.107 Manufacturers could meet the indigenization obligation only by purchasing and using Indian parts and components instead of imported ones. By the end of the third year, their production of finished vehicles could consist of 50%, 60%, or more Indian-origin parts; but that same production could include no more than 50% foreign-origin parts and components. By the end of the fifth year, Indian parts and components could comprise 70%, 80%, or more of a firm's production; but now that same firm's production could include no more than 30% imported parts and components. The indigenization requirement gave Indian goods a clear advantage: their imported counterparts will simply not be permitted to compete for the percentage of production that India expressly reserved for domestic goods. Such local content requirements had been systematically condemned. For instance, the *Canada – FIRA* panel recognized that undertakings that excluded the possibility of purchasing available imported products clearly treated such imported products less favorably than domestic products, and that such requirements were therefore not consistent with Article III:4.[193] The indigenization requirement did not disadvantage just kits and components imported in SKD/CKD form. The requirement discriminates against *any* imported part or component, from *any* non-Indian origin, that an Indian firm might use in manufacturing a motor vehicle. Any such foreign component, no matter how small or how separate from other parts, counts against a manufacturer trying to reach the mandated local content percentage. The indigenization requirement therefore accords imported parts and components treatment less favorable than it accords to like domestic items.

4.108 The **European Communities** claimed that the indigenization" requirements were inconsistent with GATT Article III:4 in that they provided less favourable treatment to imported parts and materials than to like domestic goods with respect to their internal use in the production of passenger cars. Article III:4 of GATT provided in relevant part that

> "The products of the territory of any contracting party imported into the territory of any other contracting party shall be accorded treatment no less favourable than that accorded to like products of national origin in respect of laws, regulations and requirements affecting their internal sale, offering for sale, purchase, transportation, distribution or use [...]."

---

[193] *Canada – FIRA* , para. 5.8. To the same effect is the Panel Report on *EEC - Parts and Components*, para. 5.21.

1900　　　　　　　　　　　　　　　　　　　　　　　　DSR 2002:V

India – Autos

4.109 Accordingly, in order to rule on this claim the Panel would need to address the following issues:

- first, whether the measures at issue were "laws, regulations or requirements";

- second, whether domestic products were "like" imported products;

- third, whether the measures "affect" the "internal use" of the products concerned; and

- fourth, whether the measures afforded "less favourable treatment" to imported products than to domestic products.

- *The measures in dispute were "requirements":* By now it was firmly established that Government action need not be compulsory in order to qualify as a "requirement" for the purposes of GATT Article III:4. In *Canada – FIRA* the Panel held that the legally enforceable undertakings given by some foreign investors to the Canadian Government constituted "requirements", even though the submission of such undertakings was voluntary.[194] Similarly, in *EEC – Parts and Components* the Panel concluded that the conditions accepted by a firm in order to obtain an "advantage" granted by the EC authorities also constituted "requirements".[195] Subse-

---

[194] The Panel reasoned as follows:

"The Panel first examined whether the purchase undertakings are to be considered 'laws, regulations or requirements' within the meaning of Article III:4. As both parties had agreed that the Foreign Investment Review Act and the Foreign Investment Review Regulations –whilst providing for the possibility of written undertakings- did not make their submission obligatory, the question remained whether the undertakings given in individual cases are to be considered 'requirements' within the meaning of Article III:4. In this respect the Panel noted that Section 9(c) of the Act refers to 'any written undertakings [...] relating to the proposed or actual investment given by any party thereto conditional upon the allowance of the investment' and that section 21 of the Act states that 'where a person who has given a written undertaking...fails or refuses to comply with the undertaking' a court order may be made 'directing that person to comply with the undertaking'. The Panel further noted that written purchase undertakings –leaving aside the manner in which they may have been arrived at (voluntary submission, encouragement, negotiation, etc)- once they were accepted, became part of the conditions under which the investment proposals were approved, in which case compliance could be legally enforced. The Panel therefore found that the word 'requirements' as used in Article III:4 could be considered a proper description of existing undertakings."

Panel Report on *Canada – FIRA*, adopted on 7 February 1984, BISD 30S/140, at para. 5.4.

[195] Panel Report on *EEC – Parts and Components*, BISD 37S/132, adopted on 16 May 1990, at para. 5.21:

".... Article III:4 refers to 'all laws, regulations or requirements affecting the internal sale, offering for sale, purchase, transportation, distribution or use'. The Panel considered that the comprehensive coverage of 'all laws, regulations or requirements *affecting* (emphasis added) the internal sale, etc.' of imported products suggests that not only requirements which an enterprise is legally bound to carry out, such as those examined by the *Canada – FIRA* Panel (BISD 30S/140), but also those which an enterprise voluntarily accepts in order to obtain an advantage from the government constitute 'requirements' within the meaning of that provision."

The same interpretation underlies the Report on *Italian Discrimination against Imported Agricultural Machinery*, (hereinafter "*Italy – Agricultural Machinery*"), adopted on 23 October 1958, BISD 7S/60, where the Panel concluded that an Italian law providing especial credit terms to farmers

DSR 2002:V

Report of the Panel

quent cases had clarified that the "advantage" might consist of a benefit in respect of a border measure.[196] More recently, in *Canada – Autos* the Panel went even further by holding that the "letters of undertaking" submitted by certain firms at the request of the Canadian Government were "requirements", even though they were neither legally enforceable nor a condition to obtain an advantage.[197] Public Notice No. 60 did not impose upon the joint-ventures a legal obligation to conclude an MOU with the Indian Government. Nonetheless, the conclusion of an MOU was a necessary condition for obtaining an advantage: the grant of import licenses for CKD and SKD kits. Moreover, once it was signed, the MOU is binding upon the signatory and legally enforceable under the FTDR. The European Communities submitted that, in light of the precedents cited above, either of those two features in and by itself was more than sufficient to reach the conclusion that Public Notice No. 60 and the MOUs concluded thereunder constituted "requirements" within the meaning of Article III:4.

---

for the purchase of agricultural machinery conditional upon the purchase by the farmers of Italian machinery was contrary to Article III:4 of GATT.

[196] See e.g., Panel Report on *EC – Bananas III*, WT/DS27/R/USA, adopted 25 September 1997, as modified by the Appellate Body Report, at paras. 7.179 and 7.180, DSR 1997:II, 943, where the Panel found that a requirement to purchase domestic bananas in order to obtain the right to import bananas at a lower duty rate under a tariff quota was a requirement "affecting" the internal purchase of a product within the meaning of GATT Article III:4. On appeal, this finding was upheld by the Appellate Body, WT/DS27/AB/R, at paras. 208-211 (DSR 1997:II, 591).

Similarly, in *Indonesia – Autos*, the Panel concluded that the granting of a duty exemption conditional upon compliance with a local content requirement was inconsistent with GATT Article III:4 and violated Article 2 of the TRIMs Agreement. In reaching this conclusion, the Panel rejected Indonesia's attempted defence that the measure was a "border" measure not covered by GATT Article III:4:

"We do not consider that the matter before us in connection with Indonesia's obligations under the TRIMs Agreement is the customs duty relief as such but rather the internal regulations, i.e. the provisions on purchase and use of domestic products, compliance with which is necessary in order to obtain an advantage, which advantage here is the customs duty relief. The lower duty rates are clearly 'advantages' in the meaning of the chapeau of the Illustrative List to the TRIMs Agreement and as such, we find that the Indonesian measures fall within the scope of the Item 1 of the Illustrative List of the TRIMs."

Panel Report on *Indonesia – Autos*, WT/DS54/R, WT/DS55/R, WT/DS59/R, WT/DS64/R, adopted on 23 July 1998, at para. 14.89 (DSR 1998:VI, 2201).

[197] The Panel cited the following circumstances in order to conclude that the "letters of undertaking" were "requirements":

"(i) in making the undertakings contained in the Letters, the companies acted at the request of the Government of Canada; (ii) the anticipated conclusion of the Auto Pact was a key factor in the decision of the companies to submit these undertakings; (iii) the companies accepted responsibility *vis-à-vis* the Government of Canada with respect to the implementation of the undertakings contained in the Letters, which they described as 'obligations' and in respect of which they undertook to provide information to the Government of Canada and indicated their understanding that the Government of Canada would conduct yearly audits; and (iv) at least until model year 1996, the Government of Canada gathered information on an annual basis concerning the implementation of the conditions provided for in the Letters. "

Panel Report on *Canada – Autos*, WT/DS139/R, WT/DS142/R, adopted on 19 June 2000, para. 10.122 (DSR 2000:VII, 3043).

India – Autos

- *Domestic parts and materials are "like" the imported goods:* The distinctions operated by the "indigenization" requirements were based exclusively on the origin of the products: whereas parts and materials of Indian origin contributed to satisfy the "indigenization" percentage, imported parts and materials did not. Clearly, however, the mere fact of having Indian origin was not, as such, apt to confer upon parts and materials any characteristic, property or quality which made them, by definition, "unlike" any imported good.[198]

- *The measures "affect" the internal "use" of the products concerned:* The term "affect" has been given a broad scope of application. According to the Panel Report in *Italy – Agricultural Machinery,*

  > "The selection of the word 'affecting' would imply [...] that the drafters of the Article intended to cover in [Article III:4] not only the laws and regulations which directly governed the conditions of sale and purchase but also any laws or regulations which might adversely modify the conditions of competition between the domestic and imported products on the internal market

  In the present case, the "indigenization" requirements "affect" directly the "internal use" of parts and materials because, in order to satisfy the "indigenization" percentage, the signatories must incorporate into the vehicles that they manufactured a certain amount of domestic parts and materials.[199]

- *Imported goods are afforded "less favourable treatment":* Finally, it was self-evident that, by requiring the use of a minimum amount of domestic parts and materials, the MOUs preclude the signatories from using an equivalent amount of imported parts and materials and, therefore, afford "less favourable treatment" to imported products.

- *Precedent and the TRIMs Agreement confirmed that the "indigenization" requirements were inconsistent with Article III:4:* Local

---

[198] In *Indonesia – Autos*, the Panel noted, para 14.113, that an
"... origin-based distinction in respect of internal taxes suffices in itself to violate Article III:2, without the need to demonstrate the existence of actually traded like products". (DSR 1998:VI, 2201)
   See also the Panel Report on *Canada – Autos*, para. 10.174, and the Panel Report on *Argentina – Measures Affecting the Export of Bovine Hides and the Import of Finished Leather,* (hereinafter "*Argentina – Hides and Leather*") WT/DS155/R, adopted on 16 February 2001, para.11.169 (DSR 2001:V, 1779).

[199] Panel Report on *Italy – Agricultural Machinery*, para. 12. The Appellate Body confirmed that interpretation of the term "affect" in *EC – Bananas III*, WT/DS27/AB/R, para 220 (DSR 1997:II, 591). See also the Report of the Appellate Body in *Korea – Various Measures on Beef*, WT/DS161/AB/R, WT/DS169/AB/R, adopted on 10 January 2001, paras. 130 *et seq.*(DSR 2001:I, 5)

DSR 2002:V

Report of the Panel

content requirements constituted a clear-cut violation of the national treatment requirements imposed by GATT Article III:4, which had already been condemned by GATT/WTO panels in several occasions.

- in *Canada – FIRA*, the panel found that the undertakings given to the Canadian Government by some foreign investors to, *inter alia*, purchase goods of Canadian origin in specified amounts or proportions was contrary to Article III:4[200];

- similarly, in *EEC- Parts and Components*, the panel concluded that, by making the suspension of anti-circumvention proceedings conditional upon an undertaking to limit the use of Japanese parts and materials, the European Communities acted inconsistently with Article III:4[201];

- in *Indonesia – Autos*, the panel found that the grant of certain tax and import duty benefits to a so-called "National Car" manufacturer conditional upon meeting a certain local content percentage was in violation of Article III:4[202];

- finally, in *Canada – Autos*, the panel held that the grant of a customs duty exemption to certain manufacturers of motor vehicles subject to compliance with certain "Canadian Value Added" requirements was inconsistent with Article III:4[203].

The TRIMs Agreement had confirmed beyond doubt that local content requirements were inconsistent with Article III:4 of GATT. Item 1(a) of the Illustrative List of TRIMs, included among the TRIMs that were inconsistent with Article III:4 those which require

> "a) the [...] use by an enterprise of products of domestic origin [...], whether specified in terms of [...] value of products, or in terms of a proportion of [...] value of its local production"

The "indigenization" requirements at issue in this dispute fell squarely within the terms of Item 1(a) of the Illustrative List and were, therefore, inconsistent with GATT Article III:4.

---

[200] Panel Report on *Canada – FIRA*, paras. 5.4-5.12, BISD 30S/140..

[201] Panel Report on *EEC – Parts and Components*, paras. 5.19-5.21, BISD 37S/132.

[202] Panel Report on *Indonesia – Autos*, WT/DS54/R, WT/DS55/R, WT/DS59/R, WT/DS64/R, adopted on 23 July 1998, para. 14.83 *et seq.* (DSR 1998:VI, 2201).

[203] Panel Report on *Canada – Autos*, WT/DS139/R, WT/DS142/R, adopted on 19 June 2000, as modified by the Appellate Body Report, para. 10.58 *et seq.* (DSR 2000:VI, 2985)

(b)   The Trade Balancing Requirement

4.110 In the view of the **United States**, the trade balancing requirement also modified conditions of competition in favour of Indian goods, but its discrimination affected those kits and components that were imported in SKD or CKD form. All imported SKD/CKD kits/components carried with them an obligation to export from India goods (components or finished vehicles) in a value equal to the value of the imported goods. Moreover, this obligation attached not only to SKD/CKD kits/components that the manufacturer itself imported, but also to those SKD/CKD kits or components that the manufacturer purchased within India but were imported by someone else. Domestic goods, on the other hand, were free of this obligation.

4.111 Consequently, if a manufacturer built a car with components imported in SKD/CKD form, the manufacturer must either export that car or, if it wished to sell that car on the Indian market, the manufacturer must export some other finished vehicle or auto components whose value equalled that of the SKD/CKD importation. If, instead, the manufacturer built that same car without using components imported in SKD/CKD form, the manufacturer was free to sell the car in whatever market it chose; and, if the manufacturer chose the domestic market, it did not have any export obligation to discharge. Moreover, because the requirement attached to goods purchased within India, a number of other forms of discrimination arose as well. For example, a manufacturer seeking to meet its export obligation through the export of finished vehicles would purchase domestic components rather than imported kits - because purchasing an imported kit would only further increase the manufacturer's export obligation, while purchasing the like domestic kit would not. Similarly, a manufacturer that needed to reduce an excess inventory of SKD/CKD kits or components would, all other things being equal, find a readier market for domestically produced kits than imported ones, because the imported ones carried with them the additional burden of the trade balancing requirement and the domestic ones did not. In short, the trade balancing requirement added a burden to imported goods - an interference with the distribution and other commercial choices of their user or purchaser - that did not apply to like domestic goods. That additional burden was a disincentive to the use of imported SKD/CKD kits and components, and the trade balancing requirement therefore accorded less favorable treatment to them. A similar situation had been considered in *EEC - Measures on Animal Feed Proteins* (hereinafter "*EEC – Animal Feed Proteins*"). Both disputes involved a measure that imposed a burden on those who used imported goods but not on those who used like domestic goods (the obligation to buy milk powder from intervention agencies in that case, the obligation to export finished vehicles or auto parts in this one). As the *EEC – Animal Feed Proteins* recognized, such a measure was inconsistent with Article III:4.[204]

4.112 According to the **European Communities**, the signatories of the MOUs seemed to be required to "neutralize" not only the value of the imports which they made themselves, but also the value of any imported kits and components

---

[204]   See also response to Question 10 of the Panel.

Report of the Panel

which they purchased within India from local vendors. To that extent, the "trade balancing" requirements were inconsistent not only with Article XI:1, but also with Article III:4 in that they provided less favourable treatment to imported kits and components with respect to their internal purchase than to like domestic products. (see *supra* para. 4.38)

- *The measures were "requirements":* As demonstrated above (paragraph 4.109), the Public Notice No. 60 and the MOUs were "requirements" within the meaning of Article III:4.

- *Imported products were "like" domestic product:* The distinction operated by the trade balancing requirements was based exclusively on the origin of the products: on the one hand, imported kits and components purchased within India must be neutralized with exports; on the other hand, domestic kits and components need not be neutralized.

- *The "trade balancing" requirements "affect" the internal "purchase" of imported goods:* The trade balancing requirements "affect" directly the internal purchase of imported kits and components, because they subject the purchase of those products within India to the condition that their value must be neutralized with exports.

- *The "trade balancing" requirements afforded "less favourable treatment " to imported products:* The trade balancing requirements afford "less favourable treatment" to imported products because the internal purchase of domestic products is not subject to any similar requirement. All other circumstances being equal, this creates an incentive for the signatories of MOUs to purchase local inputs, thereby modifying adversely the competitive opportunities of imported products in relation to like domestic products.

- *The TRIMs Agreement confirmed that the "trade balancing" requirements were inconsistent with Article III:4:* Item 1(b) of the Illustrative List of Prohibited TRIMs confirmed that the "trade balancing" requirements, to the extent that they apply to products imported by other parties, was inconsistent with GATT Article III:4.

4.113 **India** argued that, in the absence of import licensing, Public Notice No. 60 and the trade balancing provisions of the MOUs were consistent with Article III:4. Public Notice No. 60 merely set out criteria for the automatic grant of import licenses for SKD/CKD kits and did not apply in the absence of any requirement to obtain such a license. The European Communities and the United States claimed that the trade balancing provisions set out in the MOUs were inconsistent with Article XI:1 of the GATT because they subjected the right to import SKD/CKD kits and components to the fulfilment of an export obligation. They further claimed that the trade balancing requirements were inconsistent with Article III:4 of the GATT because they accorded the signatory an advantage, namely the relief from an export obligation, on the condition that it purchased or used domestic components. India planned to demonstrate that the trade

1906

DSR 2002:V

balancing provisions set out in the MOUs required the signatory to offset through exports only the foreign exchange expenditures for imports that had been subject to import licensing. In the absence of any requirement to obtain an import license for SKD/CKD kits and components, no export obligations accrued. The MOUs therefore did not limit in this situation the signatory's right to import SKD/CKD kits and components. Since no export obligations accrued when products not subject to licensing were imported, the signatory could also no longer acquire the advantage of reduced export obligations by purchasing or using domestic components.

4.114 The EC's claim that Public Notice No. 60 and the trade balancing provisions of the MOUs as such, that is independently of the discretionary licensing system for CKD/SKD kits, violated Articles III and XI of the GATT had no merit. The European Communities failed to explain how Public Notice No. 60, as such, restricted imports or favoured the purchase of domestic products over imported products. Public Notice No. 60 merely set out how the import restrictions on cars imposed until 1 April 2001 under the Export-Import Policy were to be administered. This was clear from paragraph 2 of this Notice which read in relevant part: " . . .import of components for motor vehicles in CKD/SKD form, which is restricted for import under the current Export-Import Policy, shall be allowed for importation against a license and such a license will be issued . . .on the basis of an MOU". Public Notice No. 60 was no longer operational because the licensing scheme it was to administer no longer existed. It was therefore not clear to India how the European Communities could claim that the Public Notice *as such* could violate WTO law in the absence of import restrictions on cars.

4.115 The **United States** noted that India had not actually attempted to defend the indigenization requirement. India had just said that car manufacturers might already be in compliance with it. If so, why was India continuing to insist that it needed to be able to enforce the requirement in its courts? Would such compliance mean anything other than that manufacturers were reluctant to test India's willingness to enforce the requirement? India also had not said what would happen to a manufacturer that slipped below the required percentage in the future. In any case, compliance by manufacturers with a WTO-inconsistent measure did not transform that measure into one that was compatible with India's WTO obligations. As India was well aware, GATT Articles III and XI protected conditions of competition, not trade flows; no demonstration of trade effects was necessary to establish a breach of those obligations. The United States added that the only response that India had advanced did not have merit. India claimed that export requirements as such were not prohibited by the GATT; India cited the *Canada – FIRA* panel report in support of its position. India overlooked, however, that the U.S. claims were directed at a *discriminatory* export obligation. Not all like products were subject to the export requirement; the requirement applied only to imported goods. An internal regulation that was otherwise consistent with the WTO Agreement became inconsistent if, like the trade balancing requirement in this case, it applied to imported products but not to like domestic ones. There was nothing to the contrary in the *Canada – FIRA* report; that dispute did not involve export requirements applied exclusively to imported goods.

Report of the Panel

2.   Article XI:1

4.116 The **United States** claimed that the indigenization and trade balancing requirements were "prohibitions or restrictions ... on ... importation", as those terms are used in Article XI:1. Panels had recognized that the scope of Article XI:1 was comprehensive: it extended not only to outright prohibitions but also to discretionary or non-automatic import licensing and to conditional suspensions of an import prohibition. Moreover, the scope of the word "restriction" itself was broad, as seen in its ordinary meaning, which was "a limitation on action, a limiting condition or regulation".

(i)   The Indigenization Requirement

4.117 The United States claimed that the indigenization requirement was a straightforward restriction or prohibition on imports. Failure to meet the 50% local content quota by the third year, or the 70% quota by the fifth year, led to the denial of the right to import parts and components in SKD/CKD form. Public Notice No. 60 was clear about this, and India had confirmed that the MOU was itself designed to limit imports of SKD/CKD kits/components when a firm failed to meet the indigenization requirement. Paragraph 3(iii) of Public Notice No. 60, and paragraph III, clause (iv) of the MOU, required that MOU signatories achieve specified levels of indigenization in order to be able to import SKD/CKD kits/components. Moreover, it was *India* that had said that the MOUs *as such* were intended to limit the importation of SKD/CKD kits/components when a firm failed to meet the indigenization requirement: "As all the companies have achieved the desired level of indigenization during the *last two years* (since issuance of Public Notice No. 60) the need *to invoke MOUs to impose limitation on them* has not arisen.[205] The indigenization requirement did not merely restrict the amount of kits that a manufacturer might import into India, it actually prohibited such imports outright. Any manufacturer that failed to achieve the local content targets in the MOU was forbidden from importing CKD/SKD kits. Thus, to the extent that the MOUs themselves prevented signatories from importing SKD/CKD kits if they did not meet the indigenization targets, the indigenization requirement was as such inconsistent with Article XI:1 of the GATT 1994 and with Article 2.1 of the TRIMs Agreement.

(ii)   The Trade Balancing Requirement

4.118 The trade balancing requirement was likewise a continuing restriction on imports of SKD/CKD kits and components. Starting in the fourth year the MOU imposed a quantitative limitation on imports - and the quantity was correlated to the degree of compliance with the trade balancing requirement. The Government of India had also confirmed that denial of an import license was effectively mandatory if the trade balancing obligation was not met. Paragraph 3(iv) of Public Notice No. 60 provides that "From 4th year [i.e. of the MOU] onwards the value

---

[205] India's responses to Questions by the United States, 13 July 2000, response to Question 5, (underlining in original, other emphasis added).

1908   DSR 2002:V

of import of CKD/SKD may be regulated with reference to the extent of export obligation fulfilled in the previous years as per the MOU." Paragraph III, clause (vi) of the MOU contained an identical provision. India had confirmed, that the MOUs were binding and enforceable.[206] In addition, the first sentence of Paragraph III, clause (vi) provided that "the party [i.e. the MOU signatory] shall achieve a broad trade balancing of foreign exchange *over the entire period of the MOU* in terms of balancing between the actual CIF value of imports of CKD/SKD kits/components and the FOB value of exports of cars and auto components over the said period." The first sentence of paragraph 3(iv) of Public Notice No. 60 was an essentially identical provision. These provisions clearly stated that the trade balancing obligation extended over the entire period of the MOU. As India had confirmed, however, the MOUs and their requirements continued to remain in force even beyond the elimination of import licensing for SKD/CKD kits and components. Furthermore, the trade balancing requirement restricted imports because it placed a maximum limit on the value of an MOU signatory's imports that was equal to the value of the signatory's exports (which, pursuant to paragraph III, clause (vi), the MOU signatory is required to specify). In practical terms, there were limits to the amount of exports which a car manufacturer might be able or willing to make (whether related to its manufacturing capacity or to the demand for its products outside India). Thus, by limiting the amount of a manufacturer's imports to that of its exports, the trade balancing requirement restricted the amount of imports. India asserted means of restricting importations by MOU signatories other than just license denials. A manufacturer's failure to comply with an MOU obligation could lead to loss of import privileges or to confiscation of the goods concerned pursuant to various provisions of the FTDR Act and the rules made thereunder. It appeared that after 1 April 2001, these additional provisions would be the instruments through which India carried out Public Notice No. 60 and the MOUs (and thus prevented SKD/CKD kits/components from being brought into India to compete with domestic parts and components). For all of these reasons, the trade balancing requirement in Public Notice No. 60 and the MOUs imposed import restrictions as such, and was therefore inconsistent with Article XI:1 of the GATT 1994 and with Article 2.1 of the TRIMs Agreement.

4.119 The **European Communities** also argued that the "trade balancing" requirements, stipulated in the MOUs, were inconsistent with GATT Article XI:1 in that they restricted imports of passenger cars, and of components therefor, by the signatories of the MOUs. The European Communities recalled, nevertheless, that the 1997 Agreement between India and the European Communities (as supplemented by the 1999 Agreement between India and the United States) allowed India to maintain import restrictions on passenger cars, and on chassis and bodies therefor (but not on imports of parts and components therefor) until 1 April

---

[206] See also India's *Replies to Questions Posed by Japan*, G/TRIMS/W/15, circulated 30 October 1998, response to Question 24; Exhibit US-5: "CKD/SKD kits imports would be allowed with reference to the extent of export obligation fulfilled in the previous year. ... There is hardly any discretion involved in determining the extent of import of CKD/SKD kits except by way of considering any genuine problems the company may have faced in achieving the export levels."

Report of the Panel

2001. Therefore, the European Communities made this claim only in so far as: the MOUs required the "trade balancing" of imports of "components" other than chassis and bodies; and the MOUs would remain binding and enforceable after 1 April 2001, both with respect to passenger cars and components therefor. Article XI:1 read as follows in pertinent part:

> "No prohibitions or restrictions other than duties, taxes or other charges, whether made effective through quotas, import or export licenses or other measures, shall be instituted or maintained by any [Member] on the importation of any product of the territory of any other [Member] or on the exportation or sale for export of any product of the territory of any other [Member]"

As noted by the Panel Report in *Japan – Trade in Semi-conductors* (hereinafter "*Japan – Semi-conductors*"), the wording of Article XI:1 was "comprehensive": it applied to "all measures instituted or maintained by a [Member] prohibiting or restricting the importation [...] other than measures that take the form of duties, taxes or charges"[207]. The test for compliance with Article XI:1 was thus three-fold: first, was the action concerned a Government "measure" second, was the measure different from a "duty, tax or other charge"? and third, did the measure "restrict" imports? In the present case, the answer to the above three questions was clearly in the affirmative. The "trade balancing" requirements were "measures". The term "measure" had been given a broad definition, indeed even broader than that of "requirements" in Article III:4.[208] In *Japan – Semi-conductors* the Panel found that non-mandatory Government action in the form of "administrative guidance" was a "measure" subject to Article XI:1 because it created sufficient incentives or disincentives for private parties to act.[209] In *Japan –Film* the Panel went even further by holding that, in certain circumstances, even purely hortatory wording in a statement of policy could qualify as a "measure".[210] As shown above, Public Notice No. 60 and the MOUs were "requirements" in the sense of Article III:4. For the same reasons, and *a fortiori*, they were also "measures" in the sense of Article XI:1. The "trade balancing" requirements were not "duties, taxes or other charges" The "trade balancing" requirements did not involve any payment or transfer of money by or on the account of the signatories of MOUs and, therefore, could not be characterized as "duties, taxes or other charges". The "trade balancing" requirements "restricted" imports. The "trade balancing" requirements "restricted" imports because they placed a maximum limit on the value of the imports which the signatories were

---

[207] *Japan – Semi-conductors*, adopted on 4 May 1988, BISD 35S/116, para. 104.

[208] See the Panel Report on *Japan – Photographic Film and Paper*, (hereinafter "*Japan – Film*") WT/DS44/R, adopted on 29 April 1998, para. 10.51 (DSR 1998:IV, 1179), where the Panel stated that

> "Given that the scope of the term requirement would seem to be narrower than that of measure, the broad reading given to the word requirement by the *(Canada – FIRA) (EEC – Parts and Components)* panel supports an even broader reading of the word measure in Article XXIII: 1 b)."

[209] Panel Report on *Japan – Semi-conductors*, BISD 35S/116, at pp. 154-155. See also the Panel Report on *Japan – Restrictions on Imports of Certain Agricultural Products*, (hereinafter "*Japan – Agricultural Products I*") adopted on 22 March 1988, BISD 35S/163, 242.

[210] Panel Report on *Japan –Film*, WT/DS44/R, para. 10.49 (DSR 1998:IV, 1179).

1910   DSR 2002:V

authorized to make equal to the value of their exports. In practice, there were limits to the amount of exports which a signatory might be able or willing to make (related both to its manufacturing capacity in India and to the demand for its products in foreign markets). Thus, by limiting the amount of a signatory's imports to that of its exports, the trade balancing requirements "restricted" the amount of imports.[211]

4.120 **India** asserted that, with respect to manufacturing and equity requirements, the law of the WTO did not regulate foreign direct investments as such[212] and therefore did not prevent India from imposing on foreign investors the obligation to manufacture (rather than merely assemble) automobiles and to make an equity investment of a specified amount. Article XI:1 of the GATT and Article 2 of the TRIMs Agreement merely prohibited the imposition of such requirements as a condition for the grant of an import license.[213] However, after 1 April 2001, the requirement to manufacture (rather than merely assemble) automobiles, and to secure an equity investment of a specified amount, would have to be performed completely independently of any right to import. It would apply equally to all signatories of MOUs, whether they imported SKD/CKD kits or not. With respect to export requirements, the GATT panel which examined Canada's Foreign Investment Review Act in 1984 correctly found that "there is no provision in the General Agreement which forbids requirements to sell goods in foreign markets in preference to the domestic market.[214] There was also no such requirement in the TRIMs Agreement. Article XI of the GATT and Article 2 of the TRIMs Agreement merely prohibited export requirements that were imposed as a condition for the grant of an import license and export requirements that vary with the level of local purchases.[215] Nowhere in WTO law were export requirements prohibited as such. As from 1 April 2001, the signatories of the MOUs would continue to be required to discharge the export obligations corresponding to the imports made by them *before* that date. They would thus be required to discharge the export obligations they have already assumed *but will no longer incur any new export obligations as a result of the further importation of SKD/CKD kits*. From 1 April 2001, the right to import SKD/CKD kits would consequently no longer in any way depend on, or vary with, the level of exports achieved. For this reason, the export requirements would no longer create any incentive to purchase local products. As a result, the export requirements would have to be performed completely independently of any imports or local purchases and would consequently be entirely consistent with both the GATT and the TRIMs Agreement.

---

[211] See also US response to Question 82 of the Panel.

[212] See the finding of the GATT Panel on *Canada – FIRA*, which noted that "the General Agreement does not prevent Canada from exercising its sovereign right to regulate foreign direct investments" (BISD 30S/157).

[213] See paragraph 2(a) of the Annex to the TRIMS Agreement.

[214] *Canada – FIRA* (BISD 30S/140).

[215] See paragraph 2(a) of the Annex to the TRIMS Agreement. Article 3.1 (a) of the Agreement on Subsidies and Countervailing Duties prohibits export requirements that are tied to subsidies. However, this prohibition does not apply to India (see Article 27.2 (a) and Annex VII of the Agreement on Subsidies and Countervailing Duties).

Report of the Panel

4.121 **India** argued that, in the absence of import licensing, Public Notice No. 60 and the trade balancing provisions of the MOUs were consistent with Article XI:1. As from 1 April 2001, India would - consistently with its undertakings towards the European Communities and the United States - no longer make the importation of SKD/CKD kits subject to the signing of an MOU. The right to import SKD/CKD kits would therefore no longer be subject to any conditions that could be deemed to constitute a restriction on the importation of a product within the meaning of Article XI of the GATT. The import liberalization would thus benefit all car manufacturers, including those who had signed an MOU. Subsequently, India informed the Panel that, since 1 April 2001, the import restrictions for SKD/CKD kits and car components had been abolished and no licenses referring to the trade balancing requirement had been issued. Since then, the signatories of the MOUs had therefore no longer incurred any new export obligations as a result of the importation of SKD/CKD kits or components.

4.122 According to India, the European Communities and the United States claimed that the provisions of Public Notice No. 60, as such, restricted imports and favoured the purchase or use of domestic products over imported products and were therefore inconsistent with Article III:4 and XI:1 of the GATT. However, Public Notice No. 60 merely set out how the import restrictions on cars imposed until 1 April 2001 under the Export-Import Policy were to be administered. This was clear from paragraph 2 of this Notice which read in relevant part:

> ... import of components for motor vehicles in CKD/SKD form, which is restricted for import under the current Export-Import Policy, shall be allowed for importation against a license and such a license will be issued . . .on the basis of an MOU.

4.123 After 1 April 2001, Public Notice No. 60 was no longer applicable because the import restrictions it was to administer no longer existed. In the absence of an import restriction on cars, this Notice could not be implemented and served no purpose. It was therefore not clear to India how the European Communities and the United States could claim that the Public Notice *as such* was capable of violating WTO law. India had requested both the European Communities and the United States to indicate which provision of the Public Notice No. 60 restricted imports or favoured domestic products in the absence of any licensing requirement for CKD/SKD kits and hence any requirement to sign an MOU. Neither the European Communities nor the United States had given a precise answer to this question. India requested the Panel to find that, in the absence of any requirement to obtain an import license for SKD/CKD kits and components, Public Notice No. 60 did not restrict imports inconsistently with Article XI:1 of the GATT.[216] The United States claimed that Public Notice No. 60 "still remains in effect" because no public notice rescinding it has been issued.[217] India submitted a copy of Notification No. 2 (RE-2001)/1997-2002 dated 31 March 2001 issued by the Ministry of Commerce, which showed that India had removed the restrictions on imports of cars in the form of CKD/SKD

---

[216] See also India's response to Question 103 of the Panel.
[217] US response to Questions 2(b) of the Panel.

1912   DSR 2002:V

India – Autos

kits and automobile components that were covered by Public Notice No. 60. In the absence of these restrictions, Public Notice No. 60 no longer applied. A new public notice rescinding Public Notice No. 60 was consequently not required to ensure the consistency of Public Notice No. 60 with Articles III:4 and XI:1 of the GATT.

4.124 The **United States** identified that India denied that Article XI:1 applied to these requirements, but India had misinterpreted that provision. India also denied that Public Notice No. 60 and the MOUs themselves imposed restrictions on imports; however, not only could that assertion not be reconciled with the actual language of the measures, but it did not appear even to be consistent with India's own statements. The United States had explained that the *trade balancing* requirement restricted imports because it limited the value of an MOU signatory's imports to the value of the signatory's exports (which, pursuant to paragraph III, clause (vi), the MOU signatory was required to specify at the time of signing). There were obviously limitations on the amount of exports which a car manufacturer might be able or willing to make. Thus, by limiting the amount of a manufacturer's imports to that of its exports, the trade balancing requirement itself restricted imports. India appeared not to accept that such a requirement was inconsistent with Article XI:1 of the GATT: India asserted that "Article XI of the GATT and Article 2 of the TRIMs Agreement merely prohibit export requirements that are imposed as a condition for the grant of an import license and export requirements that vary with the level of local purchases". This assertion was simply incorrect, as paragraph 2 of the TRIMs Agreement Illustrative List showed:

> TRIMs that are inconsistent with the obligation of general elimination of quantitative restrictions provided for in paragraph 1 of Article XI of GATT 1994 include those which are ... enforceable under domestic law ... or compliance with which is necessary to obtain an advantage, and which restrict the importation by an enterprise of products used in ... its local production ... to an amount related to the ... value of local production that it exports ... .

It was clear that the MOUs restricted importation to an amount related to the value of locally produced goods that a manufacturer exports, and it was clear that the MOU 's were "enforceable"; India had confirmed both points.[218] The trade balancing requirement thus fell within the scope of this paragraph, and consequently it was "inconsistent with the obligation of general elimination of quantitative restrictions provided for in paragraph 1 of Article XI of GATT 1994". The Panel should explicitly reject India's assertion and should make an explicit finding that the trade balancing requirement was inconsistent with India's obligations under Article XI:1 of the GATT.

---

[218] *Replies by India to Questions Posed by Japan*, G/TRIMS/W/15, circulated 30 October 1998, response to Question 24; Exhibit US-5: "CKD/SKD kits imports would be allowed with reference to the extent of export obligation fulfilled in the previous year." As discussed above, the MOUs were also "necessary to obtain an advantage".

DSR 2002:V

Report of the Panel

4.125 **India** contended that the MOU provisions on trade balancing did not apply in the absence of any requirement to obtain an import license. The United States claimed that the trade balancing provisions set out in the MOUs restricted imports inconsistently with Article XI:1 of the GATT for the following reasons:

> The trade balancing requirement restricts imports because it places a maximum limit on the value of an MOU signatory's imports that is equal to the value of the signatory's exports (which, pursuant to paragraph III, clause (vi), the MOU signatory is required to specify). In practical terms, there are limits to the amount of exports which a car manufacturer may be able or willing to make (whether related to its manufacturing capacity or to the demand for its products outside India). Thus, by limiting the amount of a manufacturer's imports to that of its exports, the trade balancing requirement restricts the amount of imports.[219]

The European Communities' and the United States' assertions were based on the incorrect assumption that the trade balancing requirement applied to all imports, irrespective of whether an import license was required or not. In fact, however, the trade balancing provisions did not apply, and had in practice never been applied, in respect of imports for which no license was required. (see IV A). Paragraph III (iv) of the MOUs declared that the MOU signatory shall discharge the export obligation corresponding to the imports made before the import licensing requirement ceased to apply. The signatories of the MOUs were therefore bound to discharge the export obligations they had already assumed before the abolition of the import restrictions on SKD/CKD kits on 1 April 2001. However, this residual export obligation would have to be performed completely independently of the level of imports or local purchases. Nowhere in WTO law were export requirements as such prohibited. The requirement to discharge the accrued export obligations would consequently be entirely consistent with both the GATT and the TRIMs Agreement. India noted that, so far, neither the European Communities nor the United States had presented any arguments challenging this position.

4.126 The issue was whether the trade balancing provisions in the MOUs gave rise to export obligations in respect of imports for which no import license was required. Contrary to the assertions of the United States, this issue was totally unrelated to the question of the duration of the MOU, the point in time at which the MOU signatory reached the 70 percent indigenization target and the enforceability of the MOUs. It was, of course, correct when the United States claimed that the MOU provisions "impose a trade balancing obligation on imports made over the full duration of the MOU" and require the trade balancing of the foreign exchange obligation incurred on imports made up to the date on which it achieves the 70 per cent indigenization target and that the MOUs are enforceable. However, it did not follow from these facts that the trade balancing requirement in the MOUs applied to imports for which no license was needed and that this requirement therefore continued to apply even after the import licensing

---

[219] US response to Question 11 of the Panel.

1914 DSR 2002:V

regime was eliminated. The evidence presented by India demonstrated that, in respect of freely importable products, the MOU signatories had never assumed, and still did not assume, any export obligations that might limit their right to import or create an incentive for them to purchase domestic components. The provisions of the MOU regulating the point in time at which the signatory moved out of the ambit of the MOU and the enforceability of the MOUs did not change this fact. The conclusion that "the signatories are required to balance **all the imports** made by them until they achieve a 70% indigenization level" simply does not follow from the fact that the indigenization requirement ceased when the 70 per cent target had been reached. The fact that the trade balancing requirement must be performed only until a 70 per cent indigenization did not change the fact the trade balancing requirement only arose **in respect of imports for which a license was required.** It followed that, in the absence of a discretionary licensing system, the right to import SKD/CKD kits and components by MOU signatories did not depend on, or vary with, the level of exports or of purchases of domestic products. It was therefore plainly incorrect to claim that the trade balancing requirements in the MOUs as such restricted imports[220] and favoured the purchase or use of domestic products over imported products. In respect of freely importable products, the MOU signatory did not assume any export obligations that might limit its right to import or create an incentive to purchase domestic components.

4.127 The **United States** understood that India had confirmed that the MOUs were measures independent of Public Notice No. 60. India also asserted, however, that any import restrictions imposed by the MOUs were eliminated when India eliminated its import licensing regime. The Panel should reject this additional argument as well. The first difficulty with India's argument came from the first sentence of Paragraph III, clause (vi) of the MOU. That sentence provided that "the party [i.e. the MOU signatory] shall achieve a broad trade balancing of foreign exchange *over the entire period of the MOU* in terms of balancing between the actual CIF value of imports of CKD/SKD kits/components and the FOB value of exports of cars and auto components over the said period." This

---

[220] There was a further, systemic reason why the Panel should reject the claim that the MOUs violate Article XI:1. The GATT made a clear distinction between measures discriminating against imports that were applied at the point and time of importation, which were covered by Articles II and XI, and those that were applied to imported products, which were covered by Article III. Article XI:1 applied to "restrictions . . . on the importation of any product". The dictionary meaning of "importation" was "the act of importing". The scope of application of Article XI:1 was therefore limited to acts affecting the process of entering products into the custom territory. By contrast, Article III:4 of the GATT applied to requirements applied to products that had already been imported into the customs territory. The exceptions applicable to Article XI:1 were wider than those applicable to Article III:4 (see for instance Article XI:2 of the GATT and Article 5 of the Agreement on Safeguards). A failure to maintain the distinction between measures applied at the border and internal measures would therefore broaden the scope of the exceptions to Article XI:1 in a manner not contemplated by the drafters of the GATT. Obviously, the provisions of the MOUs on trade balancing did not affect the process of entering products into India's customs territory and could also for this reason not constitute restrictions on importation within the meaning of Article XI:1. India invited the European Communities and the United States to reconsider their argument that the MOUs as such violated Article XI:1 in the light of its broader systemic implications.

Report of the Panel

provision imposed a trade balancing obligation on imports made over the full duration of the MOU; the trade balancing requirement in the MOU was thus independent of the elimination of the import licensing regime.[221] India had effectively confirmed this point in its answer to the Panel's questions. India said that "under paragraph 3(iv) of Public Notice 60 and paragraph III(iv) of the MOUs, the MOU signatory goes 'outside the ambit of the MOU' and will not require any import licenses once it achieves a 70% indigenization level. However, the MOU signatory will be required to achieve trade balancing of the foreign exchange obligation incurred *on imports made up to that date*".[222] Consequently, under the terms of the MOU, the export balancing requirement continued to attach to all imports made until the 70% indigenization level was reached – whenever that date arrived.[223] While India said elsewhere that no further export obligations would accrue with respect to imports made after 1 April 2001, that statement seemed impossible to reconcile with India's own description of the meaning of the MOUs.

4.128 The second difficulty with India's assertion that the MOUs imposed no separate import restriction arose from India's acknowledgment that they remained enforceable under Section 11 of the FT(DR) Act.[224] India said first that "failure to meet an export obligation after 1 April 2001 would not be an import or export prohibited by Section 11(1) of the FT(DR) Act." India added, however, that "the companies may also be liable to monetary penalties under Section 11 of the FTDR Act" and that after 1 April 2001, "MOU signatories would be treated as licensees in respect of the licences that they have utilized up to 31 March 2001."[225] Section 11 of the FT(DR) Act contained only one provision imposing monetary penalties: Section 11(2), which provided that

> ... where any person makes or abets or attempts to make any export or import in contravention of any provision of this Act or any rules or orders made thereunder or the export and import policy, he shall be liable to a penalty not exceeding one thousand rupees or five times the value of the good in respect of which any contravention is made or attempted to be made, whichever is more.

It appeared, therefore, that the imposition of monetary penalties under Section 11 – as contemplated by India for companies that fail to abide by the provisions of the MOU – depended on the making of some export or import in contravention of Indian law. India had also said, however, that failure to meet an export obligation was not an export or import prohibited by Section 11(1). It was not at all clear how these two statements could be harmonized. One possible reconciliation

---

[221] In fact, the trade balancing requirement imposed restrictions above and beyond those imposed by India's import licensing regime even when that regime was in force, because the requirement limited the amount of licenses that an MOU signatory could use.

[222] India's response to Question 50 of the Panel (emphasis added).

[223] Furthermore, according to India, at least some manufacturers have not yet reached that level; India's response to Question 33 of the Panel.

[224] Question 52(d) of the Panel.

[225] In the same Response India also confirmed once again that after 1 April 2001, "MOUs potentially can be enforced as contracts through the domestic courts".

of the provisions of Section 11 and India's statements was that while failing to export the mandated amount would not be a prohibited export or import (which was logical, since a *failure* to export hardly seemed like a *prohibited* export, let alone an import of any kind), a car manufacturer's *imports* in future years in excess of the amount of export obligation discharged would be a prohibited import to which a monetary penalty under Section 11(2) applied. For this reason as well, the export balancing requirement thus continued to impose an import restriction even after 1 April, 2001, and was inconsistent with GATT Article XI:1.

4.129 The **European Communities** noted that India contended that, in the absence of the import licenses on passenger cars, the MOUs could not restrict imports inconsistently with Article XI:1. Specifically, India argued that

> ... the MOUs as such do not in any way limit the right to import SKD/CKD kits or any other product. The non-observation of the terms of the MOUs also no longer leads to the automatic denial of an import license. Article XI of the GATT deals with 'restrictions . . . on . . . importation', that is with measures applied at the border in connection with the entry of products into the customs territory. The MOUs as such do not maintain or institute any such measure and can therefore not possibly violate Article XI.[226]

That interpretation of Article XI was unduly narrow and found no support in the wording of that provision or in the GATT/WTO jurisprudence. As noted by the panel in *Japan – Semi–Conductors*[227], the wording of Article XI:1 was "comprehensive". It applied to "all measures instituted or maintained by a [Member] prohibiting or restricting the importation, exportation or sale for export other than measures that take the form of duties, taxes or charges"[228]. Import restrictions were most commonly enforced at the border, since that was the easiest and most effective way of restricting imports. However, the scope of Article XI:1 was by no means limited to such restrictions. An agreement between the Government and the main importers of a product whereby the latter agreed to limit the value of their imports gave rise to an obvious restriction on the importation of that product. That restriction was clearly within the scope of Article XI:1, regardless of whether the agreement was enforced by means of measures taken at the border which prevented the actual entry of the goods or through other, less direct means, such as imposing fines on the signatories who import in excess of the agreed quantity or suing them for breach of contract. India's narrow interpretation of the scope of Article XI:1 was refuted by *Japan – Semi–Conductors*. In that case, the Panel concluded that:

> The requests not to export semi-conductors ... addressed to Japanese producers and exporters of semi-conductors, combined with the statutory requirement for the exporters to submit information on export prices and the systematic monitoring of company and product-specific costs and export prices by the Government,

---

[226] India's response to Question 33 of the Panel, at p. 3, para. 1 [footnotes omitted].

[227] Panel Report on *Japan – Semi-conductors*, adopted on 4 May 1988, BISD 35S/116.

[228] *Ibid.* at para. 104.

Report of the Panel

> backed up with the use of supply and demand forecasts to impress on manufacturers the need to align their production to appropriate levels, constituted a coherent system of restricting the sale for export of monitored semi-conductors ... inconsistent with Article XI:1.[229]

None of the above measures were applied by Japan "at the border ". Moreover, unlike the MOUs, the measures condemned in *Japan – Semi-conductors* were not even legally binding and enforceable. At any rate, India's argument that the MOUs as such could not be inconsistent with Article XI:1 because they were not border measures would not dispose of the EC's claims to the effect that both the balancing requirement and the indigenization requirements were inconsistent with Article III:4 of the GATT. More specifically, and contrary to India's assertions , import balancing requirements were not inconsistent with Article XI:1 only if they were enforced through the denial of import licenses. By its own terms, Article XI:1 prohibited import restrictions, whether made effective through import licenses or through any "other measures". As illustrated by *Canada – FIRA*, the obligations contained in legally binding contracts between the Government and individual firms could constitute a "requirement" prohibited by Article III:4.[230] Likewise, a binding contract between the Government and a firm whereby the latter agreed to limit its imports fell clearly within the scope of Article XI:1. (Indeed, the European Communities recalled that for a Government action to be contrary to Article XI:1, it did not even have to be legally enforceable[231]).

4.130 **India** argued that since Article XI of the GATT dealt with 'restrictions ... on ... importation', that is with measures applied at the border in connection with the entry of products into the customs territory, the MOUs as such did not maintain or institute any such measure and could therefore not possibly violate Article XI.[232] The European Communities had also failed to explain how the MOUs as such restricted imports. A failure to sign or observe the terms of an MOU could lead to a denial of an import license for SKD/CKD kits only as long as an import license for such kits was required. However, the MOUs as such did not in any way limit the right to import SKD/CKD kits or any other product. The non-observation of the terms of the MOUs also no longer led to the automatic denial of an import license.[233] Article XI of the GATT dealt with "restrictions ...on ... importation", that is with measures applied at the border in connection with the entry of products into the customs territory. The MOUs as such did not maintain

---

[229] Panel Report on *Japan – Semi-conductors*, adopted on 4 May 1988, BISD 35S/116, at para. 132.

[230] Panel Report on *Canada – FIRA*, adopted on 7 February 1984, BISD 30S/140, at para. 5.4.

[231] See the Panel Report on *Japan –Semi-conductors*, BISD 35S/116, pp. 154-155; and the Panel Report on *Japan – Agricultural Products I*, BISD 35S/163. The same is true with respect to Article III:4. See the Panel Report on *Canada – Autos*, WT/DS139/R, WT/DS142/R, adopted on 19 June 2000, as modified by the Appellate Body Report, at para. 10.122 (DSR 2000:VII, 3043) and the Panel Report on *Japan – Film*, WT/DS44/R, adopted on 22 April 1998, para. 10.49 (DSR 1998:IV, 1179).

[232] India's response to Question 33, p. 3.

[233] See the response to Question 52(b).

or institute any such measure and could therefore not possibly violate Article XI. India considered that the EC's argument that India's:

> ... interpretation of Article XI is unduly narrow and finds no support in the wording of that provision or in the GATT/WTO jurisprudence. As noted by the panel in *Japan – Semi-Conductors*[234], the wording of Article XI:1 is "comprehensive". It applies to "all measures instituted or maintained by a [Member] prohibiting or restricting the importation, exportation or sale for export other than measures that take the form of duties, taxes or charges"[235].
>
> Import restrictions are most commonly enforced at the border, since that is the easiest and most effective way of restricting imports. However, the scope of Article XI:1 is by no means limited to such restrictions.

was based on a misunderstanding of GATT law. The GATT made a clear distinction between measures that were applied in connection with or at the point or time of importation ("border measures"), which were covered mainly by Articles II and XI, and those that were applied internally to imported products, which were covered mainly by Article III. Article XI:1 applied to "restrictions ... on the importation of any product". The dictionary meaning of "importation" was "the act of importing". The scope of application of Article XI:1 was therefore limited to acts affecting the process of entering products into the custom territory. By contrast, Article III:4 of the GATT applied to requirements that were applied internally. Obviously, the provisions of the MOUs on trade balancing were not applied in connection with or at the point or time of importation and could for that reason alone not constitute restrictions on importation within the meaning of Article XI:1. The European Communities overlooked that, as far as measures affecting **exports** were concerned, the GATT did **not** distinguish between internal measures and border measures. Article XI:1 prohibited both restrictions "on the exportation **or the sale for export**". As to measures affecting exports, the drafters of the GATT had to extend the scope of Article XI to internal measures because the national treatment provisions of Article III did not cover measures favouring sales in the domestic market over sales for export. The panel report on *Japan - Semi-conductors* dealt with measures affecting **exports.** That panel did not have to distinguish between internal measures and border measures affecting exports because both were treated equally under Article XI. In fact, it made no ruling on this point at all. It merely found that the GATT jurisprudence on minimum import prices could be extended to minimum export prices. Its remark on the comprehensive nature of Article XI:1 provided the reason for this finding.[236] The panel report on *Japan - Semi-conductors* therefore did not lend any support to the EC's position. India considered that the European Communities might wish to reconsider the broader implications of its argumentation. The exceptions applicable to Article XI:1 were wider than those applicable to Article III:4 (see

---

[234] Panel Report on *Japan – Semi-conductors*, adopted on 4 May 1988, BISD 35S/116.
[235] *Ibid.*, para. 104.
[236] BISD 35S/153, paras 104-105.

Report of the Panel

for instance, Articles XI:2, XII and XVIII:B of the GATT and Article 5 of the Agreement on Safeguards). A failure to maintain the distinction between measures applied at the border and internal measures would therefore broaden the scope of the exceptions to Article XI:1 in a manner not contemplated by the drafters of the GATT.

4.131 The **United States** replied that India still appeared to deny that Article XI:1 applied to the export balancing requirement. India advanced a very limited interpretation of Article XI:1; India said that "Article XI of the GATT and Article 2 of the TRIMs Agreement merely prohibited export requirements that were imposed as a condition for the grant of an import license and export requirements that vary with the level of local purchases. Now, India said that the scope of application of XI:1 was limited to measures "affecting the process of entering products into the customs territory". Neither of these formulations was correct. It was the text of the WTO Agreement that defined the scope of Article XI:1. And, the TRIMs Agreement Illustrative List made clear that any requirement which restricted importation to an amount related to the value of locally produced goods that a manufacturer exports – such as the one in paragraph III, clause (vi) of the MOUs – was inconsistent with GATT Article XI:1. The United States considered that the Panel should reject India's proposed reformulations of Article XI:1 and should find that the trade balancing requirement was inconsistent with India's obligations under that Article.

> (a) Are the Measures Justified by Article XVIII:B of the GATT and Articles 3 and 4 of the TRIMs Agreement?

4.132 **India** argued that it maintained the restrictive import licensing regime under which the Notice and the MOU scheme operated for balance-of-payments reasons. This licensing regime, although inconsistent with the general prohibition of quantitative restrictions set out in Article XI of the GATT, was justified under Article XVIII:B of the GATT, according to which the developing country Members of the WTO could impose import restrictions to safeguard their external financial position and to ensure a level of reserves adequate for the implementation of their programme of economic development. As stipulated in Article XVIII:B, India had notified its restrictions to the WTO.[237] India had not yet disinvoked Article XVIII:B of the GATT. India noted that Article 3 of the Agreement on Trade-Related Investment Measures ("TRIMs Agreement") provided that all exceptions under the GATT should apply to the provisions of the TRIMs Agreement. Furthermore, under Article 4 of the TRIMs Agreement, in the case of developing country Members such as India, Article XVIII:B of the GATT constituted not only an exception from Article XI of the GATT but also from the obligations set out in Article 2 of the TRIMs Agreement.

4.133 India stated that the restrictions on the importation of SKD/CKD kits were imposed in order to safeguard India's external financial position.[238] When it

---

[237] WT/BOP/N/24.
[238] Question 63 of the Panel.

1920   DSR 2002:V

notified the BOPs Committee on 27 May 1997 that it was maintaining a system of non-automatic licensing for import of cars in the form of CKD/SKD kits, it had been entering into MOUs with manufacturers that wished to import CKD/SKD kits since 1995. Any differences between the discretionary licensing scheme for import of cars in the form of CKD/SKD kits applied under the MOUs entered into since 1995 and that applied after 1997 were not legally significant from the standpoint of Article XI of the GATT or of the claim that they were justified under Article XVIII:B.[239]

4.134 Prior to the establishment of the Panel, India had stated that "the main purpose of the MOU Policy is the management of balance-of-payments even while following an open door policy toward foreign investment which should not lead to a net outflow of foreign exchange" [240] The **United States** said it was not certain what India meant by that statement. For example, it was not clear how opening the door towards foreign investment might be related to a net outflow of foreign exchange. To the extent that India was concerned about capital outflows, the United States recalled that India had notified the WTO of a separate dividend balancing requirement, which required foreign-owned investments in several industries (including portions of the motor vehicle sector) to earn through exports the foreign exchange necessary to repatriate earnings to their foreign parents. India's assertion was also inconsistent with statements made when Public Notice No. 60 was adopted; at that time, Indian officials described a different purpose for the MOUs: "The objective of the new policy was to encourage local production of auto-components and thus, bring in modern technology and develop this key segment, explain ministry officials."[241]

4.135 The **European Communities** added that this statement had been made by India more than three months after the European Communities requested consultations with respect to the MOUs. The obvious purpose of the MOU policy was to promote the establishment and consolidation of a local automotive industry in India.

4.136 For the **United States**, India did not have a defense under Article XVIII:B for the measures at issue in this dispute. First, India had not complied with the procedural prerequisites for justifying these measures under the balance-of-payments provisions of the GATT Second, on 12 December 1997, when Public Notice No. 60 was adopted, India no longer had a balance-of-payments problem justifying the use of the balance-of-payments provisions of the GATT. The International Monetary Fund (IMF) had reached that conclusion several months earlier, in January of 1997[242], and the *India - Quantitative Restrictions* panel reached the conclusion that India had no valid balance-of-payments justification as of November 18, 1997 - less than a month before Public Notice No. 60

---

[239] Question 64 of the Panel.
[240] Questions from Japan, Committee on TRIMs.
[241] "Car Makers Have to Sign New MOUs in Accordance with New Automobile Policy", *Business Standard*, 11 December 1997.
[242] Panel Report on *India – Quantitative Restrictions*, WT/DS90/R, adopted on 22 September 1999, para. 3.225 (DSR 1999:V, 1799).

Report of the Panel

was issued.[243] Third, India had in any case not met its burden of proof with respect to this issue.

4.137 In elaborating on the first of these three points, the United States considered that nowhere did India actually say that the indigenization and trade balancing requirements were justified by the balance-of-payments provisions. Instead, India had simply said that if the Panel attempted to examine the US complaint, the Panel would be obliged to embark on the complicated task of re-examining India's balance-of-payments situation. The Panel should not let itself be distracted by India's suggestion, because the balance-of-payments provisions of the WTO Agreements provided no defence to the violations at issue in this case. In the first place, India was prohibited from raising those provisions as a defence to the complaint because it had never notified the measures at issue to the BOPs Committee and had never asserted a balance-of-payments justification for them. Article XVIII:12(a) of the GATT 1994 and paragraph 6 of the Uruguay Round Understanding on the Balance-of-Payments Provisions of the GATT 1994 made clear that such notification was required. However, India had never brought the indigenization or trade balancing requirements before the Committee. India could not both say that it would have been impractical for the indigenization and trade balancing requirements to be notified to and examined by the BOPs Committee, and yet also say that the *India – Quantitative Restrictions* panel ruled on these details without either knowing about them or examining them.[244]

4.138 In the second place, even if these measures had been taken for balance-of-payments reasons (and India's failure to notify them reinforced the fact that they were not), these measures dated from late 1997. Pursuant to paragraphs 2 and 3 of the Understanding, even if India had wanted to take new measures for balance-of-payments purposes, India would have been required to give preference to price-based measures. Public Notice No. 60, however, imposed quantitative restrictions and local content requirements, not tariff surcharges. Third, the balance-of-payments provisions in any case could not justify a violation of the national treatment obligations of the GATT. Article XVIII: 9 made clear that the balance-of-payments provisions could be used to "control the general level of imports" - not to deny national treatment to foreign goods. Once a foreign good had been imported, the foreign exchange for that import had been expended; there was no balance-of-payments justification for permitting discrimination against that imported good. For all of these reasons, the Panel should reject India's balance-of-payments arguments.

4.139 **India** responded to the US argument that first, the measures at issue were not new to the extent that they represented only the conditions that India applied in the context of non-automatic licensing of imports of cars in the form of CKD/SKD kits. Second, the conditions in Public Notice No. 60 and the MOUs based on it were basically the same as those contained in 1995 MOUs. Third, they did not involve either a raising of the general level of restrictions or a substantial intensification of the restrictions applied by India to imports of cars in

---

[243] *Ibid.*, paras. 5.160-5.161 and 5.236.
[244] US response to Question 74 of the Panel.

1922 DSR 2002:V

the form of CKD/SKD kits; if anything, they represented a relaxation of the restrictions. Fourth, Members did not have to notify the details of the licensing regime they applied to each of the restrictions notified under Article XVIII: B to benefit from the legal cover provided by this provision. In practice, the notifications under GATT's balance-of-payments provisions did not contain such details and Members were not expected to consult on them in the BOPs Committee. It would in any case have been totally impracticable for India to notify these details for 2,700 items and for the BOPs Committee to examine them. Finally, as from 1 April 2001, India no longer applied any balance-of-payments measures and therefore no longer invoked the balance-of-payments provisions of the GATT. The points made by the United States, expressed before 1 April 2001, were therefore no longer relevant.[245] The Panel asked us to confirm whether India was relying on Article XVIII:B of the GATT as a defence. The answer was that if the United States and the European Communities insisted on re-opening the issue of the WTO-consistency of measures which the earlier panel has already ruled upon, India also reserved its right to take up the defence that the measures were justified under Article XVIII:B of the GATT 1994. The United States argued that India could not invoke Article XVIII:B because India did not notify Public Notice No. 60 under Article XVIII:B of the GATT. However, *Public Notice No. 60, as such, did not establish an import restriction for SKD/CKD kits that would have required notification under Article XVIII:B*. The relevant import restriction was imposed under the Export-Import Policy. *Public Notice No. 60 merely set out how this import restriction was to be administered*. This was clear from paragraph 2 of this Notice which read in relevant part: " ...import of components for motor vehicle in CKD/SKD form, which is restricted for import under the current Export-Import Policy, shall be allowed for importation against a license and such a license will be issued ... on the basis of an MOU ..." Under Article XVIII:B, Members must notify the restrictions they are applying, not the import licensing schemes they use to administer those restrictions. India had explained again and again to its trading partners that Public Notice No. 60 implemented the import restrictions on SKD/CKD kits, which were notified under Article XVIII:B, and would cease to be operational once these restrictions were eliminated. It was simply not logical to tear the procedures for implementation of the import restriction on imports of CKD and SKD kits in the Public Notice out of the context of the import restriction and declare those implementing procedures in the Notice themselves to be restrictions that would have required notification under Article XVIII:B. For this reason, it was also incorrect to claim that the Public Notice No. 60 was a new measure in respect of which India was required to give preference to price-based measures pursuant to paragraphs 2 and 3 of the Understanding on the balance-of-payments provisions of the GATT.

---

[245] Question 65 of the Panel.

Report of the Panel

(i) Procedural Requirements of the Balance of Payments Provisions

4.140 The **United States** said that India had not met the procedural prerequisites for justifying these measures under the balance-of-payments provision of the GATT. GATT Article XVIII:B and the Understanding on the Balance-of-Payments Provisions of the GATT 1994 (the Understanding) established procedural prerequisites to any invocation of the balance-of-payments provisions of the GATT.[246] These prerequisites also applied to the TRIMs Agreement, Article 4 of which permitted developing country Members to deviate temporarily from the provisions of Article 2 *to the extent and in such a manner* as GATT Article XVIII and the Understanding permit These prerequisites included a requirement to consult with the BOPs Committee (the Committee) concerning any new measures immediately after applying them (or, where prior consultation was practicable, as it almost certainly was in this case, before doing so)[247]. In the view of the United States, if a Member changed an import licensing scheme that the Member justified for balance-of-payments reasons, the Member was required to notify the changes to the WTO. Significant changes must be notified within 30 days. These points flowed from paragraph 9 of the Understanding on the Balance-of-Payments Provisions of the GATT 1994 (the Understanding), which provides that "a Member shall notify to the General Council the introduction of or any changes in the application of restrictive import measures taken for balance-of-payments purposes, as well as any modifications in time-schedules for the removal of such measures as announced under paragraph 1. Significant changes shall be notified to the General Council prior to or not later than 30 days after their announcement." Paragraph 9 of the Understanding also obligated Members applying restrictions for balance-of-payments purposes to furnish to the WTO, on a yearly basis, a consolidated notification that included all changes in relevant laws, regulations, policy statements or public notices. India did not undertake such consultations; indeed, it did not even notify the measures challenged in this dispute to the Committee, despite the requirement that it do so within 30 days if they were significant or in India's annual notification if not.[248] Because India had not complied with those requirements, it could not now assert a balance-of-payments justification for those measures, and for that reason as well the Panel should reject any such assertion.

4.141 A panel might consider but should reject an Article XVIII:B defense concerning measures that the defending Member had not notified to the BOPs Committee (the Committee). In the *India - Quantitative Restrictions* dispute, the Appellate Body found that panels had the competence to review the justification of measures purportedly taken for balance-of-payments purposes, and therefore a panel was empowered to consider such a defense. It would rarely if ever be appropriate, however, for a panel to sustain such a defense if the defending Mem-

---

[246] Pursuant to GATT Article XVIII:9, a Member's right to maintain balance-of-payments measures is made subject to the provisions of Articles XVIII:10 to 12.

[247] Article XVIII:12(a). Pursuant to paragraph 6 of the Understanding, consultations are to be held within four months after the institution or intensification of restrictions.

[248] Understanding, para. 9.

ber had not complied with the procedural requirements of Article XVIII:B and the Understanding. In this case, Public Notice No. 60 had entered into effect over three years ago, and India's Article XVIII:B arguments should not be accepted.

4.142 The **European Communities** also considered that a new notification was required. Paragraph 9 of the Understanding provided in relevant part that

> "A Member shall notify the General Council the introduction of or *any* changes in the application of restrictive measures taken for balance-of-payments purposes ... Significant changes shall be notified to the General Council prior to or no later than 30 days after their announcement".

Nor, in its view, could a Panel consider an Article XVIII:B defence concerning measures not specifically notified to the Committee. Paragraph 9 of Article XVIII:B authorized a Member to take BOP measures "subject to paragraphs 10 to 12". Paragraph 12 (a) of Article XVIII:B provided that any party applying new restrictions must consult with the Committee immediately. Paragraph 6 of the Understanding specified that consultations must take place within four months.[249]

4.143 **India** recalled that according to Article XVIII:12(a) of the GATT, a new consultation was required if the Member applied new restrictions or **raised** "the **general** level of its existing restrictions by a **substantial** intensification of the measures" applied under Article XVIII:B. India's notification covered restrictions applied in the form of non-automatic licensing on imports of cars, including cars imported as CKD/SKD kits. The changes in 1997 did not entail a substantial intensification of this measure. On the contrary, the changes in 1997 had the effect of relaxing the restriction on the importation of SKD/CKD kits. India was therefore not required to re-notify and hold new consultations on the changes introduced through Public Notice No. 60 in order to benefit from the legal cover of Article XVIII:B. It was furthermore neither required nor customary to notify under Article XVIII:B the details as to the administration of the restrictions. If the Panel were to create such a requirement, the consequences would be administratively unmanageable.

(ii)   Substantive Requirements of the Balance of Payments Provisions

4.144 The **United States** argued that India did not meet the substantive requirements of the balance-of-payments provisions of the GATT. Even if India were able to overcome the legal objections described [in the foregoing paragraphs], India could not meet the substantive requirements of Article XVIII:B. The first substantive difficulty with India's assertion of a balance-of-payments justification for these measures arose from the fact that India adopted Public Notice No. 60 on 12 December 1997. Under GATT Article XVIII:9, a Member might institute balance-of-payments measures "provided that the import restrictions instituted, maintained or intensified shall not exceed those necessary: (a) to

---

[249] Question 30 of the Panel.

Report of the Panel

forestall the threat of, or to stop, a serious decline in its monetary reserves, or (b) in the case of a contracting party with inadequate monetary reserves, to achieve a reasonable rate of increase in its reserves."

4.145 However, the Panel in *India – Quantitative Restrictions* found that, as of 18 November 1997 (only 24 days before Public Notice No. 60 was issued) India's balance-of-payments situation met none of the requirements in Article XVIII:9. The Panel found that:

> Overall, we are of the view that the quality and weight of evidence is strongly in favour of the proposition that India's reserves are not inadequate. In particular, this position is supported by the IMF, the Reserve Bank of India and three of the four methods suggested by India. Accordingly, we find that India's reserves were not inadequate as of 18 November 1997.[250]
>
> [...]
>
> We find that as of the date of establishment of this Panel [18 November 1997], there was not a serious decline or a threat of a serious decline in India's monetary reserves, as those terms are used in Article XVIII:9(a).[251]
>
> [...]
>
> We find that as of the date of establishment of this Panel, India's monetary reserves of US$25.1 billion were not inadequate as that term is used in Article XVIII:9(b) and that India was therefore not entitled to implement balance-of-payments measures to achieve a reasonable rate of growth in its reserves.[252]

4.146 It strained all credulity to suggest that 24 days after 18 November 1997, India's foreign reserve situation had changed so dramatically as to justify new balance-of-payments measures. Certainly India had provided no facts to suggest that such a change occurred. And, as the United States explained in its answers to the Panel's questions, this Panel could and should be guided by those factual and legal findings of the *India – Quantitative Restrictions* panel.[253] Even if – despite the foregoing points – these measures could permissibly have been introduced under GATT Article XVIII:B in December of 1997, India would still be required to explain the basis on which it was maintaining them on 15 May and 27 July 2000, the dates on which the United States requested this Panel and on which this Panel was established.[254] Article XVIII:11 made clear that a Member

---

[250] Panel Report on *India – Quantitative Restrictions*, para. 5.176 (DSR 1999:V, 1799). This finding is a predicate for the Panel's ultimate finding under Article XVIII:9(b).

[251] Panel Report on *India – Quantitative Restrictions*, para. 5.180 (DSR 1999:V, 1799).

[252] Panel Report on *India – Quantitative Restrictions*, para. 5.183 (DSR 1999:V, 1799).

[253] US response to Panel Questions, paras. 48-50.

[254] Throughout its submissions, India said that the relevant date for a balance-of-payments analysis was the date on which a panel request is submitted. The *India – Quantitative Restrictions* panel concluded instead that the relevant date was the date of panel establishment, and it made its findings as of that date (18 November 1997). Panel Report on *India – Quantitative Restrictions*, WT/DS90/R, adopted 22 September 1999, paras. 5.160-5.161 (DSR 1999:V, 1799). In this dispute, it made no difference which date was chosen: as described below India's currency reserves on either date were

applying balance-of-payments measures "shall progressively relax any restrictions applied under this Section as conditions improve, *maintaining them only to the extent necessary* under the terms of paragraph 9 of this Article and *shall eliminate them when conditions no longer justify such maintenance.*" In fact, however, India did not have balance-of-payments difficulties at all in the spring of 2000, and therefore, under Article XVIII:11 it lacked any basis for maintaining them.

4.147 Without prejudice to the United States' position that India had failed to advance evidence required to sustain its burden to put forward at least a *prima facie* defense, the United States provided materials from the Reserve Bank of India that demonstrated that India did not face balance-of-payments difficulties that would justify maintenance of the measures at issue in this dispute at the time when this Panel was requested and established. In its Annual Report for 1999-2000, which was published in August 2000, the Reserve Bank provided information about India's currency reserves over the preceding decade. In December of 1998, those reserves had risen to US$30.1 billion (as compared to US$25.1 billion in November of 1997, the date as of which the *India – Quantitative Restrictions* panel made its rulings). In December of 1999, the reserves had risen to US$34.9 billion. According to the Reserve Bank's Weekly Statistical Supplement, on 12 May 2000, India's reserves stood at US$37.6 billion. On 28 July 2000, India's reserves stood at US$36.2 billion. In other words, between November of 1997 and the end of July 2000, India's reserves increased by more than 44%.

4.148 Furthermore, the Reserve Bank provided the following analysis of India's external position:

> The movements in India's foreign exchange reserves, in recent years, have kept pace with the requirements on the trade as well as the capital accounts. As a matter of policy, foreign exchange reserves are kept at a level that is adequate to cover the liquidity needs in the event of both cyclical and unanticipated shocks. Particularly after the South-East Asian currency crises, there has been a growing opinion that the central banks need to hold reserves far in excess of the levels that were considered desirable going by the conventional indicators. The import cover of reserves improved to about 8.2 months as at end-March 2000 as against 6.5 months as at end-March 1997 while the ratio of short-term debt to reserves declined to 10.6 per cent as at end-March 2000 from 25.5 per cent as at end-March 1997. Even in relation to a broader measure of external liabilities, foreign exchange reserves provide adequate cover. For instance, short-term debt and cumulative portfolio investment inflows taken together were only 59.3 per cent of reserves as at end-March 2000. These ratios remain, by and large, unchanged even if unencumbered reserves (gross reserves net of

---

more than adequate and not seriously declining, and consequently India lacked a balance-of-payments justification for its measures on both dates.

forward liabilities) are taken into account, given the relatively small size of forward liabilities in the Indian context. The strength of the foreign exchange reserves has also been a positive factor in facilitating flow of portfolio investment by FIIs and in reducing the 'risk premia' on foreign borrowings and Global Depository Receipts (GDR) / American Depository Receipts (ADR) issued by the Indian corporates. It is, however, important to note that unanticipated domestic or external developments, including undue volatility in asset prices in equity/bond markets, can create disproportionate pressures in the foreign exchange market in emerging economies.[255]

The Reserve Bank's confidence in the strength of India's currency reserve position - as gauged not only by measures such as the total amount of reserves, but also by measures such as import cover, ratio of reserves to short-term debt, and ratio of reserves to short-term debt plus cumulative portfolio investment inflows, among others - confirmed what the growth and absolute size of India's foreign currency reserves themselves make clear: that India was not facing inadequate reserves, seriously declining reserves or the threat of a serious decline in the spring of 2000.

4.149 Finally, there would be several other substantive difficulties with any Indian assertion of a balance-of-payments justification for these measures. First, Article XVIII:B authorized developing country Members only to "control the general level of imports".[256] India had not explained, however, how an inconsistency with national treatment "controls the general level of imports." As the United States had noted, once an item has been imported, the foreign exchange for that import has been expended; there was no balance-of-payments justification for permitting discrimination against that imported good[257] Furthermore, India had also not explained how its introduction of these measures in late 1997 would be consistent with the requirement in paragraphs 2 and 3 of the Understanding to give preference to price-based measures. The indigenization and trade balancing requirements were not import surcharges, import deposit requirements or other measures with an impact on the price of imported goods. India, however, had not provided the justification for these measures that the Understanding would require, and India therefore could not maintain them as balance-of-payments measures.

4.150 In summary, India had not provided any argumentation that would overcome the serious legal difficulties with any assertion of a balance-of-payments justification for the indigenization and trade balancing requirements. Nor had India provided any evidence that - even if those legal objections could be overcome - its foreign currency reserve position met the requirements of Article

---

[255] Annual Report, para. 6.31. Exhibit US-27 includes the paragraphs of the Annual Report devoted to India's foreign exchange reserves, paras. 6.24-6.31.
[256] GATT Article XVIII:9 and Understanding, para. 4.
[257] India did not respond to the Panel's invitation to address this point. India's response to Question 65 of the Panel.

1928

XVIII:B either at the time those measures were introduced or at the time this Panel was requested and established. To the contrary, the evidence of India's own central bank proved the opposite. India's assertion of a balance-of-payments justification for these measures should be rejected.

(iii)   The Burden of Proof

4.151 The **United States** went on to state that India had not met its burden of proof on the balance-of-payments defense; it could not surmount the procedural obstacles to any such defense; and India's external financial position had at all relevant times been so strong that it could not meet the substantive requirements for invoking Article XVIII:B. The Appellate Body had provided guidance on the allocation of burden of proof in several reports. Particularly relevant were its conclusions in the *US – Wool Shirts and Blouses* report:

> In addressing this issue, we find it difficult, indeed, to see how any system of judicial settlement could work if it incorporated the proposition that the mere assertion of a claim might amount to proof. It is, thus, hardly surprising that various international tribunals, including the International Court of Justice, have generally and consistently accepted and applied the rule that *the party who asserts a fact, whether the claimant or the respondent, is responsible for providing proof thereof.* Also, it is a generally-accepted canon of evidence in civil law, common law and, in fact, most jurisdictions, that the burden of proof rests upon the party, whether complaining or defending, who asserts the affirmative of a particular claim or defence. *If that party adduces evidence sufficient to raise a presumption that what is claimed is true, the burden then shifts to the other party*, who will fail unless it adduces sufficient evidence to rebut the presumption.[258]

In this case, India had provided no evidence whatsoever about its balance-of-payments situation. To the extent that India was asserting that its balance-of-payments position provided a legal justification for the measures at issue, it was responsible for providing proof of that assertion. It had done nothing of the sort. Having adduced no evidence of any kind on the point, India obviously had not adduced evidence sufficient to raise a presumption that it had a balance-of-payments problem justifying the measures in question. For that reason alone, any balance-of-payments defense must fail.

4.152 The **European Communities** pointed out that Article XVIII:B was an exception to other GATT provisions. Accordingly, it was for India to prove that the strict requirements of Article XVIII were met in this case. India had provided no evidence or argument whatsoever in support of its invocation of Article XVIII:B. The evidence provided by the European Communities showed that India's BOP situation had been even more buoyant when the European Commu-

---

[258] Report of the Appellate Body in *US - Wool Shirts and Blouses*, WT/DS33/AB/R, adopted on 23 May 1997, page 14 (footnotes omitted) (emphasis added) (DSR 1997:I, 323, at 335).

Report of the Panel

nities requested the establishment of this Panel than in November 1997, the date considered by the panel in *India - Quantitative Restrictions*. In addition, India had not complied with the procedural requirements imposed by Article XVIII:B and by the Understanding. In view of that, the Panel should dismiss India's attempted defence outright. In particular, the European Communities considered that it would be totally unwarranted to request the advice of the IMF. To do so would serve only to reward India's delaying tactics. For these reasons, the Panel need not address the arguments outlined by India in paragraph 42 of its First Submission (see para. 4.45 above). These arguments had already been rejected by the Panel and the Appellate Body in *India – Quantitative Restrictions* . There was no reason for the Panel to depart from that precedent in this dispute.

4.153 **India** recalled that the Appellate Body Report on *US –Woven Wool Shirts and Blouses*, stated that:

> the burden of proof rests upon the party, whether complaining or defending, who asserts the affirmative of a particular claim or defence. If that party adduces evidence sufficient to raise a presumption that what is claimed is true, the burden then shifts to the other party, who will fail unless it adduces sufficient evidence to rebut the presumption.[259]

4.154 Furthermore, the Appellate Body, in its report on *European Communities – Measures concerning Meat and Meat Products (Hormones)* (hereinafter "*EC – Hormones*"), stated that:

> The general rule in a dispute settlement proceeding requiring a complaining party to establish a *prima facie* case of inconsistency of a provision [...] before the burden of showing consistency with that provision is taken by the defending party is *not* avoided by simply describing the same provision as an exception. [260] (emphasis in original)

In the *India – Quantitative Restrictions* case, the Panel concluded from this jurisprudence:

> This implies that the United States has to prove any of its claims in relation to the alleged violation of Article XI:1 and XVIII:11. Similarly, India has to support its assertion that its measures are justified under Article XVIII:B. We also view the rules stated by the Appellate Body as requiring that the United States as the complainant cannot limit itself to stating its claim. It must present a *prima facie* case that the Indian balance-of-payments measures are not justified by reference to Articles XI:1 and XVIII:11 of GATT

---

[259] WT/DS33/AB/R, p. 16 (DSR 1997:I, 323, at 337).
[260] WT/DS26/AB/R-WT/DS48/AB/R, para. 104 (DSR 1998:I, 135).

1930   DSR 2002:V

India – Autos

1994.[261] Should the United States do so, India would have to respond in order to rebut the claim.[262]

In India's view, it was thus for the United States and the European Communities to submit a *prima facie* case that the restrictions notified by India under Article XVIII:B were inconsistent with that provision. It was only after they had done so that India was required to present a rebuttal. The complainants would have had to show in particular that India's reserves were sufficient to: safeguard its external financial position, and ensure a level of reserves adequate for the implementation of its programme of economic development[263] and that India therefore violated Article XVIII:B

4.155 India noted that, in fact, the panel in *India – Quantitative Restrictions* found (para. 5.119) that the United States had to make a *prima facie* case that India's import restrictions were not justified under Article XVIII:11. India recalled the conclusions of the Appellate Body on the burden of proof in the case of safeguard actions by the United States against imports of shirts and blouses from India:

> India has argued that it is "customary GATT practice" that the party invoking a provision which is identified as an exception must offer proof that the conditions set out in that provision are met. We acknowledge that several GATT 1947 and WTO panels have required such proof of a party invoking a defence, such as those found in Article XX[264] or Article XI:2(c)(i)[265], to a claim of violation of a GATT obligation, such as those found in Articles I:1, II:1, III or XI:1. Articles XX and XI:(2)(c)(i) are limited exceptions from obligations under certain other provisions of the GATT 1994, not positive rules establishing obligations in themselves. They are in the nature of affirmative defences. It is only reasonable that the burden of establishing such a defence should rest on the party asserting it.[266]

---

[261] Report of the Appellate Body in *Australia – Salmon*, adopted on 6 November 1998, WT/DS18/AB/R, paras. 257-259 (DSR 1998:VIII, 3327).

[262] WT/DS90/R, para. 5.119 (DSR 1999:V, 1799).

[263] See Article XVIII:9 of the GATT.

[264] *Canada – FIRA*, adopted on 7 February 1984, BISD 30S/140, para. 5.20; *United States – Section 337 of the Tariff Act of 1930*, adopted 7 November 1989, BISD 36S/345, para. 5.27; *US – Malt Beverages*, adopted on 19 June 1992, BISD 39S/206, paras. 5.43 and 5.52; and Panel Report, *United States – Standards for Reformulated and Conventional Gasoline*, as modified by the Appellate Body Report, adopted on 20 May 1996, WT/DS2/9, para. 6.20.

[265] *Japan – Agricultural Products I*, adopted on 22 March 1988, BISD 35S/163, para. 5.1.3.7; *EEC – Restrictions on Imports of Dessert Apples,* Complaint by Chile, *(hereinafter "EEC – Apples (Chile)")*, adopted on 22 June 1989, BISD 36S/93, para. 12:3; and *Canada - Import Restrictions on Ice Cream and Yoghurt*, adopted on 5 December 1989, BISD 36S/68, para. 59.

[266] Furthermore, there were a few cases that were similar in that the defending party invoked, as a defence, certain provisions and the panel explicitly required the defending party to demonstrate the applicability of the provision it was asserting. See, for example, *United States – Customs User Fee*, adopted on 2 February 1988, BISD 35S/245, para. 98, concerning Article II:2 of the GATT 1947; *Canada – Import, Distribution and Sale of Certain Alcoholic Drinks by Provincial Marketing Agencies*, adopted on 22 March 1988, BISD 35S/37, para 4.34, concerning Article XXIV:12 of the GATT

DSR 2002:V

Report of the Panel

> The transitional safeguard mechanism provided in Article 6 of the *ATC* is a fundamental part of the rights and obligations of WTO Members concerning non-integrated textile and clothing products covered by the *ATC* during the transitional period. Consequently, a party claiming a violation of a provision of the *WTO Agreement* by another Member must assert and prove its claim. In this case, India claimed a violation by the United States of Article 6 of the *ATC*. We agree with the Panel that it, therefore, was up to India to put forward evidence and legal argument sufficient to demonstrate that the transitional safeguard action by the United States was inconsistent with the obligations assumed by the United States under Articles 2 and 6 of the *ATC*. India did so in this case. And, with India having done so, the onus then shifted to the United States to bring forward evidence and argument to disprove the claim. This, the United States was not able to do and, therefore, the Panel found that the transitional safeguard action by the United States "violated the provisions of Articles 2 and 6 of the ATC".[267]

> In our view, the Panel did not err on this issue in this case.

The Appellate Body found that Article 6 of the ATC established not merely a limited exception but positive rules and that India therefore had to bear the burden of proving that the United States applied Article 6 inconsistently. What was true for the safeguard provisions of Article 6 of the ATC must also be true for balance-of-payments provisions of Article XVIII:B of the GATT. Just as Article 6 of the *ATC* was a fundamental part of the rights and obligations of WTO Members under the ATC, Article XVIII:B was a fundamental part of the rights and obligations of developing countries under the GATT. There could not be one distribution of the burden of proof for a safeguard provision that had been used extensively by the United States and another for a safeguard provision applicable to developing countries. It was consequently up to the European Communities and the United States to present a *prima facie* case of violation of Article XVIII:B and, once they had done so, for India to rebut this case. The Appellate Body ruled that "a *prima facie* case is one which, in the absence of effective refutation by the defending party, requires a panel, as a matter of law, to rule in favour of the complaining party presenting the *prima facie* case".[268] The scant and anecdotal information provided so far by the complainants would not permit the Panel to rule as a matter of law that India's reserves were adequate for the implementation of its programme of economic development. In fact, they had not even attempted to assess India's reserves in the light of its development programme. As to India's external financial position, the European Communities and the United States had merely cited statements that the Reserve Bank of India made without any reference to the requirements of Article XVIII:B. As to the

---

1947; and *US – Malt Beverages*, adopted on 19 June 1992, BISD 39S/206, para. 5.44, concerning the Protocol of Provisional Application.

[267] WT/DS33/R, para. 8.1 (DSR 1997:I, 343).

[268] Report of the Appellate Body in *EC – Hormones,* WT/DS26/AB/R, WT/DS48/AB/R, adopted on 13 February 1998, para. 104 (DSR 1998:I, 135).

1932

DSR 2002:V

relationship between India's reserves and India's programme of economic development, the complainants submitted no evidence at all. The evidence submitted by the complainants so far could not possibly be the basis of a ruling that India was violating Article XVIII:B. According to the consistent GATT and WTO practice,[269] the Panel would have to examine India's balance-of-payments situation on 15 May 2000 and 12 October 2000, the dates on which the complainants submitted their panel requests. India's balance-of-payments situation at the time of the adoption of Public Notice No. 60 was totally irrelevant. The findings of the panel on *India - Quantitative Restrictions* did not provide any evidence in respect of India's balance-of-payments situation on 15 May 2000 and 12 October 2000 and could therefore not possibly guide the present Panel.

4.156 With respect to the role of the IMF, India wished to note that the position of the European Communities and the United States was inconsistent with the position that the United States took in the proceeding of the panel on *India – Quantitative Restrictions.* The United States then asserted that Article XV:2 expressly allocated to the IMF the authority for making certain specific determinations within the scope of its particular expertise. Allocation of that authority to the IMF had been the intent of the drafters of Article XV:2, and that intent was carried out in the practice of the CONTRACTING PARTIES. Since Article XV:2 required the WTO to consult the IMF, in all cases where the WTO is called on to consider matters concerning monetary reserves, balance of payments or foreign exchange arrangements, the Panel must also do so . . . Although Article XV:2 did not mention panels, *per se*, an interpretation of WTO would include panels.[270] The position of the United States had been supported by the jurisprudence of the Appellate Body. Although the Appellate Body had found in *Argentina – Measures Affecting Imports of Footwear, Textiles, Apparel and Other Items* (hereinafter "*Argentina – Textiles and Apparel*") that the dispute did not involve "problems concerning monetary reserves, balance of payments or foreign exchange arrangements", it did find with respect to panel proceedings that Article XV:2 "*requires* the WTO to consult with the IMF when dealing with 'problems concerning monetary reserves, balance of payments or foreign exchange arrangements".[271] Also in the *India – Quantitative Restrictions* case the Appellate Body noted with approval the decision of the panel to submit questions to the IMF on India's balance-of-payments situation on the basis of Article 13 of the DSU and Article XV:2 of the GATT.[272] It followed from the above that the Panel would have to consult the IMF in accordance with Article XV:2 of the GATT if it were to find that Public Notice No. 60 and the MOUs would have restricted imports in May and October 2000 even in the absence of any requirement to ob-

---

[269] See Panel Report on *India – Quantitative Restrictions,* WT/DS90/R, adopted on 22 September 1999, as upheld by the Appellate Body Report, paras. 5.160-5.161 (DSR 1999:V, 1799).

[270] See Panel Report on *India – Quantitative Restrictions,* WT/DS90/R, adopted on 22 September 1999, as upheld by the Appellate Body Report, paras. 3.305 and 3.311 (DSR 1999:V, 1799).

[271] Report of the Appellate Body in *Argentina – Textiles and Apparel*, WT/DS56/AB/R, adopted on 22 April 1998, para. 84 (DSR 1998:III, 1003).

[272] WT/DS90/AB/R, para. 149 (DSR 1999:V, 1799).

Report of the Panel

tain a licence for imports of cars and components and an examination of India's Article XVIII:B invocation would therefore become necessary.

> (iv)   Relevance of the India – Quantitative Restrictions Case

4.157 With respect to deciding what account to take of the findings and conclusions reached by the panel in the *India – Quantitative Restrictions* dispute when considering the justification under Article XVIII:B of the measures at issue in this dispute, the **United States** considered that this Panel should be guided by conclusions reached by the panel in the *India – Patents (EC)* dispute. That panel considered the extent to which it was bound by the findings of a previous panel on the same measure and found as follows:

> It can thus be concluded that panels are not *bound* by previous decisions of panels or the Appellate Body even if the subject-matter is the same. In examining dispute WT/DS79 we are not legally bound by the conclusions of the Panel in dispute WT/DS50 as modified by the Appellate Body report. However, in the course of "normal dispute settlement procedures" required under Article 10.4 of the DSU, we will take into account the conclusions and reasoning in the Panel and Appellate Body reports in WT/DS50. Moreover, in our examination, we believe that we should give significant weight to both Article 3.2 of the DSU, which stresses the role of the WTO dispute settlement system in providing security and predictability to the multilateral trading system, and to the need to avoid inconsistent rulings (which concern has been referred to by both parties).[273]

4.158 Therefore, if the Panel decided to consider the balance-of-payments justification of the measures at issue in this dispute, the Panel should bear in mind that both the panel and the Appellate Body thoroughly analyzed the legal issues in the *India - Quantitative Restrictions* case. Furthermore, this Panel should bear in mind that the *India – Quantitative Restrictions* panel made a factual finding, after extensive factual submissions, on India's balance-of-payments situation as of 18 November 1997 - less than thirty days before the adoption of Public Notice No. 60. It would be neither necessary nor appropriate for this Panel to repeat that work. The Panel should of course consider the arguments of the parties, but it should be guided by the panel's and the Appellate Body's factual findings and recent interpretation of the provisions at issue in that case.

4.159 Moreover, the *India – Quantitative Restrictions* panel decided that, having regard to both DSU Article 13 and GATT Article XV:2, it would consult with the IMF. After giving both parties an opportunity to comment on a draft, the Panel sent the IMF a letter asking several questions about India's balance-of-payments situation as of 18 November 1997. The IMF's replies confirmed that, as of 18 November 1997, India's reserves were neither declining

---

[273] WT/DS79/R, para. 7.30 (DSR 1998:VI, 2661).

1934   DSR 2002:V

seriously nor threatened with serious decline; that India's level of foreign currency reserves was adequate; and that India's quantitative restrictions were not needed for balance-of-payments adjustment and should be removed over a relatively short period of time. The IMF also presented additional data for the period ending June 1998; the IMF indicated that this later data corroborated its views.[274] It would be entirely unnecessary to ask the IMF once again for an opinion that it had already given.

4.160 It was obvious to the **European Communities** that this Panel could not rely on the factual finding of the panel in *India – Quantitative Restrictions* to the effect that, as of the date of the establishment of that panel, India was not entitled to implement BOP measures. Rather, this Panel would have to make its own factual findings based on India's BOP situation as of the date of establishment of the panel. On the other hand, as confirmed by the Appellate Body in *Japan – Taxes on Alcoholic Beverages*[275], the Panel must take into account the findings reached by the panel (and the Appellate Body) in *India - Quantitative Restrictions* with respect to issues of legal interpretation of Article XVIII:B, (and in particular with respect to those raised by India at paragraph 4.80).

4.161 **India** contended that as the United States had submitted its request for the establishment of a panel on 15 May 2000 and the European Communities on 12 October 2000. India's external financial positions on these dates would have to be examined because they would be different from India's external financial position in November 1997 which the earlier panel examined. The panel on *India - Quantitative Restrictions* correctly found that "the determination of whether balance-of-payments measures are justified is tied to a Member's reserve situation as of a certain date".[276] The present Panel therefore could not rely on the assessment of India's balance-of-payment situation by the panel on *India – Quantitative Restrictions*.

4.162 The **European Communities** contended that Article XVIII:B was an exception to other GATT provisions. Accordingly, it was for India to prove that the strict requirements of Article XVIII:B were met in this case. So far, however, India had submitted no relevant evidence to this Panel. The European Communities recalled that the Panel on *India – Quantitative Restrictions* concluded that, as of November 1997, India's reserve position did not justify India's invocation of Article XVIII:B. India had not claimed, let alone proved that, since November 1997, India's BOP situation had deteriorated to the point where resort to Article XVIII:B of GATT would have become justified. Indeed, any claims to that effect would be untenable. India's reserve position as of 12 October 2000, as well as its current position, seemed to be, if anything, even more buoyant than in November 1997. (As evidence of this, the European Communities is providing to the Panel

---

[274] Panel Report on *India – Quantitative Restrictions*, WT/DS90/R, adopted on 22 September 1999, as upheld by the Appellate Body Report, paras. 3.360, 3.361, 3.367, and 3.368 (DSR 1999:V, 1799).
[275] Report of the Appellate Body in *Japan – Alcoholic Beverages II*, WT/DS8/AB/R, WT/DS10/AB/R, WT/DS11/AB/R, adopted on 1 November 1996, at p. 24 (DSR 1996:I, 97).
[276] WT/DS90/R, para. 5.157 (DSR 1999:V, 1799).

Report of the Panel

a copy of the relevant excerpts of the "Economic Survey 2000-2001" published by India's Ministry of Finance).

3. TRIMs Agreement

4.163 The **United States** claimed that the indigenization and trade balancing requirements fell squarely within the scope of Paragraphs 1(a), 1(b) and 2(a) of the Illustrative List, and for that reason they violated Articles 2.1 and 2.2 of the TRIMs Agreement. Separately, they also violated Article 2.1 of the TRIMs Agreement because they were inconsistent with GATT Articles III:4 and XI:1.

> *Paragraph 1(a)*: First, firms manufacturing passenger cars in India were "enterprises"; because the ordinary meaning of "enterprise" included "a business firm, a company". Second, India had affirmed that indigenization meant "local content" and "use of local materials alone". Thus, the indigenization obligation required "enterprises" manufacturing automobiles to "use" local parts and components (and effectively also to "purchase" such local parts and components if they themselves did not import them). The indigenization requirement therefore fell within the terms of Paragraph 1(a).

> *Paragraph 1(b)*: First, the measures made clear that an MOU signatory's imports of CKD/SKD kits/components "may be *regulated* with reference to the export obligation fulfilled in the previous years as per the MOU." Second, the export obligation itself was expressed in terms of value - namely, an FOB value equal to the CIF value of imported CKD/SKD kits and components. Thus, a firm manufacturing cars in India could only import and use a maximum amount of SKD/CKD components that was related to the value of its exports in previous years. If a firm wished to use a greater amount, it must purchase and use such components from an Indian source instead. The trade balancing obligation therefore fell within the terms of Paragraph 1(b).

> *Paragraph 2(a)*: Import licenses for SKD/CKD kits/components were not given to companies that do not sign and comply with an MOU. Because compliance was a condition to importation of SKD/CKD kits/components used by such companies in their motor vehicle production in India, those requirements "restrict" importation "generally" of "products used in ... local production". For that reason alone the measures fell within the scope of Paragraph 2(a). The trade balancing obligation also fell within the scope of Paragraph 2(a) for a second reason. Beginning in the fourth year, CKD/SKD kits imports were allowed with reference to the extent of export obligation fulfilled in the previous year. The trade balancing obligation thus imposed a "restriction" on a firm's imports that was "related to the ... value of local production that it [the firm] exports", as provided in Paragraph 2(a).

1936

DSR 2002:V

Illustrative list chapeaux: As required by the chapeaux to Paragraphs 1 and 2, the measures at issue either were "mandatory or enforceable under domestic law or under administrative rulings" or were measures "compliance with which is necessary to obtain an advantage." First, India has confirmed that the measures could be "enforced" at least under the provisions of the FTDR Act, through the import licensing mechanism, and under Indian contract law. Second, manufacturers must comply with the indigenization and trade balancing obligations to be permitted to import SKD/CKD kits/components. This permission constituted an "advantage" because components in SKD/CKD form were "restricted" under the Exim Policy and not generally importable into India.

Non-illustrative list violations of Article 2.1: As shown elsewhere, Public Notice No. 60 and the MOUs were inconsistent with Articles III:4 and XI:1 of the GATT 1994. Therefore, the measures were inconsistent with Article 2.1 of the TRIMs Agreement even if they discriminated against imported goods, or prohibited or restricted the importation of foreign goods, in ways that were not described in the provisions of the Illustrative List. For example, the trade balancing requirement violated Article III:4 because it obligated users and purchasers of imported SKD/CKD parts and components (but not users/purchasers of like domestic goods) to export an equal value of automobiles or automotive components. Even if this form of discrimination was not encompassed in the Illustrative List it was inconsistent with GATT Article III; and for that reason it was also inconsistent with Article 2.1 of the TRIMs Agreement.

4.164 Whether or not the TRIMs Agreement required a separate analysis of whether a measure was a "trade-related investment measure", the measures in this case definitely were such measures.

"Investment measure": First, Public Notice No. 60 and the MOUs required a minimum foreign equity of US$50 million dollars and thus were designed to increase the amount of foreign investment. Second, these measures steered foreign investment in the Indian motor vehicle manufacturing sector towards establishment of actual production facilities for "manufacture" of cars and away from "mere assembly" of imported kits/components. Third, these measures were also aimed at encouraging investment in and the development of the Indian parts and components industry generally (from whom India plainly wants automobile companies to purchase the components and parts that they need to engage in "manufacture"). The MOU made that clear when it provided that the signatory "shall aggressively pursue and achieve as soon as possible the development of the local supply base ... ." Moreover, Indian officials announcing Public Notice No. 60 said that the policy objective was "to encourage local production of auto-components and thus, bring in modern technology and develop this key segment".

Report of the Panel

The indigenization and trade balancing requirements furthered that domestic investment objective both by favoring local automotive parts and components and by restricting the entry into India of foreign components.

"Trade-related": The measures favoured domestic goods over like imported goods, and they restricted or prohibited importation of certain foreign goods. As past panels had recognized, local content requirements were trade-related by definition. Quantitative import restrictions and prohibitions (the elimination of which was a cornerstone of the GATT 1994) were no less so.

4.165 Under Article 5.2 of the TRIMs Agreement, all WTO Members benefitted from a transition period to eliminate trade-related investment measures inconsistent with Article 2. Those transition provisions, however, did not apply to this case, for three reasons. First, India introduced these measures in December of 1997, nearly three years after the entry into force of the WTO Agreement, but the transition provisions did not apply to measures adopted less than 180 days before the date of entry into force of the WTO Agreement. Second, the only measures to which the transition provisions applied were those that were notified in accordance with the provisions of Article 5.1. While India did notify a dividend balancing requirement in various sectors, India did not notify local content or trade balancing requirements. Third, India's transition period had in any case ended. Pursuant to Article 5.2, India had five years from the entry into force of the WTO Agreement to eliminate all its inconsistent measures. That five-year period had expired on 1 January 2000.

4.166 The **European Communities** pointed out that Article 2.1 of the TRIMs Agreement provided that:

> "Without prejudice to other rights and obligations under GATT 1994, no Member shall apply any TRIM that is inconsistent with the provisions of Articles III or XI of GATT."

The TRIMs Agreement did not define the notion of TRIM. Nevertheless, the Annex to that Agreement contained what Article 2.2 describes as:

> "An illustrative list of TRIMs that are inconsistent with the obligation of national treatment provided for in paragraph 4 of Article III of GATT 1994 and the obligation of general elimination of quantitative restrictions provided for in paragraph 1 of Article XI of GATT 1994 ..."

The wording of Article 2.2 indicated that any measure which fell within the List constituted *per se* a TRIM inconsistent with Article 2.1, without it being necessary for the complainant to demonstrate in each particular case that the measure concerned was an "investment measure" and was "related to trade in goods".[277] The "indigenization" requirements and the "trade balancing" requirements were

---

[277] This issue was left undecided by the Panel Report on *Indonesia – Autos*, WT/DS54/R, WT/DS55/R, WT/DS59/R, WT/DS64/R, adopted on 23 July 1998, paras. 14.64-14.72 (DSR 1998:VI, 2201).

1938

DSR 2002:V

both "investment measures" and "related to trade in goods" and, consequently, constituted TRIMs within the meaning of Article 1 of the TRIMs Agreement. Since those requirements were inconsistent with GATT Articles III:4 and XI:1, it followed that they also infringed Article 2.1 of the TRIMs Agreement. Furthermore, the "indigenization" requirements fall within Items 1(a) of the Illustrative List, whereas the "trade balancing" requirements are caught by Items 1(b) and 2(a).

- *The requirements are "investment measures":* The term "investment measure" had been interpreted in *Indonesia – Autos*, where the panel found that the grant of tax and duty incentives upon compliance with certain local content requirements was an "investment measure". The Panel reasoned as follows:

  > "[T]hose measures are aimed at encouraging the development of a local manufacturing capability for finished motor vehicles and parts and components in Indonesia. Inherent to this objective is that these measures necessarily have a significant impact on investment in these sectors. For this reason, we consider that these measures fall within any reasonable interpretation of the term 'investment measures'."[278]

  Indonesia – Autos stood for the proposition that the characterization of a measure as an "investment measure" must be based on the purpose of the measure, as discerned from the measure's structure and objectives, rather than on the measure's actual effects on investment. The measures in dispute had a similar structure and pursue the same objective as the measures at issue in *Indonesia – Autos,* namely to encourage the development of a local automotive industry. That objective is further evidenced by the other two "parameters" laid down in Public Notice No. 60, i.e. "the establishment of actual production facilities for manufacture of cars and not for mere assembly" and the minimum US$50 million investment requirement. Inherent in the objective of developing a local automotive industry was that India's measures, like Indonesia's, had a "significant impact on investment" and, therefore, constituted "investment measures" for the purposes of the TRIMs Agreement.

- *The "indigenization" requirements and the "trade balancing" requirements were "related to trade in goods":* The "indigenization" requirements were "related to trade in goods" because they favoured the use of domestic inputs over imported inputs. In turn, the "trade balancing" requirements were "related to trade in goods"

---

[278] This issue was left undecided by the Panel Report on *Indonesia – Autos*, WT/DS54/R, WT/DS55/R, WT/DS59/R, WT/DS64/R, adopted on 23 July 1998, para. 14.80 (DSR 1998:VI, 2201).

Report of the Panel

because they restricted imports, as well as the internal purchase of imported goods.

- *The "indigenization" requirements and the "trade balancing" requirements fell within the Illustrative List of prohibited TRIMs*: The "indigenization" requirements fell within Item 1(a) of the Illustrative List, which included among the TRIMs that were inconsistent with Article III:4 those which required:

  > "the [...] use by an enterprise of products of domestic origin [...], whether specified in terms [...] of [...] value of products, or in terms of a proportion of [...] value of its local production"

  To the extent that they required the trade balancing of imported goods purchased by the signatories within India, the "trade balancing" requirements fell within Item 1(b), which covered those measures that require:

  > "that an enterprise's purchases [...] of imported products be limited to an amount related to the [...] value of local products that it exports"

  Finally, to the extent that they required trade balancing of imports made directly by the signatories, the "trade balancing" requirements were caught by the terms of Item 2(a) which covered those measures which restricted

  > "the importation by an enterprise of products used in or related to its local product ion, [...] to an amount related to the [...] value of local production that it exports."

4.167 The "indigenization" and "trade balancing" requirements had not been notified under Article 5.1 of the TRIMs Agreement: The measures in dispute had not been notified by India under Article 5.1 of the TRIMs Agreement.[279] Indeed, since all these measures were introduced by India well after the entry into force of the WTO Agreement, they could never have been validly notified under that provision. Therefore, India's measures could not benefit from the five-years transitional derogation provided for in Article 5.2 with respect to prohibited TRIMs duly notified by developing countries. The European Communities further recalled that, in any event, this derogation expired as of 1 January 2000, without prejudice to the possibility under Article 5.3 that a further period may be granted for those measures previously notified under Article 5.1.

4.168 **India** responded that, according to Article 2:1 of the TRIMs Agreement, "no Member shall apply any *TRIM that is inconsistent with the provisions of Article III or XI of GATT 1994*". An inconsistency with the TRIMs Agreement could therefore arise only if there was an inconsistency with the GATT. Having

---

[279] India had confirmed that the TRIMs notified in G/TRIMS/N/1/IND/1/Add.1 do not cover the measures at issue in this dispute. See India's Replies to Questions posed by the United States in the TRIMs Committee, G/TRIMS/W/16.

1940

DSR 2002:V

demonstrated that the measures which the Panel was competent to rule upon were not inconsistent with Article III or XI of the GATT, India had therefore also demonstrated that these measures were consistent with the TRIMs Agreement. India considered that Public Notice No. 60 and the MOUs contained provisions that might possibly be regarded as "investment measures" within the meaning of Article 1 of the TRIMs Agreement because they imposed requirements relating to the investments that automobile manufacturers must make, e.g., the provisions relating to minimum foreign equity and the prohibition of mere assembly operations. However, these requirements were not at issue in these proceedings. In any case, they were no longer imposed as conditions for the grant of an import license and could therefore no longer be regarded as "related to trade" within the meaning of Article 1 of the TRIMs Agreement. The provisions of Public Notice No. 60 and the MOUs that were at issue in the present proceedings are clearly trade measures and *not* investment measures. As long as India applied its discretionary licensing system to SKD/CKD kits and car components, the trade balancing and indigenization provisions might have affected the decisions of car manufacturers as buyers of kits and components *but they did not constrain the decisions of car manufacturers as investors.* The purpose of the provisions was to minimize the foreign exchange expenditures of car manufacturers, not to regulate their investments. For these reasons, the trade balancing and indigenization provisions do not fall within the framework of the TRIMs Agreement.

4.169 The **United States** considered that India's suggestion that because the trade balancing and indigenization requirements were "trade measures", they were not "investment measures" and therefore were not within the scope of the TRIMs Agreement was a contention that should not be adopted by the Panel. The dichotomy that India tried to draw between "trade" and "investment" measures could not be sustained. Presumably any measure disciplined by GATT Article III:4 could be considered a "trade measure"; on India's logic, however, no such measure would be an "investment measure" – and therefore no measure disciplined by Article III:4 could ever fall within the scope of the TRIMs Agreement. India's hard-and-fast division between "trade" and "investment" measures was a manifestly impossible interpretation of the Agreement. Furthermore, India's position was not consistent with the conclusions of the Panel in *Indonesia – Autos*, which found as follows:

> On the basis of our reading of these measures applied by Indonesia under the 1993 and the 1996 car programmes, which have investment objectives and investment features and which refer to investment programmes, we find that these measures are aimed at encouraging the development of a local manufacturing capability for finished motor vehicles and parts and components in Indonesia. Inherent to this objective is that these measures necessarily have a significant impact on investment in these sectors. For this reason,

Report of the Panel

> we consider that these measures fall within any reasonable interpretation of the term "investment measures".[280]

The measures in question in this dispute were like those in *Indonesia – Autos*: they were aimed at encouraging local manufacturing capability, and they had a significant impact on investments (foreign and domestic) in that sector. As that panel said, the measures in this dispute "fall within any reasonable interpretation of the term 'investment measures'." India's only basis for its assertion appeared to be that the measures in question were "trade measures". But even if India was correct that these were "trade measures", there was no reason to think that they were not also "investment measures" (and therefore *a fortiori* "trade-related investment measures"). India certainly offered no reason to believe that a measure could only be one or the other, and there was no support for that position in the text of the TRIMs Agreement.[281] The indigenization and trade balancing requirements were precisely the sort of trade-distorting measures applied to foreign investment that the TRIMs Agreement was intended to address. India's assertion that these measures were not "investment measures" should be rejected. India also made a second argument – namely, that the trade balancing and indigenization requirements affected the car manufacturers as "buyers of kits" but not as "investors". However, India gave the Panel no textual or other basis for adopting that distinction as the basis of deciding whether a measure was an " investment measure" either. Even if one were to accept India's proposal, however, India was mistaken about the effect of the indigenization and trade balancing requirements. For example, these measures imposed additional costs on car manufacturers that lowered the return on their investment in India. Moreover, car manufacturers in India had to be structured to meet the indigenization and trade balancing requirements; these requirements therefore necessarily affected their investment planning. Furthermore, India had not responded to the other reasons the United States had presented for considering these measures as "investment measures". For instance, these measures were clearly intended to encourage investment in the Indian parts and components manufacturing industry. Indian officials had made that point publicly when they introduced Public Notice No. 60. Furthermore, the MOUs required signatories to "aggressively pursue and achieve as soon as possible the development of the local supply base".

4.170 In short, the United States believed that the Panel should reject India's argument that the indigenization and trade balancing requirements were outside the scope of the TRIMs Agreement. And, given that they were inconsistent with Articles III:4 and XI:1 of the GATT for reasons already discussed, the Panel

---

[280] Panel Report on *Indonesia – Autos*, WT/DS54/R, WT/DS55/R, WT/DS59/R, WT/DS64/R, adopted on 23 July 1998, para. 14.80 (DSR 1998:VI, 2201). The panel emphasized that its characterization of the measures as "investment measures" was based on an examination of the manner in which the measures at issue in that case related to investment, and that there might be other measures that qualified as investment measures within the meaning of the TRIMs Agreement because they relate to investment in a different manner.

[281] *Cf.* Panel Report on *EC – Bananas III*, WT/DS27/R/USA, adopted on 25 September 1997, as modified by the Appellate Body Report, para. 7.185 (DSR 1997:II, 943) ("the TRIMs Agreement does not add to or subtract from those GATT obligations, although it clarifies that Article III:4 may cover investment-related matters").

India – Autos

should further conclude that these measures were also inconsistent with Article 2 of the TRIMs Agreement.

V. ARGUMENTS OF THE THIRD PARTIES

Korea's submission to the Panel was as follows:

1. *The Agreements Regarding the Indian Measures must be Respected and Enforced*

5.1   This Panel should consider the years of negotiations and dispute settlement proceedings between India and the European Communities and India and the United States that preceded this dispute. With both the European Communities and the United States, India made due efforts to resolve the issues in a manner that met the concerns of the United States and the European Communities and provided India with the time and flexibility to restructure its automotive regime.

5.2   The United States concedes that the first proceeding regarding its claims ended with an agreement between the United States and India that the reasonable period of time for implementation "shall finally expire on 1 April 2001. Yet the United States seeks to readjudicate those same claims (and to challenge "measures" which do not yet exist). India correctly notes the subtle shift of focus by the United States in this proceeding. The earlier proceeding regarded, among other things, India's discretionary licensing scheme; this proceeding regards the application of the very same licensing scheme. Thus, the "distinction" upon which the United States relies does not appear to be a meaningful distinction. As India accurately notes, the DSB ruling covers both the text and the operation and application of the discretionary licensing system for all products notified under Article XVIII:B of the General Agreement on Tariffs and Trade (GATT 1994), including CKD and SKD kits. Therefore, the United States should have waited until the reasonable period had expired. Then, if the United States still believed that India had not fully implemented the recommendations and rulings of the DSB, it could have sought recourse under Article 21.5 of the DSU or requested consultations for the establishment of a new panel.

5.3   The above analysis of the US action applies also to the EC action. The European Communities and India reached a mutually agreed solution of the *India – Quantitative Restrictions* (WT/DS96) dispute that they notified under DSU Article 3.6.[282] As the European Communities concedes, the solution (as supplemented by the agreement on reasonable period of time between the United States and India) requires India to conform its Regime to its WTO commitments by 1 April 2001.[283] For its part, the European Communities agreed to "refrain from action under GATT Article XXII or Article XXIII as regards those restrictions

---

[282]   See WT/DS96/8, 6 May 1998. (Exhibit EC-8).
[283]   EC's First Submission, *India – Measures Affecting the Automotive Sector*, WT/DS146, WT/DS175, 16 January 2001, para. 61.

DSR 2002:V   1943

Report of the Panel

during the phasing-out period," i.e. for the Regime, until 1 April 2001.[284] Thus, the solution reached in the earlier, broader dispute (WT/DS96) applied to the Regime – the subject matter of this dispute. India has complied with the agreed-upon schedule and the 1 April 2001 deadline has yet to pass. Yet, the European Communities nonetheless has brought this proceeding and asked the Panel to address measures covered by the mutually agreed solution. The EC claim that the subject matter of the current dispute is not within the scope of WT/DS96 is based primarily on three assertions. Korea notes in paragraphs 30-37 of India's First Submission where India rebuts the EC assertions. As a review of India's presentation indicates, the subject of this dispute – the Regime –seems to be covered by the mutually agreed solution. The EC's action raises a systemic question for the WTO dispute settlement system enshrined in the DSU. A review of the DSU indicates that the preferred goal in *every* dispute settlement proceeding is a mutually agreed solution:

> ... The aim of the dispute settlement mechanism is to secure a positive solution to a dispute. A solution mutually acceptable to the parties to a dispute and consistent with the covered agreements is clearly to be preferred.[285]

The EC action seems to undermine this goal by removing any incentive to agree to a solution.

5.4   In the cases of both the US action and the EC action against India, fundamental values are at stake. Where two Members reach an agreement (as here) and formalize the agreement by notifying it to the WTO (as here), the agreement *must* be respected by both Members. Any other resolution will undermine the entire dispute settlement mechanism. Members must be able to rely on agreements they reach with other Members. This is *a fortiori* the case when, as here, the dispute is between a developing and a developed Member of the WTO.

> 2.   *The Measures that India May Take by 1 April 2001 are not, and as a Matter of Logic Cannot be, Properly before the Panel.*

5.5   The Panel should not consider any arguments regarding measures that India might propose. First, DSU Article 6.2 indicates that a complainant must "identify the specific measures at issue." Here, the European Communities and the United States could not possibly have identified post–1 April measures as "the *specific* measures at issue," because the measures do not yet exist. This is confirmed by a review of the panel requests.[286] Second, under DSU Article 7.1, the Panel's terms of reference, which set the scope of the proceeding, generally are based (and, in this proceeding, are based) on the "specific measures" identified in the panel request(s). Here, not having been specifically identified in the panel requests, measures that may or may not compose the post– 1 April Regime

---

[284]   WT/DS96/8, 6 May 1998, p. 2.
[285]   DSU, Article 3.7 (emphasis added).
[286]   See WT/DS146/4, 13 October 2000; WT/DS175/4, 18 May 2000.

1944   DSR 2002:V

are not part of the Panel's terms of reference and, thus, are not properly before the Panel. Third, a panel cannot possibly examine a measure not in existence when the panel is established. Once the panel is established and its terms of reference are set, all subsequent occurrences are not subject to review. This is because the scope of the panel's authority is defined when the panel is established.[287] In sum, all arguments by the United States and the European Communities regarding steps India may take after the date of each complaining party's panel request to comply with its mutually agreed solution with the European Communities and its agreement with the United States pursuant to DSU Article 21.3 have no subject matter (i.e. there is no actual measure to attack) and are untimely. If they wish, the United States and the European Communities may request consultations for a new panel or pursue a DSU Article 21.5 proceeding with India after 1 April 2001. But they cannot circumvent the procedures of the DSU and the terms of the understanding and the agreement with India by challenging in the current proceeding measures that do not yet exist.

3. *Prospective Measures*

5.6   As demonstrated above, the post– 1 April Regime is not within the scope of this proceeding. However, as an aside, Korea wishes to note that the post-1 April Regime described by India appears problematic. As India states, the exclusivity enjoyed by the manufacturers, on the one hand, and the commitments to mitigate the adverse impact of the imports on the balance of payment, on the other hand, constitute a "balanced whole." India has indicated that it does not intend to release the car manufacturers from the commitments they assumed under the memoranda of understanding (MOUs) in order to import SKD/CKD kits prior to 1 April 2001. But, India also has indicated that, from 1 April 2001, it no longer will make the importation of SKD/CKD kits subject to the signing of an MOU. The right to import SKD/CKD kits therefore no longer will be conditioned.

5.7   Thus, under India's plan, starting from 1 April 2001, companies already committed to the MOUs would be put in a situation where the MOU obligations are left, but most of the MOU benefits have been removed. The exclusivity granted under the MOUs has been the primary benefit given to MOU enterprises – abolishing the exclusive right to import SKD/CKD kits while maintaining obligations under the MOUs would compromise the "balanced whole" for the MOU enterprises. As a result, the continued enforcement of the MOU requirements would undermine the conditions of competition by disadvantaging companies that already have committed to India's market, in comparison with new entrants not subject to the MOU requirements.

5.8   India submits that MOU companies should not complain about the modified regime because they already have obtained a comparable advantage. India

---

[287] See *India — Quantitative Restrictions*, WT/DS90/R, adopted on 22 September 1999, as upheld by the Appellate Body Report, paras. 5.160-5.161 (DSR 1999:V, 1799) (a panel may examine only those facts existing on the date the panel was established).

DSR 2002:V

Report of the Panel

further asserts that the MOU requirements imposed after 1 April 2001 are merely a *pure* "obligation to manufacture" or "requirements to sell goods in foreign markets in preference to the domestic market" and, thus, are consistent with the WTO agreements.[288]

5.9   Korea reminds India that the MOU companies undertook these obligations in exchange for the exclusive right to import for the duration of the MOU period. For India to remove this right but maintain the MOU obligations would be unfair to the MOU companies. India's continuation of the MOU requirements cannot be separated from the existing Regime and interpreted as merely an imposition of a *new* "obligation to manufacture" or "requirements to sell goods in foreign markets in preference to the domestic market." Rather, it is a *continuation* of the commitments made by the MOU companies as a reward of obtaining the exclusive right to import SKD/CKD kits prior to 1 April 2001. In other words, the post-1 April Regime sketched by India would establish not merely an "obligation to manufacture" or a "requirements to sell goods in foreign markets in preference to the domestic market" – it would establish an obligation and requirement, *compliance with which is necessary to obtain an advantage (which was already exhausted)*. This, of course, would be inconsistent with India's obligations under the TRIMs Agreement and under GATT 1994.

5.10   Moreover, no provision of the WTO agreements justifies imposing disadvantages on the basis of having provided advantages in the past. If such an "cross-temporal balancing" were allowed, the basic nature – the "immediacy and unconditionality" – of the MFN obligation[289] would be compromised. Korea invites India to consider the above points as it decides how to alter the Regime.

VI.   INTERIM REVIEW

6.1   The interim report of the Panel was issued to the parties on 12 October 2001. The parties submitted their comments on 26 October 2001. India expressed its request for a meeting in conditional terms, indicating that it requested a meeting "if the Panel were to decide to make in its final report any findings on whether the violations ceased to exist as a result of events that occurred during the panel proceedings".

6.2   In the view of the Panel, the purpose of an interim review meeting is not to provide the parties with an opportunity to introduce new legal issues and evidence or to enter into a debate with the Panel. In the view of the panel, the purpose of the interim review stage is to consider specific and particular aspects of the interim report as requested by the parties. In this instance, the Panel did not feel that it would have been appropriate to make a decision to hold a meeting on the basis of the *outcome* of the interim review process, of which the meeting is a part. In addition, the Panel was of the view that it would not have been in accordance with requirements of due process for the Panel to pronounce on any

---

[288]   India's First Submission, paras. 10-12.
[289]   See GATT 1994 Article I:1; General Agreement on Trade in Services, Article II.1.

1946   DSR 2002:V

changes it may make to its findings and recommendations as suggested by India before hearing the views of the other parties on the issues raised by India. Consequently, the Panel decided to hold the meeting on the basis of India's request in order to allow the parties to exchange views on the specific and particular aspects of the interim report on which a review has been requested, without prejudice to the outcome of this interim review process.

6.3   An interim review meeting was held on 19 November 2001.

A.   Comments on the Descriptive Part

1.   Comments by the United States

6.4   All of the comments made by the United States on the draft descriptive were accepted by the Panel. A number of points, not heretofore reflected in the descriptive part, were incorporated.

2.   Comments by India

6.5   India suggested that the descriptive part of the report be restructured, in order to address the preliminary procedural issues first, and that subtitles be phrased either in terms of questions, claims or arguments but not a mix of all three. The Panel considered this acceptable and the descriptive part of the report was accordingly restructured and subtitles adjusted in accordance with India's suggestion.

6.6   At the end of the factual section (II.A), India wished to add that "Since the removal of these restrictions, importers of cars no longer have to sign an MOU to obtain an import license and the signatories of the MOUs, including those with accrued export obligations, are now free to import any amount of cars and components". The United States objected, by letter, dated 13 August 2001, as it considered that this issue was actually a subject of debate during the proceedings and should not be included in the factual section. The Panel agreed with the United States that this point was clarified by India during the panel proceedings. The section of the report titled Factual Aspects (II) records all relevant and undisputed facts available to the Panel. Since, in this case, many of the facts required clarification, the report contains a first section under Arguments of the Parties, Factual Arguments (IV.A).

6.7   India also requested that its requests to the Panel be summarized in a more coherent fashion. The Panel accepted the redraft to India's requests for findings (III.C).

6.8   In section IV.B, concerned with whether the matter had been settled and adjudicated, India wished a redraft of a concluding paragraph regarding its argument. Since the additions suggested by India were a compilation and not found as a whole in the written evidence, the Panel has included similar language found in India's second submission. (para. 4.53)

6.9   In response to comments made by the United States, India submitted additional comments on 20 August. However, many of the comments made by In-

Report of the Panel

dia had either (a) been reflected elsewhere in the report, (b) could not be found reflected in the written evidence or (c) inferred the Panel's use of editorial license to a less than comfortable degree.

3. Comments by the European Communities

6.10 The European Communities informed the panel that it had no comments on the draft descriptive part of the report.

B. Comments on the Findings and Conclusions

1. Comments by the United States

6.11 The United States made only a limited number of comments on the Panel's findings.

6.12 It suggested clarification of the language in paragraph 7.86 concerning the reference to the panel *India – Quantitative Restrictions*. The Panel found this clarification helpful and revised the paragraph accordingly. The United States also suggested clarifying paragraph 7.190 by expressly indicating that the reference to contract law concerned "Indian" contract law. The Panel agreed with this suggestion and adapted the paragraph accordingly.

6.13 The United States commented on a portion of paragraph 7.287 which, in its view, was questionable because it read it to assume a certain assignment of burden of proof to parties participating in domestic proceedings concerning safeguards, anti-dumping or countervailing determinations. While it had not been the intention of the Panel, in that paragraph, to draw any such conclusions or inferences, the Panel accepted to revise the paragraph in order to avoid any misunderstanding on this issue.

6.14 In paragraph 7.211, which describes one of the factual elements of the trade balancing obligation, the United States suggested adding a reference to the fact that the complainants had specifically claimed its existence, in order to make clear that the complainants presented a *prima facie* case on this point. The Panel added the reference suggested, because it found it to be factually correct and a useful addition to the description of the facts of the case. However, the Panel wishes to stress that, in its view, the mere statement that the complainants asserted the existence of a certain fact or measure, as in this instance, in no way amounts to the demonstration of a *prima facie* case of violation in relation to the said measure. The addition of this reference to the complainants' factual assertion therefore cannot be read to constitute in itself an assertion by the Panel that the complainants had presented a *prima facie* case on this issue. The legal analysis of the relevant claims is conducted at a later stage.

6.15 The United States requested a reflection, in footnote 464 of the fact that the meaning of the notion of moving "out of the ambit of the MOU" had been disputed and suggested that the notion should either not be reflected in its current form or clarified in light of the parties' disagreements on its meaning. The Panel did not find it necessary, for the purposes of reaching its conclusions and recommendations, to make an express finding on the meaning of the notion. However, the footnote was clarified to reflect the differences of view between the parties as to its interpretation.

2. *Comments by the European Communities*

6.16   The European Communities commented on certain paragraphs where they felt that its position had not been adequately reflected, and pointed to two instances in which it questioned the appropriateness of the Panel's statements on specific issues.

6.17   The European Communities requested a rectification in the description of their claims in paragraph 7.21. The Panel rectified this paragraph accordingly, because it agreed that the rectification requested provided a more accurate description of the claims developed by the European Communities before the Panel.

6.18   In footnote 414, the Panel added the relevant reference to the European Communities' argument as requested by it.

6.19   The European Communities argued that the Panel confused, in certain paragraphs (7.213, 7.229, and 8.13) two distinct arguments it had presented, namely (1) an argument concerning the scope of the trade balancing requirement, and (2) an argument concerning the duration of the trade balancing obligation beyond 1 April 2001. The Panel accepted the changes suggested by the European Communities and revised paragraph 7.213 of the report to reflect the European Communities' two arguments. In paragraph 7.229, the Panel deleted the last sentence and added the European Communities' second argument in paragraph 7.235. The Panel then addressed the European Communities' second argument in paragraphs 7.278 and 8.57.

6.20   The European Communities noted that paragraphs 7.230 and 7.232, which contain an analysis of the scope of the trade balancing obligation, do not fully reflect the indication provided by the European Communities that it did not have the relevant information at its disposal, or the fact that India had not presented supporting evidence for its own assertions. For the sake of clarity and completeness, the Panel added further indications of the elements before it, as submitted by all parties. However, this did not lead to any alteration of its general conclusion on the issue at stake.

6.21   The European Communities suggested that footnote 364, which elaborates on some of the systemic issues which might come into play in assessing the role of mutually agreed solutions under the DSU in subsequent disputes, was not necessary to the Panel's analysis and thus inappropriately made. The Panel is certainly fully aware that its role is not to engage in general systemic discussions divorced from what is necessary to the resolution of the dispute at hand. However, this footnote plays a specific role in the Panel's reasoning, in explaining why the Panel is not convinced by the European Communities' argument relating to the fact that a mutually agreed solution is not a "covered agreement" under the DSU as a sufficient reason for dismissing its potential relevance in subsequent

Report of the Panel

proceedings. The Panel has therefore decided to maintain the essential substance of this footnote, while clarifying its language in order to explain why it is instrumental to its reasoning.

6.22   The European Communities found that a specific assertion by the Panel on the potential impact of its rulings in these proceedings in subsequent "inter-party" determinations concerning the trade balancing conditions was beyond its jurisdiction to assess. The Panel modified this part of paragraph 7.234 in order to clarify that the objective of the disputed statement was merely to assert that it was not this Panel's mandate or objective to make or prejudge, beyond its mandate under the DSU, any future determinations which might be made on the scope of obligations on individual manufacturers in other contexts.

3.   *Comments by India*

6.23   India's comments concentrated exclusively on the Recommendations section of the report. In its view, the entire analysis conducted by the Panel under this section was inappropriate, and it suggested the deletion of the entire analysis conducted in paragraphs 8.6 to 8.26, where the Panel assessed, in light of the events argued by India to have occurred in the course of the proceedings, whether it could appropriately make recommendations under Article 19.1 of the DSU that India bring its measures into conformity with its obligations under the GATT 1994.

6.24   India suggested instead that the Panel, following its finding that India's measures were in violation of its obligations under GATT articles III and XI, simply make a recommendation as per Article 19.1 that India "bring its measures into conformity with the agreements", and "note that India claimed that it has taken measures to bring its measures into conformity with its obligations under the GATT 1994", and that since this assertion is being challenged by the complainants, it should be left to a compliance panel to assess whether that is the case.

6.25   The United States and the European Communities responded in detail to India's comments during the interim review meeting, and their arguments will be also reflected in this section. In light of all the parties' comments, and for the reasons explained below, the Panel decided to maintain a detailed analysis of the implications of the events which took place in the course of the proceedings, in particular as of 1 April 2001, but it modified its analysis in order to clarify further its approach in this section. Since India's comments affect the whole analysis under the Recommendations section, rather than merely individual paragraphs, the Panel will address here successively the legal arguments at stake rather than proceeding with a paragraph by paragraph analysis.

6.26   India raises three principal arguments in support of its position, and also raised more generally a concern of due process to the effect that the Panel's analysis of the post-April situation was entirely unexpected and that, had India realized that the Panel would engage in such an analysis, it would have presented relevant evidence. This procedural issue is addressed first.

1950   DSR 2002:V

India – Autos

(a) General Comment in Respect of India's Procedural Rights in the Proceedings

6.27   India argues that "the Panel embarked on a completely unprecedented approach not foreseen in the DSU without giving any prior indication to that effect. Neither the complainants nor India could therefore have possibly expected the Panel to make the rulings set out in the Recommendations Section. It is irreconcilable with the most basic principles of procedural justice for a tribunal to make a ruling on issues which the disputant parties could not reasonably expect any rulings and on which they could therefore not provide all the evidence available to them."[290] In particular, India argues that if the parties to the dispute could have anticipated that the Panel would determine whether the measures at issue have remained in violation, they would no doubt have exchanged further evidence and arguments on this point. India argues in this context that the Panel's analysis is factually incomplete and, *inter alia*, that it "saw no reason to inform the Panel of the fact that Public Notice No. 60 no longer exists because this was not relevant to any of the issues that the Panel had been requested to address".

6.28   The Panel disagrees with India's assertion that it was unpredictable to it that the Panel would address the issue of whether the measures remained in violation after 1 April 2001, or more generally the impact of events having occurred after the requests for establishment of this Panel, including the effect of the removal of the import licensing regime as of 1 April 2001, on the claims presented to it.

6.29   In reality, it was clear in these proceedings from the very first exchange of submissions that the elimination of India's import licensing regime in the course of the proceedings, as described by India itself, was an important part of the issues in discussion throughout the proceedings. The issue of the effects of this event was brought to the Panel's attention from the beginning of the proceedings, in the context of various arguments.

6.30   In its first submission, India divided its legal arguments in two sections, one of which related exclusively to the measures to be applied by India after 1 April 2001. Clearly, India argued principally that the Panel should have refrained in the first instance from examining these measures as they stood as of the date of its establishment, that is, in the context of the import licensing regime, and India also argued that the Panel should have found any measures India may apply as of 1 April 2001 to be outside its terms of reference. The Panel recalls that it concluded, however, that it was competent to examine the measures as they existed at the time of its establishment and that it would, indeed, not be considering any subsequent measures that India might take for the enforcement of the existing measures before it. Nonetheless, India also presented extensive arguments and evidence concerning the situation after 1 April 2001 beyond these jurisdictional arguments. India expressly argued, as part of its legal argumentation in response to the claims, that the measures that it would be applying as from 1 April would be consistent with its obligations under the GATT and the

---

[290]   Comments on Interim Report by India, para. 15.

DSR 2002:V

Report of the Panel

TRIMs Agreement. Indeed, the very first section of India's legal argument in its first submission is entirely devoted to this issue.[291]

6.31   Indeed, as reflected in Section II of this report (which was inserted using India's very own words), India's latest articulation of its requests for findings to the Panel prior to the issuance of the interim report, clearly suggests that it anticipated that these events were of potential relevance in determining the type of recommendations to be made under Article 19.1 of the DSU and requested the Panel to take them into account, were it to decide to examine the measures as they existed and operated under India's import licensing regime. It stated that:

> If the Panel were to conclude that the operation of Public Notice No. 60 and the trade balancing provisions under India's former licensing regime was inconsistent with the GATT, it should – following the practice of other panels – note that the licensing regime had been abolished on 1 April 2001 and that it was *therefore* not necessary for the Panel to recommend to the DSB in accordance with Article 19:1 of the DSU that it request India to bring these measures into conformity with the GATT. (emphasis added)

6.32   In addition, India presented arguments in the course of the proceedings to the effect that only one manufacturer had yet to achieve the required level of indigenization and, as it highlights itself in its interim comments, requested the Panel to "limit any recommendation under Article 19.1 of the DSU to the indigenization requirement that remains to be performed by that particular company with respect to that model"[292], thereby inviting a consideration of events having taken place in the course of the proceedings in the Panel's Recommendations under Article 19.1.

6.33   It is therefore clear, in the Panel's view, not only that India could reasonably have expected that the Panel would or could address the impact of the events which occurred in the course of the proceedings, but that it could also reasonably anticipate that the consideration of these issues might be specifically relevant to the Panel's recommendations under Article 19.1 of the DSU, as reflected in its own requests for findings.

6.34   It is worth noting in this respect also that the complainants, in addition to disagreeing with India's assertion that it was not provided with a full opportunity to present arguments on the events at issue, also do not deny that they themselves had the opportunity to respond to these arguments. Indeed, as will be noted below, the expression of their requests for findings to the Panel reflects this.

6.35   Paragraphs 8.4 to 8.30 of the Recommendations Section of the Report have been developed in order to present more fully the arguments of the parties to clarify further the issue before the Panel in the circumstances of this case.

6.36   Finally, with regard to India's allegation that it was not provided with adequate opportunity to present evidence and arguments in relation to the elements of relevance to the Panel's analysis in its recommendations section, the

---

[291]   See First submission of India, paras. 10 and following.
[292]   See Comments on the Interim Report by India, para. 16.

1952   DSR 2002:V

Panel notes that the only new piece of evidence presented by India was evidence of repeal of Public Notice No. 60, which it had previously stated was not a necessary action for it to take.[293]

> (b) India's Argument that the Matters Addressed in the Recommendations Section Should be Left to a Compliance Panel

6.37 India argues that the analysis conducted by the Panel under its Recommendations section should have been left to a compliance panel. In this argument, India draws a distinction between a panel's obligation under Article 19.1 of the DSU to recommend that a violating measure be brought into conformity and the distinct question of whether and how the respondent has complied with this obligation, which is a matter for a compliance panel under Article 21.5.

6.38 India argues that Article 21.5 "does not distinguish between measures taken during the panel proceeding" and those taken after the completion of its work. In the view of India, a disagreement on this issue, even occurring before the end of the initial panel proceedings, should be left to a compliance panel, and the role of the initial panel should only be to take into account the situation existing as of the request for establishment of the panel and record the parties' disagreement as to subsequent evolutions.

6.39 The Panel first wishes to clarify the scope of the issue at stake here: contrary to India's assertion, the Panel did not aim to analyze, under its Recommendations Section, any measures which it had previously found to be outside its terms of reference: the analysis relates *not* to any new measure which India might have taken in the course of the proceedings. Its exclusive objective was to examine the status of those measures which the Panel *had* identified to be covered by its terms of reference in order to determine the nature and extent of the Recommendations it should make to the DSB in relation to *those* measures.

6.40 The issue at stake here therefore relates exclusively to the extent to which it was appropriate for this Panel to seek to address any evolutions of the matter squarely within its terms of reference which might have occurred in the course of the proceedings and the form in which it may address them.

6.41 In the particular circumstances of this case, and for the reasons further elaborated in paragraphs 8.31 to 8.63, the Panel found that the most appropriate way to discharge its mandate under the DSU was to conduct an analysis of the issues presented to it regarding evolutions having arguably affected the matter before it in the course of the proceedings in the context of its section on Recommendations.

6.42 However, the Panel wishes to answer here the systemic argument raised by India that the matter it addresses in this section should have been left to a compliance panel and that "Article 21.5 does not distinguish between measures taken during the panel proceeding and those taken after the panel's work is com-

---

[293] See First Submission of India, para. 14.

DSR 2002:V

Report of the Panel

pleted", and that the issue of "how" a violating Member might bring its measures into conformity was not within the competence of this Panel under Article 19.1.

6.43   In response to India's arguments concerning the competence of an Article 21.5 panel on the matters addressed by this Panel in its Recommendations section, both complainants noted that a 21.5 compliance panel in any case only comes into play following recommendations by the DSB to bring certain measures into conformity with the relevant Agreements.[294] The role of a compliance panel is precisely to address "disagreement as to the existence or consistency with a covered agreement of measures taken to comply with the recommendations and rulings" of a previous panel. The Panel notes, in this regard, that the Appellate Body in *US – Shrimp (21.5)* stated that Article 21.5 of the DSU involves "in principle, not the original measures, but a new and different measure that was not before the original panel".

6.44   The Panel agrees that, reading the terms of Article 21.5 in their ordinary meaning in accordance with the customary rules of interpretation reflected in Article 31 of the Vienna Convention, the formal conditions of a compliance panel are in any case manifestly not met, since no ruling or recommendation had yet been made, let alone adopted in this instance. Furthermore, the Panel in this instance is no way attempting to pre-empt, in its analysis, what a compliance panel might be led to examine in the future. The definition of a compliance panel's role actually assists in distinguishing it from the analysis conducted by this Panel: as previously noted, the sole aim of the analysis conducted in the Panel's recommendations section is to determine whether it was still appropriate to make a recommendation notwithstanding India's assertion that the legal situation had fundamentally changed and that there was nothing left to bring into compliance. In concluding that such a recommendation was appropriate, the Panel did not attempt to indicate *how* India was to bring the relevant measures into compliance, or to prejudge on any future developments which may later occur following such recommendations, which might, if need be, be referred to a compliance panel.

6.45   The Panel also notes that India disputes the reference made to the Appellate Body's report on *US – Certain EC Products*, to the effect that where a panel has found a measure no longer to exist, it is logically inconsistent for it to make a recommendation that that measure be brought into conformity with the concerned Member's obligations under the covered Agreements. In India's view, this reference is inappropriate because it concerned a case where both parties agreed that the measure had ceased to apply, which is not the case here. In response to India's arguments, both complainants argued that the facts of that case did not suggest, as argued by India, that the parties were simply in agreement on discontinuation of the measure. Indeed, the Panel notes that there were some disputed factual contentions in that case concerning the definition of the measure at issue, which were addressed explicitly by the panel and the Appellate Body. These suggest that the Appellate Body's observation concerning the appropriate-

---

[294]   See Oral Statement by the European Communities at the interim review meeting, para. 3, and Oral Statement by the United States at the interim review meeting, para. 11.

1954   DSR 2002:V

ness of the recommendation foreseen in Article 19.1 of the DSU was not a mere suggestion that the panel should have simply "endorsed" an agreement of the parties on the cessation of the measures. It also suggests that, contrary to India's suggestion, the agreement of the parties on the fact that the measure has ceased to apply was not the primary source of the Appellate Body's conclusion.

6.46 More significantly perhaps, the Panel notes also that the Appellate Body's motivation in that case does not rely on the alleged fact that the *parties* had agreed that the measure no longer existed but rather on the fact that "*the Panel has found*" that the measure no longer exists. That panel was therefore not considered by the Appellate Body to be simply "endorsing" a fact agreed on by the parties, but rather had made its own finding as to the continued existence of the measure at issue. Accordingly, the Panel has not modified its reference to this report of the Appellate Body.

(c)   India's Argument that the Panel could not "properly" Conclude that the Violation is Still in Existence

6.47 While India does not contest that there can be no sense in making a recommendation to bring into conformity a measure of which a panel is properly of the view that the violation has ceased to exist, it challenges that the Panel can, in this instance, properly have *any* view on the matter. One of India's arguments in this respect is that the Panel cannot reach this conclusion because the facts are in dispute. The Panel will merely note in this respect that it is the essence of any litigation process to reach conclusions, where appropriate, on disputed issues. What is more pertinent is whether there was a proper legal basis for the Panel's analysis.

6.48 India argues in this respect that the terms of reference of a panel are limited to the matter referred to it by the DSB, which excludes, in the view of India, any matters arising in the course of the proceedings. At this point, the Panel merely wishes to recall its earlier observation that it did *not* examine any new measures adopted subsequent to the requests for its establishment, having found that such measures were not within its terms of reference and indeed, had not been the object of any claims by the complainants. The Panel's Recommendations section concerns exclusively those measures that *were in existence* at the time of both complainants' requests for establishment of panels, and which were within its terms of reference. The detailed reasons which led the Panel, in the circumstances of this case, to consider events subsequent to the Panel's establishment in the context of its recommendations are reflected in paragraphs 8.31 to 8.63 of the revised Recommendations section.

6.49 India also argues that neither the United States nor the European Communities asked the Panel to make any of the rulings set out in the Recommendations section of the Report. However, as will be also further reflected in the revised Recommendations section, both complainants, either spontaneously or in reaction to India's arguments and the Panel's questions, had clarified the nature of the findings they were requesting, and this included a request for findings that the

Report of the Panel

measures were inconsistent and a recommendation that they be brought into conformity with India's obligations. While it is true that both complainants argued that the changes subsequent to 1 April 2001 did not affect the nature of their legal claims, they both consequently also argued that the measures should be found to have *remained* inconsistent with the same provisions.

6.50   While they did not necessarily request that such findings be made separately in the context of the Recommendations section as was done by the Panel[295], the complainants certainly envisaged that the Panel may be led to consider the continued existence of violating measures, since they were arguing that these measures continued to be in violation and expected the Panel to make a finding to that effect. The fact that the complainants may not have requested the Panel's assessment of this matter in a particular form does not alter the Panel's general obligation, under Article 11 of the DSU, to make an objective assessment of the matter before it and to assess how best to fulfil its mandate in this regard within the limits of its terms of reference. This matter included, in this instance, the measures and claims identified in the requests for establishment of a panel, and the Panel was required, under its terms of reference, to make such findings as will assist the DSB in making recommendations or in giving the rulings provided for in the relevant agreements concerning this matter. For these reasons, and those further elaborated in paragraphs 8.15 and following, the Panel disagrees with India that its Recommendations section was outside the scope of what was submitted to it under its terms of reference.

6.51   India also argued that the Panel's recommendations were based on incomplete evidence, in particular because it did not, in India's view, take account of the arguments produced by India concerning the levels of indigenization reached by individual MOU signatories. The Panel notes that it had in fact reflected India's statement in this regard in paragraph 8.22 of its original recommendations. However, this had not altered the Panel's general legal conclusion on the matter. The relevant paragraphs have been expanded to further clarify the Panel's analysis in this respect and reflect the parties' most recent exchanges on this matter (see paragraphs 8.46 to 8.49).

6.52   The Panel notes also that India produced new evidence to the effect that Public Notice No. 60 has been repealed, indicating that it previously had no reason to suspect that this could be relevant to the Panel's analysis and therefore did not produce it before. The Panel cannot agree with India's argument for not producing this piece of evidence earlier, namely that it did not suspect that the issue would be of any relevance to the Panel's analysis. In fact, as noted earlier, both India and the complainants addressed this issue expressly in the course of the proceedings, and India had devoted a section of one of its earlier submissions to the argument that Public Notice No. 60 did not need to be repealed.

6.53   Leaving aside the issue that this last argument raises as to the actual relevance of the new piece of evidence produced, even in India's own view, the Panel considered whether it was appropriate to accept it at this late stage of the

---

[295]   See Oral Statement of the United States at the interim review meeting, para. 22.

1956   DSR 2002:V

proceedings. The complainants had diverging views on the matter, since the European Communities expressed no opposition while the United States thought it inadmissible.[296]

6.54 Certainly, the Panel can only regret that a piece of evidence concerning a matter which was, in its view, clearly within the purview of matters discussed in the proceedings, was produced at such a late stage in the proceedings. In the interest of completeness, and in keeping with its general approach in its recommendations, the Panel nonetheless decided to accept to consider the new evidence, in light also of the fact that this evidence only sought to confirm the official status of the measure as it had already been argued and discussed during the proceedings. It therefore did not bring into the debates any fundamentally new issue that would have required extensive additional discussion among the parties. This new evidence is taken into account in paragraphs 8.35 and following and 8.60 and following.

(d)   India's Argument that the Panel Inappropriately Prescribes a "retrospective" remedy

6.55 India challenges the Panel's analysis of "residual" export obligations as having accrued in relation to past imports and its conclusion that they are therefore not of a different nature from any of the previously accrued export obligations, even if no import licenses are currently being generated. In India's view, this implies that the Panel is requesting it to "remove the consequences of a past illegal act" and thus providing a retrospective remedy not foreseen by the DSU, whose remedies are limited to "the cessation of the illegal act".

6.56 While India's systemic concern that the DSU generally does not aim at providing "retrospective" remedies may be valid, this is not, in the Panel's view, what the Panel has done here.

6.57 The Panel has not sought, in its analysis, to determine the nature or modalities of remedies to be provided by India, beyond determining *whether* there was still a need to make a recommendation to the DSB in order to remedy an identified violation. What the Panel has sought to address in this section is what remains as of *today* of a measure found to be illegal. The Panel has said nothing of any *past* fulfilment of export obligations or of any need to compensate manufacturers for any such *past executions* of illegal obligations.

6.58 To the extent that this issue is even one of remedy, it is one of prospective remedy, not retrospective as argued by India. Indeed, the Panel's analysis corresponds to what India itself identifies as the correct interpretation of remedies under the WTO: the "cessation of an illegal act", for the future. By contrast, the implementation of the rulings in the *Australia – Automotive Leather II* case referred to by India in its interim comments[297], involved repayment of subsidies already paid over past years, which is clearly "retrospective".

---

[296] See ibid, para. 19.
[297] See Comments on the Interim Report by India, para. 28.

DSR 2002:V

Report of the Panel

6.59 Overall, including for the reasons above, the Panel was not convinced by India's arguments that it inappropriately performed the role of a compliance panel, or made rulings on issues not within its terms of reference, or provided any retrospective remedy in its Recommendations Section. However, the Panel is fully aware that the approach it has chosen to adopt here as a result of the particular circumstances of the case is not one that will necessarily be appropriate in other cases. In revising the Section in light of the parties' comments, the Panel was mindful to fully explain the purpose of its analysis and the specific circumstances which led it to adopt this approach in order to fulfill its mandate under the DSU, and to adapt as appropriate its whole analysis with a view to clarifying its exact nature and scope.

6.60 The Panel notes in this respect the concern expressed by the United States that while it was understandable in the circumstances of this case that the Panel chose to introduce this analysis, in particular in light of India's arguments, this should not be seen to suggest that there is a general obligation for panels to systematically "reassess", at the time of their recommendations, the existence of previously established violations. As is explained in detail in the revised Recommendations section, the Panel agrees that the approach it has chosen to follow here does not, indeed, imply such a general obligation. However, in conclusion, the Panel must point out to parties that the way in which they plead a case and develop their arguments cannot but have repercussions on the reasoning and conclusions of the Panel; if it were otherwise, the Panel would be derelict in its duty under Article 11 of the DSU to make an objective assessment of the matter before it.

VII. FINDINGS

7.1 This dispute is based on the facts described in Section II above. The parties' claims and requests for findings are summarized in Section III of our Report.[298]

7.2 In this case, the United States and European Communities successively requested the establishment of panels concerning certain matters. The DSB decided, in accordance with Article 9 of the DSU, to entrust a single panel with the examination of both complaints.[299]

7.3 Both the United States and European Communities allege violations of Articles III:4 and XI:1 of GATT and of Article 2 of the TRIMs Agreement in relation to certain Indian measures affecting the automotive industry. Although these claims related to the same measures, they partly differed in their specific details. As a consequence, the Panel has sought to carefully reflect these differences in its report. It has also been mindful to organize its examination and present its findings to the DSB in such a manner as to in no way impair the rights

---

[298] As will be apparent from the following section, some of the facts of the case were a subject of debate.
[299] See paragraphs 1.3 and 1.4 of this Report for details.

1958

DSR 2002:V

which the parties to the dispute would have enjoyed had separate panels examined the complaints. This is in conformity with the requirements of Article 9.2 of the DSU. Neither party having requested the submission of separate reports as foreseen in Article 9.2 of the DSU, this report addresses both the United States and the European Communities complaints in a single report.

7.4   India has raised defenses relating to the exact nature of the matter before the Panel and the extent of its jurisdiction. These jurisdictional arguments, which condition the Panel's ability to proceed further with the analysis of the claims, are addressed first. Before doing so, this Report begins with an examination of preliminary issues that arose in the course of the proceedings relating to the clarification of the claims. The Report then clarifies the measures within the Panel's terms of reference. This will assist the Panel in subsequently addressing the detail of India's procedural arguments.

A.   Clarification of the Claims in the Course of the Proceedings and Requests for Preliminary Rulings

7.5   During the first meeting with the parties, India requested the Panel to ask the complainants a number of questions in order to clarify the claims. India indicated that, depending on the complainants' answers to these questions, it would seek preliminary rulings from the Panel concerning the precise scope of the complaints. These requests for clarification and the Panel's approach to them will be detailed in this section.

7.6   At the first meeting,

(1)   India requested the Panel to ask the complainants whether the measures on which they were requesting rulings were those that India was applying at the time when the requests for the establishment of a panel were submitted to the DSB or conversely, whether the measures were those that India might be applying as from 1 April 2001. It advised that "[i]f the complainants were to respond that they consider India's future measures to be part of the present proceedings, [India] would request the Panel to issue a preliminary ruling to the effect that these measures fall outside of its mandate".[300]

(2)   India also requested the Panel to ask the complainants to clarify whether in their view, the measures at issue in this proceeding involved the enforcement of MOUs through the import licensing regime and PN60, or conversely, whether the claims were limited to the enforcement of MOUs outside the licensing regime and PN60. It advised that "[i]f the complainants were to respond that their complaints relate to the enforcement of the MOUs through the import licensing regime and Notice N° 60, India would ask the Panel to issue a preliminary ruling to the effect that both complaints are

---

[300]   See Statement of India at the First substantive meeting, para. 8.

DSR 2002:V

Report of the Panel

inadmissible because the DSU cannot be invoked in respect of the same matter twice."[301]

7.7   In response to this request, the Panel invited the parties to ask each other any questions that they felt might be useful. It indicated its own intention to ask the parties a range of questions, including questions relating to the preliminary issues raised by India. The Panel indicated that, if necessary, it would revert to the issue of preliminary rulings depending upon the parties' responses to these questions. This approach was in line with the "conditional" character of India's request for preliminary rulings. In the view of the Panel, it was also appropriate to seek further clarifications on the nature of the matter before it. [302]

7.8   In light of the complainants' responses to questions, India indicated in its second submission that:

"the European Communities and the United States appear[ed] to accept the validity of [India's] arguments because they made two matters clear. First, the European Communities and the United States clarified that their complaints are not directed against the application of discretionary licensing system to cars and components but against Public Notice No. 60 and the MOUs as such. Second, the European Communities and the United States clarified that their complaints relate to the measures applied by India at the time when they submitted their requests for the establishment to the DSB, and not to any measures that India may take in the future. With these clarifications as to the scope of the rulings requested from this Panel, two central arguments that India had advanced in its First Submission are no longer relevant. India's argument that no WTO Member may resort to the DSU on the same matter twice is no longer relevant because the European Communities and the United States have made clear that their case does not rest on the application of the discretionary licensing system that had been the subject of their prior complaints. India's argument that the Panel is not competent to rule on measures that India may take after 1 April 2001 is also no longer relevant."

7.9   At that stage therefore, India did not pursue its initial request for a preliminary ruling, and the Panel did not revert to it.

---

[301]   *Ibid.*

[302]   We recall in this respect the observation made by the panel in *Canada – Measures Affecting the Export of Civilian Aircraft*, (hereinafter "*Canada – Aircraft*"), WT/DS70/R, DSR 1999:IV, 1443, that "in our view, there is no requirement in the DSU for panels to rule on preliminary issues prior to the parties' first written submissions. Nor is there any established practice to this effect, for there are numerous panel reports where rulings on preliminary issues have been reserved until the final report. Furthermore, there may be cases where the panel wishes to seek further clarification from the parties before providing a preliminary ruling." para 9.15. In this case, the request for a preliminary ruling came at a later stage in the proceedings, and was by its own terms conditional upon further clarifications. In the view of the Panel, these clarifications helped in identifying the matter sufficiently to make it possible, to proceed without a preliminary ruling while taking care to ensure full respect for due process requirements for all parties.

1960   DSR 2002:V

India – Autos

7.10   However, India made other comments at the same stage that led the Panel to believe that there was still some confusion between the parties as to the exact scope of the claims and that India's comments above were conditional. In particular, India indicated two paragraphs below the above quotation that it would:

> "assume throughout this submission that the Panel will examine the operation of Public Notice No. 60 and the MOUs as such, that is independently of the application of the discretionary licensing system. Specifically, India will assume that the Panel will examine *whether the trade balancing and indigenization provisions set out in Public Notice No. 60 and the MOUs would have been inconsistent with Articles III:4 and XI:1 of the GATT even if India had not applied any import licensing restrictions for cars imported in the form of CKD/SKD kits and for car components at the time when the requests for the establishment of a panel were submitted.* If the Panel does not share this understanding of the scope of the complaints, India would appreciate it if the Panel were to alert India to that effect before the next meeting and give it the opportunity to make a supplementary written submission." (emphasis in original)[303]

7.11   The Panel did not consider it appropriate to simply endorse or reject India's reading of the claims before it as suggested. Rather, it believed it was appropriate, and in conformity with the requirements of due process, to ensure that the complainants were given an opportunity to clarify the claims further in order to ensure India a full opportunity to respond comprehensively to the claims as presented.

7.12   In a letter sent to the parties prior to the second meeting, the Panel therefore declined to make the interpretation of the claims before it as suggested by India. Instead, it invited the parties, including India, to present all the arguments that they felt may be of relevance in the course of the second meeting so as to allow the Panel to make an objective assessment of the matter before it, as required by Article 11 of the DSU.[304]

---

[303] Second Submission of India, para. 4.

[304] The Panel addressed the following message to the parties prior to the second meeting:
"The Panel wishes to respond to a point raised in the Indian submission, in order to ensure that all parties are in a position to prepare themselves adequately for the second substantive meeting.
       In paragraph 4 of its second submission, India indicates that "[i]n light of the clarifications provided by the complainants, India will assume throughout this submission that the Panel will examine the operation of Public Notice No. 60 and the MOUs as such, that is independently of the application of the discretionary licensing system. Specifically, India will assume that the Panel will examine whether the trade balancing and indigenization provisions set out in Public Notice No. 60 and the MOUs would have been inconsistent with Articles III:4 and Article XI:1 of the GATT even if India had not applied any import restrictions for cars imported in the form of SKD/CKD kits and for car components at the time when the requests for the establishment of a panel were submitted". India then invites the Panel to alert India before the meeting if it does not share its understanding of the scope of

DSR 2002:V   1961

Report of the Panel

7.13   The Panel then put a number of additional questions to the parties after the second meeting. These included questions to India concerning its understanding of the claims following exchanges between the parties in the course of the second meeting. The Panel wished to further ensure that India was in a position to present the arguments and defenses it wished to rely on, in light of the complainants' latest clarifications. In the Panel's view, this procedure adequately preserved the interests of all parties, including India's opportunities to respond fully to the claims presented.

7.14   In light of the evolving factual circumstances and successive clarifications in the course of the proceedings, the Panel sought to give the parties adequate opportunity at each stage to pursue the possibility of reaching a mutually satisfactory solution, as required by the final sentence of Article 11 of the DSU. The Panel thus drew the parties' attention to this provision at each of its formal meetings with them and when so requested, afforded them additional time to present their submissions to the Panel.

B.   Clarification of the Measures within the Terms of Reference of this Panel

7.15   India has raised a number of arguments relating to the competence of this Panel to examine the claims before it. Some of these arguments relate to the identification of the measures properly within the Panel's terms of reference. Since these terms of reference determine a panel's jurisdiction[305], the Panel will start its analysis with a clarification of the measures articulated within those terms. In this context, it addresses India's arguments relating specifically to the ambit of the measures under review.

7.16   This initial clarification of the measures before the Panel will also assist in addressing, in the next section of the Report, India's other arguments relating to the Panel's competence to examine the matter before it.

---

the complaint and give it the opportunity to make a supplementary written submission.

The Panel does not intend to put forward or endorse, at this stage in the proceedings, any interpretation of the "scope of the complaints", unless the parties were to reach a common understanding in this matter. In this light, we would strongly urge all parties to present to the Panel, during the second meeting, the full range of arguments which they feel are or may be of relevance to the resolution of the dispute, so as to enable the Panel to make an objective assessment of the matter before it in accordance with the terms of Article 11 of the DSU. In particular, India is not constrained in bringing forward arguments in defense in response to the claims submitted."

[305]   See Report of the Appellate Body in *India – Patents* "The jurisdiction of a panel is established by that panel's terms of reference, which are governed by Article 7 of the DSU", WT/DS50/AB/R, para 92, DSR:1998:I, 9.

1962   DSR 2002:V

India – Autos

1. Measures Identified in the Complainants' Requests for Establishment of a Panel

7.17 This Panel was established with standard terms of reference in accordance with Article 7 of the DSU. The measures and claims within those terms of reference are therefore those that have been identified in the complainants' requests for establishment of a panel.

7.18 The United States' request for establishment of a panel indicated:

"The United States considers that certain Indian measures affecting trade and investment in the motor vehicle sector are inconsistent with India's obligations under the WTO Agreement. *The measures in question require manufacturing firms in the motor vehicle sector to achieve specified levels of purchase or use of domestic content; to achieve a neutralization of foreign exchange and to balance the value of certain imports with the value of exports of cars and components over a stated period; and to limit imports to a value based on previous exports.* These requirements are enforceable under Indian law and rulings (including under the Foreign Trade (Development and Regulation) Act 1992). In addition, manufacturing firms in the motor vehicle sector must comply with these requirements in order to obtain certain Indian import licenses. The United States believes that the Indian measures in question are therefore inconsistent with India's obligations under Article III:4 and XI:1 of the General Agreement on Tariffs and Trade 1994 (GATT 1994) and Articles 2.1 and 2.2 of the Agreement on Trade-Related Investment Measures.

The measures in question are Public Notice No. 60 ((PN)/97-02) of the Indian Ministry of Commerce, published in the Gazette of India Extraordinary, effective 12 December 1997; the Foreign Trade (Development and Regulation) Act 1992; the Export and Import Policy, 1997-2002; memoranda of understanding signed by the Government of India with manufacturing firms in the motor vehicle sector pursuant to Public Notice No. 60; as well as amendments thereto, other legislative and administrative provisions implemented thereby or consolidated therein, and implementing measures or associated administrative actions taken thereunder." (emphases added)[306]

7.19 The European Communities indicated in its request for establishment of a panel:

"The measures concerned are contained in:

-	Public Notice No. 60 (PN 97-02) of the Indian Ministry of Commerce, effective 12 December 1997; and

---

[306] WT/DS175/4.

DSR 2002:V

1963

Report of the Panel

-    the Memorandums of Understanding (MOUs) entered into
     by certain manufacturers of automobiles with the Govern-
     ment of India pursuant to Public Notice No. 60.

The above measures require manufacturers of automobiles to sign
an MoU as a condition for obtaining licenses for importing automotive products that are currently subject to import restrictions.
According to the Indian authorities, the MOUs are "binding" and
"enforceable" instruments, which shall remain valid after the date
when those restrictions are eliminated. The MOUs require (i) to establish "actual production facilities" in India; (ii) to make a minimum investment; (iii) to achieve a certain level of "indigenization"; and (iv) to export a certain amount of automotive products.

The European Communities considers that the requirements imposed by the above measures are in violation of Articles III:4 and
XI:1 of GATT and of Article 2.1 of the TRIMs Agreement."

7.20   Both requests thus included express reference to Public Notice No. 60 and
the MOUs signed thereunder and to the specific conditions provided for under
those measures. As will be detailed below, the complainants explained in their
submissions that they were specifically challenging two of these conditions,
namely, the "indigenization" and "trade balancing " conditions.

7.21   The United States requested the Panel to find that the indigenization and
the trade balancing requirements imposed by Public Notice No. 60 and the
MOUs, were inconsistent with Article III:4 and XI:1 of GATT 1994 and Articles
2.1 and 2.2 of the TRIMs Agreement and to request India to bring these measures into conformity with its obligations.[307] The European Communities, similarly, requested the Panel to find that the trade balancing requirements contained
in Public Notice No. 60 and in the MOUs concluded thereunder were inconsistent with Articles III and XI of the GATT 1994 and Article 2 of the TRIMs
Agreement and that the indigenization requirements contained in these measures
are inconsistent with Article III of the GATT 1994 and with Article 2 of the
TRIMs Agreement.[308]

7.22   It is not disputed that Public Notice No. 60 was in existence and in operation at the time of both requests for establishment of a panel. It is also not disputed that most major car manufacturers had already, at that time, entered into
MOUs as foreseen in Public Notice No. 60, which included, *inter alia*, the two
conditions specifically referred to by the complainants. These measures as they
existed at the time of the complainants' requests for establishment of this Panel
are thus expressly contained in the Panel's terms of reference and are conse-

---

[307]   See para. 3.1 above.

[308]   Both complainants also referred in their requests to related measures, concerning which they did
not make distinct claims in the course of the proceedings.

1964   DSR 2002:V

quently within its jurisdiction in accordance with the terms of Articles 6.2 and 7 of the DSU.[309]

2. Evolution of the Measures in the Course of the Proceedings

7.23 India indicated in the course of the proceedings that import licensing requirements were to be removed on the products at issue in this dispute as of 1 April 2001, in order to comply with the implementation obligations agreed with the United States and the European Communities in prior disputes concerning quantitative restrictions maintained by India for balance-of-payments purposes.[310] Nevertheless, India also explained that the provisions of existing MOUs would continue to apply, to the degree that they were operative as of 1 April 2001.

7.24 India advised that the implications of these changes would be that as of 1 April 2001, no new MOUs would be required under Public Notice No. 60 and imports of previously restricted kits and components could be made freely as from that date. However, signatories of existing MOUs under Public Notice No. 60 would continue to be required to discharge outstanding obligations under the MOUs they had entered into. In particular, they would continue to be required to meet the indigenization condition foreseen in Public Notice No. 60 and their MOU and to discharge export obligations accrued in relation to previously restricted imports under the "trade balancing" condition.

7.25 In India's view, the events of 1 April 2001 modify the legal situation before the Panel. It argues in particular that any measures which India might apply as of 1 April 2001 would fall outside the terms of reference of this Panel.[311] It also argues that the measures before the Panel "as applied after 1 April 2001" (i.e. the remaining obligations under the MOUs), will in any case be consistent with the GATT and TRIMs Agreements.[312]

7.26 A WTO panel is generally competent to consider measures in existence at the time of its establishment. This power is not necessarily adversely affected simply because a measure under review may have been subsequently removed or

---

[309] This observation on the basis of the terms of reference is without prejudice to the examination, in the next section of this report, of India's further challenges to the Panel's competence to examine the case on distinct grounds.

[310] *India – Quantitative Restrictions* (complaint by the United States) (WT/DS90), and *India - Quantitative Restrictions on Imports of Agricultural, Textile and Industrial Products* (complaint by the European Communities) (WT/DS96). The agreed period for implementation of the DSB recommendations in the case concerning the United States is contained in document WT/DS90/15, circulated on 17 January 2000 (US Exhibit – 9). The mutually agreed solution reached between India and the European Communities in their dispute is contained in document WT/DS96/8, circulated on 6 May 1998 (European Communities Exhibit – 8).

[311] See paras. 4.73 to 4.80 above for a more complete description of India's arguments.

[312] See for example paras. 4.113 and 4.121 above.

Report of the Panel

rendered less effective. Panels in the past have examined discontinued measures where there was no agreement of the parties to discontinue the proceedings.[313]

7.27   In any event, the complainants dispute India's contentions about the ramifications of the events of 1 April 2001.The complainants have clearly indicated that they are requesting the Panel to find that the measures were inconsistent with the cited provisions as of the date of this Panel's establishment and that they have *remained* so subsequently.[314]   The complainants consider that the events of 1 April 2001 have no effect on their legal claims, because these do not rest on the continued existence of import licensing after 1 April 2001.

7.28   While India has indicated that Public Notice No. 60 has ceased to apply as of 1 April 2001, it is not disputed that the MOUs signed in accordance with its terms did not *ipso facto* cease to exist at the same time. India has in particular confirmed that "it is not the intention of India to release the car manufacturers from the commitments they have assumed under the MOUs as a result of imports of SKD/CKD kits prior to 1 April 2001"[315] and that signatories were still required to fulfill the indigenization condition, although India indicated in the later stages of the proceedings that as a matter of fact, all but one of the signatories had achieved the required level of indigenization. Therefore, while the framework governmental measure which initially led to the signature of the MOUs may have ceased to "operate", the MOUs themselves have remained in existence. Indeed, the practical implications of this dispute rest primarily on their *continued* existence after 1 April 2001.

7.29   In light of the foregoing, the Panel is of the view that it is not prevented by subsequent events which impacted upon the measures before it, from examining these measures as they stood at the date of establishment of the Panel.

7.30   However, the Panel also recognizes that it may need to consider whether these developments affect the continued relevance in the post-April 2001 period,

---

[313]   See for instance the Panel Report on *US – Wool Shirts and Blouses*, WT/DS33/R, adopted on 23 May 1997, as upheld by the Appellate Body Report, para. 6.2 (DSR 1997:I, 343), where the measure was withdrawn following the issuance of the interim report, and the panel nonetheless issued a complete report. See also the Panel Report on *Indonesia – Autos* where the panel proceeded with its examination of the claims despite a notification in the course of the proceedings by the respondent that the programme in issue had expired: "(...) In any event, taking into account our terms of reference, and noting that any revocation of a challenged measure could be relevant to the implementation stage of the dispute settlement process, we consider that is appropriate for us to make findings in respect of the National Car Programme. In this connection, we note that in previous GATT/WTO cases, where a measure included in the terms of reference was otherwise terminated or amended after the commencement of the panel proceedings, panels have nevertheless made findings in respect of such a measures" (WT/DS54/R, WT/DS55/R, WT/DS59/R, WT/DS64/R, para. 14.9, DSR 1998:VI, 2201). As mentioned by that panel, there have also been such instances of continued proceedings despite expiry or partial disappearance of the measures at issue under the GATT: see for instance *EEC –Apples I (Chile)* (BISD 27S/98) paras 2.2 and 2.4; *United States – Prohibition of Imports of Tuna and Tuna Products from Canada* (BISD 29S/91), paras. 2.8, 4.2 and 4.3, where despite some evolution in the measures in the course of the proceedings and encouragement from the Panel to reach a mutually agreed solution, there was no agreement among the parties that such a solution had been found and the panel issued a complete report.

[314]   See paras. 3.1, 3.5 and 4.92 to 4.94 above.

[315]   First Submission, para. 11

of any findings and conclusions it might make as to the consistency of the measures as at the date of its establishment. Article 19.1 requires a panel that has made a finding that a measure is in violation of a covered Agreement, to recommend that the Member concerned bring the measure into compliance with that Agreement. The Panel's ability to make meaningful recommendations to the DSB under Article 19.1 of the DSU may be affected if any changes in the measures had occurred which would affect the continued existence of any violations that might be identified as at the date of establishment. However, the Panel does not believe that these issues relate to its initial competence to examine the measures as they stood as of that date, but rather, to the nature and scope of any recommendations it might make. It will therefore address these aspects more fully at a later stage in the context of its conclusions and recommendations.[316]

3. *Measures not within our Terms of Reference*

7.31   India has also raised a distinct argument to the effect that any future measures which India may take after 1 April cannot be within the terms of reference of this Panel. This argument requires a separate analysis.

7.32   India indicated in its First Submission that it was unclear from the complainants' submissions whether they were challenging measures that India was applying as of the date of their requests for establishment of a panel, or measures that India "might" take in the future.

7.33   India argued that a valid complaint required that "both the measures at issue before a panel and the legal issues to which they give rise must have existed at the time of the request for establishment of a panel". It indicated that "the measures which India will apply as from 1 April 2001 to comply with the mutually agreed solution negotiated with the European Communities and the DSB ruling sought by the United States fall outside the Panel's terms of reference". India highlighted that "[a]lthough the European Communities and the United States allege that India is currently violating its obligations under the GATT and the TRIMs Agreement, many of their arguments relate to measures India *might* take after 1 April 2001 and legal issues that *might* consequently arise at that time."[317] India argued that any future enforcement measures which India might take after 1 April to enforce the MOUs are not within the terms of reference of this Panel, because "[u]nder the DSU, Members may not bring complaints on proposed measures nor may they request advisory rulings on potential future issues".[318] It also argued that "... these complaints - should events substantiate

---

[316]   See Section VIII:B below.

[317]   First Submission, para. 20 (emphases in original).

[318]   First Submission, para. 17. In India's view,

"although the European Communities and the United States allege that India is currently violating its obligations under the GATT and the TRIMs Agreement, many of their arguments relate to measures that India might take after 1 April 2001 and legal issues that might consequently arise at that time. Both submissions often leave the reader confused as to whether the legal arguments relate to the factual situation before or after the elimination of the discretionary licensing regime for SKD/CKD kits."

Report of the Panel

them – should appropriately be made in a dispute settlement proceeding initiated after 1 April 2001."[319]

7.34   The Panel agrees with India's contention that hypothetical future measures which it could, but might not take, including any future action that India might take for the enforcement of Public Notice No. 60 or the MOUs, would not fall within the scope of this Panel's terms of reference.

7.35   The complainants subsequently clarified that they were not seeking rulings on any measures which India might take after 1 April 2001 for the future enforcement of the conditions being challenged. Their claims concerned the measures that India was applying at the date of establishment of the Panel and would continue to apply subsequently.[320]

7.36   Further to the complainants' clarifications, India indicated in its second submission that

> "(...) the European Communities and the United States clarified that their complaints relate to the measures applied by India at the time when they submitted their requests for the establishment to the DSB, and not to any measures that India may take in the future. With these clarifications as to the scope of the rulings requested from this Panel, two central arguments that India had advanced in its First Submission are no longer relevant. India's argument that no WTO Member may resort to the DSU on the same matter twice is no longer relevant because the European Communities and the United States have made clear that their case does not rest on the application of the discretionary licensing system that had been the

---

[319]   First Submission, para 26.

[320]   The European Communities thus explained that it was

"not asking the Panel to rule that India would infringe the GATT and the TRIMs Agreement if 'India were to do this or do that' in order to enforce the MOUs. The European Communities claims that already the existence of binding and enforceable MOUs is as such inconsistent with the GATT and the TRIMs Agreement, regardless of whether any specific action needs to be taken. (...) 'Finally, the European Communities agrees with India that the Panel 'must base its rulings on inconsistencies that had already occurred at the time of the request for the [establishment of the Panel]. However, the continued existence and enforceability of the MOUs after 1 April 2001 does not result from any additional measure taken by the Indian Government after that request, but exclusively from the terms of the MOUs concluded by the Indian Government before that date. Thus, the inconsistencies claimed by the European Communities existed from the moment of the conclusion of the MOUs."

The United States, for its part, clarified that:

"the US complaint is not directed at any particular method or means of enforcing the MOUs and Public Notice No. 60. The US complaint is instead directed to the indigenization and trade balancing requirements as such, and these requirements have not changed. These requirements have imposed the same obligations on car manufacturers since the date that the MOUs were signed, and it is the US position that those obligations are themselves inconsistent with India's WTO commitments. What matters is that those obligations are binding and enforceable; what means India chose or will choose to enforce them is simply not relevant to the US legal claims in this dispute."

subject of their prior complaints. *India's argument that the Panel is not competent to rule on measures that India may take after 1 April 2001 is also no longer relevant."(emphasis added).*[321]

7.37   The Panel will thus not be considering any future measures which India might take after 1 April 2001.

C.   The Panel's Competence to Consider the Matter before it

7.38   The Panel recalls its conclusion that both complainants have specifically identified two conditions under Public Notice No. 60 and the MOUs signed thereunder in their requests for establishment of a panel in this case: the "indigenization" and "trade balancing" conditions. It is against these particular conditions that their claims are directed. The Panel has also concluded that these measures are expressly within the Panel's terms of reference and thus within its jurisdiction in accordance with the terms of Articles 6.2 and 7 of the DSU. As explained in paragraph 7.32, the claims should be considered as of the date of establishment of the Panel, as was requested by both complainants and as was recognized to be appropriate by India.[322]

7.39   India has not disputed that Public Notice No. 60 and the MOUs, including the trade balancing and indigenization conditions thereunder, are properly within the Panel's terms of reference. However, it has raised a number of additional arguments to those addressed above, to the effect that this Panel still cannot validly examine these claims. The Panel's observations as to its express terms of reference were without prejudice to the consideration of these arguments of India.

7.40   India has expressly raised three distinct challenges in this respect:

(a)   India argued that certain claims have already been decided on between it and the United States through the rulings adopted by the DSB in the *India – Quantitative Restrictions* dispute, and that the principle of *res judicata* applies to prevent the re-litigation of these claims;

(b)   It also asserts that these claims have already been resolved between India and the European Communities through the notification of a mutually agreed solution (hereafter "MAS"), and that the terms of the MAS bind the European Communities and this Panel;

(c)   India also argued in its First Submission that the claimants may not raise new legal claims with respect to a measure that must be eliminated in any case as a result of the abovementioned DSB ruling and MAS. It supports this proposition in two ways, by alluding to a suggested principle of "abusive splitting" in the context of different legal claims brought at different stages in relation to the same measures, and by separately arguing that it would be need-

---

[321]   Second Submission, para. 2.
[322]   First Submission, para. 19.

Report of the Panel

less to consider new grounds to determine the validity of measures that are to be brought into compliance in any event.

7.41 The Panel addresses each of these arguments in turn in order to ascertain its competence to examine the claims before proceeding further.

1. *Are any of the United States' Claims Barred by the Principle of res judicata?*

7.42 In India's view, the United States' initial submission suggested that it was attempting to obtain a new ruling on a matter which had already been decided on between India and the United States through the recommendations of the DSB in their *India – Quantitative Restrictions* dispute, namely, the inconsistency of India's discretionary import licensing system under its Export Import Policy of 1997-2002 (hereafter "EXIM Policy") with Article XI of GATT 1994.

7.43 India's reliance on the principle of *res judicata* evolved in the course of the proceedings. This has coincided with its evolving view as to the nature and ambit of the United States claims as they were further clarified. India's reliance on the principle was conditional upon the way the claims were clarified and upon the way the Panel would choose to view the measures before it. The Panel must therefore first clarify whether the conditions on which India considered *res judicata* to be raised as a defense are met, to determine whether there is a need to proceed further with the examination of this argument.

(a) Arguments of the Parties and Scope of India's Invocation of the Doctrine of *res judicata*

7.44 As noted above, India argued in its First Submission that the matter before the Panel was *res judicata* with respect to at least some of the United States claims. India argued that *res judicata* is a firmly established principle in international law which must be considered to constitute an inherent part of the WTO dispute settlement process.[323] In India's view, the principle prevents the resubmission of the same dispute between the same parties to a new panel. It considered that the United States had already obtained a ruling that "the discretionary licensing scheme administered by the Ministry of Commerce is inconsistent with Article XI" in the *India – Quantitative Restrictions* ruling. In India's view, that ruling also covers the "operation and application of the discretionary licensing system in respect of all products that were notified under Article XVIII:B", including the products of which CKD/SKD kits are composed.

7.45 The United States, on the contrary, considered that India has not demonstrated the relevance of the principle of *res judicata* to WTO dispute settlement. It argued that in any case, the measures and claims in this dispute are different from those at issue in *India – Quantitative Restrictions*. Consequently, it asserted that the *India – Quantitative Restrictions* panel could not and did not address the

---

[323] See First Submission, para. 40.

1970

DSR 2002:V

India – Autos

matter brought before this Panel and that this Panel should not engage in an analysis of legal notions not called for by the circumstances of the case.

7.46 In its second written submission, India considered that through their clarifications, the claimants had confirmed that their assertion was essentially that the measures as identified in the terms of reference, namely, conditions contained in Public Notice No. 60 and the MOUs executed under Public Notice No. 60, impose requirements and restrictions within the meaning of Articles III:4 and XI:1 of the GATT and the corresponding provisions of the TRIMs Agreement independently of the application of the discretionary licensing scheme that India was obliged to eliminate as a result of the prior proceedings. Based on that perception of the claims, it indicated that it "assumed that the issue before the Panel is no longer the scope of the principle of *res judicata* but rather, the question of whether Public Notice No. 60 and the MOUs impose requirements and restrictions even in the absence of the licensing scheme for CKD/SKD kits"[324] and confirmed in its second submission that its argument on *res judicata* was no longer relevant to the case.[325]

7.47 Nevertheless, India also indicated in its second submission that in its view, the Panel was required to examine whether the measures would have been inconsistent with the covered Agreements "even if" there had been no import licensing.[326] It later confirmed that if the Panel were to examine these measures "in the presence" of import licensing, then India was continuing to argue that the matter had been adjudicated upon already and could not be examined by the Panel.[327] Thus by that stage, it seemed that India's invocation of the doctrine of *res judicata* was conditional, depending on whether the claimant was calling for its claims to be considered "in the presence of" import licensing or as "if there had been no import licensing in place" at the date of the Panel's establishment.

7.48 In order to determine whether the Panel needs to examine India's *res judicata* argument, it therefore needs to give further attention to the clarifications made by the United States as to the exact role of the import licensing system in its claims and determine whether the existence of import licensing at the time of establishment of the Panel is a factor to be taken into account in the Panel's analysis.

(b)   Role of India's Import Licensing System in the United States' Claims

7.49 Further questions between the parties and from the Panel sought to resolve this issue. Paragraphs 7.78 to 7.80 below outline the clarification of the claims between the parties in order to accurately identify the matter before this

---

[324] See response to Question 36 of the Panel.
[325] See Second Submission para. 2.
[326] See Second Submission para. 4.
[327] See response to Question 109 of the Panel, where India indicated that "[t]he principle of *res judicata* would only be relevant if the Panel were to decide to examine the operation of Public Notice No. 60 and the trade balancing provisions in the MOUs *under the licensing scheme* that India was obliged to eliminate as a result of the complainants prior invocations of the DSU (emphasis added)".

DSR 2002:V   1971

Report of the Panel

Panel in the context of a *res judicata* analysis. For present purposes, it merely needs to be noted that those clarifications confirmed that the United States was asking for a ruling on the identified conditions in the context of India's discretionary licensing regime.

7.50   In response to a question by India, the United States indicated that it would not be a correct reflection of the facts for the Panel to assume in its legal analysis that there was no import licensing in place at the time of establishment of the Panel. It further clarified the role of import licensing in its claims as follows : "the limited relevance of these licenses is that India used them to induce car manufacturers in India to accept the indigenization and trade balancing requirements (...) What is relevant, therefore, is that import licensing existed in 1997 and 1998, when the MOUs were signed. (...)".[328] The United States thus confirmed that it was asking the Panel to rule on the conditions in Public Notice No. 60 and the MOUs in the context of that licensing regime, i.e. neither a ruling on the licensing regime *per se* nor a ruling "in abstraction" of the undisputed fact that import licensing existed for these products at the time of establishment of the Panel.[329]

7.51   In the Panel's view, the normal role of a panel under the DSU does not contemplate consideration of measures in isolation from their circumstances. To do so would be to rule on a hypothetical abstraction divorced from the circumstances of the particular matter that is within the Panel's terms of reference. In this case, import licensing was part of the factual circumstances present at the time of establishment of this Panel. The Panel is required to take this fact into account in order to make the objective assessment of the matter required by Article 11 of the DSU.

7.52   The Panel therefore agrees that the United States' articulation correctly reflects the way it should approach the examination of the matter before it. The Panel is requested and required to examine these measures as they existed as of the date of establishment of the Panel in their actual context, which includes the existence of import licensing. The Panel therefore concludes that it is necessary to address India's *res judicata* argument.

7.53   While the Panel has concluded that the presence of import licensing is something that must be taken into account as a factual matter, the extent to which this will be relevant to its deliberations will depend upon the nature of the claims. In turn, this will impact upon the Panel's analysis of the relationship between this dispute and the *India – Quantitative Restrictions* dispute.

(c)   General Approach to the *res judicata* Arguments

7.54   As a preliminary matter, the Panel first notes that the conclusions reached in the *India – Quantitative Restrictions* dispute - namely that the discretionary import licensing system applied by India to certain restricted products under the

---

[328]   See response to Question 9(a) of the Panel, para. 27.

[329]   The European Communities, although not directly concerned by the *res judicata* issue, confirmed a similar understanding of how the Panel was being asked to assess the claims.

1972   DSR 2002:V

India – Autos

EXIM policy was inconsistent with Article XI - were not disputed in these proceedings. The issue before this Panel is rather whether the *scope* of the *India – Quantitative Restrictions* dispute and the rulings adopted in it can be such as to preclude any further litigation concerning the claims and measures in *these* proceedings between the same parties.

7.55   This issue has two aspects. It first raises a general question as to the applicability of the doctrine of *res judicata* in the WTO. Secondly, it raises a specific question as to whether the facts in this dispute and in the *India – Quantitative Restrictions* dispute are such as to satisfy the requirements of the doctrine, if it were applicable to WTO dispute settlement.

7.56   India refers to a number of general provisions in the DSU highlighting the objective of settlement of disputes through the DSU, in support of its contention that *res judicata* may apply. India has referred to the jurisprudence of the International Court of Justice and to two specific provisions of the Court's statute concerning the status of its own decisions. India has also invoked *res judicata* as a general principle of law applicable in WTO dispute settlement.[330] The United States, however, does not believe that India has demonstrated the relevance of this doctrine to WTO dispute settlement or that it is necessary or desirable for the Panel to consider this systemic issue.

7.57   The general question as to the applicability of the doctrine of *res judicata* to WTO dispute settlement is of systemic importance. It does not appear to have been explicitly considered in WTO dispute settlement.[331] A general principle of *res judicata* has also not been otherwise referred to or endorsed by any WTO panel or by the Appellate Body, although it is certainly true that certain widely recognized principles of international law have been found to be applicable in WTO dispute settlement, particularly concerning fundamental procedural matters.[332]

---

[330]   In its responses to the second set of questions from the Panel, India also suggests that the *res judicata* principle is "but one facet of the broader principle of judicial economy". It suggests that the Appellate Body's rulings to the effect that a panel need only address those claims which must be addressed in order to resolve the matter at issue should also apply when a panel is being asked to rule on a matter already resolved in prior proceedings (see response to Question 104 (b) from the Panel). The Panel is not convinced, however, that the application of the principle of *res judicata* could appropriately be reduced or equated to the guidance given to panels to address, within the matter in their jurisdiction, only those issues which are necessary to the resolution of the dispute at issue. The issue of *res judicata* involves an argument of quite a distinct nature concerning the very competence of the adjudicatory body to address the issue submitted to it at all. The exercise by panels of judicial economy as recalled by India is a totally different concept allowing panels to address the matter properly within their jurisdiction in the most efficient way to achieve the objectives of WTO dispute settlement.

[331]   The doctrine does not appear to have been directly raised as a defense in any dispute to date, although it has been referred to by India before the panel in *India – Patents (EC)*, WT/DS79/R, DSR 1998:VI, 2661.

[332]   See for instance *US – Shrimp*, Report of the Appellate Body, WT/DS58/AB/R, DSR 1998:VII, 2755, para. 158, on the principle of good faith as a general principle of law and general principle of international law, or *Indonesia - Autos*, Panel Report, WT/DS54/R, WT/DS55/R, WT/DS59/R, WT/DS64/R, para. 14.28, DSR 1998:VI, 2201, concerning the "presumption against conflict" in international law.

DSR 2002:V   1973

Report of the Panel

7.58   The text of the DSU does not directly address this issue. More generally, the DSU does not contain any express provision concerning the status of adopted panel or Appellate Body reports, or concerning their potential impact in separate proceedings under the DSU concerning the same matter.[333] Nevertheless, when considering the status of adopted panel reports, the Appellate Body has indicated that they are binding on the parties "with respect to that particular dispute".[334] This statement was not directly addressed at the notion of *res judicata*, but rather, appears to have been made primarily in the context of determining the status of adopted reports *per se* and their relevance to subsequent panels as a matter of precedent. It is thus not necessarily determinative of the status of the doctrine of *res judicata* in the WTO as a bar to re-litigation of the same issues, although it may be open to debate whether this could form the basis, or a basis, for the application of the principle of *res judicata*.

7.59   In the absence of any clear guidance, many important interpretative issues would thus need to be considered in determining whether the doctrine of *res judicata* applies in WTO dispute settlement in circumstances where the facts would support such an assertion. However, the potential relevance of the notion of *res judicata* to this case would only arise if its commonly understood conditions of application were met on the facts.

7.60   The Panel recalls in this regard that its mandate under the DSU requires it only to address those issues which need to be addressed in order to resolve the dispute. Thus the Panel finds it appropriate, in this instance, to first consider whether the factual circumstances for the application of *res judicata* could be met in the circumstances of this case. If the basis of this dispute is sufficiently similar to that of *India – Quantitative Restrictions* so as to come within accepted notions of the doctrine, the Panel would need to rule on its applicability as a doctrine. Conversely, if the Panel were to find, as a matter of fact, that the matter ruled on by the *India – Quantitative Restrictions* panel is distinct from that sub-

---

[333]   Two adopted panel reports under the WTO have considered claims in situations involving the establishment of "successive" panels concerning the same matter. However, this was in circumstances where the complainants were distinct or where the first panel was not pursued, so that in either case *res judicata* would not be directly relevant, in the first case for lack of identity of parties, and in the second instance for lack of a prior decision on the same issue between the parties.

The first of these cases was *India – Patents (EC)*, where the second panel, established shortly after a first report had been circulated concerning the same measures, but at the request of a different complainant, found that it was competent to examine in full the claims, taking account of the reasoning and conclusions of the previous panel. In another case, *Australia – Subsidies Provided to Producers and Exporters of Automotive Leather* (hereinafter "*Australia – Automotive Leather II*"), a second panel was established at the request of the same complainant, in circumstances where the composition of the panel established a short time before was not pursued and the first proceedings never led to any further developments. The responding party having challenged the validity of the establishment of the second panel in these circumstances, the panel found that Australia was asking this panel to read into the DSU an implicit prohibition on multiple panels between the same parties regarding the same matter that does not exist in the text of the DSU, noting that this was not a case where a complainant was actively pursuing two procedures with respect to the same matter, since the first panel was never composed and then never began its work. (Cf. Panel Report, WT/DS126/R, adopted on 16 June 1999, DSR 1999:III, 951, para. 9.14).

[334]   *Japan – Alcoholic Beverages II*, Report of the Appellate Body, WT/DS8/AB/R, WT/DS10/AB/R, WT/DS11/AB/R, p. 14, DSR 1996:I, 97, at 108.

India – Autos

mitted to it in this dispute, it would not be necessary to make a general ruling on the role of *res judicata* in WTO dispute settlement.

7.61   To conduct such an analysis, the Panel must at least identify a benchmark by which disputes might be seen as distinct or similar for the purposes of rejecting or applying *res judicata*.

7.62   In international jurisdictions where it is applicable, the doctrine is generally understood to mean that an issue that has been decided on in a final adjudication, that is, after exhaustion of any available appeal rights, must be considered as a settled matter between the parties to the dispute. Consequently the issue previously resolved cannot be re-opened in subsequent proceedings. [335] This doctrine has found application in the jurisprudence of the International Court of Justice, whose Statute contains express provisions concerning the binding and final character of its judgments.[336]

7.63   In this instance, while the United States was of the view that India had not demonstrated the relevance of this principle to WTO dispute settlement, the

---

[335]   While there may be variations in the exact understanding of the doctrine depending on the jurisdiction concerned or commentators' interpretation of its scope, it can be noted that *res judicata* is broadly understood to encompass three elements: a final decision, on a given issue, between the same parties. Black's Law Dictionary defines *res judicata* as follows:

> "A matter adjudged; a thing judicially acted upon or decided; a thing or matter settled by judgment. Rule that a final judgment rendered by a court of competent jurisdiction on the merits is conclusive as to the rights of the parties and their privies, and, as to them, constitutes an absolute bar to a subsequent action involving the same claim, demand or cause of action. (…) And to be applicable, requires identity in thing sued for as well as identity of cause of action, of persons and parties to action, and of quality in persons for or against whom claim is made. The sum and substance of the whole rule is that a matter once judicially decided is finally decided (…)".

[336]   In the context of the International Court of Justice, two provisions of its Statute, Articles 59 and 60, as referred to by India, are frequently cited as the source of the principle of *res judicata* concerning its own decisions, although some divergences appear to emerge among commentators as to the exact role of either of the two provisions or even the need to consider them as the source of this principle since it is arguably a general principle of law in any case (see Collier and Lowe, *The Settlement of Disputes in International Law. Institutions and Procedures*, Oxford University Press, p. 177). In the words of Sir Gerald Fitzmaurice,

> "A judgment of the [International] Court [of Justice] has, internationally, the authority of res judicata, and this covers all matters which are actually the subject of decision in the judgment. Thus in the *Haya de la Torre* case, the Court (*I.C.J., 1951, 77*) referred to
>
>> '… questions which the Judgment of November 20th, 1950, had already decided with the authority of *res judicata*'
>
> (…) Unless, however, the point is duly covered by the previous decision, there is no res judicata, and therefore nothing (on that particular score) to prevent it being raised in later proceedings. Thus, again in the *Haya* case, the Court said (ibid, 80):
>
>> ' As mentioned above, the question of the surrender of the refugee was not decided by the judgment of November 20th. This question is new; it was raised by Peru in its Note to Colombia of November 28th, 1950, and was submitted to the Court by the Application of Colombia of December 13th, 1950. There is consequently no *res judicata* upon the question of surrender.'"

(in *The Law and Procedure of the International Court of Justice*, Sir Gerald Fitzmaurice, Volume Two, Cambridge, Grotius Publications Limited, 1986, pp. 584-585).

DSR 2002:V

Report of the Panel

submissions did not display any fundamentally different view of either party as to the nature of the concept.[337] On the other hand, the parties have generally provided limited guidance as to how they would expect a panel to assess the similarity of two cases to determine the relevance of *res judicata* in the context of WTO dispute settlement.

7.64   Because the policy underlying *res judicata* is to bring litigation of a particular nature to an end at an appropriate stage, the key to its application should be to compare what has already been ruled on to what is being brought before the adjudicating body in the subsequent proceedings. Both India and the United States have used a comparison between the "matter" ruled on in the *India - Quantitative Restrictions* case and the "matter" brought before this Panel in identifying the similarities or dissimilarities between the two disputes for the purposes of assessing whether the issues before this Panel can be considered to be *res judicata*.[338]

7.65   In the context of WTO dispute settlement, the notion of "matter", as referred to in Article 7.1 of the DSU, determines the scope of what is submitted, and what can be ruled upon, by a panel. As confirmed by the Appellate Body in the *Guatemala – Cement* case, the matter referred to the DSB consists of two elements: the specific measures at issue and the legal basis of the complaint (or the claims). This appears to the Panel to be the most appropriate minimal benchmark by which to assess whether the conditions of *res judicata* could conceivably be met, if such a notion was of relevance.[339]

7.66   The Panel therefore considers that for *res judicata* to have any possible role in WTO dispute settlement, there should, at the very least, be in essence identity between the matter previously ruled on and that submitted to the subsequent panel. This requires identity between both the measures and the claims pertaining to them. There is also, for the purposes of *res judicata*, a requirement of identity of parties which is clearly met with regard to the United States in this instance.

---

[337]   The United States thus indicated that "[g]enerally speaking, a principle of *res judicata*, if applicable, would presumably relate to the effect of a previously adopted panel report on a subsequent dispute involving the same matter between the same parties".

[338]   The European Communities, which is not directly concerned by this issue of *res judicata*, has also used this benchmark in explaining the contours of the notion and its relevance to this case.

[339]   This might only be a minimal benchmark. Where respondents have made allegations as to a lack of specificity of the matter articulated in panel requests, some cases have upheld very general claims. The more broadly claims are stated in two distinct cases, the more it might superficially appear that the issues are similar. Nevertheless, the policy behind such considerations in cases challenging specificity under Article 6.2 of the DSU differs from the policy behind the *res judicata* concept. Thus to finally determine the applicability of the *res judicata* concept to the facts of a particular case, a tribunal may need to identify a more detailed articulation of the claims in each case and might even need to integrate this with a consideration of which arguments were addressed in each dispute. Whether this is so or not, it remains the case that if even the "matters" are not the same, the doctrine could not apply. The Panel will therefore proceed with an examination of the scope of each dispute through a comparison between the matter before this Panel and the matter ruled on by the *India - Quantitative Restrictions* panel. If they are the same, the Panel would then need to consider this subsidiary question of whether further refinement of the notion is necessary.

1976   DSR 2002:V

(i) The Matter before this Panel

7.67 While the measures at issue and the legal basis of the complaint are identified in the United States request for establishment of a panel, it was perhaps not fully apparent from its terms what the precise role of India's discretionary import licensing scheme was intended to be in the matter submitted to the Panel.[340] The Panel has already resolved that this dispute cannot be conducted on a hypothetical basis as if the licensing scheme did not exist. The Panel believes it is appropriate, in considering the potential application of *res judicata*, to consider in more detail the subsequent elaboration by the United States of its claims, in order to clarify the exact scope of the complaint identified in our terms of reference.[341]

7.68 In its First Submission, the United States explained that :

> "The present dispute (...) concerns not the import licenses themselves; maintaining them beyond April 1 would in any case be inconsistent with India's existing obligation to remove them. Instead, this dispute concerns discriminatory, trade-restricting conditions that India exacts from investors in the motor vehicle manufacturing sector and that it intends to continue to exact.
>
> The United States contends that the local content and trade balancing requirements in Public Notice No. 60 and the MOUs, together with the Indian domestic legislation under which they have come into force, are inconsistent with the obligations of India under the General Agreement on Tariffs and Trade 1994 ("GATT 1994") and the Agreement on Trade-Related Investment Measures ("TRIMs Agreement"). The United States respectfully requests this Panel to make findings to this effect, and to recommend that India bring all such measures into conformity with its obligations."

7.69 This explanation made it clear that the United States did not seek to challenge the import licensing regime or its application to the products at issue, as such. Nevertheless, it referred in a number of its arguments to the import licensing system and to the possible denial of import licenses as a consequence of failing to comply with the requirements at issue.[342] In view of these arguments of the United States and India's assertions as to the nature of this claim, the Panel sought further clarification as to the scope of this dispute and the exact extent to

---

[340] Thus it was not necessarily clear on the face of the document that the measures were alleged to be in violation *per se*, or because they were enforceable, or because failure to comply would lead to the refusal of import licences. The use of the term "therefore" after such statements in the sentence which articulates the provisions in dispute does not make clear whether these are distinct claims or whether each feature is a necessary element of the alleged violation.

[341] In the view of the Panel, such recourse to subsequent clarifications of the claims is appropriate in order to determine exactly the scope of the matter that the complainant intended to refer to the Panel. This is with the clear understanding that the full scope of the matter referred to the panel is determined by its terms of reference, and that subsequent elaborations can only serve to clarify the meaning of a matter already *within* such terms of reference. See, in this respect the Report of the Appellate Body in *Guatemala – Cement I*.

[342] See for example paragraph 101 of the First US Submission, which refers to the possible denial of import licenses as a source of restriction on importation.

Report of the Panel

which the claimants saw the licensing scheme as relevant to these proceedings, but still distinct from the issues considered in *India – Quantitative Restrictions*.

7.70   Subsequent exchanges of submissions, as well as answers to questions from the Panel, further confirmed that the United States in this case was not seeking a ruling from this Panel on the consistency with the WTO agreements of the import licensing regime *per se*. Instead, its claims related to the "indigenization and trade balancing requirements" in Public Notice No. 60 and in the MOUs.[343] It has requested the Panel to find that these requirements "are inconsistent with Article III:4 and XI:1 of the GATT 1994 and Articles 2.1 and 2.2 of the TRIMs Agreement." Nevertheless, as noted above, the United States considered that the Panel must address these measures in the context of the discretionary licensing scheme that applied at the time of the Panel's establishment, and that this licensing scheme constituted an advantage used to induce the manufacturers to sign the MOUs. It contended that the measures at issue in these proceedings were in violation of those provisions, independently of the violation of the licensing scheme *per se* and requests the Panel to recommend that India bring these measures into conformity with its obligations under the GATT 1994 and the TRIMs Agreement.[344]

---

[343]   The United States thus further clarified that "[t]he measures at issue in this dispute are those set forth in the US panel request: (...). The US claims relate to the indigenization requirement and the trade balancing requirement found in these measures" and that the limited relevance of the licenses is that India used them to induce manufacturers to sign the MOUs and they constitute the advantage gained in signing the MOUs.

In its Second Submission, the United States further indicated:

"it is not the licensing requirements but the indigenization and trade balancing requirements that are the subject of the US complaint in this dispute. Because the indigenization and trade balancing requirements did not change on April 1, 2001 (or on any other date), and because those requirements are independent of India's now-eliminated licensing regime, India's elimination of import licensing is not relevant to – and certainly does not resolve – this dispute."

[344]   In its final set of responses to the Panel's questions, India argued that while it was legitimate for complainants to narrow the focus of their claims in the course of the proceedings, they cannot legitimately successively narrow or broaden them at will as India alleges they did here (see response to Question 102 of the Panel). This is a distinct argument from the *res judicata* claim and is distinct from any assertion that the claim as finally relied upon is outside the terms of reference.

The Panel agrees with India that parties in a dispute should avoid successive shifts or modifications in the presentation of their arguments. In some circumstances this could jeopardize the ability of the other parties to present their arguments in sufficient time and prejudice the fulfilment of requirements of due process. In this case we believe that the successive exchanges between the United States and India constituted a clarification of the United States claim rather than a shifting back and forth as alleged, although the Panel notes that the United States' articulation of the relevance of the licensing scheme to its claims in its first written submission was at the very least confusing (as reflected for instance in paragraphs 101 and 103 of that submission).

However, we also recall that it is normal for claims to be clarified in the course of proceedings. While the clarification process might have been more lengthy in this case than would normally be expected, we also find that the United States has sought to clarify its claims in good faith in a manner that enabled India to properly understand the nature of the claims before this Panel. These claims remain within the Panel's terms of reference. The Panel also feels that India's ability to defend itself was not jeopardized, in particular because at all stages of the proceedings it was accorded ample opportunity to develop its arguments in light of the complainants' clarifications.

1978   DSR 2002:V

(ii) The Matter Ruled on by the India –
Quantitative Restrictions Panel

7.71   The Panel is mindful that in seeking to consider the ambit of the *India – Quantitative Restrictions* case, it is only analyzing the nature and scope of that case and its resultant rulings and recommendations to consider the relevance of India's jurisdictional arguments. This analysis is without prejudice to any determination an Article 21.5 compliance panel in the context of the *India - Quantitative Restrictions* case might make as to the scope of that case and its rulings and their potential impact on India's subsequent behaviour.

7.72   A consideration of the matter resolved before the *India – Quantitative Restrictions* panel should also begin with an examination of its terms of reference, which in turn, incorporate the United States request for establishment of a panel in that case. That request provided that:

> "quantitative restrictions maintained by India, including, but not limited to, the more than 2700 agricultural and industrial product tariff lines notified to the WTO in Annex I, Part B of WT/BOP/N/24 dated 22 May 1997, appear to be inconsistent with India's obligations under Articles XI:1 and XVIII:11 of GATT 1994 and Article 4.2 of the Agreement on Agriculture. Furthermore, the import licensing procedures and practices of the Government of India are inconsistent with fundamental WTO requirements as provided in Article XIII of GATT 1994 and Article 3 of the Agreement on Import Licensing Procedures.
>
> The quantitative restrictions referred to above include all import prohibitions, bans, restrictions, import licenses, special import licenses and the prohibition of non-commercial (sample) quantities as well as the procedures to implement and administer these measures".[345]

7.73   The factual section of the *India – Quantitative Restrictions* panel report indicates that "(a)t the time the panel was established, India maintained quantitative restrictions on imports of products falling in 2,714 tariff lines at the eight-digit level of HS96 for which it claimed balance-of-payments justification. These restrictions had been notified to the BOPs Committee in May 1997 in the course of consultations being held with India. The restrictions that are within the scope of the dispute appear in Annex 1, Part B of WT/BOP/N/24".

7.74   During the *India – Quantitative Restrictions* proceedings, the United States requested the panel to find that "the quantitative restrictions at issue violate Article XI:1 and XVIII:11 of the GATT 1994 and Article 4.2 of the Agriculture Agreement". The United States identified four specific measures that it asked the panel to rule upon.

7.75   The panel then articulated the measures at issue in that case as follows:

---

[345] WT/DS90/8.

Report of the Panel

> "India regulates the importation of goods found in a 'Negative List of Imports', contained in Chapter 15 of India's Export and Import Policy 1997-2002. The United States identifies four measures which are implemented under India's Export and Import Policy and which it claims constitute quantitative restrictions within the meaning of Article XI:1: (a) discretionary import licensing; (b) canalization of imports through government agencies; (c) the Special Import Licensing (SIL) system; (d) the 'Actual User' condition on import licensing. (...) To the extent that India applies these four measures as balance-of-payments restrictions on the products specified in Annex I, Part B of WT/BOP/N/24, we refer to these measures as the 'measures at issue' in this dispute."[346]

7.76   The measures which the panel ruled on were therefore those specific measures, to the extent that India applied them as balance-of-payments restrictions on the products specified in Annex 1 part B of its notification WT/BOP/N/24.[347] In stating its conclusions, the panel referred to the "measures at issue", as described in this paragraph.[348]

7.77   The report further explains that imports of goods are regulated in the EXIM policy through the Negative List and explains the general rules applicable

---

[346]   Panel Report on *India – Quantitative Restrictions*, WT/DS90/R, adopted on 22 September 1999, as upheld by the Appellate Body Report, para. 5.122, DSR 1999:V, 1799.

[347]   Annex 1, Part B of India's notification contains a reference to a number of items under the HS heading "8703", at the 8 digit level, which relate to automotive vehicles. These are marked as restricted on grounds of "AUTO/BOP-XVIII-B", and under the QR symbol "NAL", "AL/NAL" or "SIL/NAL". The reference "AUTO/BOP-XVIII-B" is explained in a note as follows: "When imports of passenger cars and automotive vehicles are permitted without a license on fulfilment of conditions specified in a Public Notice issued in this behalf, and restrictions on imports through NAL are otherwise maintained". "SIL/AUTO/BOP" is defined as "when imports of passenger cars and automotive vehicles are permitted without a license on fulfilment of conditions specified in a Public Notice issued in this behalf, and imports are otherwise permitted against Special Import Licenses." See also responses to Questions 48 and 49 of the Panel.

In response to a question by this Panel, India confirmed that the following tariff lines in Chapter 87 notified as restricted for Auto/BOP reasons cover cars in the form of CKD/SKD kits: 870321.04, 870322.04, 870323.04, 870331.04, 870332.04, 870333.03 (sic). In addition a number of tariff lines covering components restricted for balance-of-payments reasons as considered in *India – Quantitative Restrictions* were also subject to the MOU privileges (870600.01, 870600.09, 870710.01 and 870710.02). All of these tariff lines were identified in India's BOP notification as restricted under "AUTO/BOP" grounds and subject to non-automatic licensing ("NAL").

[348]   With regard to the legal basis for import restrictions and import licensing, the descriptive part of the report notes the following factual aspects. "Indian domestic legislation governing import licensing can be found in: (i) section 11 of the Customs Act 1962, (ii) the Foreign Trade (Development and Regulation) Act, 1992, (iii) the rules and orders promulgated under the Foreign Trade (Development and Regulation) Act, 1992, and (iv) the Export and Import Policy 1997-2002." It is further explained that the Customs Act and the FT(DR) Act foresee the possibility for the Indian Government to regulate imports through rules and orders. It is further explained that the FTDR Act authorizes the Central Government to formulate and announce by notification in the Official Gazette the export and import policy, which is done on a five yearly basis, the current EXIM being the 1997-2002 policy, which "includes, *inter alia*, the Negative List of Imports ("Negative List") found in Chapter 15 of the Export and Import Policy. The list sets forth various prescribed procedures or conditions for imports, and the eligibility requirements including export performance that must be met to qualify for Special Import Licenses".

to the issuance of import licenses by the DGFT. In this context, none of the specific criteria for various products are mentioned, other than the "Actual user" condition, which required that only the "actual users" of the product could obtain an import license. With regard to the "Special Import Licensing" (SIL), which applied to a limited number of goods identified with the symbol SIL in the notification, it is explained that these licenses were granted on the basis of export performance criteria.

7.78   The panel went on to analyze the four measures it had identified in the light of Article XI of GATT 1994. In respect of India's import licensing system for products on the "Negative List of Imports", the panel considered the United States claim that "imports of these products into India are subject to an arbitrary, non-transparent and discretionary import licensing system, under which licenses are granted "on merit" and only to a category of operators called "actual users". The panel noted that it was agreed that India's licensing system for goods in the Negative List of Imports is a discretionary import licensing system, in that licenses are not granted in all cases, but rather on unspecified "merits". The panel concluded that this licensing system, to the extent that it applied to the products specified in WT/BOP/N/24, Annex 1, Part B, operated as a restriction on imports within the meaning of Article XI:1.

7.79   The Actual User condition and SIL, having been identified as distinct and specific measures in the request, were examined separately and were the basis of distinct findings of violation of Article XI.

> (iii)   Comparison between the Matter Ruled on by the India – QR*s* Panel and the Matter before this Panel

7.80   As noted above, the notion of "matter" in the context of the DSU encompasses both the specific measures at issue and the claims, that is, the legal basis on which the complaint is made with respect to those measures. If the application of *res judicata* at the very least requires that the same matter which has already been adjudicated on be the object of a new complaint, then it seems to require as a minimum, that both the measures and the legal basis of the claims be essentially the same. The Panel will consider both aspects in turn, although there may be some artificiality in separating the analysis. This is because it may be difficult to know how to describe and characterize the measures without understanding the nature of the claims and vice versa. For this reason the Panel will first analyze each separately and then consider them together in drawing its conclusions.

7.81   India, in its second submission, seemed to concede that if the complaint concerned the consistency with the WTO Agreements of these specific conditions under Public Notice No. 60 and the MOUs rather than the consistency of the application of discretionary import licensing to the products at issue *per se*, then its *res judicata* argument was no longer relevant. Nonetheless, it later indicated that any examination of these conditions as they operated *in the presence of* import licensing was also covered by *res judicata*. This suggests that India considers that even if the application of the discretionary import licensing system

Report of the Panel

to restricted kits and components is not the direct object of this claim, *res judicata* would apply to preclude the litigation of this claim concerning any administration or application measure of the import licensing regime considered in the *India – Quantitative Restrictions* ruling. This seems to imply that even an "indirect" coverage of these measures would, in the view of India, make them *res judicata*.

7.82   The Panel would only need to rule on the role of indirect coverage in the doctrine of *res judicata* if the facts supported India's contention. The Panel will therefore consider this factual question also. The Panel will first compare the measures submitted to it with those expressly ruled on in the context of the *India – Quantitative Restrictions* dispute, before comparing the express claims in both disputes. The Panel will then assess overall whether the matters ruled on in *India – Quantitative Restrictions* can be considered to include, directly or indirectly, the matter it is requested to rule on in these proceedings.

A Comparison of the Measures Expressly Considered

7.83   The Panel has determined that the specific measures in dispute before it are the indigenization and trade balancing conditions contained in Public Notice No. 60 and the MOUs entered into under it. Although the products at issue in this case fell within the scope of restricted items within the meaning of the EXIM policy at issue in the *India – Quantitative Restrictions* case, it is clear from an analysis of the terms of reference and panel report in *India – Quantitative Restrictions* that *these* specific conditions were not expressly considered by that panel.

7.84   In any event, neither Public Notice No. 60 nor the MOUs signed thereunder could have been expressly within the terms of reference of the *India – Quantitative Restrictions* panel, since they were only adopted after its establishment.[349] It would only have been possible to expressly refer to measures that preceded Public Notice No. 60 in respect of these products. India has explained that prior to the existence of Public Notice No. 60, a number of MOUs had been signed with automotive manufacturers that called for some indications of indigenization and export intent.[350] These, however, were also not expressly referred to or considered by the *India – Quantitative Restrictions* panel.

7.85   In fact that panel never evaluated, or made any ruling on, any element of the administration of the discretionary licensing system, other than an Actual User condition provided for in the EXIM policy. This was specifically identified by the complainant in the *India – Quantitative Restrictions* case and was the object of a distinct ruling of violation of Article XI. The parties' arguments in that case further document that none of the specific criteria or conditions for the granting of non-automatic licenses were otherwise considered or directly ruled

---

[349]   The *India – Quantitative Restrictions* panel was established on 18 November 1997. Public Notice No. 60 was adopted on 12 December 1997.

[350]   See India's First Submission, para. 4 and its responses to Questions 43 and 110 of the Panel.

1982   DSR 2002:V

India – Autos

on. By contrast, the "Special Import Licensing" system, or "SIL", was analyzed in light of its export obligation component.

7.86   The Panel therefore concludes that the measures before it were not expressly considered by the *India – Quantitative Restrictions* panel. Nor did that panel expressly consider the earlier MOUs applicable to restricted kits and components at the time of establishment of that panel. The *India – Quantitative Restrictions* panel based its finding of violation in relation to the discretionary import licensing on the more general observation that licenses were granted on the basis of "unspecified 'merits'". India's BOPs notification, which served as the basis for the definition of the measures before that panel, included some general indication of the type of measure that could apply to specific products, but not in any detail, including for the products at issue in this proceeding. However, the *India – Quantitative Restrictions* panel, more generally, did not consider directly any of the specific application measures or criteria relating to specific product categories subjected to discretionary non-automatic import licensing.

A Comparison of the Express Claims

7.87   India does not appear to argue that *res judicata* applies to the claims under Articles III:4 of GATT and 2 of the TRIMs Agreement.[351] These claims could not constitute the "same" claims as those examined by the previous panel, which did not address either of these provisions. The issue therefore only arises with respect to the claims based on Article XI of GATT.

7.88   Leaving aside the references to provisions other than Article XI:1, in a minimal sense at least, the legal bases for the claims have some superficial similarity: a violation of Article XI:1 is claimed in both cases. Nevertheless, to argue that the claims are the same merely because the same provision is in issue would be a strained usage of the notion of claim, at least in the context of an analysis of the potential application of *res judicata*.

7.89   The Panel believes that in considering the factual potential for a *res judicata* defense, it must go beyond a mere identification of the provision claimed to have been violated.[352] It must at the very least accurately identify the precise legal basis for the claimed violation in relation to the measure at issue.

---

[351]   In its First Submission, India argued exclusively in its section on *res judicata* in relation to a possible "re-examination" of claims under Article XI (see for instance paragraphs 41 and 43). On the other hand, it made distinct arguments in a subsequent section concerning the reasons why this Panel should not, in its view, be examining the claims based on other legal bases invoked by the complainants in this case (see paragraphs 45 to 49). Despite a specific question from the Panel at a later stage inviting India to clarify whether it was only invoking the principle of *res judicata* in respect of violations of Article XI or was also invoking it with respect to claims of violation of Article III:4 of GATT 1994 or the TRIMS Agreement, it declined to answer this point expressly (see response to Question 109 of the Panel).

[352]   The Panel is mindful of the fact that in the context of procedural challenges as to the specificity of claims, the Appellate Body has indicated that a mere identification of the provision of the covered Agreement at issue may be sufficient for the purposes of identifying the matter within the meaning of Article 6.2 of the DSU. This was in the context of determining whether the nature of the claim was sufficiently identified to put the defendant on notice of the challenge faced. Even in this context the jurisprudence makes it clear that this assessment should be made on a case by case basis. This Panel

DSR 2002:V

Report of the Panel

7.90   As was noted above, the consistency with Article XI:1 of the trade balancing and indigenization conditions was not expressly examined by the *India –
Quantitative Restrictions* panel. They were not expressly examined in any context. The *India – Quantitative Restrictions* panel addressed the claim that India's
discretionary licensing system under the EXIM policy was inconsistent with Article XI. The United States in this case is claiming, *inter alia*, that the trade balancing and indigenization conditions subsequently introduced through Public
Notice No. 60, in and of themselves, are distinctly in violation of Article XI. In
the Panel's view, this is a distinct question. While the *India – Quantitative Restrictions* panel considered whether it was consistent with the terms of Article XI
for a member to apply discretionary or non-automatic licensing to certain products, this panel is being asked to consider whether two specific obligations are
consistent with the same provision. The Panel concludes that the *India – Quantitative Restrictions* panel did not rule on the specific claims before this Panel.

Are the Matters the Same?

7.91   The Panel has identified that neither the specific measures in this case,
nor any comparable measures in existence at the time of that panel's establishment, were expressly considered in the *India – Quantitative Restrictions* case.
The ruling on India's discretionary import licensing scheme in that case was in
the context of a very broad-ranging challenge relating to measures taken by India
on products covering over 2,700 tariff lines in the context of India's general
EXIM policy, which included quantitative restrictions instituted for balance-of-
payments purposes. The ruling on discretionary import licensing was accordingly broad-ranging and sought to address the existence of discretionary licensing rather than any of the specific conditions foreseen for the granting of any
individual licenses. Where specific conditions were identified within the policy
itself, such as the Actual User condition, or the export requirements under the
"Special Import Licenses" (SIL), these were specifically addressed. Under the
ruling concerning discretionary import licensing, no specific conditions were
even identified, and certainly, the consistency of specific "trade balancing" and
"indigenization" conditions was never considered.

7.92   As was noted above, India, in its second submission, considered that even
if the application of the discretionary import licensing system to restricted kits
and components was not the direct object of the claim, any examination of these
conditions as they operated *in the presence of* import licensing was also covered
by *res judicata*.

7.93   In India's view, such claims would be covered because the *India – Quantitative Restrictions* ruling "covers the operation and application of the discretionary licensing system in respect of all products that were notified under Article XVIII:B".[353] In India's view, the specific measures now referred to this Panel
are an "inherent part" of the licensing scheme that India is required to eliminate

---

is comparing the claims in the cases for a different reason and should look to see if there has previously been a final determination of a specific issue that is now before it.

[353]   First Submission, para 39.

1984   DSR 2002:V

as a result of the previous ruling.[354] The Panel previously noted that it would look to see if the facts supported this contention.

7.94   It might be expected that a ruling that a particular broad-ranging scheme is in violation of provisions of the covered Agreements and must be brought into conformity may have implications for a number of administrative features of the system. This is not determinative however. In the context of a *res judicata* analysis, the question to determine is whether a particular issue was ruled on and decided upon, and not merely whether the implementation of a previous ruling may have practical implications for particular measures in the later dispute.

7.95   Furthermore, it cannot be assumed that all measures related to the application or administration of such a broad system would necessarily be so closely connected to it that they could not form the object of a discrete challenge. This is illustrated by the fact that the "Actual user" condition for import was discretely challenged and ruled on in the *India – Quantitative Restrictions* dispute.

7.96   In this regard, it is notable that the specific measures challenged before us were not even in existence at the time of establishment of the previous panel. These measures could thus hardly be argued to be in themselves "inherent" in the licensing scheme as considered by the *India - Quantitative Restrictions* panel. Although another MOU scheme preceded that foreseen in Public Notice No. 60, that scheme itself was not envisaged in the *India - Quantitative Restrictions* panel.

7.97   Furthermore, the 1997 scheme of which Public Notice No. 60 and its ensuing MOUs were part, was a new and legally distinct measure taken at Cabinet level that introduced a new auto licensing policy. This replaced an ad-hoc voluntary scheme. Public Notice No. 60 established a very significant, more permanent and binding regime. Companies had to have been prepared to invest US$50 million and undertake a range of other binding contractual commitments. These commitments included the two elements of indigenization and trade balancing which are the subject of this dispute. These were long-term contracts. The two schemes thus seem to imply significant commercial differences for the companies concerned and the Indian government.[355] While the policy change may have been motivated by issues of transparency and objectivity as argued by India, the Panel finds that it does significantly more than that.

---

[354]   See response to Question 37 of the Panel.

[355]   On the basis of the facts available to the Panel, it seems that there may have been other significant differences between both schemes. There was also evidence presented that no one had been denied a license under the 1995 regime. Even if the same were true for the 1997 scheme, that would have depended upon a corporations agreement to the investment and other commitments. In addition, as is evident in this dispute, under the 1997 regime, India maintains that the MOUs continue to have a life even after discretionary import licensing has been removed. This would not have been likely with the 1995 regime if the earlier MOUs involved voluntary projections leading to annual licenses. If the projections were not met in one year under the earlier scheme, they would more likely than not, have simply been taken into account in the discretionary decision about the following years licence. If the licensing regime ceased at that stage, it is not shown on balance that any other repercussions would have been likely to ensue.

Report of the Panel

7.98   Had the United States sought to challenge in these proceedings the mere existence or application of discretionary import licensing to the specific products at issue here, such a request may indeed have merely duplicated one part of the broader ruling of the *India – Quantitative Restrictions* panel. In this instance, however, the challenge before this Panel is different and concerns discrete measures which in themselves constitute an "Auto Licensing Policy". This Panel is being asked to rule on conditions which are specific to this policy, and the legal issue to consider here, i.e. whether the trade balancing and indigenization conditions are compatible with certain provisions of the covered Agreements, was neither expressly nor implicitly asked of, or addressed by, the *India - Quantitative Restrictions* panel.

7.99   In this instance, the most that can be said in aid of India's argument is that the existence of the import licensing scheme is a significant element of the factual context of the case, since the provisions of the MOUs were entered into with a view to obtaining the right to import some of the products restricted under India's EXIM policy and subject to import licensing. In a broad sense, the MOUs and the conditions foreseen in Public Notice No. 60 contributed to the continued application of one part of the discretionary licensing system examined by the *India – Quantitative Restrictions* dispute. However, this does not mean that the specific terms and conditions of the MOUs in themselves cannot be of such a nature as to be inconsistent with the same or other provisions of the Agreements, beyond the import restriction generated by the import licensing itself.

7.100 Complex measures or sets of measures may involve different aspects, which generate distinct violations of the WTO Agreements. This has been recognized through the acknowledgement in dispute settlement proceedings that different aspects of a single measure may be covered by different WTO Agreements. In this respect, the Panel also notes the comment by the *Korea – Measures Affecting Imports of Fresh, Chilled and Frozen Beef* panel (hereinafter "*Korea – Various Measures on Beef*"), that "where a discretionary licensing system is implemented in conjunction with other restrictions, such as in the present dispute, the manner in which the discretionary licensing system is operated may create additional restrictions independent of those imposed by the principal restriction".[356] The converse must also be possible. This led to the finding in *India – Quantitative Restrictions* as to the Actual User condition.

---

[356] WT/DS161/R, DSR 2001:I, 59, para. 782. Another illustration of the diverse legal consequences which a complex licensing scheme can have is to be found in the *EC – Bananas III* case. In that case, an issue arose as to whether the EC's procedures and requirements concerning the allocation of import licenses among operators who fulfilled the requirements in the European Communities fell within the scope of Article III:4. The European Communities having appealed the Panel's finding that these measures fell within the scope of Article III, the Appellate Body found as follows:

"At issue in this appeal is not whether *any* import licensing requirement, as such, is within the scope of Article III:4, but whether the European Communities procedures and requirements for the *distribution* of import licences for imported bananas among eligible operators *within* the European Communities are within the scope of this provision. The European Communities licensing procedures and requirements include the operator category rules, under which 30 per cent of the import licences for third-country and non-traditional ACP bananas are allocated to operators that market European Communities or traditional ACP bananas, and the activity function rules, under which Category A

1986   DSR 2002:V

India – Autos

7.101 The question put to this Panel relates to aspects of Public Notice No. 60 and the MOUs that are specific to the auto policy expressed in Public Notice No. 60, and which are not, in the Panel's view, "inherent" components of the import licensing system. To put it differently, knowing that the discretionary import licensing system is inconsistent with Article XI does not necessarily answer the question of whether indigenization and trade balancing obligations constitute restrictions on imports within the terms of Article XI. Indeed, the terms of India's BOPs notification suggest that with regard to these products, measures existed not only for balance-of-payments purposes but also for the purposes of an "auto policy".[357] It is some specific aspects of *that* policy that this panel is being asked to review. Whether they needed to be altered as a result of the ruling in *India – Quantitative Restrictions* is not a matter for this Panel's determination.

Conclusion

7.102 In view of the foregoing, the Panel concludes that the matter before it concerns

new claims never brought before the original panel,

concerning *specific conditions* applicable to automotive manufacturers wishing to import restricted kits and components

(1)   *never envisaged* by the *India - Quantitative Restrictions* panel, and

(2)   contained in *legally distinct measures*, adopted subsequent to the initiation of the *India – Quantitative Restrictions* panel, which constitute, in their own terms a "new auto licensing policy".

7.103 On the basis of the foregoing, the Panel further concludes that the matter referred to it in these proceedings is not the same as the matter adjudicated upon by the *India – Quantitative Restrictions* dispute, to the extent that it relates to violations resulting from the trade balancing and indigenization provisions in the MOUs under Public Notice No. 60, and not from the discretionary import licensing as such. For this reason the Panel considers that the doctrine of *res judicata* could not apply to the facts in this dispute. The Panel does not seek to rule on whether the doctrine could potentially apply to WTO dispute settlement.

7.104 India has also asked that, in the event the Panel rules that the United States claim is not barred by *res judicata*, it rule that India's balance-of-payments

---

and B licences are distributed among operators on the basis of their economic activities as importers, customs clearers or ripeners. *These rules go far beyond the mere import licence requirements needed to administer the tariff quota* for third-country and non-traditional ACP bananas or Lomé Convention requirements for the importation of bananas. *These rules are intended, among other things, to cross-subsidize distributors of European Communities (and ACP) bananas and to ensure that European Communities banana ripeners obtain a share of the quota rents. As such, these rules affect "the internal sale, offering for sale, purchase, ..." within the meaning of Article III:4*, and therefore fall within the scope of this provision. Therefore, we agree with the conclusion of the Panel on this point."

[357] The terms of India's notification to the BOPs Committee, in referring to "AUTO/BOP" as the grounds for restrictions for the products at issue, suggested that measures existed concerning these products *both* in the context of quantitative restrictions for balance-of-payments purposes and in specific "Auto" purposes.

DSR 2002:V
1987

Report of the Panel

defense in this dispute is also not barred. Given that an analysis of a balance-of-payments defense considers the evidence in existence at the date of a particular panel's establishment,[358] such defense cannot be precluded by another panel's consideration of economic factors on a wholly distinct date. Thus, regardless of the relevance of the *res judicata* doctrine to WTO dispute settlement, India is not prevented from raising a balance-of-payments defense in this case simply as a result of the panel in *India – Quantitative Restrictions* having held that the defense was not made out in that dispute.

1. *Has Any Part of the Matter before this Panel Been Settled Through a Mutually Agreed Solution?*

7.105 India has argued that with regard to the EC claim, the mutually agreed solution concluded in 1997 in settlement of their dispute on India's quantitative restrictions, (hereafter the "MAS"), prevents the European Communities from bringing this dispute to this Panel.[359]

7.106 This argument by India, if successful, would lead to the same result as a successful *res judicata* argument, in that it aims at excluding from the scope of these proceedings issues alleged to have already been resolved. Nevertheless, its legal basis is quite distinct. Here it is necessary to consider the terms of the agreement and the express provisions of the DSU dealing with such agreements.

(a) The Mutually Agreed Solution in the *India – Quantitative Restrictions* Dispute with the EC

7.107 The MAS reached with the European Communities was notified to the DSB in accordance with Article 3.6 of the DSU. This agreement, which was in the form of an exchange of letters, provides for three stages for the phasing out of import restrictions maintained on a number of products as notified by India to the Committee on Balance-of-Payments Restrictions (hereafter "BOP Committee"). It provided that

> "the European Communities will refrain from action under GATT Article XXII or Article XXIII as regards those restrictions during the phasing-out period (...) as long as India complies with its obligations [under their agreement]."[360]

7.108 The phasing out period ended on 1 April 2001, a point in time after the European Communities made its panel request in this matter.

7.109 In its First Submission, the European Communities argued that, not being a "covered Agreement" under the DSU, the MAS cannot be invoked by India "in order to justify the violation of its obligations under the GATT and the TRIMs Agreement".[361] India argued that the issue is not whether the MAS is a covered

---

[358] See Panel Report on *India – Quantitative Restrictions*, WT/DS90/R, adopted on 22 September 1999, as upheld by the Appellate Body Report, DSR 1999:V, 1799, para. 5.159.
[359] India's First Submission, para. 29, citing WT/DS96/8.
[360] WT/DS96/8, p. 2 (EC exhibit EC-8).
[361] EC First Submission, para. 98 (in footnote 73).

1988   DSR 2002:V

India – Autos

agreement. The issue is whether the DSU may be invoked again in respect of a matter formally raised under the DSU and settled through a mutually agreed solution notified under the DSU. It asserts that this issue is related to the EC's procedural rights under the DSU, not India's substantive obligations under a covered agreement.[362]

7.110 India further argues that a mutually agreed solution to a matter formally raised under a covered agreement and jointly notified to the DSB as such "must be regarded as a formal settlement of the dispute that makes the re-submission of the same dispute inadmissible".[363]

7.111 In addition to arguing that the agreed solution is not a covered agreement, the European Communities has also argued that the MAS did not settle this dispute, since both the measures and the claims are different. In particular, the European Communities stresses that the MOUs and Public Notice No. 60 were introduced after the negotiation of the MAS and are not an "inherent part" of the licensing scheme, which could have been administered in many different ways.

7.112 Like the issue of *res judicata* concerning the *India – Quantitative Restrictions* ruling, the issue before the Panel involves two questions: the first, and more general question, is that of the legal effect of a previously agreed and notified solution under Article 3.6 of the DSU in relation to subsequent proceedings concerning the same matter. The second question is, to the extent that such agreements may have legal implications for a panel's jurisdiction, whether the facts support its application in this case. The Panel will consider each question in turn.

(b) Relevance of Mutually Agreed Solutions in Subsequent Proceedings

7.113 The status of mutually agreed solutions under the DSU and their impact in subsequent dispute settlement proceedings is not expressly indicated in the DSU and has not been previously addressed in WTO dispute settlement proceedings. As was the case with the issue of *res judicata,* the Panel is thus unaided by any jurisprudence. Unlike that issue, however, such agreements are expressly referred to and supported by the DSU. It is certainly reasonable to assume, particularly on the basis of Article 3 of the DSU, as cited by India, that these agreed solutions are intended to reflect a settlement of the dispute in question, which both parties expect will bring a final conclusion to the relevant proceedings.

7.114 This does not necessarily resolve the issue of what can be done if, despite the agreed solution, a subsequent disagreement emerges relating to the scope of the solution or to compliance with it. This is not an issue expressly addressed in the DSU, nor has it been previously examined by another panel established under the DSU.

---

[362] India's First Submission, para. 33.
[363] *Ibid*, para. 35.

DSR 2002:V

Report of the Panel

7.115 Without clear guidance in the DSU, this question raises an important systemic issue.[364] On the one hand, the Panel recognizes that the right for any WTO Member to bring a dispute to the DSB is one of the fundamental tenets of the DSU, and that it could not be lightly assumed in what particular circumstances the drafters of the DSU might have intended such right to be foregone. On the other hand, it may also be the case that it could not be lightly assumed that those drafters intended mutually agreed solutions, expressly promoted by the DSU, to have no meaningful legal effect in subsequent proceedings. There may be significant differences between the provisions of mutually agreed solutions from case to case, which may also make it difficult to draw general conclusions as to the relevance of such solutions to subsequent proceedings other than on a case by case basis.

7.116 At the very least, the Panel sees merit in India's argument that the issue in this respect is not solely whether the mutually agreed solution is a covered agreement, but rather, what effects it may have on the exercise of procedural rights under the DSU in subsequent proceedings. As was the case with the question of *res judicata*, this systemic legal question of the effect of a mutually agreed solution in subsequent proceedings concerning the same matter only needs to be answered if the facts support the argument that the matter before us is covered by the MAS. In light of the European Communities' argument that the matter referred to this Panel has not been settled by the MAS, the Panel will proceed first with an analysis of whether the MAS can be considered to relate to the same matter. If that is the case, the Panel must then rule on the legal effect of such agreements. If it is not the case, there is no need for it to do so.

(c)   The Scope of the Mutually Agreed Solution between the European Communities and India

7.117 To determine the coverage of the MAS the Panel needs to consider its provisions and also the ambit of the previous dispute to which it was addressed. In that dispute, the European Communities called for formal consultations but did not proceed to a panel request. Thus the Panel needs to consider the terms of the consultation request as well as the terms of the MAS. Ultimately it is the terms of the MAS that are the only possible source of any restriction on our jurisdiction, since it is the scope of the matter that has been resolved through this solution that is at stake in the current determination. The consultation request

---

[364] In the absence of any express mechanism foreseen in the DSU for the consideration of such agreements, there would be a need to determine whether such a power can be implied from various provisions of the DSU. Alternatively, there may be an argument that a general principle such as *estoppel* may apply to WTO dispute settlement. These possibilities suggest that the issue cannot necessarily be resolved simply through an acknowledgement that an MAS is not a covered agreement as was argued by the EC. That argument simply is another way of noting that the DSU does not expressly give a panel a mandate to consider whether a "violation" of such an agreement might exist as a distinct basis for a dispute under the DSU. It does not necessarily prove that a panel may not in some circumstances need to consider the terms of such agreed solutions in order to fulfill its duties under the DSU. Here the Panel notes that disputes concerning the application of the DSU itself can be the object of proceedings under the DSU. This might possibly include disputes concerning mutually agreed solutions, since these are expressly referred to in the DSU.

1990   DSR 2002:V

may merely aid in an understanding of those terms. Because an MAS does not involve a specific adjudicatory ruling that would allow a precise identification of the matter actually "decided on", the Panel must rely on the articulation within the solution of the scope of what the parties intended to settle.[365]

7.118 As the MAS is not a covered agreement, it is not expressly subject to the DSU requirement to utilize customary rules of interpretation of international law. Nevertheless, since this is an agreement among States, the Panel finds it appropriate to address the terms of this agreement in accordance with the customary rules of interpretation of international law. It will therefore consider the ordinary meaning of the terms of the MAS in light of their context and taking into account their object and purpose.

7.119 The EC's initial request for consultations in the dispute which gave rise to the MAS with India (WT/DS96) identified the following measures:

> "quantitative restrictions maintained by India on importation of a large number of agricultural, textile and industrial products. The restrictions include those notified to the WTO in document WT/BOP/N/24 of 22 May. Annex 1 of this document lists more than 3,000 quantitative restrictions maintained as per 1 April 1997."[366]

These measures were alleged to be inconsistent with, *inter alia*, Articles XI, XIII, XVII and XVIII of GATT 1994.

7.120 The MAS reached by exchange of letters on 12 November 1997 was notified in accordance with Article 3.6 of the DSU, and circulated on 6 May 1998.[367] This agreement begins with the following provisions:

> "Desiring to reach a satisfactory settlement of the difference regarding quantitative restrictions maintained by India on import of industrial, agricultural and textile products, as notified by India to the WTO by Annex 1, Part B (Notification on Quantitative Restrictions Maintained on Imports Under the Export and Import Policy (as on 1 April 1997)) of document WT/BOP/N/24 of 22 May, and for which the European Communities requested consultations with India under GATT Article XXII on 18 July 1997, India, on the understanding that nothing in this Agreement prejudices the respective rights and obligations of the European Communities and India under the WTO Agreement and that *the European Communities will refrain from action under GATT Article XXII or Article XXIII as regards those restrictions during the phasing-out period*

---

[365] In this analysis, the Panel again adopts the notion of "matter", as referred to in the DSU, as a minimal benchmark by which to assess the respective scopes of the MAS and the matter brought before it. The nature of the comparison, however, varies *mutatis mutandis* in considering an MAS rather than a ruling argued to be *res judicata*. In this instance, what should be the basis for the comparison is the scope of the MAS, as defined essentially by the parties themselves, rather than any legal issues actually ruled on in previous proceedings.

[366] WT/DS96/1.

[367] WT/DS96/8.

DSR 2002:V

Report of the Panel

as defined below, as long as India complies with its obligations under this exchange of letters, agrees as follows:

> 1. India will eliminate all quantitative restrictions on imports maintained by reference to GATT Article XVIII and notified to the WTO in Annex I, Part B of document WT/BOP/N/24 of 22 May, in accordance with the time schedules contained in Annex III of that document, as modified by the attached Annex. The modifications in the attached Annex concern the duration of each of the three phases of the period for the elimination of quantitative restrictions on imports imposed by India for balance-of-payments purposes and the shifting of certain products from Phase II to Phase I or Phase III to Phase I or II. This is without prejudice to India's rights and obligations under the WTO Agreement." (emphasis added)

7.121 The scope of the solution is identified in this initial part of the MAS as relating to "quantitative restrictions maintained by India on import of industrial, agricultural and textile products, as notified by India to the WTO by Annex 1, Part B (Notification on Quantitative Restrictions Maintained on Imports Under the Export and Import Policy (as on 1 April 1997)) of document WT/BOP/N/24 of 22 May, and for which the European Communities requested consultations with India under GATT Article XXII on 18 July 1997". These are thus in essence the same measures as were brought to the panel on *India – Quantitative Restrictions* by the United States at approximately the same period.[368]

7.122 The MAS further provides a timetable for "the elimination of quantitative restrictions imposed by India and notified to the WTO in Annex I, Part B of document WT/BOP/N/24 over three phases". While the period for elimination of the restrictions foreseen for the products at issue in the instant proceedings extended beyond 1 April 2001, an MFN clause in the solution allowed the European Communities to benefit from the more favourable solution subsequently reached with the United States. This meant that the date of 1 April 2001 was the relevant date for elimination of the quantitative restrictions maintained by India on kits and components as contemplated in the MAS with the EC.[369]

7.123 India refers, in its argument, to the final part of the above introductory paragraph, and more particularly, to the European Communities' commitment not to initiate proceedings under Articles XXII or XXIII of GATT "as long as it complied with its phase-out obligations".

7.124 In considering that argument, the Panel notes that both the consultation request and the MAS refer exclusively to the "quantitative restrictions" maintained by India on a number of products as notified to the BOP Committee. The European Communities promise is merely to "refrain from action ... with regard

---

[368] The panel on *India – Quantitative Restrictions* was established on 18 November 1997, while the mutually agreed solution between India and the European Communities, although only notified in May 1998, was reached on 12 November 1997.

[369] See MAS paragraph 3, in WT/DS96/8.

1992

DSR 2002:V

to those measures." There is no express reference in the MAS to any such promise with regard to supplementary or subsidiary measures. Indigenization and trade balancing are not mentioned. Where the MAS is concerned, there is no direct or indirect reference in the definition of the scope of the solution to any specific criteria, Public Notices or other instruments used for the administration of these restrictions, nor to any specific criteria applied in conjunction with the restrictions maintained.

7.125 As in the case of the dispute between the United States and India, the Panel also notes that the specific measures before it could not have been expressly dealt with in the consultations or the MAS as negotiated. This is because Public Notice No. 60 was adopted exactly one month after the exchange of letters which sealed the MAS, albeit several months before its notification to the DSB.[370]

7.126 The Panel also notes that there is no express reference in the MAS to the indigenization or trade balancing elements of the MOUs which were utilized prior to the 1997 changes. Thus those changes cannot be seen to be a mere continuation of similar measures expressly covered.

7.127 The Panel again considers that a claim that contractual conditions as to indigenization and trade balancing in and of themselves constitute a violation of Article XI, is different from a claim that a general quantitative restrictions regime is itself in violation of that Article. The MAS only expressly precluded resort to formal dispute settlement in respect of the quantitative restrictions, although it did address other provisions as well. Indeed, India's argument in relation to the MAS only refers to the European Communities' promise relating to the obligation to "phase-out" these restrictions. The phase-out obligation is contained in paragraph 1 of the MAS. This leads us to a preliminary conclusion that the ordinary meaning of the European Communities' promise in the MAS concerning the phase-out of the quantitative restrictions referred to, does not expressly preclude the initiation of a dispute aimed at questioning the validity *per se* of subsequently introduced specific conditions employed in the administration of a part of India's then applicable quantitative restrictions.

7.128 The MAS also contains additional provisions that address the relations of the parties in the course of the implementation period. The Panel feels that it must consider these as part of the context of the provisions of the MAS principally raised by India, in order to ensure a complete interpretation of the scope of the MAS. These are as follows:

> "Without prejudice to the rights and obligations of the European Communities and India under the WTO Agreement, India will refrain during the phase-out period from making more restrictive the import arrangements for the products in the attached Annex and in Annex III of document WT/BOP/N/24.

---

[370] As previously noted, the MAS was reached on 12 November 1997. Public Notice No. 60 was adopted on 12 December 1997.

Report of the Panel

> During the transition period India will operate the SIL and the NAL arrangements in a transparent and non-discriminatory manner so as to ensure that they do not have trade-restrictive or distortive effects additional to those caused by the restrictions themselves. This is without prejudice to India's rights and obligations under the Agreement on Import Licensing Procedures. India will notify licensing procedures, and changes in these procedures, in accordance with Article 5 of the Agreement on Import Licensing Procedures.
>
> (...)
>
> This agreement shall be reviewed annually by India and the EC. For the purposes of this review, India will provide information on the implementation of the phasing-out schedule. In this framework, there will be an opportunity for India and the European Communities to discuss the implementation of the time schedules and for the European Communities to raise questions regarding the functioning of licensing procedures during the phasing-out period."

7.129 These clauses suggest that the parties contemplated that modifications might be made to the arrangements the subject of the MAS. They imply that during the phase-out period, if India met the interim phase-out targets it would only be in breach of the MAS if such modifications were "more restrictive" or caused "additional distortive effects."

7.130 The express promise to refrain from bringing a challenge against the quantitative restrictions refers to the condition of India complying with its obligations under the agreement. This could be argued to include the obligations as to changes in the licensing "arrangements". These clauses however do not address the separate question of whether a change which raises a distinct claim can be separately challenged. The plain meaning of the European Communities' promise with respect to "those restrictions" is thus not, in the view of the Panel, affected by these clauses.. This is the interpretation that the Panel adopts.[371]

7.131 In addition, the Panel also notes that the claims invoked in the request for consultations in the earlier dispute, which formed the basis of the subsequent agreed solution, referred to a number of provisions of the GATT, including Arti-

---

[371] If the Panel were wrong in that view, the next question would be whether the facts support the application of those provisions in a way which precludes the European Communities' express DSU rights to bring an action where it deems it appropriate. Those clauses refer to modifications and alterations. It is not in dispute that some changes were made. For the same reasons as articulated with respect to the *res judicata* issue, the Panel believes that the changes were significant and were more than merely measures that made existing provisions more transparent and objective. That conclusion does not however lead to the conclusion that they are necessarily more restrictive or distortive. Nor is it clear what evidentiary elements would be appropriate to rely on in considering whether the 1997 changes are more restrictive or distortive. Nevertheless, as India seeks to rely on the MAS as a defense, it would have been for it to address this issue and provide a prima facie case and convince us that these changes alter the plain meaning of clause 1 of the MAS. The Panel does not find that they have done so.

India – Autos

cle XI, but not to any inconsistency with Article III. In addition, while other covered Agreements were identified, the TRIMs Agreement was not one of those. From these observations, the Panel cannot conclude that the scope of the agreed solution with regard to the measures actually covered, encompasses any claims of violation of either Article III or the TRIMs Agreement.

7.132 The Panel now turns to consider whether it can be successfully argued that the matter raised before it by the European Communities is indirectly or by implication precluded from further dispute by reason of the terms of the MAS. As in the case of the *res judicata* analysis, the Panel acknowledges that such a broad-ranging dispute as that which gave rise to the MAS could not be reasonably expected to have such a solution list every single measure which may have some bearing on the application of the quantitative restrictions at issue. The Panel again acknowledges that compliance by India with the terms of the MAS would no doubt have had implications for many such administrative elements. Again, that does not determine whether those elements are covered by the promise not to resort to dispute settlement. In much the same way as it held that the specific trade balancing and indigenization requirements were not implicitly covered by the *India – Quantitative Restrictions* panel ruling, the Panel concludes on balance that the mutually agreed solution concerning India's quantitative restrictions for balance-of-payments purposes does not indirectly encompass the specific conditions before it.

7.133 The Panel considers that the reference to "those restrictions" in the introductory paragraph of the MAS is, as far as discretionary import licensing is concerned, a reference to the licensing scheme *per se* and not to future elements of it that are argued to violate provisions of the covered agreements in and of themselves. Thus, the Panel does not consider that the plain meaning of the promise relating to challenges to quantitative restrictions, impliedly deals with the two conditions now in dispute. Nor does it consider that it should be interpreted to cover distinct challenges to all administrative features. The Panel does not read in the terms of the MAS an all-encompassing promise barring litigation of any subsequent administrative aspect of the measures expressed to come within the covered solution. The Panel would therefore not interpret a promise by the European Communities to "refrain from action … as regards those restrictions" as impliedly applying to the measures in dispute before it. This plain meaning and contextual interpretation is sufficiently clear but in any event does not, in the Panel's view frustrate the object and purpose of the MAS, which from its terms is to bring to an end the particular dispute it dealt with: i.e. the European Communities' concerns with a broad range of quantitative restrictions taken by India for balance-of-payments purposes.

(d)   Conclusion

7.134 In view of the foregoing, the Panel concludes that the terms of the mutually agreed solution notified by the European Communities and India do not preclude it from examining the matter brought before it by the European Communities. In view of that factual finding the Panel does not intend to rule on the legal

DSR 2002:V

Report of the Panel

question as to whether a notified mutually agreed solution can ever operate as a bar to a panel's express mandate from the DSB.

7.135 The European Communities also argues, as a subsidiary matter, that if the Panel were to find that the issues raised in this dispute are covered by the MAS, then these measures violate that agreement for a further reason, since they are alleged to continue beyond 1 April 2001. Having found that the Panel's competence is not precluded by the MAS in any event, it does not need to consider this argument further.

2. *Measures to be Eliminated in the Course of Implementing the Results of the India - Quantitative Restrictions Dispute and Abusive Splitting of a Dispute*

7.136 India invokes further arguments in support of its contention that the Panel should not consider the claims referred to it, because the MOUs are an inherent part of the import licensing scheme which India is required to eliminate as of 1 April 2001 as a result of the ruling of the *India - Quantitative Restrictions* dispute and of its mutually agreed solution with the EC.

7.137 India argues that it would be pointless for this Panel to "add" new grounds of violations concerning them. This argument relates to the Article III of GATT and TRIMs allegations not dealt with or referred to in either *India – Quantitative Restrictions* or the MAS. India also argues that a complainant may not abusively "split" a dispute into successive actions instead of raising all the issues relating to a single matter in one proceeding.

7.138 The Panel has already concluded that the matter before it is different to the matter before the *India-QR* panel and the matter dealt with in the MAS. Thus this is not, in the Panel's view, a case of a new claim being expressly directed against a distinct measure previously addressed under another provision. The remaining underlying assumption in both of these arguments appears to be that all issues relating to measures which may need to be eliminated as a result of a specific proceeding should all have been dealt with at once and a separate dispute should not be engaged in where the issues at stake are arguably already disposed of through the outcome of the initial disputes.

(a) Abusive Splitting

7.139 India argues that it should not be possible to "split" a dispute into separate successive cases. Although India seems to invoke an autonomous "principle" of prohibition of "abusive splitting" of disputes, it has not explained any source for this specific principle. Rather, its argument appears to rest essentially on the basis that this would be an abusive exercise of the right to bring complaints before the DSB.

7.140 Such a principle could be sought to be argued to fit within general principles of due process or some equitable principle such as good faith or abuse of rights. While such notions might be of relevance to WTO dispute settlement in some circumstances, the Panel is not convinced that the conditions which might

1996   DSR 2002:V

justify such a decision are present in this instance. This is not a case where it is alleged that a complainant knowing all the facts about a measure, chooses to deliberately burden a respondent with a range of separate actions dealing with distinct WTO provisions. Here it is not in dispute that new measures were introduced in 1997. These measures themselves contain a range of provisions specific to the auto sector and constitute a distinct "auto licensing policy". These measures may have significantly affected the legal and commercial implications of the indigenization and trade balancing undertakings made by signatories to earlier MOUs.

7.141 In such circumstances, the Panel recalls the terms of Article 3.7 of the DSU, according to which "Before bringing a case, a Member shall exercise its judgment as to whether action under these procedures would be fruitful". The DSU thus entrusts Members with the responsibility of being essentially self-regulating in deciding to bring a case to the attention of the DSB. In this instance, as noted above, the specific measures brought before this Panel, although they have some relation with the matter ruled on in QRs are in themselves distinct measures concerning a specific industrial sector. In addition, while India disputes the significance and overall distortive effects brought about by the 1997 changes, it has never presented any evidence that the complainants were acting in bad faith or contrary to the spirit of Article 3.7 in coming to a different view about the 1997 measures. Consequently the Panel does not find any evidence to support an allegation of abusive splitting, even if such a principle could ever allow a panel to make a discretionary determination not to pursue its express mandate.

7.142 In view of the above factual finding the Panel does not rule on whether such a power could in theory exist.

(b) Unnecessary Litigation

7.143 This argument seems to rely on the notion that matters which have not been expressly ruled on, (in this case, in India's view, the claims based on provisions other than Article XI of GATT), should not be re-considered on the basis that it would be, in its view, "pointless" to examine these additional claims in relation to measures which are required to be eliminated in any case.

7.144 The assumption seems to be that if full compliance with previous rulings incidentally requires the elimination of part or all of the measures considered in the subsequent dispute, then these distinct claims should not be examined by the second panel.

7.145 The argument seems to assume a certain interpretation of what is required in terms of implementation of the previous panel ruling. As outlined below, however, this Panel takes the view that this assessment is not for it to perform. Therefore, the question of whether the measures before the *India - Quantitative Restrictions* panel need to be brought into compliance to a degree which would make the issues before this Panel without practical significance, is not one which can be part of this Panel's mandate.

Report of the Panel

7.146 In any event the Panel does not believe that the facts support an assertion that the new claims can have no practical significance. This argument by India relates to claimed violations that the Panel has concluded were *not* ruled on by the *India – Quantitative Restrictions* panel. Even if the proper implementation of the rulings in that case may involve the elimination of measures in a way that will incidentally dispose of other violations also, this cannot be presumed in all instances. For example, if Public Notice No. 60 and the MOUs were to involve violations of Article III, it cannot be presumed that these violations would necessarily disappear with the disappearance of the import licensing scheme in implementation of the *India – Quantitative Restrictions* rulings. There may be many ways for India to implement the results of the *India - Quantitative Restrictions* ruling in order to eliminate the import restrictions maintained for balance-of-payments purposes on different products, and depending on the structure of the specific measures at stake, this may or may not entail the elimination of other violations of the Agreements.

7.147 In concluding its consideration of these arguments relating to measures that India may be "required to eliminate" as a result of the *India - Quantitative Restrictions* disputes, the Panel wishes to stress that it does not intend, in these proceedings, to draw any conclusions on what the implementation of the rulings adopted in the *Quantitative Restrictions* case with the United States and of the MAS with the European Communities may or may not require. This would be a matter for a compliance panel to establish, if so requested. This Panel's mandate, however, is quite distinct from that of a compliance panel under Article 21.5.

7.148 It was never argued that the measures as they existed at the dates of request for establishment of the Panel were taken in order to comply with the rulings and recommendations of the DSB in the *India – Quantitative Restrictions* dispute. On the contrary, at the time of their adoption, they supported and contributed to the continued application of the import licensing scheme which India was subsequently required to bring into conformity with the WTO Agreements under the *India – Quantitative Restrictions* case.

7.149 Nor do subsequent events alter this distinction between this Panel's jurisdiction and any possible compliance panel's jurisdiction. It is true that, in the parties' own description of the facts, the evolution of the measures in the course of these proceedings is directly linked to actions taken with a view to implementing the *India – Quantitative Restrictions* rulings. Nevertheless, the Panel does not see this question as affecting its jurisdiction to consider the measures as they existed as of the date of its establishment. A compliance panel might, at most, if so requested, consider these measures as of the date for compliance with the *India – Quantitative Restrictions* rulings. Any potential for overlap between views expressed under this Panel's mandate and views which might be expressed by a hypothetical compliance panel under *India – Quantitative Restrictions* may be a systemic issue of significance, but it is not for this Panel to resolve. [372] The po-

---

[372] Nor is there any reason to presume that any panel subsequently examining an issue considered by a previous panel would not take the outcome of such ruling into consideration, to the extent relevant.

1998 DSR 2002:V

tential ambit of a compliance panel's findings does not in any way diminish this Panel's obligation to comply with its express mandate from the DSB to consider the measures before it.

3. Conclusion

7.150 In examining each of India's arguments, the Panel has given careful consideration to the concerns expressed by India concerning the possible reopening of the same disputes between the same parties. It is apparent to the Panel that the measures before it have operated in direct relation to the discretionary import licensing system which India has committed itself to eliminate in accordance with the recommendations of the DSB and its agreed solution with the European Communities. Nonetheless, the Panel is of the view that this dispute raises distinct legal issues from those resolved through the *India – Quantitative Restrictions* disputes, and that it must consider these issues. In view of the foregoing analysis, the Panel rejects each of India's arguments to the effect that it does not have jurisdiction or should exercise some discretion not to consider the matter before it. The Panel now turns to a consideration of the substantive issues.

D. Order of Examination of the Claims

7.151 Both complainants have made claims that the measures in issue are in violation of both GATT 1994 and the TRIMs Agreement (Article 2). The Panel first wishes to consider whether it is desirable to consider these claims in any particular order.

7.152 A number of factors should be considered in that regard. The Panel recalls the Appellate Body's comment in *European Communities – Regime for the Importation, Sale and Distribution of Bananas* (hereafter "*EC – Bananas III*") suggesting that a panel would normally be expected to examine the more specific agreement before the more general, where two Agreements apply simultaneously.[373] The Panel also recalls that it is permitted to apply judicial economy in considering matters before it, so that "a panel need only address those claims which must be addressed in order to resolve the matter in issue in the dispute".[374]

---

[373] See Report of the Appellate Body in *EC – Bananas III*, WT/DS27/AB/R, adopted on 25 September 1997, para. 204 (DSR 1997:II, 591): "Although Article X:3(a) of the GATT 1994 and Article 1.3 of the Licensing Agreement both apply, the Panel, in our view, should have applied the Licensing Agreement first, since this Agreement deals specifically, and in detail, with the administration of import licensing procedures. If the Panel had done so, then there would have been no need for it to address the alleged inconsistency with Article X:3(a) of the GATT 1994".

[374] Report of the Appellate Body in *US – Wool Shirts and Blouses*, WT/DS33/AB/R, adopted on 23 May 1997, p.19 (DSR 1997:I, 323, at 340). The Appellate Body noted more generally in that paragraph that "[n]othing in [Article 11 of the DSU] or in previous GATT practice *requires* a panel to examine *all* legal claims made by the complaining party. Previous GATT 1947 and WTO panels have frequently addressed only those issues that such panels considered necessary for the resolution of the matter between the parties, and have declined to decide other issues. (...) Given the explicit aim of dispute settlement that permeates the DSU, we do not consider that Article 3.2 of the DSU is meant to encourage either panels or the Appellate Body to "make law" by clarifying existing provi-

Report of the Panel

7.153 The Panel has also taken into account the fact that two complaints are effectively being addressed in this report, the scopes of which are not in all respects identical. In considering these questions of order and judicial economy, the Panel has been mindful of its obligations under Article 9 of the DSU in preserving the rights of all parties where multiple complaints are involved.

7.154 Where the order of analysis of claims is concerned, it is important to consider if a particular order is compelled by principles of valid interpretative methodology, which, if not followed, might constitute an error of law.[375]

7.155 In circumstances other than where a proper application of one provision might be hindered without prior consideration of other issues, the adoption by a panel of a particular order of examination of discrete claims would rarely lead to any errors of law. A panel would always be required to consider, *inter alia,* contextual aspects of interpretation of each of the relevant provisions in accordance with customary rules of interpretation, and to take account of the principle of effectiveness in such interpretation, whichever agreement it chooses to examine first. Here the Panel notes the comments of the Appellate Body in *US – FSC* concerning the United States' argument that the Panel erred by failing to begin its examination of the European Communities' claim under Article 3.1(a) of the *SCM Agreement* with footnote 59 of that Agreement. In the Appellate Body's view,

> "it was not a legal error for the Panel to begin its examination of whether the FSC measure involves export *subsidies* by examining the general definition of a "*subsidy*" that is applicable to export *subsidies* in Article 3.1(a). In any event, whether the examination begins with the general definition of a "subsidy" in Article 1.1 or with footnote 59, we believe that the outcome of the European Communities' claim under Article 3.1(a) would be the same. The appropriate meaning of both provisions can be established and can be given effect, irrespective of whether the examination of the claim of the European Communities under Article 3.1(a) begins with Article 1.1 or with footnote 59.[376]

7.156 In this case, the Panel is dealing with separate claims to the effect that a particular factual situation falls foul of both GATT 1994 provisions and provisions of the TRIMs Agreement. Previous panels confronted with concurrent claims concerning these two agreements have had diverse approaches to the choice of order of analysis of such claims.[377]

---

sions of the *WTO Agreement* outside the context of resolving a particular dispute. A panel need only address those claims which must be addressed in order to resolve the matter in issue in the dispute".

[375] An example of a situation where a proper order of examination of different elements of a certain provision can be identified would be Article XX of GATT 1994, as highlighted by the Report of the Appellate Body in *US – Shrimp*, WT/DS58/AB/R, adopted on 6 November 1998, DSR 1998:VII, 2755, para. 120.

[376] Report of the Appellate Body in *US – FSC*, WT/DS108/AB/R, adopted on 20 March 2000, DSR 2000:III, 1619, para. 89.

[377] One panel decided to examine claims under Article III:4 and Article 2.1 of the TRIMs Agreement together, but having found a violation of Article III:4, did not consider it necessary to make a

India – Autos

7.157 As a general matter, even if there was some guiding principle to the effect that a specific covered Agreement might appropriately be examined before a general one where both may apply to the same measure, it might be difficult to characterize the TRIMs Agreement as necessarily more "specific" than the relevant GATT provisions. Although the TRIMS Agreement "has an autonomous legal existence", independent from the relevant GATT provisions, as noted by the *Indonesia – Autos* panel,[378] the substance of its obligations refers directly to Articles III and XI of the GATT, and clarifies their meaning, *inter alia*, through an Illustrative list. On one view, it simply provides additional guidance as to the identification of certain measures considered to be inconsistent with Articles III:4 and XI:1 of the GATT 1994. On the other hand, the TRIMs Agreement also introduces rights and obligations that are specific to it, through its notification mechanism and related provisions. An interpretative question also arises in relation to the TRIMs Agreement as to whether a complainant must separately prove that the measure in issue is a "trade-related investment measure". For either of these reasons, the TRIMs Agreement might be arguably more specific in that it provides additional rules concerning the specific measures it covers. [379] The Panel is therefore not convinced that, as a general matter, the TRIMs Agreement could inherently be characterized as more specific than the relevant GATT provisions.

7.158 In some circumstances, there may be a practical significance in determining a particular order of examination of claims based on the TRIMS and GATT 1994.[380] One example might be where the temporary cover offered to notified

---

finding on Article 2.1 of the TRIMS Agreement (See Panel Report on *EC – Bananas*, WT/DS27/R, DSR 1997:II, 695-803-943 and DSR 1997:III, 1085, para. 7.168).

Another panel decided to examine first the claims under the TRIMs Agreement, "since the TRIMs Agreement is more specific than Article III:4 as far as the claims under consideration are concerned". In doing this, the panel was seeking to follow the approach endorsed by the Appellate Body in *EC – Bananas III* and referred to above that claims on the more specific agreement should be examined before the more general (See Panel Report on *Indonesia – Autos*, WT/DS54/R, WT/DS55/R, WT/DS59/R, WT/DS64/R, adopted on 23 July 1998, para. 14.63, DSR 1998:VI, 2201).

A third and subsequent panel, however, was "not persuaded that the TRIMS Agreement can be properly characterized as more specific than Article III:4 in respect of the claims raised by the complainants in the present case". That panel chose to examine first the claims under the GATT 1994, following the parties' order of presentation (See Panel Report on *Canada – Autos*, WT/DS139/R, WT/DS142/R, adopted on 19 June 2000, as modified by the Appellate Body Report, para. 10.63 (DSR 2000:VII, 3043)).

[378] Panel Report on *Indonesia – Autos*, WT/DS54/R, WT/DS55/R, WT/DS59/R, WT/DS64/R, para. 14.63 (DSR 1998:VI, 2201).

[379] To say, for instance, that the TRIMs Agreement is more specific because it contains a specific criterion of the presence or absence of a trade-related investment measure depends upon whether that is a distinct criterion and whether the lack of such a criterion in Articles III and XI of GATT 1994 makes these provisions more general as opposed to merely having a broader range of coverage on the same criteria. The only practical difference and potential advantage in looking at the TRIMs agreement first in this instance seems to be the possible utilization of the Illustrative List, to the extent that it would be relevant to the claims at issue and may facilitate the identification of a violation of Articles III:4 or XI:1 of GATT 1994.

[380] Determining order of analysis is different to the question of resolution of conflict between provisions. The latter entails the use of conflict resolution rules or interpretative techniques. The Panel notes that both GATT 1994 and the TRIMs Agreement are part of Annex 1A of the WTO Agreement. A general interpretative note to Annex 1A provides that "[i]n the event of a conflict between a

---

DSR 2002:V

2001

Report of the Panel

TRIMs would be of relevance. In this instance, India has not claimed to have notified the measures at issue under the TRIMs Agreement. This issue therefore does not arise here. Indeed, in response to a question from the Panel, India has indicated that "the TRIMs Agreement (...) no longer entails rights and obligations in respect of India that are different from those under the GATT", and has encouraged the Panel to refrain from examining the TRIMs Agreement.[381] For the purposes of this case, therefore, there appears to be, in that respect, no particular reason to start our examination on any particular order. Nor does it find that the end result would be affected by either determination of order of analysis.

7.159 Both complainants have also addressed their claims under GATT 1994 prior to their claims under the TRIMS Agreement. Their responses to specific questions from the Panel on the proper order of examination of their claims suggest that both would be in agreement with an approach leading to an examination of the GATT 1994 claims first.[382]

7.160 In these circumstances, the Panel does not see that there is anything improper in either addressing the GATT claims or the TRIMs claims first.

7.161 The order selected for examination of the claims may also have an impact on the potential to apply judicial economy. It seems that an examination of the GATT provisions in this case would be likely to make it unnecessary to address the TRIMs claims, but not vice-versa. If a violation of the GATT claims was found, it would be justifiable to refrain from examining the TRIMs claims under the principle of judicial economy. Even if no violation was found under the GATT claims, that also seems an efficient starting point since it would be difficult to imagine that if no violation has been found of Articles III or XI, a violation could be found of Article 2 of the TRIMs Agreement, which refers to the same provisions. Conversely, if no violation of the TRIMs Agreement were found, this would not necessarily preclude the existence of a violation of GATT Articles III:4 or XI:1 because the scope of the GATT provisions is arguably broader if India's argument was accepted that there is a need to prove that a measure is an investment measure and its assertion that this is not the case with the measures before this Panel.

7.162 For all of these reasons the Panel will therefore examine the GATT claims first.

7.163 Violations of Articles III and XI have been alleged with regard to two of the conditions foreseen under Public Notice No. 60 and in the MOUs, namely "indigenization" and "trade balancing". The Panel will address claims relating to these two conditions in turn.

---

provision of the General Agreement on Tariffs and Trade 1994 and a provision of another agreement in Annex 1A (...) the provision of the other agreement shall prevail to the extent of the conflict." No conflict has been alleged to exist in this instance, in the absence of any issue relating to any TRIMs which would have been notified under the TRIMs Agreement.

[381] Response to Question 128 of the Panel.

[382] See the response of the EC to Question 99 of the Panel, and the response of the US to Question 84 of the Panel.

E.   Consistency of the Indigenization Condition with the GATT 1994

7.164 Paragraph 3 (iii) of Public Notice No. 60 provides that the MOUs shall be based on a number of parameters, including:

> "Indigenization of components up to a minimum level of 50% in the third year or earlier from the date of clearance of first import consignment of CKD/SKD kits/components and 70% in the 5th year or earlier. Once the MOU signing firm has reached an indigenization level of 70%, there will be no need for further import licences from DGFT. Consequently, as and when the firms achieve 70% indigenization, they would go outside the ambit of the MOU automatically. However, they will discharge the export obligation corresponding to the imports made by them till that time."

7.165 The standard MOU annexed to Public Notice No. 60 reflects this obligation by requiring:

> "that the party shall achieve indigenization of components up to a minimum level of 50% in the third year or earlier from the date of clearance of first import consignment of CKD/SKD kits and 70% in the fifth year of earlier. Once the party has reached an indigenization level of 70% there will be no need for further import licence from DGTF. However, the party shall discharge the export obligation corresponding to the imports made by them till that time.
>
> That the party intends to achieve the following levels of indigenization of their product, year-wise:
>
> Year   Percentage (%) of indigenization
>
> The party shall aggressively pursue and achieve as soon as possible the development of the local supply base and increased local content, since the same will allow a higher level of indigenization."

7.166 It is not disputed that MOUs have been signed with most major car manufacturers in India in accordance with these terms, including the "indigenization" condition.

7.167 The European Communities and United States claim that this obligation is inconsistent with Article III:4 of the GATT 1994. The United States also claims that the measure is inconsistent with Article XI:1 of GATT 1994.

7.168 The Panel does not believe that it is required as a matter of proper interpretation to consider one of these claims prior to the other as they are distinct Articles and the proper application of one does not require a prior determination of the other. The Panel will consider first the claims concerning an alleged violation of Article III:4, since this claim is common to both complainants. This would provide the greatest opportunity to at least consider the application of the judicial economy principle, since any finding which might be first made on the

Report of the Panel

basis of Article XI, would not have addressed the claim of the European Communities.

1. Claims under Article III:4 of GATT 1994

7.169 In accordance with the terms of Article 3.2 of the DSU, the Panel is required to clarify the existing provisions of the covered agreements in accordance with customary rules of interpretation of public international law. As has been recalled by the Appellate Body, these rules are embodied in particular in Articles 31 and 32 of the Vienna Convention on the Law of Treaties. Accordingly, this Panel is required to interpret the text of the agreements by way of reference to the "the ordinary meaning of the terms of the treaty in their context and in the light of its object and purpose".

7.170 Article III:1 provides in relevant part that:

> "[t]he contracting parties recognize that internal taxes and other internal charges, and laws, regulations and requirements affecting the internal sale, offering for sale, purchase, transportation, distribution or use of the products (...) should not be applied to imported or domestic products so as to afford protection to domestic production".[383]

7.171 Article III:4 provides in relevant part:

> "The products of the territory of any contracting party imported into the territory of any other contracting party shall be accorded treatment no less favourable than that accorded to like products of national origin in respect of all laws, regulations and requirements affecting their internal sale, offering for sale, purchase, transportation, distribution or use."

7.172 To determine whether the Indian measure is consistent with Article III:4, it is necessary to examine whether (1) imported products and domestic products are like products; (2) the measures constitute a "law, regulation or requirement"; (3) they affect the internal sale, offering for sale, purchase, transportation, distribution or use; and (4) imported products are accorded less favourable treatment than the treatment accorded to like domestic products.[384]

---

[383] The Appellate Body has recently clarified the contextual role of Article III:1 in the interpretation of Article III:4:

> "the "general principle" set forth in Article III:1 "informs" the rest of Article III and acts "as a guide to understanding and interpreting the specific obligations contained" in the other paragraphs of Article III, including paragraph 4. Thus, in our view, Article III:1 has particular contextual significance in interpreting Article III:4, as it sets forth the "general principle" pursued by that provision." Report of the Appellate Body on *European Communities – Measures Affecting Asbestos and Asbestos-Containing Products*, WT/DS135/AB/R, adopted on 5 April 2001, para. 93.

[384] Report of the Appellate Body in *Korea – Various Measures on Beef*, WT/DS161/AB/R, WT/DS169/AB/R, adopted on 10 January 2001, para. 133 (DSR 2001:I, 5).

2004   DSR 2002:V

(a) Like Products

7.173 This claim deals with the treatment of certain specified imported automotive parts and components and their domestic equivalent.

7.174 The Panel notes that the only factor of distinction under the "indigenization" condition between products which contribute to fulfilment of the condition and products which do not, is the origin of the product as either imported or domestic. India has not disputed the likeness of the relevant automotive parts and components of domestic or foreign origin for the purposes of Article III:4 of the GATT 1994. Origin being the sole criterion distinguishing the products, it is correct to treat such products as like products within the meaning of Article III:4.

7.175 The panel in *Canada - Autos* reached the same conclusion in similar conditions.[385] More recently, the compliance panel in *US – FSC (Article 21.5)* noted that :

> "the distinction made between imported and domestic products in the Act's foreign Articles/labour limitation concerning the limitation on fair market value attributable to 'articles' is solely and explicitly based on origin. We do not believe that the mere fact that a good has US origin renders it "unlike" an imported good."[386]

7.176 The Panel therefore concludes that automotive parts and components of domestic and foreign origin are like products within the meaning of Article III:4 of GATT 1994.

(b) "Laws, regulations or requirements"

7.177 While the Panel is at this stage considering the indigenization condition, it does not arise in a vacuum. It emanates from Public Notice No. 60 and the MOUs entered thereunder. The Panel thus needs to look at these measures as identified in our terms of reference to consider whether they constitute "laws, regulations or requirements".

7.178 Public Notice No. 60 and the MOUs operate together, so that in combination, the obligations actually accrue: the proper application of Public Notice No. 60 required MOUs to be signed by an entity that wished to obtain licenses. The legal obligations on individual firms therefore resulted from the combination of both instruments: the MOUs were signed in accordance with Public Notice No. 60, and once signed, they embodied for the manufacturers the obligations foreseen in the Public Notice No. 60.

7.179 The Panel has therefore chosen to examine these legal instruments together as the combined foundation for the indigenization obligation. If between the two instruments, it is appropriate to conclude that the indigenization condition is an element of certain "laws, regulations or requirements", then this should be enough for this part of the Article III analysis. The situation may be different at the stage of considering any recommendations and rulings. The provision call-

---

[385] Panel Report on *Canada – Autos*, WT/DS139/R, WT/DS142/R, adopted on 19 June 2000, as modified by the Appellate Body Report, para. 10.74 (DSR 2000:VII, 3043).
[386] WT/DS108/RW circulated on 20 August 2001 (DSR 2002:I, 119).

Report of the Panel

ing for the conditions being challenged in this dispute is contained in Public Notice No. 60 itself. This might mean that this measure in itself might be in violation to the extent that it requires action inconsistent with GATT obligations. The European Communities has asked for a separate ruling in that regard. The US has not. The European Communities request will be considered separately at a later stage. In the meantime, because both instruments contain the indigenization and trade balancing conditions at issue, and in light of the close relationship between Public Notice No. 60 and the signature of the MOUs, the Panel will first complete its analysis of the two conditions in issue taking both instruments into account.

7.180 The United States argues that the measures constitute "at least 'regulations' or 'requirements', as those terms in Article III:4 are ordinarily understood".[387] The European Communities considers the measures to be "requirements" within the meaning of Article III:4.[388] Thus both complainants consider that Public Notice No. 60 and the MOUs at least impose "requirements" under Article III:4. The Panel turns to a consideration of this term.

> (i)   The Notion of "requirement" within the Meaning of Article III:4

7.181 An ordinary meaning of the term "requirement", as articulated in the New Shorter Oxford Dictionary, is "Something called for or demanded; a condition which must be complied with". The *Canada – FIRA* panel further suggested that there must be a distinction between "regulations" and "requirements" and that requirements could not be assumed to mean the same, i.e. "mandatory rules applying across the board".

7.182 The European Communities argues that "it is firmly established that Government action need not be compulsory in order to qualify as a "requirement" for the purposes of GATT Article III:4". It acknowledges that "Public Notice No. 60 does not impose upon the joint-ventures a legal obligation to conclude an MOU with the Indian Government. Nonetheless, the conclusion of an MOU is a necessary condition for obtaining an advantage: the grant of licenses for SKD and CKD kits. Moreover, once it is signed, the MOU is binding upon the signatory and legally enforceable under the FTDR." The United States argues similarly that once the MOUs are entered into, the commitments in them become part of the conditions under which the MOU signatories are permitted to receive import licenses. These conditions are to be enforced through the import licensing scheme and also as a legal contract between the Government of India and the manufacturer.[389] The United States argues that the fact that the firms could have chosen not to sign such contracts does not affect the analysis: "the term "requirement", in its ordinary meaning, encompasses such preconditions to obtaining a benefit from the Government".[390]

---

[387] First Submission, para 62.
[388] First Submission, para 46.
[389] First Submission, para. 67.
[390] First Submission, para 68.

2006   DSR 2002:V

7.183 In previous instances, the term "requirement" has been interpreted to encompass commitments entered into on a voluntary basis by individual firms as a condition to obtaining an advantage.[391] Under GATT 1947, in *EEC – Parts and Components*, the panel noted that:

> "Article III :4 refers to 'all laws, regulations or requirements affecting the internal sale, offering for sale, purchase, transportation or use'. The Panel considered that the comprehensive coverage of 'all laws, regulations or requirements *affecting'* (emphasis added) the imported sale, etc. of imported products suggests that not only requirements which an enterprise is legally bound to carry out, such as those examined by the 'FIRA panel' (BISD 30S/140, 158), but also those which an enterprise voluntarily accepts in order to obtain an advantage from the government constitute 'requirements' within the meaning of that provision."[392]

7.184 GATT jurisprudence thus suggests two distinct situations which would satisfy the term "requirement" in Article III:4:

(i)   obligations which an enterprise is "legally bound to carry out";

(ii)   those which an enterprise voluntarily accepts in order to obtain an advantage from the government

7.185 This interpretation was confirmed in the panel report on *Canada – Autos*) under the WTO. In that instance, "letters of undertaking" submitted by certain firms at the request of the Canadian Government were considered to be "requirements". That panel stated in particular that:

> "We note that it has not been contested in this dispute that, as stated by previous GATT and WTO panel and appellate body reports, Article III:4 applies not only to mandatory measures but also to conditions that an enterprise accepts in order to receive an advantage, including in cases where the advantage is in the form of a benefit with respect to the conditions of importation of a product. The fact that compliance with the CVA requirements is not mandatory but a condition which must be met in order to obtain an ad-

---

[391] See *Canada – FIRA*: "the Panel first examined whether the purchase undertakings are to be considered "laws, regulations or requirements" within the meaning of Article III :4. As both parties had agreed that the FIRA and the FIR Regulations – whilst providing for the possibility of written undertakings – did not make their submission obligatory, the question remained whether the undertakings given in individual cases are to be considered "requirements" within the meaning of Article III :4. In this respect the Panel noted that Section 9(c) of the Act refers to "any written undertakings … relating to the proposed or actual investment given by any party thereto conditional upon the allowance of the investment" and that Section 21 of the Act states that "where a person who has given a written undertaking … fails or refuses to comply with such undertaking" a court order may be made "directing that person to comply with the undertaking". The Panel further noted that written purchase undertakings – leaving aside the manner in which they may have been arrived at (voluntary submission, encouragement, negotiation, etc.) once they were accepted, became part of the conditions under which the investment proposals were approved, in which case compliance could be legally enforced. The Panel therefore found that the word "requirement" as used in Article III :4 could be considered a proper description of existing undertakings."

[392] Panel Report on *EEC – Parts and Components*, para .5.21, BISD 37S/132.

Report of the Panel

vantage consisting of the right to import certain products duty-free therefore does not preclude application of Article III:4."[393]

7.186 This Panel supports and adopts that interpretation.

(ii) The Indigenization Condition as a "requirement"

7.187 The Panel recalls that the indigenization condition is contained in two distinct instruments: Public Notice No. 60 and the MOUs signed by manufacturers under the terms of Public Notice No. 60. The Panel will consider both of these instruments in determining whether the indigenization condition can be considered to constitute a "requirement within the meaning of Article III:4.

7.188 Public Notice No. 60, a governmental measure adopted under the authority of the EXIM policy, clearly requires that an MOU must be signed in order to gain the right to apply for an import license: import licenses will only be granted to manufacturers who sign an MOU containing certain conditions, including indigenization and trade balancing. Under Public Notice No. 60, the signing of an MOU is therefore in itself a condition to obtaining a license. In other words, acceptance of the indigenization condition was necessary under Public Notice No. 60 in order to obtain the right to import the restricted items addressed in Public Notice No. 60. Thus, the indigenization condition, as contained in Public Notice No. 60, constitutes a condition to the granting of an advantage, namely, in this instance, the right to import the restricted kits and components. It therefore constitutes a requirement within the meaning of Article III:4.[394]

7.189 The MOUs themselves also contain the same conditions, including the indigenization condition, whose acceptance as legal obligations by the signatories was necessary in order to obtain the right to import the restricted kits and components under license. They were thus entered into in order to gain an advantage, consisting in the right to import these products. In and of itself, this leads to the conclusion that they constitute "requirements" as per the interpretation from *Canada –Autos* that this Panel has endorsed.

7.190 In addition, manufacturers are expected to comply with the terms of the MOUs they have signed. Once signed, the MOUs became binding and enforceable, first under Public Notice No. 60 itself, and also under the FTDR Act and under general principles of contract law. Prior to 1 April 2001, failure to comply with these conditions could lead to the denial of an import license. The MOUs have thus been binding and enforceable since their signature. A binding enforce-

---

[393] Panel Report on *Canada – Autos*, WT/DS139/R, WT/DS142/R, adopted on 19 June 2000, as modified by the Appellate Body Report, para. 10.73 (DSR 2000:VII, 3043).

[394] We recall in this regard that in the context of this analysis, it is not the WTO-consistency or inconsistency of the advantage granted that is at stake. In other words, the fact that these products were restricted and subject to import licensing is not what is at stake in this determination. In this regard, previous jurisprudence has clarified that the advantage to be gained might be of very diverse natures.

2008

DSR 2002:V

able condition seems to fall squarely within the ordinary meaning of the word "requirement", in particular as "a condition which must be complied with".[395]

7.191 The enforceability of the measure in itself, independently of the means actually used or not to enforce it, is a sufficient basis for a measure to constitute a requirement under Article III:4. As far as a manufacturer having entered into an MOU is concerned, the commitments have existed since they were entered into and would affect its commercial behaviour. This further supports the conclusion that the "indigenization" condition as contained in the MOUs themselves also constitutes a "requirement" within the meaning of Article III:4.

7.192 The Panel is supported in this view by the jurisprudence[396] and by the fact that the TRIMs agreement expressly refers to mere enforceability in the context of the introductory paragraph of the Illustrative List, Item 1. Where the jurisprudence is concerned, the Panel recalls that the panel in *US - Malt Beverages* found the mandatory price affirmation laws in Massachusetts and Rhode Island inconsistent with Article III:4 because they accorded imported beer and wine less favourable treatment than the like domestic products even though the States concerned might not have been using their police powers to enforce the legislation. The panel noted that this did not change the fact that the measures were mandatory legislation that may influence the decision of economic operators.

7.193 Therefore, the Panel finds that the indigenization condition, as contained in Public Notice No. 60 and in the MOUs signed thereunder, constitutes a "requirement" within the meaning of Article III:4.

7.194 India has confirmed that the MOUs have remained binding and enforceable since then, even though the means through which enforcement might be pursued may have changed and may currently not have been decided on. India has argued that there is a fundamental difference between a requirement that has to be fulfilled to obtain an import license under the Indian trade laws and a requirement under private contract law with the Government of India, which the Government is free to enforce or not. In the view of India, the MOUs have become, since 1 April 2001, private contractual obligations that amount to discretionary legislation, and thus cannot be challenged as such under WTO dispute

---

[395] New Oxford English Dictionary, as cited above.

[396] The *Canada – FIRA* panel, in considering an argument by Canada that the undertakings were "private contractual" arrangements, found that:

> "The Panel carefully examined the Canadian view that the purchase undertakings should be considered as private contractual obligations of particular foreign investors vis-à-vis the Canadian government. The Panel recognized that investors might have an economic advantage in assuming purchase undertakings, taking into account the other conditions under which the investment was permitted. The Panel felt, however, that even if this was so, private contractual obligations entered into by investors should not adversely affect the rights which contracting parties, including contracting parties not involved in the dispute, possess under Article III :4 of the General Agreement and which they can exercise on behalf of their exporters. This applies in particular to the rights deriving from the national treatment principle, which – as stated in Article III :1 – is aimed at preventing the use of internal measures 'so as to afford protection to domestic production'." (paras 5.4 to 5.6).

Report of the Panel

settlement.[397] This argument relates to an alleged distinction between the situation pre- and post-April 2001. The Panel recalls in this respect its earlier conclusion that it would address arguments relating to any changes in the measures after 1 April 2001 when considering what recommendations may appropriately be made to the DSB.

(c)   ... Affecting the Internal Sale, Offering for Sale, Purchase (...) of the Products

7.195 Having determined that the indigenization condition is a "requirement", the Panel next examines whether the Indian measures affect the internal sale, offering for sale, purchase or use of the imported products within the meaning of Article III:4.

7.196 Under GATT and WTO jurisprudence, the term "affecting" has consistently been defined broadly. In particular, it has been well established that it "implies a measure that has "an effect on" and this indicates a broad scope of application".[398] This term therefore goes beyond laws and regulations which *directly* govern the conditions of sale or purchase to cover also any laws or regulations which might adversely modify the conditions of competition between domestic and imported products.

7.197 The Indian measure at issue requires the MOU signatories to commit to achieving a level of indigenization of components up to a minimum level of 50% in the third year or earlier and 70% in the fifth year or earlier, in order to obtain import licenses. To meet the indigenization requirement, car manufacturers must purchase Indian parts and components rather than imported goods. This provides an incentive to purchase local products. Such a requirement "modifies the conditions of competition between the domestic and imported products" and therefore affects the internal sale, offering for sale, purchase and use of imported parts and components in the Indian market within the meaning of Article III:4 of the GATT 1994.

7.198 The Panel also notes that the indigenization requirement affects not only SKD and CKD kits, but also any imported parts or components. This is because indigenization is required over all automotive parts and components. Any required components that are sourced from imports would not count towards fulfilling the level of indigenization requirement that increases over a period of time.

(d)   Whether Imported Products are Accorded Less Favourable Treatment

7.199 Finally, it is necessary to determine whether the measure is such as to accord less favourable treatment to the imported goods. In determining whether

---

[397] Second Submission, para. 30.

[398] See *Italy – Agricultural Machinery*, BISD 7S/60, para. 12. See also the Panel Report on *Canada – Autos*, WT/DS139/R, WT/DS142/R, adopted on 19 June 2000, as modified by the Appellate Body Report, para. 10.80 (DSR 2000:VII, 3043).

2010

DSR 2002:V

India – Autos

imported products are treated less favourably than domestic products, the Panel is obliged to examine whether the Indian measure modifies the conditions of competition in the Indian market to the detriment of imported products. The Appellate Body stated in *Korea—Beef* that "[a]ccording treatment 'no less favourable' means…according conditions of competition no less favourable to the imported product than to the like domestic product."[399]

7.200 In *Japan—Alcoholic Beverages*, the Appellate Body stated:

> "The broad and fundamental purpose of Article III is to avoid protectionism in the application of internal tax and regulatory measures. More specifically, the purpose of Article III "is to ensure that internal measures 'not be applied to imported or domestic products so as to afford protection to domestic production'".[400] Toward this end, Article III obliges Members of the WTO to provide equality of competitive conditions for imported products in relation to domestic products.[401] "[T]he intention of the drafters of the Agreement was clearly to treat the imported products in the same way as the like domestic products once they had been cleared through customs. Otherwise indirect protection could be given".

7.201 As noted previously, the very nature of the indigenization requirement generates an incentive to purchase and use domestic products and hence creates a disincentive to use like imported products. This requirement is more than likely to have some effect on manufacturers' choices as to the origin of parts and components to be used in manufacturing automotive vehicles, since they need to take into account the requirement to use a certain proportion of products of domestic origin. Car manufacturers are required to purchase a certain amount of parts and components that are of Indian origin for the simple reason that this is the only way to meet the indigenization requirement. This amount increases over a period of time and hence so too does the disincentive to the use of imported components. Car manufacturers are thus not free to choose to purchase imported parts and components over domestic parts and components in excess of a certain proportion. In these circumstances, imported products cannot compete on an equal footing with Indian-origin parts and components because the indigenization requirement explicitly sets out the percentage of domestic parts and components that must be used. [402]

---

[399] Report of the Appellate Body in *Korea – Various Measures on Beef*, WT/DS161/AB/R, WT/DS169/AB/R, adopted on 10 January 2001, para. 135 (DSR 2001:I, 5).

[400] United States - Section 337 of the Tariff Act of 1930, BISD 36S/345, para. 5.10.

[401] United States - Taxes on Petroleum and Certain Imported Substances, BISD 34S/136, para. 5.1.9; Japan - Customs Duties, Taxes and Labelling Practices on Imported Wines and Alcoholic Beverages, BISD 34S/83, para. 5.5(b).

[402] A GATT panel on *EEC – Parts and Components* made a finding of violation of Article III:4 involving relatively similar circumstances: "The Panel noted that the EEC made the *grant of an advantage*, namely the suspension of proceedings under the anti-circumvention provision, *dependent on undertakings to limit the use of parts or materials of Japanese origin without imposing similar limitations on the use of like products of EEC or other origins* hence dependent on undertakings to accord treatment to imported products less favourable than that accorded to like products of national origin in respect of their internal use".

Report of the Panel

7.202 Such a requirement clearly modifies the conditions of competition of domestic and imported parts and components in the Indian market in favour of domestic products. The Panel therefore finds that the indigenization requirement foreseen in Public Notice No. 60 and incorporated in the MOUs signed thereunder, by requiring manufacturers to use specified percentages of parts and components of domestic origin is a requirement affecting the internal sale of like imported products, and which affords these imported products less favourable treatment than that accorded to like products of national origin.

7.203 The Panel also recalls in particular the conclusions of the Panel on Canada – Autos, in examining a "Canadian Value Added" requirement (CVA) that "the CVA requirements accord less favourable treatment within the meaning of Article III:4 to imported parts, materials and non-permanent equipment than to like domestic products because, by conferring an advantage upon the use of domestic products but not upon the use of imported products, they adversely affect the equality of competitive conditions of imported products in relation to like domestic products".[403]

(e)   Conclusion

7.204 The Panel thus finds the "indigenization" condition, as contained in Public Notice No. 60 and in the MOUs entered into thereunder, is in violation of Article III:4 of GATT 1994 as at the date of its establishment.

7.205 This conclusion is consistent with the fact that the TRIMs Agreement Illustrative List identifies measures which require "the purchase or use by an enterprise of products of domestic origin or from any domestic source, whether specified in terms of particular products, in terms of volume or value of products, or in terms of a proportion of volume or value of its local production" as being TRIMs inconsistent with Article III:4 of GATT 1994. In this instance, MOU signatory manufacturers are required to use a certain proportion of products of domestic origin in their local production.

2.   Claim under Article XI

7.206 The United States has claimed that the indigenization requirement is also inconsistent with Article XI:1 of GATT 1994. The Panel has found this requirement to be in violation of Article III:4 of the GATT 1994.

7.207 The Panel recalls that, under the terms of Article 11 of the DSU, it is only required to address "those issues which must be addressed in order to resolve the matter in issue in the dispute".[404] This implies that if a particular measure is found to be in violation of a particular provision, the Panel does not necessarily need to go on to consider whether the same measure is also inconsistent with another provision of the GATT.

---

[403]   Panel Report on *Canada – Autos*, WT/DS139/R, WT/DS142/R, adopted on 19 June 2000, as modified by the Appellate Body Report, para. 10.85 (DSR 2000:VII, 3043).
[404]   See Report of the Appellate Body in *US – Wool Shirts and Blouses*, WT/DS33/AB/R, adopted on 23 May 1997, p.18 as cited above (DSR 1997:I, 323, at 339).

2012   DSR 2002:V

7.208 In this instance, the Panel has found the indigenization condition in its entirety to be inconsistent with Article III:4. In these circumstances, the Panel does not see any need to address in addition whether the same condition is also inconsistent with Article XI:1 of the GATT. It therefore exercises judicial economy with respect to that claim.

F.   GATT Claims Concerning the Trade Balancing Condition

1.   Factual Aspects of the Measure

7.209 Subparagraphs 3(i) through (iv) of Public Notice No. 60 set out four obligations which an MOU imposes on a manufacturing company that is a signatory. Subparagraph 3(iv) contains the "trade balancing" obligation.

7.210 MOU signatories must achieve "broad trade balancing of foreign exchange over the entire period of the MOU", in terms of balancing between the actual CIF value of imports of CKD/SKD kits/components and the FOB value of exports of cars and auto components over that period. Other parts of the MOU indicate the time-frame for that obligation. While a signatory has a trade balancing obligation over the period of the MOU, there is a two-year moratorium during which the firm does not need to fulfill that commitment. The period of execution of the export obligation therefore begins from the third year of commencement of production. However, imports made during the moratorium count towards the firm's total export obligation under the MOU.

7.211 Two other aspects of the alleged administration of this measure are of particular relevance to the Panel's deliberations and will be addressed at a later stage of analysis. The first is that, although there is no express provision to that effect in Public Notice No. 60, it has been argued by the complainants and confirmed by India that purchases by an MOU signatory within India of previously imported CKD/SKD kits/components that were subject to a license requirement on their importation, also count towards the signatory's export balancing requirement.[405]

7.212 The second is the assertion by India that the trade balancing obligation has only ever applied in respect of products that were subject to discretionary import licensing. India has indicated that since 1 April 2001, the import restrictions for SKD/CKD kits and car components have been abolished and no licenses are required. As from that date, the signatories of existing MOUs would continue to be required to discharge the export obligations corresponding to the imports made by them *before* that date. They would no longer incur any *new* export obligations as a result of the further importation of SKD/CKD kits since these are no longer restricted.[406]

---

[405] There is no dispute between the parties as to this assertion and we address its legal significance separately below.

[406] It is not clear, despite a question put to all three parties on the issue, what the time-frame is for the execution of outstanding export requirements. Nothing turns on this from a legal point of view, although it affects the degree of commercial significance of the residual obligation.

Report of the Panel

7.213 There is a factual dispute between the European Communities and India on this aspect of the scope of the export obligation. The European Communities argues that under the terms of the MOUs and of Public Notice No. 60, the requirement applies to "imports of kits/components" generally, i.e. not just those kits and components which are or were subject to licensing.[407] The European Communities also argues that the trade balancing requirement, irrespective of the scope of the products covered, would continue to apply so long as the signatories have not achieved the 70% indigenization level.

2. Order of Analysis of the Claims

7.214 The Panel recalls that in considering the order of examination of the claims concerning the indigenization condition, it decided to first examine the claim of violation of Article III:4 which was common to both complainants. On the trade balancing issue, the Panel again wishes to follow the same approach, namely to seek to determine whether common ground between the claims can be identified to assist in determining the order of their examination. This seem to the Panel the best means of allowing for the possible exercise of judicial economy while respecting its obligation under Article 9 of the DSU with regard to the preservation of the rights and obligations of parties in cases involving multiple complaints.

7.215 Both complainants assert that Articles III and XI respectively apply to at least some aspects of the measure. However their claims differ somewhat in their coverage:

-   the European Communities merely makes a claim of violation of Article III:4 in relation to its impact upon purchases made on the domestic market. It considers all other aspects of the measure to fall under Article XI.

-   The United States makes a claim of violation of Article III:4 in relation to both purchases on the domestic market and in relation to imports made directly by the signatories. While it thus takes a broader view than the European Communities as to the relevance of Article III, it also makes a distinct comprehensive claim of violation based on Article XI:1.[408]

7.216 While the claim that the trade balancing condition is inconsistent with Article XI is common to both complainants, the claim of inconsistency with Article III:4 argued by the United States involves aspects of that condition which the European Communities does not argue to be inconsistent with Article III.4. The scope of the United States's claim under Article III:4 is therefore much broader than that of the European Communities. In this instance, because both

---

[407] The Panel will address this factual question and its legal ramifications below in the context of analyzing the scope of the EC's claim. See below, section 4 b.

[408] The United States appears to have ultimately argued in the alternative. It has stated in its responses to the Panel's questions that the measure might be covered by one or the other provision, but in any case it should be found contrary to at least one of the two.

2014

DSR 2002:V

the European Communities' and the United States' claims seek to bring the entire measure within Article XI and because the European Communities addresses a wider range of effects under that Article than under Article III, the Panel has resolved to begin its analysis of trade balancing under Article XI.

3. Relationship between Articles III and XI

7.217 While the Panel has resolved to begin its analysis with Article XI, the parties have addressed the relative scope of Articles III and XI and their relationship to each other, in light of India's arguments concerning these issues. In light of this, the Panel felt it appropriate to begin by outlining its general interpretative approach to this Article and these submissions.

7.218 India has argued that the trade balancing condition cannot fall within the purview of Article XI. It asserts that Article XI only applies to border measures. It considers that this measure is not a border measure because it does not relate to the "process" of importation. It suggests that it should be considered as an internal measure and hence be analyzed under Article III. This argument will be addressed in due course in our analysis under Article XI.

7.219 More generally, India has warned of the systemic implications of applying Article XI to other than "border" measures, as to the effect on the respective scopes of Articles III:4 and XI:1 of GATT. In particular, there may be a concern that too broad an interpretation of Article XI might lead to it inappropriately covering ground intended for Article III. Others might assert a contrary concern with a broad interpretation of Article III:4.

7.220 In that regard the Panel notes that Articles III and XI seem to have been considered to have distinct scopes of application. In *Canada –FIRA* a panel stated that:

> "The Panel shares the view of Canada that the General Agreement distinguishes between measures affecting the 'importation' of products, which are regulated in Article XI:1, and those affecting 'imported products', which are dealt with in Article III. If Article XI:1 were interpreted broadly to cover also internal requirements, Article III would be partly superfluous."[409]

7.221 Only in the very specific circumstance of state trading enterprises involving a monopoly over both importation and distribution of goods has a blurring of the traditional distinction between measures affecting imported products and measures affecting importation been acknowledged.[410]

---

[409] Panel Report, L/5504, adopted on 7 February 1987, para. 5.14.

[410] See the Panel Report on *Korea – Various Measures on Beef*, WT/DS161/R, WT/DS169/R, adopted on 10 January 2001, as modified by the Appellate Body Report, para. 766 (DSR 2001:I, 59): "Based on the panel findings in the *Canada – Marketing Agencies (1988)* case, the Panel considers that to the extent that LPMO fully controls both the importation and distribution of its 30 per cent share of Korean beef quota, the distinction normally made in the GATT between restrictions affecting the importation of products (i.e. border measures) and restrictions affecting imported products (i.e. internal measures) loses much of its significance."

Report of the Panel

7.222 The Panel feels that it is vital that the task be approached solely through an application of the customary rules of interpretation of public international law as required by Article 3.2 of the DSU. This should occur without any presumption as to some preordained or systemic balance between the two Articles. The customary rules provide sufficient mechanisms to ensure an appropriate outcome that should deal with such concerns, as they require consideration of ordinary meaning in context and in the light of object and purpose of the treaty. In this regard, context includes a reading of each Article in relation to other potentially relevant provisions and an analysis, where necessary, of any differences in terminology. The principle of effectiveness would also apply to prevent reducing any provision to inutility.

7.223 While other provisions in the WTO Agreement may usefully be considered as part of the context which informs the meaning of a given provision, the scope of that provision should not be assumed *a priori* to vary depending on the mere presence of other provisions which may have some relevance to the situation: the contours of a provision should flow from its terms, as read in context alongside the other provisions of the agreement. The Panel is also mindful of the fact that different aspects of a particular measure may legitimately be covered by distinct provisions of the WTO Agreements.

7.224 For all the foregoing reasons, it therefore cannot be excluded *a priori* that different aspects of a measure may affect the competitive opportunities of imports in different ways, making them fall within the scope either of Article III (where competitive opportunities on the domestic market are affected) or of Article XI (where the opportunities for importation itself, i.e. entering the market, are affected), or even that there may be, in perhaps exceptional circumstances, a potential for overlap between the two provisions, as was suggested in the case of state trading. Any analysis of the applicability of either Article III:4 or XI:1 should thus be based on the principles within Article 3.2 of the DSU. This is how the Panel will proceed in its examination.

4. Claims under Article XI:1

7.225 Both the United States and the European Communities argue that the trade balancing requirement is inconsistent to Article XI:1 of GATT. Although the substance of their claims is essentially similar, they differ somewhat in that the European Communities initially made its claim subject to some specific conditions. This will need to be considered as a preliminary matter.

(a) Scope of the European Communities' Claim

7.226 The European Communities' request for establishment of a panel indicated the following:

"The measures concerned are contained in:

- Public Notice No. 60 (PN 97-02) of the Indian Ministry of Commerce, effective 12 December 1997; and

2016   DSR 2002:V

> - the Memorandums of Understanding (MOUs) entered into by certain manufacturers of automobiles with the Government of India pursuant to Public Notice No. 60.
>
> The above measures require manufacturers of automobiles to sign an MOU as a condition for obtaining licenses for importing automotive products that are currently subject to import restrictions. According to the Indian authorities, the MOUs are "binding" and "enforceable" instruments, which shall remain valid after the date when those restrictions are eliminated. The MOUs require (i) to establish "actual production facilities" in India; (ii) to make a minimum investment; (iii) to achieve a certain level of "indigenization"; and (iv) to export a certain amount of automotive products.
>
> The European Communities considers that the requirements imposed by the above measures are in violation of Articles III:4 and XI:1 of GATT and of Article 2.1 of the TRIMs Agreement."

7.227 In its First Submission, however, the European Communities indicated that it was making the claim of violation of Article XI:1 concerning the trade balancing obligation only in so far as:

- prior to 1 April 2001, the MOUs required the "trade balancing" of imports of "components" other than chassis and bodies; and

- the MOUs would remain binding and enforceable after 1 April 2001, both with respect to passenger cars and components therefor.

7.228 In the course of the proceedings, the European Communities further clarified the scope of its claims, and as was noted above, a disagreement arose and persisted between the European Communities and India as to the scope of application of the trade balancing condition. The Panel will address this issue first.

(i) The Scope of the Trade Balancing Obligation

7.229 The European Communities contends that because the plain meaning of Public Notice No. 60 and the MOUs does not limit the reference in the trade balancing obligation to imports subject to licensing, it remains concerned that accrued export obligations might include calculations based on non-restricted imports.

7.230 India argues that the regime has never been interpreted or administered in that way. It asks the European Communities to rely on its assurances to that effect. In response to questions from the Panel as to the way this distinction was effectively administered, India explained that ongoing calculation of the export obligation was based on the actual imports made under the import licenses themselves. In response to similar questions, the European Communities was not able to provide any evidence of calculations made contrary to India's assertions. It indicated that evidence concerning calculations performed in the past and signa-

Report of the Panel

tories' annual report under the MOUs were not available to it, and relied on the plain meaning of the documents concerned.[410 bis]

[410 bis] See EC's response to Question 94 of the Panel."

7.231 The Panel notes that the terms of Public Notice No. 60, as reflected in the standard MOU, refer to an obligation to balance "the actual CIF value of imports of CKD/SKD kits/components" (subparagraph 3(iv)). It is true that it is not expressly mentioned in this phrase that this refers exclusively to *restricted* kits and components. Nevertheless, these terms should be considered in their proper context. Paragraph 2 of Public Notice No. 60 provides as follows: "Pursuant to the above, imports of components for motor vehicles in CKD/SKD form, *which is restricted for import under the current Export Import Policy*, shall be allowed against a license (...)" (emphasis added). This suggests that in the context of Public Notice No. 60, it could be argued that where "imports of CKD/SKD kits/components" are referred to, the reference may be to those "components for motor vehicles in CKD/SKD form" defined in paragraph 2 of the Public Notice No. 60, i.e. the restricted items under the EXIM Policy. The Panel is not persuaded that the ordinary meaning of these words, in this context, would encompass any non-restricted components. At most, the plain meaning of the expression, in context, appears ambiguous.

7.232 In addition, as noted above the European Communities has adduced no additional evidence to suggest that the reading it suggests is indeed that which prevails, while India has provided an indication of how it assesses the obligation which suggests a direct reliance on the licenses themselves.

7.233 In these circumstances, the European Communities has not proven on balance that the trade balancing requirement accrues in relation to non-restricted imports. A mere reference to a plain meaning which, read in context, is debatable, without reference to any evidence of relevant domestic Indian interpretations or reference to evidence from any signatory in support of the contention and in the face of India's clear assertions as to methodology to the contrary, is not sufficient to support a factual finding of that nature. There is thus no basis for any specific ruling on the consistency with Article XI of the trade balancing condition as it allegedly applies to non-restricted imports as requested by the European Communities and the Panel declines to do so.

7.234 In ruling on this factual question, the Panel wishes to point out that it has no jurisdiction to make any binding inter-party determination as to the actual level of the export obligation accrued by any signatory under individual MOUs. It is merely saying that it has not been demonstrated, for the purposes of this proceeding, that this condition applies to the importation of non-restricted parts or components. The Panel's ruling does not seek to determine, or prejudge, any determination which might be made in other contexts relating to the extent of specifications under individual MOUs.

2018

DSR 2002:V

(ii)   The Continued Enforceability of the MOUs
after 1 April 2001

7.235 The European Communities also indicated in its First Submission that it was making a claim of violation of Article XI in relation to the trade balancing only to the extent that the MOUs remained binding and enforceable after 1 April 2001. The European Communities specifically argued that the trade balancing requirement would continue to apply so long as the MOU signatories have not achieved the 70% indigenization level. The Panel has previously noted India's confirmation that the MOUs did remain binding and enforceable after that date.[411] More specifically, India confirmed that it did not intend to release signatories from obligations incurred in relation to imports made before 1 April and that the indigenization condition remained in place.

7.236 In response to questions from the Panel, the European Communities further explained the qualified submission it had made at that stage. It confirmed its view that the violation it was referring to would have existed as of the date of establishment of the Panel already, but that as a factual matter, since India had been otherwise authorized to maintain quantitative restrictions on these products beyond that date, there would have been little practical interest in challenging the measures earlier unless India intended to maintain them after 1 April 2001. The European Communities further clarified in the course of the proceedings that it was nonetheless generally requesting the Panel to make findings that the measures were in violation of the WTO Agreements as of the date of establishment of the Panel, and also that they subsequently remained in violation of the same provisions.

7.237 The Panel finds the European Communities' explanations of the scope of its claim under Article XI to have been somewhat confusing at the early stages of the proceeding.[412] Nevertheless, the European Communities referred to this claim in its request for establishment of a panel and has clarified that it is essentially requesting the Panel to rule on the measures as they existed as of the date of its request for establishment of a panel and as they, in its view, continued to exist subsequently. In the context of the Panel request and terms of reference, the statements as a whole lead the Panel to conclude that the claim presented by the European Communities under Article XI concerning trade balancing is appropriately within its terms of reference.

7.238 The Panel understands the European Communities' articulation of its claim in its First Submission as meaning that it wished to pursue this particular claim only if, as a factual matter, the MOUs remained binding and enforceable

---

[411]   See First Submission, paras. 11 ff.

[412]   The confusion arose because at one stage it seemed to have been implied that the claim related only to the post-April situation. The Panel is on balance satisfied that the explanations provided by the European Communities in the course of the proceedings have clarified that they intended the Panel to examine a claim of violation which would have existed as of its date of establishment, which is appropriate, although the motivation for the European Communities' request, which is not for a Panel to pass judgment upon, may have rested principally on the expectation of the effects of a finding after the 1 April 2001. The DSU allows Members to exercise their own judgment as to when a case is worth pursuing.

Report of the Panel

beyond 1 April 2001, rather than as a suggestion that the Panel's legal assessment of the claim should be on the basis exclusively of the situation as of 1 April 2001. The European Communities confirmed that any violations it was requesting the Panel to make were violations that would have existed at the time of establishment of this Panel.

7.239 In light of the foregoing, the Panel considers it appropriate to rule on the EC's claim on the basis of the measures as they existed as of the date of their request for establishment of this Panel, in accordance with the approach determined in section B above. Any implications of the events of 1 April 2001 in relation to the continuation of these violations will be addressed, as determined in the same section, at a later stage.

(b) Arguments of the Parties

7.240 The United States argues that starting in the fourth year, each MOU imposed a quantitative limitation on imports through the trade balancing obligation. It asserts that the trade balancing requirement restricts imports because it limits the value of an MOU signatory's imports to the value of the signatory's exports (which, pursuant to paragraph III, clause (vi), the MOU signatory was required to specify at the time of signing). Because there would obviously be limitations on the amount of exports which a car manufacturer might be able or willing to make, it argues that the trade balancing obligation itself restricts imports.

7.241 In addition, the United States notes that the obligation is clearly enforceable. The Government of India had confirmed that denial of an import license was effectively mandatory if the trade balancing obligation was not met. A manufacturer's failure to comply with an MOU obligation could lead to loss of import privileges or to confiscation of the goods concerned pursuant to various provisions of the FTDR Act and regulations thereunder. It appeared that after April 1, 2001, these additional provisions would be the instruments through which India would enforce Public Notice No. 60 and the MOUs (and thus prevent SKD/CKD kits/components from being brought into India to compete with domestic parts and components). For all of these reasons, it considered that the trade balancing obligation in Public Notice No. 60 and the MOUs imposed import restrictions as such, and was therefore inconsistent with Article XI:1 of the GATT 1994.

7.242 The United States further refers to Item 2(a) of the Illustrative List of the TRIMs Agreement to support its argument, asserting that the MOUs restricted importation to an amount related to the value of locally produced goods that a manufacturer exports, as foreseen by that item, and the MOUs were "enforceable". The Untied States argued that India had confirmed both points.[413] The trade balancing requirement thus fell within the scope of this paragraph, and con-

---

[413] India's First Submission, para. 14, and *Replies by India to Questions Posed by Japan*, G/TRIMS/W/15, circulated 30 October 1998, response to Question 24; Exhibit US-5: "CKD/SKD kits imports would be allowed with reference to the extent of export obligation fulfilled in the previous year." As discussed above, the MOUs were also "necessary to obtain an advantage".

2020 DSR 2002:V

India – Autos

sequently it was "inconsistent with the obligation of general elimination of quantitative restrictions provided for in paragraph 1 of Article XI of GATT 1994".

7.243 The European Communities argues that the trade balancing obligation stipulated in the MOUs is inconsistent with GATT Article XI:1 in that it restricts imports of passenger cars, and of components therefor, by the signatories of the MOUs. In the view of the EC, it does so because it places a maximum limit on the value of the imports that the signatories are authorized to make, equal to the value of their exports. In practice, there were limits to the amount of exports which a signatory might be able or willing to make, related both to its manufacturing capacity in India and to the demand for its products in foreign markets. Thus, by limiting the amount of a signatory's imports to that of its exports, the trade balancing obligation "restricted" the amount of imports.[414] The European Communities also refers to Item 2(a) in the TRIMs Illustrative List to support its argument under Article XI:1.

7.244 As noted above, India first argues that the trade balancing obligation does not fall within the purview of Article XI because it is not a border measure and does not relate to the "process" of importation. It also argues that in any case, after 1 April 2001, the execution of outstanding export obligations will in no way be tied to imports and therefore will be a straight export requirement, which is not in itself prohibited by any provision of GATT 1994. This second aspect of India's defense, which relates to a distinction between the measures as they applied prior to 1 April 2001 and after that date, will be addressed as necessary in our section on Recommendations.

      (c)   Scope of Article XI:1

            (i)   The Notion of "measures" within the Meaning of Article XI:1

7.245 Article XI:1 provides that:

> "No prohibition or restriction other than duties, taxes or other charges, whether made effective through quotas, import or export licenses or other measures, shall be instituted or maintained by any [Member] on the importation of any product of the territory of any other [Member] or on the exportation or sale for export of any product destined for the territory of any other [Member]."

7.246 Article XI:1 refers to restrictions "made effective through quotas, import or export licenses or other measures". This formulation, which includes a "broad residual category"[415] of "other measures", suggests a broad scope to the types of measures which can be considered to fall within the meaning of Article XI:1.

7.247 Past jurisprudence supports such a broad interpretation. The Panel recalls in particular the conclusion of the panel in *Japan – Semi-conductors* that

---

[414] See First Submission of the European Communities, para. 74. See also US response to Question 82 of the Panel.
[415] As described in the Panel Report on *Argentina – Hides Leather*, WT/DS155/R, adopted on 16 February 2001, para. 11.17 (DSR 2001:V, 1779).

DSR 2002:V

Report of the Panel

> "Article XI:1, unlike other provisions of the General Agreement, did not refer to laws or regulations but more broadly to measures. This wording indicated clearly that any measure instituted or maintained by a contracting party which restricted the exportation or sale for export of products was covered by this provision, irrespective of the legal status of the measure"[416]

7.248 Such a broad interpretation of the notion of "measure" has also been subsequently endorsed in the context of an analysis of that notion under Article XXIII:1 (b),[417] and more generally in the context of WTO dispute settlement.[418]

7.249 Thus, under past jurisprudence, a network of non-binding incentive measures has been considered to constitute "measures" and a restriction within the meaning of Article XI:1 of GATT. Such a broad interpretation is consistent both with the express terms of the provision, which are all-encompassing, and also more generally with its context, including other provisions defining the type of measures which can be validly be submitted to dispute settlement.

7.250 It is notable in this respect that the more specific terms of Article III:4 ("laws, regulations or requirements"), as noted in our analysis of the indigenization, has been broadly interpreted to cover measures which are not mandatory but are either binding and enforceable or necessary in order to obtain an advantage. The Panel sees no reason to interpret the more general notion of "measure" under Article XI:1 more restrictively, especially as these two provisions, as the *Superfund* panel stated, have "essentially the same rationale, ***namely to protect expectations of the contracting parties as to the competitive relationship between their products and those of the other contracting parties***".[419]

7.251 In this instance, India does not seem to dispute that Public Notice No. 60 constitutes a governmental measure which could properly be the object of dispute settlement. It is less clear, however, whether it accepts that the MOUs as

---

[416] Report of the Panel on *Japan – Semi-conductors*, adopted on 4 May 1988, BISD35S/116, para. 106.

[417] See Panel Report on *Japan – Film*, WT/DS44/R, adopted on 22 April 1998, para. 10.45 (DSR 1998:IV, 1179).

[418] See Report of the Appellate Body in *Guatemala – Cement I*, WT/DS60/AB/R, adopted on 25 November 1998, footnote 47 (DSR 1998:IX, 3767): "In the practice established under the GATT 1947, a "measure" may be any act of a Member, whether or not legally binding, and it can include even non-binding administrative guidance by a government (see *Japan – Semi-conductors*, adopted 4 May 1988, BISD 35S/116). A measure can also be an omission or a failure to act on the part of a Member (see, for example, *India – Patents (US)*, WT/DS50/R (DSR 1998:I, 41) and WT/DS50/AB/R (DSR 1998:I, 9), adopted 16 January 1998, and also *India – Patents (EC)*, WT/DS79/R (DSR 1998:VI, 2661), adopted 22 September 1998)." Interestingly, this analysis appears to encompass together analyses of the notion of "measure" as contained in different provisions of the GATT 1994, including Article XI:1.

[419] The Panel is further comforted in this analysis by the fact that the Illustrative List of the TRIMs Agreement, in its introductory paragraph to item 2 concerning TRIMs that are inconsistent with Article XI:1, refers to "those which are mandatory or enforceable under domestic law or under administrative rulings, or compliance with which is necessary to obtain an advantage". This reference also suggests an endorsement, in the context of recourse to Article XI:1 for the purposes of the TRIMs Agreement, of a broad notion of "measures".

such can constitute such "measures", including within the meaning of Article XI:1 of the GATT 1994.

7.252 As previously noted, the MOUs have been signed between the Government of India and automotive manufacturers, in accordance with the terms of Public Notice No. 60, a government measure which provides the framework and basis for these MOUs. As noted above in the context of our analysis of the indigenization condition, the MOUs constitute binding and enforceable contracts, whose signature with all the specified conditions, including trade balancing, was necessary in order to obtain an advantage, namely the right to import restricted auto kits and components. The acceptance of this particular condition was thus in itself necessary to obtain the advantage sought (namely, the right to import restricted items). Although they were not mandatory in the sense of being directly applicable to any manufacturer outside of that manufacturer's acceptance of it, a manufacturer wishing to import restricted kits and components had no choice but to sign an MOU. In addition, the terms of these MOUs, including the trade balancing condition, were dictated by a pro-forma required by a governmental measure, Public Notice No. 60, which clearly set out the requirements to be accepted by car manufacturers for importation of restricted kits and components. The MOUs emanate directly from a government measure, Public Notice No. 60, which requires car manufacturers to execute an MOU and comply with the terms contained therein to be able to import the kits and components.

7.253 For these reasons, the Panel finds that the trade balancing condition, as contained in both Public Notice No. 60 and the MOUs constitutes a "measure" within the meaning of Article XI:1.

> (ii) "Restriction on importation" within the Meaning of Article XI:1 and "border measures"

7.254 The restrictions envisaged by Article XI:1 are exclusively restrictions "*on importation*". Since India argues that the measure at issue cannot fall under Article XI because it is not a "border measure", it is necessary to analyze first whether the phrase "restriction.... on importation" suggests such a limitation on the scope of Article XI:1. This argument is considered first, before considering more generally whether the type of obligation at issue can be said to constitute such a "restriction".

7.255 In its second submission, in support of its argument that the trade balancing obligation was an internal measure not subject to Article XI, India argued that

> "Obviously, the provisions of the MOUs on trade balancing do not affect the process of entering products into India's customs territory and can also for this reason not constitute restrictions on importation within the meaning of Article XI:1".[420]

---

[420] Footnote 8, para 20, Second Submission. See also Annex 1 to second oral statement.

Report of the Panel

7.256 As indicated above, the Panel will address any such contentions through an application of the customary rules of interpretation of public international law.

7.257 The Panel turns therefore to consider the ordinary meaning of the phrase "restriction...on importation". An ordinary meaning of the term "*on*", relevant to a description of the relationship which should exist between the measure and the importation of the product, includes "with respect to", "in connection, association or activity with or with regard to".[421] In the context of Article XI:1, the expression "restriction... *on importation*" may thus be appropriately read as meaning a restriction "with regard to" or "in connection with" the importation of the product. On a plain reading, this would not necessarily be limited to measures which directly relate to the "process" of importation. It might also encompass measures which otherwise relate to other aspects of the importation of the product. Thus, at this stage of our analysis, the Panel does not find that the ordinary meaning of the words supports India's contentions.

7.258 India also makes contextual arguments in support of its contentions in pointing out the difference between the use of the term "importation" alone, in Article XI:1, as compared to "exportation or sale for export". It appears from these terms that Article XI does not intend to deal directly with measures relating to the "sale for importation", but this otherwise suggests no limitation on the *manner* in which a given measure might affect or relate to "importation".

7.259 Nor would a contextual comparison with other Articles, such as Article III, support India's contentions. The use of the term "importation" in Article XI, rather than "imports", or "imported products", clearly suggests that what is targeted in Article XI:1 is exclusively those restrictions which relate to the importation itself, and not to *already* imported products. This does not, however, support a conclusion that the only manner in which a measure can be a restriction "*on importation*" is by being a "border measure", or a measure relating to "the process of importation", as described by India.

7.260 Contextual and purposive interpretation support this initial conclusion by the Panel. The text of the Ad note to Article III clarifies that some measures applied "at the point or time of importation" for imported products are nonetheless to be considered as internal measures under Article III. This would appear to confirm that the application of the measure "at the point of importation" is not necessarily the decisive criterion. If that note requires a particular measure to be considered as an internal measure, it would mean that application at the point of importation would not be decisive in determining the scope of Article XI:1.[422]

---

[421] Webster's New Encyclopedic Dictionary, 1994 ed.

[422] The Panel's conclusions are not dependant on the Ad Note as it could also be read to the contrary to argue that the expression "at the point or time of importation" reflects a description of what measures would naturally fall within the scope of Article XI, some of them then falling "out" of the scope of the provision by express derogation in certain circumstances. Such a view would contend that such derogation would not have been necessary if it had been evident that border application of the measure was not sufficient to make it fall under Article XI.

2024

DSR 2002:V

India – Autos

7.261 Purposive interpretation suggests rather that it is the nature of the measure as a restriction *in relation to importation* which is the key factor to consider in determining whether a measure may properly fall within the scope of Article XI:1.

7.262 Even if the trade balancing requirement cannot necessarily be considered to relate to the actual "process" of importation, or to constitute a "border" measure, this would therefore not be a sufficient reason to conclude that it cannot come within the scope of Article XI:1.

7.263 However, it still must be determined how it might constitute a "restriction.... on importation" within the meaning of that provision. A rejection of India's suggested test for the conditions of applicability of the provision does not imply that the claimants' contentions are made out. The Panel turns to address those contentions.

> (d) The Trade Balancing Condition as a "restriction ... on importation"

> (i) The Notion of "restriction ... on importation"

7.264 Although the title of Article XI refers to the elimination of "quantitative restrictions", the text of the provision makes no distinction between different types of restrictions on importation. On the contrary, the words "*No* prohibitions or restrictions ... *whether made effective through* quotas, import or export licenses *or other measures*" (emphases added) suggest an intention to cover any type of measures restricting the entry of goods into the territory of a Member, other than those specifically excluded, namely, duties, taxes or other charges. As was noted by the *India – Quantitative Restrictions* panel,

> "the text of Article XI:1 is very broad in scope, providing for a general ban on import or export restrictions or prohibitions 'other than duties, taxes or other charges'. As was noted by the panel in *Japan - Trade in Semi-conductors*, the wording of Article XI:1 is comprehensive: it applies 'to all measures instituted or maintained by a [Member] prohibiting or restricting the importation, exportation, or sale for export of products other than measures that take the form of duties, taxes or other charges.'[423] The scope of the term 'restriction' is also broad, as seen in its ordinary meaning, which is 'a limitation on action, a limiting condition or regulation'."[424]

7.265 This Panel endorses the ordinary meaning of the term "restriction" as identified by the *India - Quantitative Restrictions* panel and its view as to the generally broad scope of the prohibition expressed in Article XI:1. As a result, it can be concluded that any form of *limitation* imposed on, or in relation to importation constitutes a restriction on importation within the meaning of Article XI:1.

---

[423] Panel Report on *Japan – Semi-conductors*, BISD 35S/116, para. 104.
[424] Panel Report on *India – Quantitative Restrictions*, WT/DS90/R, para. 5.128 (DSR 1999:V, 1799).

DSR 2002:V

Report of the Panel

7.266 As far as the trade balancing obligation is concerned, it is a condition placed on importation of the product. It results both from the signature of the MOU (whereby the principle of the obligation is agreed to, as part of the conditions to gain the right to import the restricted products) and from the actual importation of products (which determines the "quantum" of the export obligation). The MOUs are signed "on the basis of" projections regarding indigenization and trade balancing.[425] After entering into the MOU, signatories had the opportunity to apply for licenses whenever they wished to import kits or components subject to restrictions. It seems that the licenses themselves, before 1 April 2001, made a reference to the trade balancing obligation.

7.267 Both complainants describe the measure as a "limitation" on imports, and highlight the practical threshold imposed by the export requirement on the value of imports that can be made, which, they assert, amounts to a restriction.

7.268 The trade balancing condition does not set an absolute numerical limit on the amount of imports that can be made. It does, however, limit the value of imports that can be made to the value of exports that the signatory intends to make over the life of the MOU. If all signatories could at all times have an unlimited desire and ability to export, this obligation would be unlikely to have any impact upon import decisions. That is not a realistic scenario, however and was not contended for by India. In reality, therefore, the limit on imports set by this condition is induced by the practical threshold that a signatory will impose on itself as a result of the obligation to satisfy a corresponding export commitment. The amount of imports is therefore linked to a certain amount of anticipated exports. The more a signatory would be concerned about its ability to export profitably at significant levels, the more it would be induced by the trade balancing obligation to limit its imports of the relevant products.

7.269 The question of whether this form of measure can appropriately be described as a restriction on importation turns on the issue of whether Article XI can be considered to cover situations where products are technically allowed into the market without an express formal quantitative restriction, but are only allowed under certain conditions which make the importation more onerous than if the condition had not existed, thus generating a disincentive to import.

7.270 On a plain reading, it is clear that a "restriction" need not be a blanket prohibition or a precise numerical limit. Indeed, the term "restriction" cannot mean merely "prohibitions" on importation, since Article XI:1 expressly covers both "prohibition or restriction". Furthermore, the Panel considers that the expression "*limiting condition*" used by the *India – Quantitative Restrictions* panel to define the term "restriction" and which this Panel endorses, is helpful in identifying the scope of the notion in the context of the facts before it. That phrase suggests the need to identify not merely a condition placed on importation, but a

---

[425] What is perhaps not entirely clear in the operation of the MOUs is the extent to which these export projections by the manufacturers might "bind" them to the extent of preventing them from applying for licenses over the period of the MOU *beyond* the initial projections. Nothing turns on this from a legal perspective in terms of the Panel's analysis.

2026   DSR 2002:V

condition that is limiting, i.e. that has a limiting effect. In the context of Article XI, that limiting effect must be on importation itself.

7.271 The Panel believes that a substance over form approach should be taken to the analysis of the facts in the context of this test. Such an approach is consistent with that taken by the panel on *Japan-Semi-conductors*.[426] The panel examined a series of actions taken by the Government of Japan after concluding an Agreement on trade in semi-conductors with the United States. These included requests which the Japanese Government addressed to Japanese producers and exporters of semi-conductors not to export semi-conductors at prices below company-specific costs to contracting parties other than the United States. There was also a statutory requirement for exporters to submit information on export prices and systematic monitoring of company and product-specific costs and export prices by the Government. This was backed up with the use of supply and demand forecasts to impress on manufacturers the need to align their production to appropriate levels. The panel concluded that:

> "the complex of measures exhibited the rationale as well as the essential elements of a formal system of export control. The only distinction in this case was the absence of formal legally binding obligations in respect of exportation or sale for export of semi-conductors. However, the Panel concluded that this amounted to a difference in form rather than substance because the measures were operated in a manner equivalent to mandatory requirements. The Panel concluded that the complex of measures constituted a coherent system restricting the sale for export of monitored semi-conductors at prices below company-specific costs to markets other that the United States, inconsistent with Article XI:1."[427]

7.272 This finding suggests that measures which involve no formal restriction but rather a network of strong suggestions can fall within the scope of Article XI:1. It is true that in that instance, exports were being restricted, rather than imports, and the panel referred in its final conclusion to a restriction on "the sale for export". This Panel acknowledges that this phrase has no matching phrase under Article XI:1 with regard to imports. However, the rest of the *Semi-conductors* panel's conclusions suggest that the restrictions found by the panel also concerned exportation (e.g. "The Panel considered that the complex of measures exhibited the rationale as well as the essential elements of a formal system of *export control*. The only distinction in this case was the absence of formal legally binding obligations in respect of *exportation or sale for export* of semi-conductors."). This report thus seems to support a reading of Article XI:1 encompassing import limitations made effective through disincentives to importation, without a formal numerical limit on imports.

7.273 The same panel also found that "export licensing practices by Japan, leading to delays of up to three months in the issuing of licences for semi-conductors destined for contracting parties other than the United States, had been non-

---

[426] See Panel Report cited above in footnote 410.
[427] *Ibid*, para. 117.

DSR 2002:V

2027

Report of the Panel

automatic and constituted restrictions on the exportation of such products inconsistent with Article XI:1." This finding suggests that a measure that does not preclude any exportation but rather makes it more burdensome can also amount to a restriction on exportation. *Mutatis mutandis*, the same reasoning could apply to a restriction on importation.

7.274 The Panel Report on *EEC – Programme of Minimum Import Prices, Licences and Surety Deposits for Certain Processed Fruits and Vegetables* also made a finding on Article XI:1 which is of interest in identifying its scope. In that case, the panel examined a minimum import price and associated security system for tomato concentrate. The United States was arguing that the system prohibited importation of goods below a certain price and was, therefore, a restriction within the meaning of Article XI on the importation of these goods. The EC, on the contrary, was arguing that the system was a non-tariff barrier measure and that, in principle, imports of tomato concentrates into the Community were allowed, but not below the minimum price. The panel found that "the minimum price system, as enforced by the additional security, was a restriction "other than duties, taxes or other charges" within the meaning of Article XI:1".[428]

7.275 That report was adopted by the CONTRACTING PARTIES and cited by the *Japan - Semi-conductors* panel as having decided that "the import regulation allowing the import of a product in principle, but not below a minimum price level, constituted a restriction on importation within the meaning of Article XI:1".[429] The Panel also notes, in this regard, the observation made by the panel in *Argentina –Hides and Leather* that "[t]here can be no doubt, in [its] view, that the disciplines of Article XI:1 extend to restrictions of a *de facto* nature". [430]

7.276 As noted above, the *India – Quantitative Restrictions* panel endorsed the broad scope of the provision articulated by *Japan – Semi-conductors* in finding that a discretionary import licensing scheme, where licenses were not granted automatically but rather on "unspecified" merits, was contrary to Article XI:1. This Panel agrees with and adopts these interpretations. For reasons outlined above, the Panel does not consider that it is a separate requirement of Article XI that a measure can be described as a border measure. It is the impact of a meas-

---

[428] There was a dissenting opinion on this point. One panelist (out of a panel of five), however, "considered that the minimum import price system, as enforced by the additional security, could well be applied in a way which would qualify it as a "restriction "other than duties, taxes or other charges" within the meaning of Article XI:1. However, having noted the explanation given with respect to the functioning of the system, this member considered that importation of tomato concentrates at a price lower than the minimum price could still be carried out by exporters who had an interest in doing so. He further considered that the system operated in a way to levy an additional charge which raised the price of tomato concentrate imported at a price lower than the minimum price. Therefore, he concluded that the minimum import price system was not being enforced in a manner which would qualify it as a restriction within the meaning of Article XI." This suggests that, for that panelist, the measure operated so as to levy an additional *charge*, rather than as an import restriction (i.e. it was possible to import below the minimum price, but with an additional charge). BISD 25S/68.

[429] Panel Report on *Japan – Semi-conductors*, BISD 35S/116, para. 105.

[430] Panel Report on *Argentina – Hides and Leather*, WT/DS155/R, adopted on 16 February 2001, para. 11.17 (DSR 2001:V, 1779).

2028   DSR 2002:V

India – Autos

ure by way of a "restriction ...on importation" that counts, not the physical place of its application.

(ii) Analysis of the Trade Balancing Condition

7.277 With regard to the trade balancing condition, the Panel finds that as at the date of its establishment, there would necessarily have been a practical threshold to the amount of exports that each manufacturer could expect to make, which in turn would determine the amount of imports that could be made. This amounts to an import restriction. The degree of effective restriction which would result from this condition may vary from signatory to signatory depending on its own projections, its output, or specific market conditions, but a manufacturer is in no instance free to import, without commercial constraint, as many kits and components as it wishes without regard to its export opportunities and obligations.

7.278 The Panel therefore finds that the trade balancing condition contained in Public Notice No. 60 and in the MOUs signed thereunder, by limiting the amount of imports through linking them to an export commitment, acts as a restriction on importation, contrary to the terms of Article XI:1. With respect to the European Communities' argument that the MOU signatories that have yet to achieve the 70% indigenization requirement would continue to incur export obligations after 1 April 2001, the Panel notes that no evidence was presented to show that any such new export obligations have in fact accrued.

7.279 The Panel is comforted in this finding by the fact that it appears consistent with Item 2(a) of the Illustrative list of the TRIMs Agreement which suggests that measures linking the amount of imports to a certain quantity or value of exports can constitute restrictions on importation within the meaning of Article XI:1. The Illustrative List thus provides that:

> "TRIMS that are inconsistent with the obligation of general obligation of elimination of quantitative restrictions provided for in paragraph 1 of Article XI of GATT 1994 include those which are mandatory or enforceable under domestic law or under administrative rulings, or compliance with which is necessary to obtain an advantage, and which restrict:
>
> > (a)   the importation by an enterprise of products used in or related to its local production, generally or to an amount related to the volume or value of local production that it exports."[431]

7.280 In particular, the Panel notes that this item does not limit the linkage to past exports.

7.281 Nevertheless, the Panel is not ruling on whether the specific type of measure under consideration here is necessarily the precise type of measure envisaged in the Illustrative List or on the extent to which this list may operate as an aid to interpretation of Article XI itself. The Panel also notes that to fall

---

[431] The Illustrative List of the TRIMs Agreement is referred to in its Article 2.2 and contained in the Annex to that Agreement.

DSR 2002:V

Report of the Panel

within the terms of item 2(a), the measures in question may in any case need to be characterized as measures that "restrict" imports in certain ways. The essence of our analysis has been to consider the proper meaning of a similar term under Article XI:1 itself. Nonetheless, this item is at least consistent with the finding that a measure linking imports to a certain amount of exports constitutes a restriction on importation within the meaning of Article XI.1.

5. Balance-of-Payments Defense

7.282 To the extent that a violation of Article XI would be found, India is claiming a defense under Article XVIII:B, although India also indicates that it will not be applying any measures for balance-of-payments purposes after 1 April 2001.

7.283 India argues that for the purposes of the present proceedings, its balance-of-payments situation should be assessed as of the dates of each request for the establishment of this Panel. This is not disputed by the complainants.

7.284 India has not presented any evidence as to its balance of payments situation as at the relevant dates. Instead, India considers that the burden of proof is on the complainants to establish that its measures are not justified on balance-of-payments grounds. It cites the *India – Quantitative Restrictions* report as support for its position, as well as the Appellate Body's ruling on burden of proof in the context of the *US – Wool Shirts and Blouses* case under the Textiles and Clothing Agreement (ATC).

7.285 The Panel does not agree with India's contentions as to burden of proof. In both of these cases cited by India, the rule applied was the general rule on burden of proof as consistently affirmed by the Appellate Body and panels. That rule is to the effect that a party claiming a violation must assert and prove its claim, and that a party asserting a defense is required to prove that the conditions for invoking that defense are met. In the *India – Quantitative Restrictions* case, while the panel found that the United States had the burden of proving its own claim that Article XVIII:11 had been violated by India, it also clearly held that India had the burden of proving its own defense under Article XVIII:B. Similarly, in the *US – Wool Shirts and Blouses* case, India, as the complainant, had the burden of proving its own claim that Article 6 of the ATC was violated by the United States. Thus in both of these cases, the party asserting a particular claim or defense was required to prove its assertions.

7.286 In this instance, the United States and European Communities asserted their claims that India had violated Articles III and XI of GATT 1994 and Article 2 of TRIMs. They made no representations concerning Article XVIII:B. It is India who invoked Article XVIII:B as a defense to any violations of Article XI which the Panel might find. Therefore, it is for India to assert this defense.

7.287 India suggests that applying the burden of proof to a party claiming a balance of payments defense but not a party applying a safeguard measure would be systemically unfair to developing countries. The Panel does not agree that this is an accurate policy consideration that might inform a purposive interpretation on this issue. Safeguards actions may be taken by any country. More importantly,

2030

DSR 2002:V

areas of coverage such as safeguards, anti-dumping and countervailing duties require domestic analysis where affected foreign interests may be represented and may use local courts to challenge bureaucratic determinations. It is only where the foreign interest alleges through the WTO that the procedures and principles were not properly followed that the burden then lies on it. There is no such domestic process with balance of payments issues. Thus the Panel does not find the analogy to be relevant.

7.288 Thus the Panel holds that the burden is on India in relation to this defense. To successfully assert this defense it must at a minimum, present a *prima facie* case that these measures can be considered to be maintained under Article XVIII:B.

7.289 Article XVIII:B foresees the possibility for developing country Members to apply certain measures to safeguard their external financial position and to ensure a level of reserves adequate for their level of development. Article XVIII:9 lists the substantive conditions which should be met in order to apply such measures. In addition, Article XVIII:B and the Understanding on Balance-of-payments provisions require the notification of such measures to the BOPs Committee.

7.290 In support of its assertion that its measures were justified under Article XVIII:B, India invokes the notification which it submitted to the BOPs Committee in 1997. It asserts that no new notification was required in respect of Public Notice No. 60 because the measures it contained were not significant changes to the measures within the terms of Article XVIII:B.

7.291 Other than that assertion, India has presented no evidence of any discussion in the BOPs Committee subsequent to the rulings of the panel and Appellate Body in the *India – Quantitative Restrictions* dispute. It has also not explained how any of the substantive conditions foreseen by Article XVIII:B might be fulfilled. It has also presented no evidence whatsoever concerning its actual balance of payments during the period which it itself has defined as the relevant time of examination for this Panel.

7.292 In the light of the foregoing, the Panel finds that India has failed to make a *prima facie* case that its measures were justified under Article XVIII:B.

7.293 The Panel also notes that the complainants have, in response to India's defense, presented some arguments and figures suggesting that India's balance-of-payments situation was not such as to justify the application of balance-of-payments measures under Article XVIII:B. India has also not provided evidence to refute those contentions.

7.294 India has also indicated that it would expect the Panel to consult with the IMF in determining India's balance-of-payments situation as of the dates of each claimant's request for establishment of this Panel. The Panel does not rule on whether consultation with the IMF is compulsory or not before the final factual resolution by a panel of a balance-of-payments matter, where there is conflicting evidence presented. Whatever the proper view as to this question, such a consultation could not be used as a total substitute for asserting and providing a prima facie case as to a defense under Article XVIII:B, and in the absence of any indi-

Report of the Panel

cation of how the measures might fall within the terms foreseen in that provision. It is clear that a panel's fact finding mandate should not be utilized so as to make out a *prima facie* case where that is not achieved by the relevant party.[432] At an appropriate stage in proceedings, consultation of appropriate international experts or authorities could be helpful in establishing whether one of the specific situations foreseen in Article XVIII:B applied to India's situation. As stated by the *India – Quantitative Restrictions* panel, such consultation could "assist in assessing the claims submitted" to the Panel. However, the arguments presented did not even lead the Panel to that point.

6. *Claims under Article III:4*

7.295 In light of the Panel's findings that the trade balancing condition contained in Public Notice No. 60 and the MOUs is inconsistent with Article XI:1, it wishes to apply the principle of judicial economy and does not consider it necessary in this instance, to separately consider the United States' general claim that the trade balancing condition is inconsistent also with Article III:4 of the GATT 1994.

7.296 Nevertheless, the Panel wishes to make one observation in that regard owing to India's general claim that the measure should be considered under Article III and the implication that the provisions are necessarily mutually exclusive. In support of the conclusion that while Articles III:4 and XI:1 deal with "imported products" and "importation" respectively, but without thereby prejudging what the outcome of such an Article III:4 examination might have been in this instance, the Panel wishes to note that it sees merit in the proposition that there may be circumstances in which specific measures may have a range of effects. In appropriate circumstances they may have an impact both in relation to the conditions of importation of a product and in respect of the competitive conditions of imported products on the internal market within the meaning of Article III:4.[433] This is also in keeping with the well established notion that different aspects of the same measure may be covered by different provisions of the covered Agreements.

---

[432] The Panel recalls in this regard the Appellate Body's observation that "Article 13 of the DSU and Article 11.2 of the SPS agreement suggest that panels have a significant investigative authority. However, this authority cannot be used by a panel to rule in favour of a complaining party which has not established a prima facie case of inconsistency based on specific legal claims asserted by it. A panel is entitled to seek information and advice from experts and from any other relevant source it chooses, pursuant to Article 13 of the DSU and, in an SPS case, Article 11.2 of the SPS Agreement, to help it understand and evaluate the evidence submitted and the arguments made by the parties, but not to make the case for a complaining party". (Report of the Appellate Body, *Japan – Agricultural Products II*, WT/DS76/AB/R, adopted on 19 March 1999, para. 129 (DSR 1999:I, 277)).

[433] The Panel notes that the TRIMS Agreement Illustrative List envisages measures relating to export requirements both in the context of Article XI:1, as noted above in the context of our analysis under Article XI:1, and in the context of Article III:4 of the GATT 1994, by listing as inconsistent with that provision measures which require "that an enterprise's purchases or use of imported products be limited to an amount related to the volume or value of local products that it exports" TRIMS Illustrative List, Item 1 (b).

2032   DSR 2002:V

India – Autos

7.297 While the Panel refrains from further consideration of the broader application of Article III:4 to the same features dealt with in the Article XI analysis, there is one distinct element of the trade balancing measure that was not factually in dispute between the parties and which was alleged by the complainants to constitute a distinct aspect of violation of Article III:4. This was the export obligation that India acknowledged to be incurred in relation to previously imported products acquired by manufacturers directly on the Indian market. This specific aspect was not considered in the examination under Article XI:1. Because it is a discrete condition attached to the administration of the trade balancing obligation and because it was addressed by the complainants in their Article XI analysis, the Panel feels it is appropriate to make a separate ruling on it.

(a) Purchases of Restricted Imported Kits and Components on the Domestic Market

7.298 Both the United States and European Communities argue that the trade balancing condition is inconsistent with Article III:4 in that it requires MOU signatories who purchase restricted kits and components on the Indian market to count the value of these purchases towards their trade balancing obligations. India has confirmed that,

> "if an MOU signatory purchased a component that was subject to import restrictions in India from either a trading company or another MOU signatory that had imported such a component on the basis of an import license, the value of such components would be taken into account for purposes of the neutralization requirement."[434]

7.299 The Panel recalls that Article III:4 provides that:

> "The products of the territory of any [Member] imported into the territory of any other contracting party shall be accorded treatment no less favourable than that accorded to like products of national origin in respect of all laws, regulations and requirements affecting their internal sale, offering for sale, purchase, transportation distribution or use."

7.300 As previously noted, for a violation of Article III:4 to be established, it is necessary to examine whether (1) imported products and domestic products are like products; (2) the measures constitute a "law, regulation or requirement"; (3) they affect the internal sale, offering for sale, purchase, transportation, distribution or use; and (4) imported products are accorded less favourable treatment than the treatment accorded to like domestic products. The Panel will consider these points successively.

---

[434] Response to Question 47 (b) of the Panel.

Report of the Panel

(i) Like Products

7.301 In this instance, the products at stake are the imported kits and components to which the trade balancing requirement applies. India asserts that these products are those that are/were subject to import licensing, since these are the only ones for which the trade balancing requirement applies. The Panel has already separately addressed the factual disagreement on this issue and concluded that the European Communities have not demonstrated that trade balancing applied in the past, or would still apply, to non-restricted items.

7.302 For the purpose of this analysis, the Panel will therefore consider only those products that were subject to restriction, i.e. kits and certain listed components. As was the case with the analysis under Article III:4 concerning the indigenization requirement, the only distinguishing factor between imported kits and components and kits and components of domestic origin would be their origin. Such differences in origin would not alone be such as to make products unlike. The Panel also recalls that it need not, for the purpose of this analysis, demonstrate actual trade in the products concerned to establish the likeness of the products at stake. The Panel therefore concludes that kits and components of imported and domestic origin are like products within the meaning of Article III:4.[435]

(ii) Laws, Regulations or Requirements

7.303 The Panel recalls its earlier conclusion that indigenization conditions in Public Notice No. 60 and the MOUs signed thereunder are "requirements" within the meaning of Article III:4 of GATT 1994. This conclusion is equally applicable to the trade balancing, obligation which is, like the indigenization requirement, one of the conditions provided for in Public Notice No. 60 and to be accepted by MOU signatories as a condition for obtaining the advantages of a license. Thus the Panel concludes that it is a requirement.

(iii) Affecting Internal Sale, Use, ...

7.304 Having established that the trade balancing condition foreseen in Public Notice No. 60 and the MOUs signed thereunder is a requirement within the meaning of Article III:4, the Panel must now consider whether this requirement is one "affecting the internal sale, offering for sale, purchase, use or distribution" of the products at issue, in that it requires MOU signatories purchasing restricted kits and components within India to count their value towards their export obligation.

---

[435] See for example the Panel Report on *Indonesia – Autos*, WT/DS54/R, WT/DS55/R, WT/DS59/R, WT/DS64/R, adopted on 23 July 1998, para. 14.113 (DSR 1998:VI, 2201) ("... an origin-based distinction in respect of internal taxes suffices in itself to violate Article III:2, without the need to demonstrate the existence of actually traded like products.")

See also the Panel Report on *Canada – Autos*, WT/DS139/R, WT/DS142/R, adopted on 19 June 2000, as modified by the Appellate Body Report, para. 10.74 (DSR 2000:VII, 3043).
See also the Compliance Panel Report on *US – FSC (Article 21.5)*, WT/DS108/RW, circulated on 20 August 2001, para. 8.133 (DSR 2002:I, 119).

India – Autos

7.305 The Panel recalls that the ordinary meaning of the term "affecting" has been understood to imply "a measure that has "an effect on" and this indicates a broad scope of application".[436] The disciplines of Article III:4 thus govern a broad range of measures, i.e. not only measures which are directly intended to regulate the product, but in addition, any law, regulation or requirement which "has an effect" on either the internal purchase, offering for sale etc. of the product. The fact that a provision is not necessarily primarily aimed at regulating the offering for sale or use of the product on the domestic market is thus not an obstacle to its "affecting" them. Nonetheless, it applies only to situations where either internal sale, or purchase (...) or use are affected.

7.306 The fact that the measure applies only to imported products need not, in itself, an obstacle to its falling within the purview of Article III.[437] For example, an internal tax, or a product standard conditioning the sale of the imported but not of the like domestic product, could nonetheless "affect" the conditions of the imported product on the market and could be a source of less favorable treatment. Similarly, the fact that a requirement is imposed as a condition on importation is not necessarily in itself an obstacle to its falling within the scope of Article III:4.[438]

7.307 In the present instance, an MOU signatory choosing to purchase an imported kit or component within the Indian market will incur an additional export obligation of a value at least equivalent to that of the product, whenever the product has been imported subject to restrictions (which is normally the case for these products). On the other hand, were it to purchase a locally-made kit or component, the manufacturer would not incur such an additional export obligation. The purchase of the imported good thus carries with it an additional burden not incurred upon the purchase of a like domestic product. This obviously affects the competitive conditions of the imported product on the Indian market and more specifically, affects the conditions of internal offering for sale or purchase of these products.

---

[436] Panel Report on *Canada – Autos*, WT/DS139/R, WT/DS142/R, adopted on 19 June 2000, as modified by the Appellate Body Report, para. 10.80 (DSR 2000:VII, 3043).

[437] Article III:1 refers to the application of measures "to imported *or* domestic products", which suggests that application to both is not necessary.

[438] Thus, the "advantage" to be obtained could consist in a right to import a product. See for instance, the Report of the second GATT panel on *EC – Bananas II* as cited and endorsed in *EC – Bananas III*, WT/DS27/R/USA, adopted on 25 September 1997, as modified by the Appellate Body Report, para. 4.385 (DSR 1997:II, 943):

"The Panel further noted that previous panels had found consistently that this obligation applies to any requirement imposed by a contracting party, including requirements 'which an enterprise voluntarily accepts to obtain an advantage from the government.' In the view of the Panel, a requirement to purchase a domestic product in order to obtain the right to import a product at a lower rate of duty under a tariff quota is therefore a requirement affecting the purchase of a product within the meaning of Article III:4."

Report of the Panel

(iv) Whether the Measure Affords Less Favourable Treatment to Imported Products

7.308 By requiring that the purchaser of an imported kit or component take on an additional obligation to export cars or components of equal value when such domestic purchases occur, the trade balancing requirement creates a disincentive to the purchase of these products, and consequently makes them more difficult to dispose of on the internal market. This element of the trade balancing obligation therefore distinctly accords less favorable treatment to these imported products than to like products of domestic origin, within the meaning of Article III:4 of GATT 1994.

7.309 The Panel therefore finds that, by requiring that MOU signatories count towards their export obligation under the MOU any purchases of imported restricted kits and components on the Indian market, the trade balancing condition is in violation of Article III:4 of the GATT 1994.

7. Ruling on the Consistency of Public Notice No. 60 with the GATT 1994

7.310 To date the Panel has considered the claims concerning the indigenization and trade balancing successively, examining each time both Public Notice No. 60 and the MOUs together. The Panel previously indicated that it thought this to be the appropriate approach, since both instruments contain the two specific obligations that are the measures in issue. Indeed, it is only through the existence of Public Notice No. 60 that manufacturers were induced to sign the MOUs. While the European Communities has not objected to such an approach, it has also requested the Panel to make a separate ruling that Public Notice No. 60 itself is inconsistent with the GATT and TRIMs Agreement.[439]

7.311 This request is not simply a further claim about an identified measure that could be the subject of a decision to apply judicial economy. It is instead a distinct claim as to a more restrictively defined measure, albeit still relating to the two conditions of indigenization and trade balancing. As such, the Panel feels bound to rule on it.

7.312 In order to consider this separate claim, the Panel will address successively the claims of inconsistency with Articles III:4 and XI of the GATT 1994.

---

[439] In response to the Panel's question whether the European Communities was seeking a distinct ruling on Public Notice No. 60, separate from whether any MOU has been executed, the European Communities replied that it was seeking a distinct ruling. The European Communities argued that "[t]o the extent that the MOUs impose obligations that are inconsistent with the GATT and the TRIMs Agreement, a requirement to enter into an MOU is also inconsistent with those agreements, regardless of whether any manufacturer actually concludes a MOU." See EC's Response to Question 88.

2036

DSR 2002:V

India – Autos

(a) Consistency of Public Notice No. 60 with Article III:4 of GATT 1994

7.313 In addressing whether Public Notice No. 60 is consistent with Article III:4 of the GATT 1994, the Panel notes that the following elements must be considered: whether the imported products and domestic products are "like products"; whether Public Notice No. 60 is a "law, regulation, or requirement affecting the internal sale, offering for sale, purchase...or use"; whether the imported products are accorded "less favourable treatment" than that accorded to like domestic products. In the previous analysis, the Panel found that automotive parts and components of domestic and foreign origin are like products within the meaning of Article III:4.

7.314 In respect of whether Public Notice No. 60 constitutes a "requirement" under Article III:4, the Panel first noted that commitments entered into on a voluntary basis by individual firms to obtain an advantage constituted a "requirement". In this instance, the Panel noted that auto manufacturers were required to accept the indigenization condition set out in Public Notice No. 60 to obtain an import license to be able to import the restricted items contained in Public Notice No. 60. The Panel went on to conclude that the indigenization condition contained in Public Notice No. 60 is a condition to the granting of an advantage, i.e. the right to import restricted kits and components, and therefore constituted a requirement within the meaning of Article III:4.

7.315 The Panel subsequently found that the indigenization condition affects the internal sale, offering for sale, purchase and use of the imported parts and components in the Indian market and that, by requiring auto manufacturers to use a certain percentage of domestic products, it affects the internal sale of like imported products which affords less favourable treatment to the imported products.

7.316 The Panel is mindful that Public Notice No. 60 does not, in and of itself, impose a "direct" obligation on individual manufacturers as it is the execution of the MOUs that imposes such obligations. However, the Panel notes that it is not necessary for actual MOUs to have been signed under Public Notice No. 60 in order for the indigenization condition, as contained in Public Notice No. 60, to afford less favourable treatment to imported products within the meaning of Article III:4. The Panel recalls in particular, in this respect, that the purpose of Article III:4 is to protect the competitive opportunities of imported products on the domestic markets. It is a well established principle under WTO jurisprudence that Article III of the GATT 1994 is to provide equality of competitive conditions for imported products in relation to domestic products. That is, Article III requires Members to provide equality of competitive conditions for imported products in relation to domestic products. These competitive conditions are affected even in the absence of actual trade flows, wherever the conditions afforded to imported products are such as to affect their competitive opportunities on the market.[440] In this instance, Public Notice No. 60 imposes the acceptance

---

[440] The Appellate Body stated that "Article III protects expectations not of any particular trade volume but rather of the equal competitive relationship between imported and domestic products." See

DSR 2002:V

2037

Report of the Panel

of the indigenization condition on any manufacturer wishing to import restricted kits or components. This in itself adversely affects the competitive opportunities of all automotive parts and components, as far as the indigenization condition is concerned because it can be assumed that certain car manufacturers will wish to import restricted goods and will therefore choose to accept the indigenization condition.

7.317 In light of the foregoing, the Panel finds that Public Notice No. 60, independent of whether the MOUs have been executed, is a requirement that is inconsistent with Article III:4 of the GATT 1994.

> (b)   Consistency of Public Notice No. 60 with Article XI:1 of the GATT 1994 in so far as it Contains the Trade Balancing Condition

7.318 In determining whether Public Notice No. 60 is inconsistent with Article XI:1 of the GATT 1994, the Panel recalls its earlier analysis of the trade balancing condition as contained in the previous section.

7.319 First, it recalls its conclusion that Public Notice No. 60, as a governmental measure requiring manufacturers to accept certain conditions in order to be allowed to import restricted automotive kits and components, constituted a "measure" within the meaning of Article XI:1. This conclusion remains relevant to this analysis and the Panel confirms its earlier conclusion in this respect.

7.320 Second, in order to establish whether Public Notice No. 60, in itself, can be considered to be inconsistent with Article XI:1, it has to be established that it constitutes a "restriction ... on importation" within the meaning of that provision. The Panel recalls in this respect its earlier conclusion that the trade balancing condition, as contained both in Public Notice No. 60 and in the MOUs signed thereunder, constituted a restriction on importation contrary to Article XI:1 in that it effectively limits the amount of imports that a manufacturer may make by linking imports to commitment to undertake a certain amount of exports. Under such circumstance, an importer is not free to import as many restricted kits or components as he otherwise might so long as there is a finite limit to the amount of possible exports.

7.321 While the Panel, in reaching its earlier conclusion, analyzed both instruments containing the trade balancing condition, the conclusion that this condition is inconsistent with Article XI:1 is not dependent on the signature by individual manufacturers of MOUs as such condition contained in Public Notice No. 60 is a measure that restricts the import of kits or components.

7.322 The Panel therefore concludes that Public Notice No. 60 in itself, to the extent that it requires the acceptance of the trade balancing condition in order to gain the advantage of importing the restricted products, imposes a restriction on imports and is inconsistent with Article XI:1 of the GATT 1994.

Appellate Body Report in *Japan – Alcoholic Beverages II*, WT/DS8/R, WT/DS10/R, WT/DS11/R, adopted on 1 November 1996, p. 16 (DSR 1996:I, 97, at 110).

2038

DSR 2002:V

India – Autos

G. *Claims under the TRIMs Agreement*

7.323 Both complainants argue that the indigenization and neutralization conditions are in violation of Article 2 of the TRIMs Agreement, which prohibits the use of trade-related investment measures inconsistent with Articles III or XI of GATT 1994.

7.324 However, having found that these measures are respectively in violation of Articles III:4 and XI:1 of the GATT, the Panel applies the principle of judicial economy and finds that it is not necessary to consider separately whether they are also inconsistent with the provisions of the TRIMs Agreement.

VIII. CONCLUSIONS AND RECOMMENDATIONS

A. *Conclusions*

8.1 In light of the foregoing findings, the Panel concludes that:

    (a) India acted inconsistently with its obligations under Article III:4 of the GATT 1994 by imposing on automotive manufacturers, under the terms of Public Notice No. 60 and the MOUs signed thereunder, an obligation to use a certain proportion of local parts and components in the manufacture of cars and automotive vehicles ("indigenization" condition);

    (b) India acted inconsistently with its obligations under Article XI of the GATT 1994 by imposing on automotive manufacturers, under the terms of Public Notice No. 60 and the MOUs signed thereunder, an obligation to balance any importation of certain kits and components with exports of equivalent value ("trade balancing" condition);

    (c) India acted inconsistently with its obligations under Article III:4 of the GATT 1994 by imposing, in the context of the trade balancing condition under the terms of Public Notice No. 60 and the MOUs signed thereunder, an obligation to offset the amount of any purchases of previously imported restricted kits and components on the Indian market, by exports of equivalent value;

8.2 The Panel recalls that it has examined the foregoing measures as of the date of the complainants' requests for establishment of a panel. However, the Panel also recalls that a number of arguments were exchanged in the course of the proceedings concerning events which took place during the Panel's proceedings and their potential impact on the rulings or recommendations to be made by the Panel.

8.3 The Panel had earlier concluded that events subsequent to the requests for establishment of the Panel had not removed the Panel's initial competence to consider the validity of the measures as at the date of its establishment. It had also noted that separate consideration would be given to the issue whether the events which took place subsequently, including on or after 1 April 2001, might have affected the existence of any violations identified and that it would consider

DSR 2002:V

2039

Report of the Panel

whether those events affect the nature or range of any recommendations it may make to the DSB in accordance with Article 19.1 of the DSU. This issue will be addressed now.

> ### B. Consequences of Events Having Taken Place in the Course of the Proceedings

> #### 1. Presentation of the Issue: Arguments of the Parties

8.4   India principally argued that the Panel could not rule on the measures at issue because they had already been the subject of a DSB ruling and a mutually agreed solution. It also argued that any future measures which India might take as of after 1 April would be outside of this Panel's terms of reference. In addition, India made a number of arguments to the effect that the situation in respect of the measures at issue had changed after 1 April 2001 and that in any event, India's measures as applied after 1 April 2001, in the absence of any import licensing restrictions, could not be in violation of the GATT 1994 or of the TRIMs Agreement.

8.5   India thus argued generally that "Public Notice No. 60 is no longer applicable because the import restrictions it was to administer no longer exist. In the absence of an import restriction on cars, this notice cannot be implemented and serves no purpose. It is therefore not clear to India how the European Communities and the United States can claim that the Public Notice as such is capable of violating WTO law." As for Public Notice No. 60 itself, in its first submission (prior to April 2001), India indicated that Public Notice No. 60 would no longer apply as of 1 April 2001 and explained what the consequences of this absence of further application of Public Notice No. 60 would be: no new MOUs would be required and no licenses would be required for the importation of previously restricted kits and components. In its second submission, India confirmed that Public Notice would no longer be applicable in the absence of import restrictions[441]. In response to a concern raised by the United States that the notice appeared to still remain in effect,[442] India explained in its second submission that "a new public notice rescinding Public Notice No. 60 is (..) not required to ensure the consistency of Public Notice No. 60 with Articles III:4 and XI:1 of the GATT."[443]   The Panel was not advised by India until the interim review stage that Public Notice had, nonetheless, been repealed in September 2001.[444]

8.6   It is clear that India's arguments relating to the elimination of its import licensing regime were relevant to a number of its legal arguments, including its principal arguments concerning the inadmissibility of the claims, as having already been the object of dispute settlement procedures. Nonetheless, India also envisaged the possibility that the Panel might conclude that it was competent to

---

[441]   Second Submission by India, para. 12.
[442]   Response to Question 2(b) by the Panel.
[443]   Second submission by India, para. 14.
[444]   See document annexed to the Oral Statement of India at the interim review meeting.

examine the matter before it and examine "the operation of Public Notice No. 60 and the trade balancing provisions under India's former licensing regime".[445]

8.7   In this respect, India requested that:

> If the Panel were to conclude that the operation of Public Notice No. 60 and the trade balancing provisions under India's former licensing regime was inconsistent with the GATT, it should – following the practice of other panels – note that the licensing regime had been abolished on 1 April 2001 and that it was *therefore* not necessary for the Panel to recommend to the DSB in accordance with Article 19:1 of the DSU that it request India to bring these measures into conformity with the GATT (emphasis added).[446]

8.8   In addition, India suggested in its first submission that it was quite possible that a number of MOU signatory manufacturers may have reached, or be close to reaching, the required level of indigenization in manufacturing. At the second substantive meeting, India presented the results of a survey following a meeting with "the most important car manufacturers from the EC, Japan and the United States to verify their performance under the MOUs" which led to written confirmation by these signatories that they had reached the required levels of indigenization, except for one of the surveyed companies, who remained below the 70% threshold for one car model.[447]

8.9   India thus also requested that:

> "If the Panel were to rule that the indigenization requirements in the MOUs are inconsistent with Article III:4, it should find that, according to the evidence submitted by the parties, there remained as of May 2001 only one company that was still bound by the indigenization requirement with respect to one car model. India therefore requested the Panel to limit any recommendation under Article 19:1 of the DSU to the indigenization requirement that remains to be performed by that particular company with respect to that model."[448]

8.10   Both complainants, to the contrary, generally considered that the disappearance of India's licensing system did not affect their legal claims and that the measures, as they would remain in place after 1 April 2001, would continue to be inconsistent with the provisions invoked by them. They also confirmed the nature of their requests for findings in light of these elements, which suggested an expectation that the Panel would take them into account.

8.11   The United States thus requested the Panel to find that the measures at issue in this dispute, the indigenization and the trade balancing requirements, imposed by Public Notice No. 60 and the MOUs, were inconsistent with Article III:4 and XI:1 of GATT 1994 and Articles 2.1. and 2.2 of the TRIMs Agree-

---

[445] See para. 3.7 above.
[446] Para. 3.8 of the report.
[447] Statement of India at the second meeting, para. 29 and Annex II to that statement.
[448] Para. 3.8 of the report.

DSR 2002:V

Report of the Panel

ment.[449] The United States requested this Panel to make findings to this effect, and to recommend that India bring all such measures into conformity with its obligations.[450] In response to questions from the Panel, the United States confirmed that it was "requesting the Panel to make findings with respect to the indigenization requirement and the trade balancing requirement as such. Those requirements were in existence at the time the Panel was established, and remain in existence today. There is therefore no distinction to be drawn between the measures as they existed at the time of the Panel establishment and now."[451] The United States also indicated in response to a question from the Panel that "the Panel must of course consider the arguments that India has advanced about the relevance of the situation after April 1, 2001, since India has made those arguments a central part of its defense (...)".[452]

8.12   The European Communities requested the Panel to find that the trade balancing and indigenization requirements contained in Public Notice No. 60 and in the MOUs concluded thereunder were inconsistent with Articles III:4 and XI:1 of the GATT 1994 and Article 2.1 of the TRIMs Agreement as of the date of establishment of this Panel and had remained so after 1 April 2001.[453] It clarified that the measures applied after 1 April 2001 continued to be inconsistent with the GATT 1994 and the TRIMs Agreement because they were the same as the measures applied before that date.[454] Furthermore, the European Communities requested the Panel to find that, at the time when the Panel was established, Public Notice No. 60 was inconsistent with Article XI:1 and III:4 of the GATT 1994 and Article 2.1 of the TRIMs Agreement.

8.13   The issue of the impact of certain events subsequent to the request for establishment of the Panel was therefore clearly raised before the Panel, and it appears from the terms of their arguments and requests for findings that this issue was relevant in the findings of violation which the Panel might make with respect to the measures as they were applied as of its establishment. In these circumstances, the Panel found it necessary to determine whether it was still appropriate to make a recommendation notwithstanding India's assertion that the legal situation had fundamentally changed and that there may be nothing left to bring into conformity.

---

[449]   See also Questions 1 and 17 of the Panel.

[450]   See para 3.1. The United States also considered it would be appropriate for the Panel to rule on Public Notice No. 60 given that the requirements were still in place through the MOUs. The United States said it was not requesting the Panel to make findings on Public Notice No. 60 that were separate from its findings on the MOUs executed thereunder. The United States was, however, requesting that the Panel's findings encompass both Public Notice No. 60 and the individual MOUs (see para 3.2). See also para. 38 of the First Submission of the United States to the Panel.

[451]   Response to Question 2 (a) from the Panel.

[452]   Response to Question 72 from the Panel para. 10.

[453]   See Second Oral Statement para. 41.

[454]   Para. 3.5. See also Question 87 of the Panel.

2042   DSR 2002:V

2. Approach of the Panel

8.14 Article 19.1 of the DSU provides that "[w]here a panel or the Appellate Body concludes that a measure is inconsistent with a covered agreement, it shall recommend that the Member concerned bring the measure into conformity with that Agreement."

8.15 This provision thus envisages a situation where a violation *is* in existence. Indeed, this formulation reflects the usual situation which panels encounter, examining a matter which does not significantly evolve in the course of the proceedings. It is only natural in such circumstances for a panel, following a finding that a measure is inconsistent with a covered agreement, to simply recommend, without the need for any further substantive analysis, that this measure be brought into conformity with that Agreement.

8.16 In this instance, however, a number of arguments have been presented, as was noted, to suggest that certain events having occurred in the course of the proceedings fundamentally affect the existence or persistence of the alleged violations. In fact, issues relating to the elimination of India's import licensing regime and its particular impact on the measures at issue in this dispute were discussed before this Panel from the very first stages of the proceedings. As noted above, India itself had suggested in its requests for findings that, should the Panel examine the measures and find them to be inconsistent with India's obligations under the GATT 1994, these factors be taken into account in the context of the Panel's recommendations under Article 19.1, either to preclude the need for such recommendations or to limit their scope. The complainants, on the other hand, have expected the Panel to make certain findings and recommendations implying that the events having taken place in the course of the proceedings have been taken into account.

8.17 The determination the panel therefore needs to make is whether it is appropriate for it, in the circumstances of the case, to take these developments into account and determine in this light whether it still should make a recommendation under Article 19.1, and, if so, whether the content of this recommendation should be affected by these developments.

8.18 In most instances of dispute settlement under the WTO, the measures at issue are not affected, or argued to be affected, by events having occurred during the course of the proceedings in relation to the measures at issue.[455] Some panels have, however, had to consider whether to take into account amendments made to the measures in the course of the procedure. While some panels have declined to examine subsequent amendments to the measures and their conformity with the agreements,[456] at least one panel has taken into account the most recent evo-

---

[455] The Panel notes, as a general matter, that if a respondent could make changes of any degree to a measure subject to challenge and then always be able to successfully argue that the Panel's report can have no ultimate normative effect because the changes are distinct measures from those originally envisaged, this could entirely frustrate the dispute settlement system.

[456] In *Indonesia – Autos*, the National Car program was terminated and the regulations and decrees thereunder were revoked during the panel process. Citing previous GATT and WTO panel reports, the panel proceeded to make findings on the National Car program. In *US – Section 337*, the challenged measure was amended during the panel process but the panel refused to take into account such

Report of the Panel

lutions of the measures where this allowed it to find the "current" measures no longer to be in violation[457].

8.19   In situations where the withdrawal of the entire measure in dispute has taken place, it may understandably be possible for the Panel, assuming that it nonetheless had examined the consistency of the relevant measure, to conclude that that there is no recommendation left to make under Article 19.1. However, the situation arising in this instance is quite distinct. While it is not disputed that some evolutions have taken place in the more general context of India's import restrictions, the parties are in strong disagreement as to the effect of these evolutions on the specific measures at issue in this dispute.

8.20   It should first be stressed that the issue arising in this instance is *not* whether the Panel might be entitled to examine the WTO-consistency of any new measures which might have been taken by India after the beginning of these proceedings. Such subsequent measures have been clearly stated not to be within this Panel's terms of reference. None of the parties contended that the measures themselves were no longer those that were within the Panel's initial terms of reference. The issue is limited solely to the question of whether, as argued by the respondent, certain events subsequent to the Panel's establishment are such as to affect the continued relevance of the Panel's initial findings with regard to measures clearly within its terms of reference. This raises the issue of whether they should be considered, in this light, before the Panel can make appropriate recommendations as to the need for India to bring its measures into conformity with the GATT 1994. [458]

8.21   In approaching this question, the Panel considers it appropriate to seek guidance in the definition of the mandate given to it by the DSB under the DSU. The Panel recalls in particular the terms of Article 11 of the DSU, which describes the function of panels as follows:

> "The function of panels is to *assist the DSB in discharging its responsibilities under this Understanding and the covered agreements.* Accordingly, a panel should make an objective assessment

---

amendments. See also *Argentina – Textiles*, Report of the Appellate Body, para. 64 (DSR 1998:III, 1003).

[457] See under the GATT, the *Thailand – Cigarettes* case: the panel took into account, in drawing its conclusions as to the compatibility of the measure submitted to it, an amendment in the measure on the basis of which it was able to conclude that the measure was no longer in violation of the relevant GATT provision:

> "the Panel observed that the new Thai measure, by eliminating business and municipal taxes on cigarettes, removed the internal taxes imposed on imported cigarettes in excess of those applied to domestic cigarettes. The Panel noted that (...) the Tobacco Act continued to enable the executive authorities to levy the discriminatory taxes. However, the Panel (...) found that the possibility that the Tobacco Act might be applied contrary to Article III:2 was, by itself, not sufficient to make it inconsistent with the General Agreement".

The panel concluded that "the current regulations relating to the excise, business and municipal taxes on cigarettes are consistent with Thailand's obligations under Article III".

[458] It should be stressed in this respect that none of the issues raised here relate to any alleged "worsening" of the situation likely to generate additional violations resulting from the measures at stake, but rather to whether the situation as examined has lost part or all of its legal or practical relevance.

2044   DSR 2002:V

of the matter before it, including an objective assessment of the facts of the case and the applicability of and conformity with the relevant covered agreements, and make such other findings as will assist the DSB in making the recommendations or in giving the rulings provided for in the covered agreements. (emphasis added and final sentence omitted)"

8.22   The Panel also recalls its own terms of reference in this case:

"To examine, in the light of the relevant provisions cited by the United States in WT/DS175/4 and by the European Communities in WT/DS146/4, the matters referred to the DSB by the United States and the European Communities in those documents and to *make such findings as will assist the DSB in making the recommendations or in giving the rulings provided for in those agreements.* (emphasis added)"[459]

8.23   The Panel believes that it has an important responsibility to the DSB to "assist [it] in making the recommendations or giving the rulings" provided for under the covered agreements, and, more generally, to "assist it in discharging its responsibilities under this Understanding and the covered agreements" as foreseen in Article 11 of the DSU. As recalled by the Appellate Body, the aim of dispute settlement is "to resolve the matter at issue and 'to secure a positive solution to a dispute'".[460]

8.24   The responsibilities of a panel under the DSU include the requirement under Article 19.1 of the DSU that "[w]here a panel or the Appellate Body concludes that a measure is inconsistent with a covered agreement, it shall recommend that the Member concerned bring the measure into conformity with that Agreement".

8.25   If only as a matter of logic, there can be no sense in making such a recommendation if a Panel is of the view that the violation at issue has ceased to exist when its recommendation is being made.[461] The Panel does not believe that Articles 11 and 19 of the DSU should be interpreted to demand that a panel must make a formalistic statement that a measure needs to be brought into compliance when it is faced with factual and legal arguments that this is no longer the case and must do so without being entitled to resolve those contentions.

8.26   Indeed, were these issues not taken into account at all in the Panel's assessment of the matter, there may be a significant risk that the resulting ruling could remain of very uncertain value even as of the date of release of the Panel's

---

[459]   See para. 1.4.

[460]   *Australia – Salmon*, Report of the Appellate Body, para. 223 (DSR 1998:VIII, 3327).

[461]   This was recalled by the Appellate Body in its report on *US – Certain EC Products*, where it observed that "there is an obvious inconsistency between the finding of the Panel that 'the 3 March Measure is no longer in existence' and the subsequent recommendation of the Panel that the DSB request that the United States bring its measure into conformity with its WTO obligations. The Panel erred in recommending that the DSB request the United States to bring into conformity with its WTO obligations a measure which the Panel has found no longer exists" (*US – Certain EC Products*, Report of the Appellate Body, WT/DS165/AB/R, adopted on 10 January 2001, para. 81 (DSR 2001:I, 373)).

Report of the Panel

report, as well as potentially be internally inconsistent in making a recommendation to bring into conformity measures alleged to have ceased to have an effect.

8.27   In the circumstances of the case, the respondent itself has requested that the events which occurred in the course of the proceedings be taken into account in the context of making the recommendations under Article 19.1. The complainants, while they had not specifically requested the Panel to consider these issues at this stage of its analysis, did make requests for findings which called for these subsequent events to be taken into account, in requesting the Panel to find that the measures had "remained" in violation subsequent to 1 April.

8.28   In light of the foregoing, the Panel felt that it would not be making an "objective assessment of the matter before it", or assisting the DSB in discharging its responsibilities under the DSU in accordance with Article 11 of the DSU, had it chosen not to address the impact of events having taken place in the course of the proceedings, in assessing the appropriateness of making a recommendation under Article 19.1 of the DSU.

8.29   This is, in the Panel's view, an entirely distinct question from the issue of *how* India might appropriately remedy this situation and bring its measures into conformity in the future. The Panel does not seek here to engage in such an analysis. Any future issues arising as to whether India has complied with any recommendations resulting from the adoption of this report would be for a compliance panel to assess.

8.30   It should be highlighted in concluding this section that the decision taken by this Panel to proceed in this way in the particular circumstances of this case is in no way intended to imply that panels have a general duty to systematically re-evaluate the existence of any violations identified before proceeding with making their recommendations under Article 19.1. This Panel is simply responding to the particular arguments placed before it, where the parties disagree as to the implications of subsequent events on the Panel's power to make recommendations and rulings. The principal aim of the Panel in proceeding in this manner is to discharge its duty in the most efficient way towards resolving the matter at issue in this dispute.

3.   *Analysis*

8.31   The parties agree that as from 1 April 2001 India removed its discretionary import licensing regime on the products at issue and that Public Notice No. 60 and the MOUs were originally introduced and operated in the context of this licensing system. This was obviously a significant change in the situation affecting the conditions of importation of these previously restricted products. In particular, India clarified that no new MOUs would be required to be signed and no import licenses would be required for future non-restricted imports.

8.32   However, the question to consider is not whether these changes were significant *per se*, but rather, what effect they may have on the foregoing legal and factual analysis of the two measures before the Panel, namely the indigenization and trade balancing obligations, and consequently, on the recommendations the Panel might make under Article 19.1 of the DSU.

8.33   India raises essentially two lines of argument:

(a)   the general import licensing framework under which the measures operated had disappeared and that, as a result, there could be no further violation of the relevant provisions; more specifically, India argued that one of the instruments containing the challenged obligations (i.e. Public Notice No. 60), first "ceased to operate" and then was formally repealed; it also argued that after 1 April 2001, the MOUs signed under Public Notice No. 60 became mere private contracts;

(b)   as a factual matter, all signatories but one had fulfilled their indigenization obligations and the Panel's recommendation in that regard could therefore be limited to that signatory who had not yet reached required indigenization level. This is a separate issue from the consequences of the repeal of Public Notice No. 60 as such. The Panel will however also address it here, since it is raised as a fact of potential relevance to the scope of the Panel's recommendations.

8.34   The Panel notes that after 1 April, the situation appears to differ somewhat between the two instruments in which the violating measures are to be found, i.e. Public Notice No. 60 and the MOUs signed thereunder. It was alleged that Public Notice No. 60 no longer applied, and then that it was repealed. It is not alleged that the MOUs, as such, have ceased to apply. Indeed, it has been confirmed that while no new MOUs will be required and that previously restricted products could now be freely imported without licenses, manufacturers are expected to fulfill their indigenization requirements and outstanding export obligations under existing MOUs. However, India has also presented specific arguments to the effect that the nature of the MOUs as mere private contracts since 1 April has also affected how they might be considered as measures for the purposes of WTO dispute settlement.

8.35   As in its principal findings, the Panel will address successively the two challenged measures, i.e. the indigenization and trade balancing provisions, and consider within these sections the different issues at stake.

(a)   Indigenization Provisions

8.36   The Panel recalls that the indigenization provisions, as contained in both Public Notice No. 60 and the MOUs signed thereunder, were found to be inconsistent with the provisions of Article III:4 of the GATT.

Report of the Panel

> (i) The Cessation of the Application of Public Notice No. 60 and the MOUs as Private Contracts

8.37   It is not in dispute that the indigenization requirements contained in MOUs already signed by individual manufacturers in accordance with Public Notice No. 60 have remained under the same terms as of 1 April 2001 or any other date. India confirmed that, even after the elimination of import restrictions and licensing requirements on the products subject to Public Notice No. 60, it did not intend to release these manufacturers from their legal obligations under those terms. Nevertheless, because no new MOUs would be signed, there would be no new violation in respect of any person not a signatory as of that date.

8.38   However, India considers that since 1 April 2001, the MOUs have become enforceable merely as private contracts. It argues that there is a fundamental difference between a requirement that has to be fulfilled to obtain an import license under the Indian trade laws and a requirement under private contract law with the Government of India, which the Government is free to enforce or not. It has thus argued that India is free to waive or enforce them, and that they have therefore become discretionary measures which cannot be challenged as such under WTO dispute settlement.[462]

8.39   India's argument in this regard concentrates on the means of enforcement rather than the existence and enforceability of the primary obligation itself. The fact that the Indian government may have some "discretion" in seeking the actual enforcement of the requirements, in that it could choose to pursue or not pursue its legal rights under the MOUs and enabling legislation, does not fundamentally alter the fact that the obligation already exists. The measure's status as a requirement as at the date of the Panel's establishment does not fundamentally alter, simply because a change has been made in the background circumstances which may then alter the potential means of enforcement.

8.40   A distinction must be made between the binding character and enforceability of the commitment, and its actual enforcement. As far as a manufacturer having entered into an MOU is concerned, the commitments already exist and affect commercial behaviour, whether or not the Indian Government ultimately would choose to seek their enforcement through specific administrative or judicial action in the event of breach.[463]

---

[462]   Second Submission, para. 30.

[463]   The *Canada – FIRA* panel, in considering an argument by Canada that the undertakings were "private contractual" arrangements, found that:

> "The Panel carefully examined the Canadian view that the purchase undertakings should be considered as private contractual obligations of particular foreign investors vis-à-vis the Canadian government. The Panel recognized that investors might have an economic advantage in assuming purchase undertakings, taking into account the other conditions under which the investment was permitted. The Panel felt, however, that even if this was so, private contractual obligations entered into by investors should not adversely affect the rights which contracting parties, including contracting parties not involved in the dispute, possess under Article III :4 of the General Agreement and which they can exercise on behalf of their exporters.

2048

DSR 2002:V

India – Autos

8.41   The Panel is supported in this view by the fact that the Illustrative List of the TRIMs agreement expressly refers to mere enforceability in the context of defining measures which may fall within the scope of Article III:4 as well as Article XI:1.

8.42   This view is also supported by the jurisprudence. This Panel has previously alluded to *US - Malt Beverages* where a panel found the mandatory price affirmation laws in Massachusetts and Rhode Island inconsistent with Article III:4 because they accorded imported beer and wine less favourable treatment than the like domestic products even though the States concerned might not have been using their police powers to enforce the legislation. The panel noted that this did not change the fact that the measures were mandatory legislation which may influence the decision of economic operators.

8.43   Changing the historical inducement for entering and then complying with the relevant commitments from the potential denial of import licensing under Public Notice No. 60 to inducement for compliance with existing commitments through the potential for contractual or penalty-based litigation, does not change the legal and historical basis upon which the relevant companies came to adopt the obligations in the first place.

8.44   The Panel therefore cannot accept India's argument that the legal nature of the MOUs would have been altered after 1 April so as to make them discretionary measures not subject to review under WTO dispute settlement. On the contrary, the MOUs in place after 1 April are those very same legal instruments signed by manufacturers prior to 1 April 2001 and that it is only by virtue of this prior commitment that they remain binding after 1 April 2001, despite the disappearance of the supporting government measure which served to induce their signature. Suppressing the advantage that served to induce the manufacturers to sign the MOUs does not fundamentally alter the analysis of the commitments they undertook.

8.45   Any signatories who have not attained the stipulated levels are still required to do so. Thus they would still be induced to favour domestic products if they are concerned to comply with their contractual commitments to the government of India. As indicated above, the only potential change relates to the means by which any enforcement of a breach of that obligation would occur, and that change alone does not alter the nature of the commitment entered into. Hence, the Panel concludes that the indigenization obligations contained in the MOUs have not been essentially altered by the events of 1 April 2001.

8.46   The indigenization requirements as they stand in existing MOUs thus remain in violation of Article III:4. The cessation or repeal of Public Notice No. 60 has not suppressed this inconsistency. Public Notice No. 60 served to induce the signature of these MOUs, and these instruments contain the effective commitments of manufacturers in relation to indigenization and trade balancing. In-

---

This applies in particular to the rights deriving from the national treatment principle, which – as stated in Article III :1 – is aimed at preventing the use of internal measures 'so as to afford protection to domestic production'." (paras 5.4 to 5.6).

DSR 2002:V

2049

Report of the Panel

dia has clearly indicated that these MOUs remain in existence. It has also clearly indicated that it was not its intention to release signatories from their remaining obligations thereunder, including the indigenization requirement generally.[464]

8.47   In light of the foregoing, the Panel concludes that the indigenization conditions contained in Public Notice No. 60 and in the MOUs, as they have continued to exist and apply after 1 April 2001, have remained in violation of the relevant GATT provisions.

(ii)   Achievement of the Required Levels of Indigenization by MOU Signatories

8.48   India informed the Panel in the course of the proceedings that among the "most important manufacturers" surveyed in April-May 2001, only one remained below the indigenization threshold with regard to one car model. On that basis, India requested the Panel to "limit any recommendations under Article 19:1 of the DSU to the indigenization requirement that remains to be performed by that particular company with respect to that model".[465]

8.49   However, the Panel notes that India indicated that the survey on which this assessment is based concerned "the most important manufacturers". It is therefore not clear that the figures given would concern all signatories and that it could be legitimately assumed on the basis of that survey alone that among all those manufacturers having signed the MOUs, this would be the only one still required to fulfil an indigenization requirement.

8.50   Indeed, in the course of the interim review meeting, the European Communities suggested the name of one company that was not covered by the survey. The European Communities also noted during the interim review meeting that the survey provided by India reflected the manufacturers' own assessment of their fulfilment of their obligations, which may not preclude Indian authorities from reaching a different conclusion. The European Communities also recalls that it is, in its view, still unclear what the effects of falling below the 70% threshold in the future might be.[466]

8.51   On the basis of the elements before it, the Panel is not in a position to conclude that it has been established that only one signatory remains who needs

---

[464]   The Panel also notes in this regard that signatories who might have reached the required level, at whatever date, would have, in India's own description, "moved out of the ambit of the MOU" in that regard regardless of the events of 1 April 2001: to the extent that manufacturers would have reached the 70% indigenization level, their situation would arguably not have been fundamentally altered by the continued application or not of Public Notice No. 60: Moving "out of the ambit of the MOU altogether" as described by India, arguably would have the same practical consequences as the general suppression of the import licensing regime, regardless of the continuation of Public Notice No. 60. We note however that there is a persisting disagreement on this issue among the parties, since both complainants remain concerned that it is unclear what the consequences of subsequently "slipping" below the required level may be. The Panel does not find it necessary, for the purpose of its analysis, to rule on this particular issue.

[465]   Para. 3.8, cited above.

[466]   Oral Statement at the interim review meeting, para. 12. This concern is also shared by the United States.

2050   DSR 2002:V

to fulfill the indigenization requirement and would not be able to limit its recommendation to the obligation to be performed by one of the signatories only. Indeed, it is not in a position to assess the exact modalities under which existing MOU signatories still have to discharge their indigenization obligations. Nor is it, in its view necessary to attempt such an assessment for the purposes of this analysis. In India's own admission, at least one manufacturer yet has to achieve the required level of indigenization and it can thus not be concluded that this issue has lost any practical relevance so as to preclude the Panel from making recommendations with regard to the indigenization requirements as contained in the MOUs.

(b) Trade Balancing Provisions

8.52   The Panel recalls its earlier finding that the trade balancing obligations, as contained in Public Notice No. 60 and in the MOUs signed thereunder, and as applied as of the date of establishment of this Panel, were in violation of Articles XI:1 and III:4 of the GATT 1994.

(i) Accrued Obligations as Independent from Imports

8.53   India has argued that outstanding trade balancing obligations accrued under the MOUs before 1 April 2001 cannot be in violation of its obligations under GATT 1994 or the TRIMs Agreement, since these obligations will be executed independently of any new imports. In India's view, these obligations will therefore not be inconsistent with India's obligations under the WTO, since the WTO does not generally prohibit export obligations as such. In particular, India argues that they can no longer be in violation of Article XI:1, because they will be executed independently of any new imports.

8.54   The Panel notes in the first instance that this argument concerning the fact that these accrued obligations will be executed independently of any new imports appears to be addressed towards the Panel's finding of violation of Article XI:1, and would not be of relevance to its finding on the basis of Article III:4, which was not tied to a link between imports and the amount of exports required.

8.55   This argument draws a distinction between the conditions in which the obligations were entered into and accrued in the first place and the circumstances in which they will be executed. In this instance, it is not disputed that any remaining export obligations accrued in relation to restricted imports prior to 1 April 2001. While they might be actually executed independently of the conditions of any *future* imports, this would in fact already have always been the case. Future restricted imports would have generated *additional* export obligations. They would not as such have affected previously accrued obligations.

8.56   The fact that, at the time of *execution* of any outstanding export obligations, there will be no future import restrictions does not alter the fact that these particular obligations were *accrued* in relation to imports, in the same way as any other export obligations accrued under the MOUs. They were certainly not accrued independently of any imports and they are to be executed under the same

DSR 2002:V

Report of the Panel

terms as were found to be inconsistent with the provisions of both Articles XI:1 and Article III:4 of the GATT 1994. These residual obligations are therefore not different in that respect from any other accrued obligations under the MOUs. Signatories continue to be bound to the execution of conditions which were found to be inconsistent with the provisions of Articles III:4 and XI:1 of the GATT 1994.

8.57   The Panel notes that the events of 1 April 2001 did not alter the nature of any export obligation *previously* accrued under the MOUs. The Panel also notes that no evidence was presented to show that any new export obligations have in fact accrued for any imports taking place *after* 1 April 2001.

8.58   The essential issue here is that the obligation foreseen in Public Notice No. 60 and reflected in the individual MOUs, which was found to be inconsistent, continues to be binding and to produce effects on those signatories who have not yet fully discharged their export obligations. This issue does not relate to whether any *past execution of* trade balancing obligations might be required to be "undone" or otherwise called into question, but merely to establishing whether the measure previously found to be in violation of two of the GATT provisions continues to have an existence today, so that the Panel would be justified in making a recommendation that this measure be brought into conformity with the relevant agreement as of today.[467]

(ii)   Cessation of the Application of Public Notice No. 60 and the MOUs as Private Contracts

8.59   India's argument concerning the alleged changed nature of the MOUs, as constituting mere private contracts, has already been addressed in the previous section. The Panel refers to its analysis under that section to draw the same conclusion in the context of the trade balancing provisions, namely that the MOUs in place after 1 April are those very same legal instruments signed by manufacturers prior to April 2001 and that it is only by virtue of this prior commitment that they remain binding after 1 April 2001, despite the disappearance of the supporting government measure which served to induce their signature.

8.60   With regard to the cessation or repeal of Public Notice No. 60, the Panel notes that Public Notice No. 36 (RE-2000) which provides that Public Notice No. 60 "stands repealed", also indicates that "however, export obligation incurred by the MOU signatories in respect of imports made up to 31/3/2001 shall be fulfilled by them within the stipulated period unless extended by the Govern-

---

[467]   The Panel also notes that it does not seek to engage, in this analysis, in an assessment of the exact levels of any currently existing trade balancing obligations to be fulfilled. Indeed, none of the parties have provided any relevant evidence in that regard. While this is an issue which may be relevant in relation to the implementation of any recommendations the DSB might adopt in this case, such an analysis is not required in this context.

2052   DSR 2002:V

ment for good and sufficient reasons."[468] It thus appears that the repeal of Public Notice No. 60 has in any case not altered the continued existence of export obligations accrued under existing MOUs.

8.61   In light of the foregoing, the Panel concludes that the trade balancing conditions contained in Public Notice No. 60 and in the MOUs, as they have continued to exist and apply after 1 April 2001, have remained in violation of the relevant GATT provisions.

8.62   As to the question of any future enforcement of the current obligations of MOU signatories, the Panel takes note of and welcomes India's statement that any future measures it may take to enforce the MOUs will not involve any inconsistencies with its WTO obligations. However, the Panel also recalls its earlier conclusion that such future actions would in any case not be part of its terms of reference.

8.63   Finally, the Panel recalls that India has asserted that it did not apply any balance-of-payments measures after 1 April 2001, so that any defense which it might have been able to establish for the period prior to that date would in any case not have justified the subsequent continuation of the violation by India of Article XI:1 of the GATT 1994.

C.   Recommendations

8.64   In accordance with the terms of Article 3.8 of the DSU, the Panel notes that the violations by India of its obligations under the GATT 1994 is considered *prima facie* to constitute a case of nullification and impairment of benefits under that Agreement, and that this has not been rebutted.

8.65   The Panel consequently recommends that the DSB request India to bring its measures into conformity with its obligations under the WTO Agreements.

---

[468]   Public Notice No. 36 (RE-2000) / 1997-2002, 4th September 2001, as annexed by India to its Oral Statement during the interim review meeting, with the indication "To be published in the Gazette of India Extraordinary".

Report of the Panel

TABLE 1

AUTO COMPONENTS LICENSING POLICY

The cabinet decision on the new policy for import of cars in CKD and SKD condition was announced by the principal information officer who acts as the spokesperson for the cabinet subsequently. The DGFT released a notice on 12 December, 1997 to announce the import licensing policy for CKD and SKD imports in the auto industry. Essentially, the public notice requires minimum foreign investment of $50 mn for joint ventures. Further, indigenization up to 70 percent is required by the fifth year. Last, foreign exchange outflow over the five year period of the MOU must be balanced by corresponding inflow from export of cars and auto components subsequently, relaxations have been made in specific cases. Interpretation of the policy too has been simplified. However, the basic Public Notice of 12.12.97 continuous as before without amendment.

Subject: Export and Import Policy April, 1997 – March 2002 – Policy relating to import of CKD/SKD kits/components by Joint Venture Car manufacturer companies under MOU to be signed with the Government of India.

60-PN In exercise of the powers conferred under Paragraph 4.11 of the Export and Import Policy, 1997-2002 as

12.12.97 amended from time to time, Director General of Foreign Trade hereby draws attention to the above subject and the parameters stipulated in the year 1995 for import of CKD/SKD kits/components by the Joint Venture Motor Vehicle manufacturer companies under Memorandum of Understanding to be signed by them with the Government of India. These parameters have now been reviewed in the light of the changed circumstances and joint venture motor vehicle manufacturing companies (both existing and new) are required now to sign a fresh MOU with the Government of India as per the revised parameters.

2. Pursuant to the above, import of components for motor vehicle in CKD/SKD form, which is restricted for import under the current Export-Import Policy, shall be allowed for importation against a licence and such a licence will be issued only to joint venture automobile manufacturing companies. Thus, all joint venture manufacturers shall enter in to an MOU DGFT for import CKD/SKD kits/components.

3. The MOU shall be based on the following parameters:-

   (i)   Establishment of actual production facilities for manufacture of cars and not for mere assembly of imported kits/components.

   (ii) A minimum foreign equity of US$50 Million to be brought in by the

2054   DSR 2002:V

foreign partner within the first three years of start of operations, if the Joint Venture involves majority foreign equity ownership. However, this condition will apply to new Joint Venture companies only.

(iii) Indigenization of components up to a minimum level of 50% in the third year or earlier from the date of clearance of first import consignment of CKD/SKD kits/components and 70% in the 5th year or earlier. Once the MOU signing firm has reached an indigenization level of 70%, there will be no need for further import licences from DGFT. Consequently, as and when the firms achieve 70% indigenization, they would go outside the ambit of the MOU automatically. However, they will discharge the export obligation corresponding to the imports made by them till that time.

(iv) Regarding export obligation, the firms entering into MOU would achieve broad trade balancing of foreign exchange over the entire period of the MOU in terms of balancing between the actual CIF value or imports of CKD/SKD kits/components and the FOB value of exports of cars and auto components over the said period. The period of export obligation would commence from the third year of commencement of production. The date of commencement of production would be deemed to be the date of the first release of consignment from factory after payment of excise duty, but there would be a moratorium to two years from this particular date of commencement of production during which the firm need not fulfill any export commitment. However, from the third year onwards, (effective from date of release of first consignment), the MOU signing firm would have an export obligation equivalent to the CIF value of imports made by them till that time for the remainder of the MOU period till they complete the entire export obligation. From 4th year onwards, the value of import of CKD/SKD may be regulated with reference to the export obligation fulfilled in the previous years as per the MOU. The export commitment would be met by export of cars as well as auto components. This export obligation will be over and above the EPCG related export obligation.

4. The MOU Scheme would be enforced through the import licensing mechanism and MOU signing firms would be granted import licences by DGFT based on above parameters.

5. To monitor the progress in respect of the elements stipulated above all the Joint Ventures would submit annual reports to the GFT on the parameters outlined above and a Joint Annual Review of the progress made in respect of these parameters would be undertaken by Ministry of Commerce, DIPP and Department of Revenue.

6. These revised guidelines will apply to all existing and future entrants into this sector.

7. By way of exception to the foregoing, companies intending to set up manu-

facturing units under foreign collaboration for light or heavy commercial vehicles, tractors, earthmoving equipments etc. will not be required to enter into any MOU. Their requests for CKD/SKD imports shall be considered by the Special Licensing Committee on merits on an annual basis.

8. A standard format for MOU is enclosed as appendix to this Public Notice and MOU is required to be signed as per this format.

TABLE 2

MEMORANDUM OF UNDERSTANDING (MOU)

I.   This MOU has been made on   day of 1997-98

between

Government of India acting through the Director-General of Foreign Trade (hereinafter referred to as the DGFT) Udyog Bhawan, New Delhi,

and

M/s. ......(hereinafter referred to as the party which expression shall be deemed to include their executors, successors, administrators and assignee).

II.   Whereas the party has sought issue of an import licence to cover import of CKD/SKD parts for manufacture of cars.

III. And whereas the party shall do the following by way of implementation of the Joint Venture:

(i)   that the party shall make an investment of Rs. in this joint venture with equity share of US$ (Rs....) of M/s...., the foreign partner, which will be in freely convertible currency as per the time frame mentioned hereunder:

Year   Foreign Collaborator's
       Equity Contribution in freely
       convertible currency.
       (Rs. in crores)
       (US$ millions)

       Total investment
       (RS. in crores) (US$ in millions)

(ii)   That a minimum foreign equity of US$ 50 million to be brought in by the foreign partner within the first three years of start of operations, if the joint venture involves majority foreign equity ownership.

(iii) that the party shall establish actual manufacturing facilities, and not mere assembly facilities, in India to produce cars. The following will be production volumes year-wise:

Report of the Panel

Year   Production Volumes (Numbers)

(iv)   that the party shall achieve indigenization of components up to a mini-
        mum level of 50% in the third year or earlier from the date of clearance of
        first import consignment of CKD/SKD kits and 70% in the fifth year or
        earlier. Once the party has reached an indigenization level of 70% there
        will be no need for further import licence from DGTF. However, the
        party shall discharge the export obligation corresponding to the imports
        made by them till that time.

That the party intends to achieve the following levels of indigenization of their
product, year-wise:

Year   Percentage (%) of indigenization

The party shall aggressively pursue and achieve as soon as possible the development of the local supply base and increased local content, since the same will
allow a higher level of indigenization.

(v)   that the party intends to import the following number of kits with CIF
        value as indicated in the first five years:

Year   No. of Kits   CIF value   (Rs. in crores)

                                    (US$ in millions)

(vi)   That the party shall achieve a broad trade balancing of foreign exchange
        over the entire period of the MOU in terms of balancing between the ac-
        tual CIF value of imports of CKD/SKD/components and the FOB value
        of export of cars and auto components over the said period. The period of
        export obligation would commence from the third year of commencement
        of production. The date of commencement of production would be
        deemed to be the date of the first release of consignment from factory af-
        ter payment of excise duty, but where would be a moratorium of two
        years from this particular date of commencement of production during
        which the firm need not fulfill any export commitment. However, from
        the third year onwards (effective from date of release of first consign-
        ment), the MOU signing firm would have an export obligation equivalent
        to the CIF value of imports made by them till that time for the remainder
        of the MOU period till they complete the entire export obligation. From
        4th year onwards the value of imports of CKD/SKD may be regulated
        with reference to the export obligation fulfilled in the previous year as per
        the MOU. The export commitment would be met by export of only cars
        as well as auto components,. This export obligation will be over and
        above the EPCG related export obligation.

That the party intends to achieve export of cars and auto components as under
year-wise:

India – Autos

Year   Exports   (RS. crores)

       Exports   (US$ in million)

IV.   To monitor the progress in respect of the elements stipulated above the party shall submit annual reports to the DGFT on the parameters outlined above and further licences will be issued to the party on the basis of an annual report of the progress made in relation to these parameters.

V.   The MOU Scheme would be enforced through the import licensing mechanism and MOU signing firms would be granted import licences by DGFT based on the progress made in respect of the parameters mentioned at para. III above.

Managing Director	Director General of Foreign Trade
On behalf of	On behalf of Govt. of India
M/s……….	M/s……….
Witnesses:	Witnesses:
1.	1.
2.	2.

DSR 2002:V

UNITED STATES – DEFINITIVE SAFEGUARD MEASURES ON IMPORTS OF CIRCULAR WELDED CARBON QUALITY LINE PIPE FROM KOREA

Arbitration
under Article 21.3(c) of the
Understanding on Rules and Procedures
Governing the Settlement of Disputes

Report of the Arbitrator

Yasuhei Taniguchi

WT/DS202/17

Circulated to Members on 26 July 2002

1.   On 8 March 2002, the Dispute Settlement Body (the "DSB") adopted the Appellate Body Report [1] and the Panel Report [2], as modified by the Appellate Body Report, in *United States – Definitive Safeguard Measures on Imports of Circular Welded Carbon Quality Line Pipe from Korea* ("*US – Line Pipe*"). [3] At the DSB meeting of 5 April 2002, the United States informed the DSB, pursuant to Article 21.3 of the *Understanding on Rules and Procedures Governing the Settlement of Disputes* (the "DSU"), that it would implement the recommendations and rulings of the DSB in this dispute in a manner that respects its obligations and that it would require a "reasonable period of time" to do so, pursuant to the terms of Article 21.3 of the DSU. [4]

2.   In view of the parties' inability to reach an agreement on the period of time reasonably required for implementation of those recommendations and rulings, Korea requested, in a letter dated 29 April 2002, that such period be determined by binding arbitration pursuant to Article 21.3(c) of the DSU. [5]

3.   In the absence of an agreement between the parties on the appointment of an arbitrator within 10 days after referring the matter to arbitration, Korea requested, in a letter dated 13 May 2002, the Director-General of the World Trade Organization (the "WTO") to appoint the arbitrator, as provided for in footnote 12 to Article 21.3(c) of the DSU. After consultations with the parties, the Director-General decided, on 23 May 2002, to appoint me as the arbitrator in this mat-

---

[1] Appellate Body Report, WT/DS202/AB/R, adopted 8 March 2002 (DSR 2002:IV).
[2] Panel Report, WT/DS202/R, adopted 8 March 2002, as modified by the Appellate Body Report, WT/DS202/AB/R (DSR 2002:IV).
[3] WT/DS202/13.
[4] WT/DSB/M/122.
[5] WT/DS202/14.

Award of the Arbitrator

ter.[6] On the same day, the parties were informed of my acceptance of the designation as arbitrator.

4.   In subsequent letters to me, the parties indicated that they agreed to extend the deadline for completion of the arbitration to 12 July 2002. Notwithstanding this extension of the 90-day time period stipulated in Article 21.3(c) of the DSU, the parties confirmed that the arbitration award shall be deemed to be an award issued under Article 21.3(c) of the DSU.[7]

5.   Written submissions were received from the United States and Korea on 3 June 2002, and an oral hearing was held on 12 June 2002.

6.   By joint letter of 12 July 2002, the parties requested that I delay the issuance of the award until 22 July 2002, in order to allow time for additional bilateral discussions. The parties also confirmed that should the arbitration award be issued on 22 July 2002, it would be deemed to be an award issued pursuant to Article 21.3(c) of the DSU.

7.   I informed the parties by letter dated 12 July 2002 that I agreed to delay the issuance of the award until 22 July 2002, to give the parties a further opportunity to seek agreement on a reasonable period of time for compliance in this matter.

8.   Additional joint requests for delay were received on 19 and 22 July 2002, wherein the parties requested that the award pursuant to Article 21.3(c) of the DSU be delayed until 24 July 2002 and 26 July 2002, respectively. I informed the parties by letters dated 19 and 22 July 2002 that I agreed to the requests.

9.   By letters dated 24 July 2002, the parties informed me that they had reached agreement on the reasonable period of time for compliance in this matter. Under the circumstances, it will not be necessary for me to issue an award in this arbitration.

---

[6]   WT/DS202/16.
[7]   Korea's letter of 30 May 2002; United States' letter of 3 June 2002.

2062   DSR 2002:V

Cumulative Index of Published Disputes

Argentina – Definitive Anti-Dumping Measures on Imports of Ceramic Floor Tiles from Italy
Complaint by the European Communities (WT/DS189)
Report of the Panel .... DSR 2001:XII, 6241

Argentina - Measures Affecting Imports of Footwear, Textiles, Apparel and Other Items

Complaint by the United States (WT/DS56)
Report of the Appellate Body .... DSR 1998:III, 1003
Report of the Panel .... DSR 1998:III, 1033

Argentina - Measures Affecting the Export of Bovine Hides and the Import of Finished Leather
Complaint by the European Communities (WT/DS155)
Report of the Panel .... DSR 2001:V, 1779
Award of the Arbitrator under Article 21.3(c) of the DSU .... DSR 2001:XII, 6013

Argentina - Safeguard Measures on Imports of Footwear
Complaint by the European Communities (WT/DS121)
Report of the Appellate Body .... DSR 2000:I, 515
Report of the Panel .... DSR 2000:II, 575

Australia - Measures Affecting Importation of Salmon
Complaint by Canada (WT/DS18)
Report of the Appellate Body .... DSR 1998:VIII, 3327
Report of the Panel... DSR 1998:VIII, 3407
Award of the Arbitrator under Article 21.3(c) of the DSU ....DSR 1999:I, 267
Report of the Panel - Recourse to Article 21.5 of the DSU.......DSR 2000:IV, 2031

Australia - Subsidies Provided to Producers and Exporters of Automotive Leather
Complaint by the United States (WT/DS126)
Report of the Panel .... DSR 1999:III, 951
Report of the Panel - Recourse to Article 21.5 of the DSU.......DSR 2000:III, 1189

Brazil - Measures Affecting Desiccated Coconut
Complaint by the Philippines (WT/DS22)
Report of the Appellate Body ....DSR 1997:I, 167
Report of the Panel ....DSR 1997:I, 189

Brazil - Export Financing Programme for Aircraft
Complaint by Canada (WT/DS46)
Report of the Appellate Body .... DSR 1999:III, 1161
Report of the Panel .... DSR 1999:III, 1221
Report of the Appellate Body - Recourse to Article 21.5
of the DSU .... DSR 2000:VIII, 4067

DSR 2002:V

2063

Cumulative Index of Published Disputes

Report of the Panel - Recourse to Article 21.5 of the DSU.......DSR 2000:IX, 4093

Report of the Panel - Second Recourse to
Article 21.5 of the DSU ....DSR 2001:XI, 5481

Decision by the Arbitrators - Recourse to Arbitration by Brazil under
Article 22.6 of the DSU and Article 4.11 of the SCM Agreement...DSR 2002:I, 19

Canada - Certain Measures Affecting the Automotive Industry

Complaint by the European Communities (WT/DS142);
complaint by Japan (WT/DS139)

Report of the Appellate Body ....DSR 2000:VI, 2985

Report of the Panel .... DSR 2000:VII, 3043

Award of the Arbitrator under Article 21.3(c) of the DSU .... DSR 2000:X, 5079

Canada - Certain Measures Concerning Periodicals

Complaint by the United States (WT/DS31)

Report of the Appellate Body ....DSR 1997:I, 449

Report of the Panel ....DSR 1997:I, 481

Canada - Export Credits and Loan Guarantees for Regional Aircraft

Complaint by Brazil (WT/DS222)

Report of the Panel.. DSR 2002:III, 849

Canada - Measures Affecting the Importation of Milk and the Exportation of Dairy Products

Complaint by New Zealand (WT/DS113); complaint by the United States
(WT/DS103)

Report of the Appellate Body .... DSR 1999:V, 2057

Report of the Panel...DSR 1999:VI, 2097

Report of the Appellate Body - Recourse to Article 21.5
of the DSU .... DSR 2001:XIII, 6829

Report of the Panel - Recourse to Article 21.5 of the DSU.... DSR 2001:XIII, 6865

Canada - Measures Affecting the Export of Civilian Aircraft

Complaint by Brazil (WT/DS70)

Report of the Appellate Body .... DSR 1999:III, 1377

Report of the Panel .... DSR 1999:IV, 1443

Report of the Appellate Body - Recourse to Article 21.5
of the DSU ....DSR 2000:IX, 4299

Report of the Panel - Recourse to Article 21.5 of the DSU.......DSR 2000:IX, 4315

Canada - Patent Protection of Pharmaceutical Products

Complaint by the European Communities (WT/DS114)

Report of the Panel .... DSR 2000:V, 2289

Award of the Arbitrator under Article 21.3(c) of the DSU ....DSR 2002:I, 3

Canada - Term of Patent Protection

Complaint by the United States (WT/DS170)

Report of the Appellate Body .... DSR 2000:X, 5093

Report of the Panel ....DSR 2000:XI, 5121

2064

DSR 2002:V

Award of the Arbitrator under Article 21.3(c) of the DSU ......DSR 2000:IX, 4537

Chile - Taxes on Alcoholic Beverages
Complaint by the European Communities (WT/DS87), (WT/DS110)

Report of the Appellate Body ....DSR 2000:I, 281

Report of the Panel ....DSR 2000:I, 303

Award of the Arbitrator under Article 21.3(c) of the DSU ....DSR 2000:V, 2583

European Communities - Anti-Dumping Duties on Imports of Cotton-Type Bed Linen from India
Complaint by India (WT/DS141)

Report of the Appellate Body ....DSR 2001:V, 2049

Report of the Panel ....DSR 2001:VI, 2077

European Communities - Customs Classification of Certain Computer Equipment
Complaint by the United States (WT/DS62); complaint by the United States – Ireland (WT/DS68); complaint by the United States – United Kingdom (WT/DS67)

Report of the Appellate Body ....DSR 1998:V, 1851

Report of the Panel ....DSR 1998:V, 1891

European Communities - Measures Affecting Asbestos and Asbestos-Containing Products
Complaint by Canada (WT/DS135)

Report of the Appellate Body ....DSR 2001:VII, 3243

Report of the Panel ....DSR 2001:VIII, 3305

European Communities - Measures Affecting the Importation of Certain Poultry Products
Complaint by Brazil (WT/DS69)

Report of the Appellate Body ....DSR 1998:V, 2031

Report of the Panel ....DSR 1998:V, 2089

European Communities - Measures Concerning Meat and Meat Products (Hormones)
Complaint by Canada (WT/DS48); complaint by the United States (WT/DS26)

Report of the Appellate Body ....DSR 1998:I, 135

Report of the Panel (Canada)...DSR 1998:II, 235

Report of the Panel (United States)..DSR 1998:III, 699

Award of the Arbitrator under Article 21.3(c) of the DSU ....DSR 1998:V, 1833

Decision by the Arbitrators under Article 22.6 of the DSU (Canada) ....DSR 1999:III, 1135

Decision by the Arbitrators under Article 22.6 of the DSU (United States) ....DSR 1999:III, 1105

European Communities - Regime for the Importation, Sale and Distribution of Bananas
Complaint by Ecuador; Guatemala; Honduras; Mexico; and the United States (WT/DS27)

Report of the Appellate Body ....DSR 1997:II, 589

Report of the Panel (Ecuador)..DSR 1997:III, 3

Cumulative Index of Published Disputes

Report of the Panel (Guatemala, Honduras)............................... DSR 1997:II, 695

Report of the Panel (Mexico).. DSR 1997:II, 803

Report of the Panel (United States).. DSR 1997:II, 943

Award of the Arbitrator under Article 21.3(c) of the DSU ....DSR 1998:I, 3

Decision by the Arbitrators under Article 22.6
of the DSU (US).. DSR 1999:II, 725

Report of the Panel - Recourse to Article 21.5 of the DSU
(European Communities) .... DSR 1999:II, 783

Report of the Panel - Recourse to Article 21.5 of the DSU
(Ecuador) .... DSR 1999:II, 803

Decision by the Arbitrators under Article 22.6
of the DSU (Ecuador) .... DSR 2000:V, 2237

European Communities – Trade Description of Scallops

Complaint by Canada (WT/DS7); complaint by Chile (WT/DS14); complaint by Peru
(WT/DS12)

Report of the Panel (Canada) ....DSR 1996:I, 89

Report of the Panel (Chile, Peru) ....DSR 1996:I, 93

Guatemala – Anti-Dumping Investigation Regarding Portland Cement From Mexico

Complaint by Mexico (WT/DS60)

Report of the Appellate Body ....DSR 1998:IX, 3767

Report of the Panel ....DSR 1998:IX, 3797

Guatemala - Definitive Anti-Dumping Measures on Grey Portland Cement from Mexico

Complaint by Mexico (WT/DS156)

Report of the Panel ....DSR 2000:XI, 5295

India - Patent Protection for Pharmaceutical and Agricultural Chemical Products

Complaint by European Communities (WT/DS79); complaint by the United States
(WT/DS50)

Report of the Appellate Body (United States)...................................DSR 1998:I, 9

Report of the Panel (European Communities)..........................DSR 1998:VI, 2661

Report of the Panel (United States)..DSR 1998:I, 41

India - Quantitative Restrictions on Imports of Agricultural, Textile and Industrial Products

Complaint by the United States (WT/DS90)

Report of the Appellate Body ....DSR 1999:IV, 1763

Report of the Panel.. DSR 1999:V, 1799

Indonesia - Certain Measures Affecting the Automobile Industry

Complaint by European Communities (WT/DS54); complaint by Japan (WT/DS55,
WT/DS64); complaint by the United States (WT/DS59)

Report of the Panel..DSR 1998:VI, 2201

Award of the Arbitrator under Article 21.3(c) of the DSU ......DSR 1998:IX, 4029

Japan - Measures Affecting Agricultural Products
Complaint by the United States (WT/DS76)
Report of the Appellate Body ....DSR 1999:I, 277
Report of the Panel ....DSR 1999:I, 315

Japan - Measures Affecting Consumer Photographic Film and Paper
Complaint by the United States (WT/DS44)
Report of the Panel ....DSR 1998:IV, 1179

Japan – Taxes on Alcoholic Beverages
Complaint by Canada (WT/DS10); complaint by the European Communities
(WT/DS8); complaint by the United States (WT/DS11)
Report of the Appellate Body ....DSR 1996:I, 97
Report of the Panel...DSR 1996:I, 125
Award of the Arbitrator under Article 21.3(c) of the DSU ....DSR 1997:I, 3

Korea - Definitive Safeguard Measure on Imports of Certain Dairy Products
Complaint by the European Communities (WT/DS98)
Report of the Appellate Body ....DSR 2000:I, 3
Report of the Panel ....DSR 2000:I, 49

Korea – Measures Affecting Imports of Fresh, Chilled and Frozen Beef
Complaint by Australia (WT/DS169); complaint by the United States (WT/DS161)
Report of the Appellate Body ....DSR 2001:I, 5
Report of the Panel ....DSR 2001:I, 59

Korea - Measures Affecting Government Procurement
Complaint by the United States (WT/DS163)
Report of the Panel ....DSR 2000:VIII, 3541

Korea - Taxes on Alcoholic Beverages
Complaint by the European Communities (WT/DS75); complaint by the United States
(WT/DS84)
Report of the Appellate Body ....DSR 1999:I, 3
Report of the Panel ....DSR 1999:I, 44
Award of the Arbitrator under Article 21.3(c) of the DSU .... DSR 1999:II, 937

Mexico - Anti-Dumping Investigation of High Fructose Corn Syrup (HFCS) from the United States
Complaint by the United States (WT/DS132)
Report of the Panel ....DSR 2000:III, 1345
Report of the Appellate Body - Recourse to Article 21.5
of the DSU ....DSR 2001:XIII, 6675
Report of the Panel - Recourse to Article 21.5 of the DSU.... DSR 2001:XIII, 6717

Cumulative Index of Published Disputes

Thailand – Anti-Dumping Duties on Angles, Shapes and Sections of Iron or Non-Alloy Steel and H-Beams from Poland
Complaint by Poland (WT/DS122)
    Report of the Appellate Body .... DSR 2001:VII, 2701
    Report of the Panel .... DSR 2001:VII, 2741

Turkey - Restrictions on Imports of Textile and Clothing Products
Complaint by India (WT/DS34)
    Report of the Appellate Body ....DSR 1999:VI, 2345
    Report of the Panel ....DSR 1999:VI, 2363

United States - Anti-Dumping Act of 1916
Complaint by the European Communities (WT/DS136); complaint by Japan (WT/DS162)
    Report of the Appellate Body .... DSR 2000:X, 4793
    Report of the Panel (European Communities)........................... DSR 2000:X, 4593
    Report of the Panel (Japan).. DSR 2000:X, 4831
    Award of the Arbitrator under Article 21.3(c) of the DSU .... DSR 2001:V, 2017

United States - Anti-Dumping Duty on Dynamic Random Access Memory Semiconductors (DRAMS) of One Megabit or Above from Korea
Complaint by Korea (WT/DS99)
    Report of the Panel .... DSR 1999:II, 521

United States – Anti-Dumping Measures on Certain Hot-Rolled Steel Products from Japan
Complaint by Japan (WT/DS184)
    Report of the Appellate Body .... DSR 2001:X, 4697
    Report of the Panel .... DSR 2001:X, 4769
    Award of the Arbitrator under Article 21.3(c) of the DSU ......DSR 2002:IV, 1389

United States – Anti-Dumping Measures on Stainless Steel Plate in Coils and Stainless Steel Sheet and Strip from Korea
Complaint by Korea (WT/DS179)
    Report of the Panel ....DSR 2001:IV, 1295

United States – Definitive Safeguard Measures on Imports of Circular Welded Carbon Quality Line Pipe from Korea
Complaint by Korea (WT/DS202)
    Report of the Appellate Body ....DSR 2002:IV, 1403
    Report of the Panel...DSR 2002:IV, 1473

United States – Definitive Safeguard Measures on Imports of Wheat Gluten from the European Communities
Complaint by the European Communities (WT/DS166)
    Report of the Appellate Body .... DSR 2001:II, 717
    Report of the Panel .... DSR 2001:III, 779

2068   DSR 2002:V

Cumulative Index of Published Disputes

United States – Import Measures on Certain Products from the European Communities
Complaint by the European Communities (WT/DS165)
    Report of the Appellate Body ....DSR 2001:I, 373
    Report of the Panel .... DSR 2001:II, 413

United States - Imposition of Countervailing Duties on Certain Hot-Rolled Lead and Bismuth Carbon Steel Products Originating in the United Kingdom
Complaint by the European Communities (WT/DS138)
    Report of the Appellate Body ....DSR 2000:V, 2595
    Report of the Panel ....DSR 2000:VI, 2623

United States - Import Prohibition of Certain Shrimp and Shrimp Products
Complaint by India (WT/DS58); complaint by Malaysia (WT/DS58); complaint by Pakistan (WT/DS58); complaint by Thailand (WT/DS58)
    Report of the Appellate Body .... DSR 1998:VII, 2755
    Report of the Panel .... DSR 1998:VII, 2821
    Report of the Appellate Body - Recourse to Article 21.5
    of the DSU (Malaysia) .... DSR 2001:XIII, 6481
    Report of the Panel - Recourse to Article 21.5
    of the DSU (Malaysia) .... DSR 2001:XIII, 6529

United States - Measure Affecting Imports of Woven Wool Shirts and Blouses from India
Complaint by India (WT/DS33)
    Report of the Appellate Body ....DSR 1997:I, 323
    Report of the Panel ....DSR 1997:I, 343

United States - Measures Treating Export Restraints as Subsidies
Complaint by Canada (WT/DS194)
    Report of the Panel ....DSR 2001:XI, 5767

United States - Restrictions on Imports of Cotton and Man-made Fibre Underwear
Complaint by Costa Rica (WT/DS24)
    Report of the Appellate Body ....DSR 1997:I, 11
    Report of the Panel ....DSR 1997:I, 31

United States – Safeguard Measures on Imports of Fresh, Chilled or Frozen Lamb Meat from New Zealand and Australia
Complaint by Australia (WT/DS178); complaint by new Zealand (WT/DS177)
    Report of the Appellate Body ....DSR 2001:IX, 4051
    Report of the Panel ....DSR 2001:IX, 4107

United States - Section 110(5) of the US Copyright Act
Complaint by the European Communities (WT/DS160)
    Report of the Panel .... DSR 2000:VIII, 3769
    Award of the Arbitrator under Article 21.3(c) of the DSU .... DSR 2001:II, 657
    Award of the Arbitrator under Article 25 of the DSU................. DSR 2001:II, 667

Cumulative Index of Published Disputes

United States - Sections 301-310 of the Trade Act of 1974
Complaint by the European Communities (WT/DS152)
Report of the Panel .... DSR 2000:II, 815

United States – Section 211 Omnibus Appropriations Act of 1998
Complaint by the European Communities (WT/DS176)
Report of the Appellate Body .... DSR 2002:II, 589
Report of the Panel.. DSR 2002:II, 683

United States – Standards for Reformulated and Conventional Gasoline
Complaint by Brazil (WT/DS4); complaint by Venezuela (WT/DS2)
Report of the Appellate Body ....DSR 1996:I, 3
Report of the Panel ....DSR 1996:I, 29

United States - Tax Treatment for "Foreign Sales Corporations"
Complaint by the European Communities (WT/DS108)
Report of the Appellate Body ....DSR 2000:III, 1619
Report of the Panel ....DSR 2000:IV, 1675
Report of the Appellate Body - Recourse to Article 21.5
of the DSU ....DSR 2002:I, 55
Report of the Panel - Recourse to Article 21.5
of the DSU ....DSR 2002:I, 119

United States – Transitional Safeguard Measure on Combed Cotton Yarn from Pakistan
Complaint by Pakistan (WT/DS192)
Report of the Appellate Body .... DSR 2001:XII, 6027
Report of the Panel .... DSR 2001:XII, 6067

2070   DSR 2002:V

For EU product safety concerns, contact us at Calle de José Abascal, 56–1°, 28003 Madrid, Spain or eugpsr@cambridge.org.

www.ingramcontent.com/pod-product-compliance
Ingram Content Group UK Ltd.
Pitfield, Milton Keynes, MK11 3LW, UK
UKHW030654060825
461487UK00011B/955